# STUDIES AND TEXTS

## 35

### PART ONE

# A BOOK OF SHOWINGS
# TO THE ANCHORESS
# JULIAN OF NORWICH

Part One

Introduction and The Short Text

Edited by

EDMUND COLLEDGE O.S.A.

and

JAMES WALSH S.J.

PONTIFICAL INSTITUTE OF MEDIAEVAL STUDIES
TORONTO 1978

ACKNOWLEDGMENT

This book has been published with the help of a grant
from the Humanities Research Council of Canada,
using funds provided by the Canada Council.

Canadian Cataloguing in Publication Data

Juliana, anchoret, 1343-1443.
  A book of showings to the anchoress Julian of Norwich

(Studies and texts - Pontifical Institute of Mediaeval Studies ;
35 ISSN 0082-5328)

Text in Middle English.
Bibliography: pt. 2, p.
Includes index.

ISBN 0-88844-035-9

1. Devotional literature. I. Colledge, Edmund, 1910-    II. Walsh, James, 1920-
III. Title. IV. Series: Pontifical Institute of Mediaeval Studies. Studies and
texts - Pontifical Institute of Mediaeval Studies ; 35.

BV4831.J8 1978  *Pt 1*                   231'.74                     C77-001104-7

*46,539*

PRINTED BY UNIVERSA PRESS, WETTEREN, BELGIUM

# TABLE OF CONTENTS

## *PART ONE*

## A Book of Showings

## PART TWO

## A Book of Showings

# PREFACE

This edition has its origin in the critical texts of both the short and long versions of Julian's *Showings* presented for the Ph. D. degree of Leeds University by Sr. Anna Maria Reynolds, C. P., working under the direction of Professor R. M. Wilson. Later, when Sr. Anna Maria was preparing a modernized English translation of the short text for publication and James Walsh was similarly at work on the long text, she invited him to collaborate with her in preparing a critical edition of both texts. Then, when her new professional commitments forced Sr. Anna Maria to abandon the work, James Walsh invited Edmund Colledge to share in it ; and for the past eleven years it has engaged them from time to time. At an early stage it was realised that Sr. Anna Maria's texts could not be used ; but even so the editors are much in her debt for generous help and advice. They know that she would wish them to mention the guidance and counsel she received from Professor Wilson, who, more recently, has greatly assisted the present editors with his expert opinions, as has also Fr. Leonard Boyle, O. P.

In recent years the Pontifical Institute of Mediaeval Studies in Toronto has given this work invaluable support, both moral and financial. Generous grants from the Canada Council and the American Philosophical Society made possible much necessary travelling and photography; and the work is being published with the help of a subvention from the Humanities Research Council of Canada.

The editors are indebted to all the libraries who have allowed them to consult their manuscripts and printed books, especially to those owners of copies of Julian's text who have permitted their use for this edition. They are conscious of the special obligation they are under, in Toronto, to Fr. Donald Finlay, C.S.B., librarian of the Pontifical Institute, to Fr. Walter Hayes, S. J., its director of publications, and to Mrs. Margaret McGrath, reference librarian of St. Michael's College. They must thank Denise Critchley, Theresa Gerson, Bernard Muir, Michael Sargent and Linda Spear for their skilled and devoted help in the preparation of the work for the press.

Finally, it remains for them to express their gratitude to their respective orders, to their religious superiors over the years who have permitted them to pursue their researches, and to the many Augustinian and Jesuit houses, in two continents, who have given them hospitality and kindness.

# SIGLA OF MANUSCRIPTS AND OTHER ABBREVIATIONS

| | |
|---|---|
| A | London British Museum Add. 37790 |
| C | Cressy 1670 edition |
| P | Paris Bibliothèque Nationale Fonds anglais 40 |
| S1 | London British Museum Sloane 2499 |
| S2 | London British Museum Sloane 3705 |
| SS | S1 and S2 |
| U | Upholland Seminary Library |
| W | Westminster Diocesan Archives |
| | |
| AFH | *Archivum Franciscanum Historicum* |
| AFr | Anglo-French |
| AISP | *Archivio Italiano per la Storia della Pietà* |
| ASS | *Acta Sanctorum* |
| BL | British Library (Museum) |
| BM | British Museum (Library) |
| BN | Bibliothèque Nationale |
| C. Brown, XIII | *English Lyrics of the XIIIth Century* |
| C. Brown, XIV | *Religious Lyrics of the XIVth Century* |
| C. Brown, XV | *Religious Lyrics of the XVth Century* |
| CCCM | *Corpus Christianorum Continuatio Mediaeualis* |
| CCSL | *Corpus Christianorum Series Latina* |
| CSEL | *Corpus Scriptorum Ecclesiasticorum Latinorum* |
| DACL | *Dictionnaire d'Archéologie Chrétienne et de Liturgie* |
| DNB | *Dictionary of National Biography* |
| DSp | *Dictionnaire de la Spiritualité* |
| DTC | *Dictionnaire de Théologie Catholique* |
| EETS (ES) | Early English Text Society (Extra Series) |
| EETS (OS) | Early English Text Society (Original Series) |
| FEW | *Französisches etymologisches Wörterbuch* |
| HBS | Henry Bradshaw Society |
| LCI | *Lexikon der christlichen Ikonographie* |
| MÆ | *Medium AEvum* |
| ME | Middle English |
| MED | *Middle English Dictionary* |
| MGH | *Monumenta Germaniae Historica* |
| MS | *Mediaeval Studies* |
| NCE | *New Catholic Encyclopedia* |
| NED | *New English Dictionary* |
| OE | Old English |
| OFr | Old French |
| OHG | Old High German |
| PL | *Patrologiae Latinae Cursus Completus* |
| RAM | *Revue d'Ascétique et de Mystique* |
| RES | *Review of English Studies* |
| RTAM | *Recherches de Théologie Ancienne et Médiévale* |
| SC | *Sources chrétiennes* |
| SCN | Summary Catalogue Number (Bodleian Library) |
| TLL | *Thesaurus Linguae Latinae* |
| UL | University Library |
| VCH | *Victoria County History* |

# INTRODUCTION

## I Description of Manuscripts and of the Cressy Printed Text[1]

### 1 A: London, MS British Museum[2] Additional 37790[3]

Ff. 236 + 2 stubs + f. 238, 180 × 266 mm, vellum. Binding nineteenth-century. Written in a single hand, clear, bold and well-formed, of the mid-fifteenth century, which is also responsible for the rubrication. The scribe's larger lettering occupies c. 34 lines to the page, the smaller c. 38. The margins, but not the lines, are ruled. There are numerous indications that this is the product of a monastic scriptorium. There are few guide-letters for the coloured initials, which shows that the limner for whom blank spaces were left was expected to consult the master-copy or a scribe. He has in fact made several mistakes (his very first letter, f. 1ʳ, is 'T' instead of 'Þ'), including the first two initials in the Julian text. (Such accidents, common enough, explain the instruction in chapter 13, 'De rubricatore', of the fifteenth-century statutes of the Cologne Brethren of the Common Life: 'Scripturarij directionibus in illuminandis libris sibi per eum traditis obtemperabit'[4]). Throughout, there are numerous hands at work correcting errors. Two contemporary with that of the scribe are of interest for the Julian text. One (using plummet) has emended 'worlde' to 'worme' (cf. 219.5); on f. 158ᵛ, in *The Mirror of Simple Souls,* the same hand corrects 'drawis' to 'drinkyth', showing that this emendator's dialect had not that mixture of Northern forms which is to be found throughout A, the last Bridget fragment only excepted; and Margaret Amassian points out that elsewhere, when the scribe wrongly used black ink, the other has noted 'rubrica'. She

---

[1] No other mention is made, here or elsewhere, of MS British Museum Stowe 42, an eighteenth-century copy of the Cressy printed text with no identifiable marks of ownership. For the brief quotation in a Colwich Abbey manuscript, see II, 'Scribes and Owners'.

[2] Now officially designated as the 'British Library'.

[3] Cf. *Catalogue of Additions to the Manuscripts in the British Museum in the Years MDCCCCVI-MDCCCCX*, 153-156. This is often given the name of its last private owner and called 'the Amherst MS'.

[4] K. O. Meinsma: *Middeleeuwse bibliotheken*, 131.

tells us that in the Rolle texts he shows close and accurate concern for their purity. However, in the Julian text the chief corrections are in yet another contemporary hand, called in this edition 'the corrector', which is remarkably like that of the scribe, and probably formed by the same writing master.

Though the well-known copy of the English *Stimulus amoris* and *The Poor Caitiff* which is now MS Downside 26542 is written in a hand not identical with that of A, the two manuscripts resemble one another so much, in handwriting, rubrication, lay-out and contents, that it is hard to suppose that they are not the products of the same scriptorium. In addition to the *Stimulus* (ff. 1ʳ-90ʳ) and *The Poor Caitiff* (ff. 94ʳ-168ᵛ), the Downside manuscript contains 'How a man shall knowe whiche is the speche of the flesshe in his hert ... seynt Bernard techith and seieth thus: If thou feele a thought or a stiryng in thyn hert of mete or of drynke ..', exp. '.. yt is spekyng of god and not of thyself. Jhesu mercy. Lady helpe' (ff. 90ᵛ-92ᵛ, f. 91 blank), which also follows the English *Stimulus* in MS Trinity College Cambridge B.14.19;[5] Latin excerpts from the *Horologium sapientiae* and from the revelations of Mechtild of Hackborn;[6] and 'Sermo beati Augustini notabilis ad par(o)chianos. Rogo vos fratres karissimi vt attencius cogitemus ... si vos libenter audiatis et nobis facitis gaudium et vos feliciter peruenietis ad regnum. Amen' (ff. 172ʳ-173ᵛ).[7] Before the Dissolution the Downside manuscript was in the private possession of two Dominican nuns of Dartford, one of whom, Emma Winter, is also recorded in MS Society of Antiquaries of London 717, a collection of psalms and offices, as having commissioned its writing.[8] It is very probable that both this Downside manuscript and A are such commissioned pieces. The general character of A, as an anthology of less popular spiritual classics which comprises the unique copies of Julian's short text and of the English Ruysbroek *Treatise of Perfection* has previously been remarked.[9] That the Downside manuscript should contain Latin extracts from the *Horologium* and from Mechtild of Hackborn is evidence of the same kind of connoisseurship.

[5] We owe this identification to A. I. Doyle.

[6] We owe this identification to Roger Lovatt.

[7] PL 39 2237-2240, 'De christiano nomine cum operibus non christianis'. The ascription to Augustine is spurious (Dekkers, no. 368), and its true author is Caesarius of Arles; Germain Morin, ed. *Sancti Caesarii Arelatensis sermones* 1, no. XIII, 64 e.s.

[8] N. R. Ker, *Medieval Manuscripts in British Libraries* 1, 315.

[9] J. Bazire and E. Colledge, *Chastising,* Introduction, 83-87.

Since it has long been known that A was at one time in the care of James Grenehalgh[10] (his monogram occurs on f. 33$^r$, and there are numerous emendations and marginalia — none of them in the Julian text — which may be his), one is tempted to suppose that the manuscript may have been written at Sheen; but this can be no more than a supposition. It would be strengthened, had the Dartford manuscript been owned in Sheen or Syon and not Dartford. The evidence suggests that Grenehalgh worked only for the benefit of Syon and of English Carthusian houses. There may however have been other Carthusian scribes copying volumes intended for sale outside their monasteries. G. I. Lieftinck has produced numerous references from the chronicles of the houses of the Windesheim Congregation to religious who copied or illuminated 'pro pretio'; usually such references appear in obituary notices, praising the scribes' pious zeal.[11] This practice existed also in England.[12]

Collation: gatherings of eight, the first four in each with signatures and arabic numbers, the gatherings signed a-h, j-t, v, x-z, &, *con,* a$^2$-d$^2$ + 7 unsigned sheets.

Ff. 237 and 238 have been excised. The stub of f. 237 shows on the recto the first two letters of 13 lines of script; the rest of the folio evidently blank, as is f. 238 (recte 239)$^r$, except for a rough plummet sketch of a madonna and child, and a contemporary note, in a hand not found elsewhere, inc.: 'Augustinus de civitate dei 14. Dum huius vite infirmitatem si passiones nullas habeamus ...'

The chief contents of A are as follows:

f. 1$^r$ inc.: T(h)is boke is off mendynge of lyfe or ellys off the rewle off lyfynge destinct into xij chapiters ...

f. 18$^r$ exp.: Thus endis the xij chapetyrs off Richarde Hampole into englys *translate* be frere Rycharde Misyn to informacio*nn* off crystyn saulis *anno domini* millesimo cccc$^{mo}$ xxxiiij.

f. 18$^v$ inc.: At the reu*erence* off oure lorde Jhe*s*u Criste to the askynge of thy desyre sistyr Margarete couetynge asethe to make ...

f. 68$^v$ exp.: Explicit liber pr*imus* Incendij Amoris R*icardi* Hampole h*er*emite *translatus* a latino in anglicu*m* per fra*trem* Ri*cardum* Misyn*n*

[10] E. Colledge: '*The Treatise of Perfection of the Sons of God'*, a Fifteenth-Century English Ruysbroek Translation'.

[11] 'Windesheim, Agnietenberg en Mariënborn' (*Dancwerk: opstellen aangeboden aan Prof. Dr. D. Th. Enklaar,* 188-207), passim.

[12] Cf. E. Colledge: 'The Capgrave "Autographs"', 11 and notes 37, 38.

heremitam et ordinis carmelitarum ac sacre theologie bachalari(um)
anno domini millesimo cccc xxxv^to.

f. 69^r inc.: Why perfitte contemplatife to vtwarde songe takes no hede ...

f. 95^r exp.: Explicit liber de Incendio Amoris Ricardi Hampole heremite
translatus in anglicum instancijs domine Margarete Heslyngtonn
recluse per fratrem Ricardum Misynn sacre theologie bachalarium
tunc priorem Lyncoln ordinis carmelitarum anno domini m^o cccc^o
xxxv^to in festo translacionis sancti Martini episcopi quod est iiij nonas
julij per dictum Ricardum Misynn scriptum et correctum. [13]

f. 95^v inc.: This pistill made saynt Barnerde vnto his cosynn the whiche
is calde a goldynn pystill for the grete abundannce of gostely fruyte
that is contynede in it.

My frende yf ye will come perfitely ...

f. 96^v exp.: ... that he of my syns will haue mercye. Amenn.
Jhesu mercy. Lady helpe. JS. [14]

ff. 97^r-115^r: the short text of Julian's *Revelations*.

ff. 115^r-130^r: *The Treatise of Perfection of the Sons of God*, the English translation of John Ruysbroek's treatise. [15]

f. 130^v inc.: De triplici genere amoris spiritualis.
The fyrste degre of loue is called insuperabill ...

f. 132^r exp.: ... bot ȝif he ware disposede as I was in saule. [16]
Incipit tractatus de diligendo deo.
Amore langueo. Thyr two wordes are writtene ...

f. 132^v exp.: ... as is writtene now here aftyre. [17]
Thou that lyste to loue, heelde thy nere ...

f. 135^v exp.: ... And fra the neuer twynne botte ay be in thy louynge.

---

[13] R. Harvey edited these English translations of Rolle: *The Fire of Love, and the Mend-
ing of Life*. Both are being re-edited by Margaret Amassian, who is re-examining the at-
tributions to Misyn.

[14] For a transcript, see E. Colledge: 'Fifteenth and Sixteenth-Century English Versions of "The Golden Epistle of St. Bernard"'. He no longer thinks, as he did in 1952,
that the scribe's 'J.S.' on f. 96^v refers to Joanna Sewell of Syon; the script of A an-
tedates her residence there by some forty or fifty years.

[15] Edited J. Bazire and E. Colledge: *The Chastising*, 229-258.

[16] This is a compilation from chapters 8, 9 and 10 of Rolle's *Form of Living* (Hope
Emily Allen: *English Writings*, 104-116; *Rolle*, 260). There are numerous omissions, very
few additions or major variants, but a markedly inferior text of the *Cantus amoris*
(*English Writings*, 107), written as prose. The dialect is of as distinctly Northern quality
as is the text in *English Writings*, from MS Cambridge University Library Dd. v. 54.

[17] Part of chapter 7 and the first sentence of chapter 8 of the *Form*; *English Writings*,
103.

Amen.[18] The fyrste degree of lufe is insup*er*abill, the seconnde insep*er*abill, the thyrde synguler*e*.[19]

Formula compendiosa vite sp*iritu*alis.

In the felaschippe of sayntis whilke as þe morne sterne schone ...

f. 136ᵛ exp.: ... Thise he sayde ar*e* the pr*i*nciples of gostely hele. Deo gracias.[20]

ff. 137ʳ-225ʳ: *The Mirror of Simple Souls.*[21]

f. 225ᵛ inc.: O glorious trinite in whom is alle godnes ... exp.: ... *and* magnifie euerlastingly with outen ende. Amen. Jh*es*u merci. Amen.

f. 226ʳ inc.: Sequitur hic quedam introductiua ad co*n*templac*i*on*em* ... Qui di*u*initate*m* do*m*ini n*os*tri Jhesu Chr*is*ti contemplari desiderat ...

f. 233ᵛ exp.: ... qui est tr*i*nus *et* vnus deus b*e*nedictus in *secu*la *secu*lor*um*. Amen.[22]

f. 234ʳ inc.: Via ad conte*m*placion*em*. Capiat *qu*i pot*est* caper*e* ... Therefore eu*er*e new discipull ascende to the p*er*feccion*n* of this scyence ...

f. 236ʳ exp.: ... þou hase woundyd my herte in on of thyne eyne. Deo gracias. Amen.[23]

Labure hastely for the tyme is schorte ...

f. 236ᵛ exp.: ... than a synner*e* can haue of hymselfe *et cetera.*[24] God almyghty apered to seynte Bryde sayinge to hyr ... ... *and* in pr*a*yers *and* oþer goode dedys, for all/.[25]

---

[18] *Ego dormio* (*English Writings*, 61-72), with many omissions and unique variants. Hope Allen knew of no other such compilation from *Ego dormio* and the *Form,* and commented: 'It is unlikely that this arrangement, occurring, as far as I know, only in this manuscript, should have been due to Rolle' (*Rolle,* 248).

[19] This sentence repeats the beginning of chapter 8 of the *Form; English Writings,* 104. Hope Allen also knew of no other such Rolle compilation as this on ff. 130ᵛ-135ᵛ, and considered it an editor's work; ibid., 248.

[20] This is from chapter 4 of the English translation of Henry Suso's *Horologium sapientiae*; cf. the Horstman text (from MS Douce 114), *Anglia* 10, 353-355.

[21] Edited by M. Doiron: '"The Mirror of Simple Souls". A Middle English Translation' (basing her text on MS St. John's College Cambridge 71, collated with A and with MS Bodley 505; the St. John's and Bodley manuscripts both belonged to the London Charterhouse).

[22] A compilation which 'includes the greater part of ch. xxxi-xxxvii of the spurious *Liber soliloquiorum animae ad Deum* ... (PL 40 888-898), extracts from St. Bernard, etc.' (BM Catalogue, 156).

[23] Edited and described by Peter Jolliffe: 'Two Middle English Tracts on the Contemplative Life' (MS 37, 1975, 85-121).

[24] A separate piece, though it may well be by the same editor-translator as the preceding one.

[25] Imperfect through the excision of f. 237, this translates part of Bridget of Sweden's *Revelationes* II 16, inc.: Ideo humilia te in omnibus ... (ed. Durante, Munich 1680, 127). The thirteen lines of script of which the first two letters of each line survive on the stub

## 2 C: the Cressy printed text[26]

> Title page: + / XVI / REVELATIONS / OF / Divine Love, /
> Shewed to a Devout Servant / of our Lord, called / MOTHER
> JULIANA, / AN / Anchorete of NORWICH: / Who lived in the
> Dayes of *KING* / *EDWARD* the Third. / Published by *R.F.S. Cressy.*
> / *Accedite ad Deum et Illuminamini.* Psal. 33 v. 5 / Printed in the
> Year, *MDCLXX.* / *Permissu Superiorum.*
> Pp. 1-215. Collation: title page, A²⁻³ + 1, B¹⁻⁴ + 4 - I¹⁻⁴ + 4, K¹⁻⁴
> + 4, O¹⁻⁴ + 4, P¹⁻³, end page, 4 unsigned pages.

Throughout, archaic words are marked with an asterisk or other
sign, repeated in the margin with a gloss. Running titles, e.g. (verso)
*Revelations of Love*, (recto) *The First Revelation*. Occasionally the recto titles
are misnumbered; e.g. pp. 31, 46-47, 49-51.

David Rogers of the Bodleian Library sent this communication:
'Though I cannot name you a printer, I am absolutely certain that
Cressy's edition of Julian of Norwich was printed in England, where
Cressy seems to have lived between his being sent on the mission in the
Southern Province in 1660 and his death at West Grinstead (not East
Grinstead, surely, as DNB has it) in 1674. The reason I am so certain is
the presence, on the second and third leaves, of a band of small type or-
naments known as "printers' flowers". These include a small two-
handled vase and two sorts of fleur-de-lys which can all be matched in
English books of the same date, but are quite unlike French or Flemish
ornaments of the same period. For example, I find what may be the
same three small ornaments used in a pamphlet entitled *Toleration disap-
prov'd and Condemn'd* by William Assheton, printed at Oxford by
William Hall in 1670, and again in John Gadbury's *A brief relation of the
Life and death of Mr. Vincent Wing,* printed in London in the same year'.

## 3 P: Paris, MS Bibliothèque Nationale Fonds anglais 40.[27]

Ff. iii + 1-23, 23^(bis)-174 + i (ruled, blank) — iv, 80 × 117 mm,

---

of f. 237 would be just sufficient to end chapter 16. There are in the English numerous
phrases, whether of the translator or from a variant text, not found in Durante's Latin.
This is not one of the passages in the manuscript edited by W. P. Cumming. Unlike the
other contents of A, this Bridget fragment is non-Northern in dialect, and gives the impression of coming from a quite separate source.

[26] For the purpose of this description the perfect copy at Trinity College, Cambridge
(in its original binding with tooled and gilt spine) has been used.

[27] Cf. Gaston Raynaud: *Catalogue des manuscrits anglais de la Bibliothèque Nationale,* 15-
16.

paper. Ruled 22 lines to the page. Binding nineteenth-century.

The only contents are the long text of the *Revelations*. It is written in a single hand, a sedulous but unskilled and unconvincing imitation, each letter individually formed, of a hand of c. 1500. It is certainly of the seventeenth century, probably c. 1650. There are running titles in red; e.g. (f. 7$^r$) 'The fourthe Chapter *and* the first revelacion'. Red paraphs, chapter initials in blue (with no guide letters). The scribe has written numerous words and phrases in red; these are usually, but not invariably, divine locutions.

Signatures of gatherings: (f. 16$^r$): B; (f. 31$^r$-i.e. 32$^r$ with 23$^{(bis)}$): C; (f. 47$^r$): D; (f. 59$^r$):E; (f. 75$^r$): F; (f. 91$^r$):G; (f. 105$^r$): H; (f. 119$^r$): J; (f. 135$^r$): K; (f. 151$^r$): L; (f. 167$^r$): M. Catchwords to almost every page.

The only indication of ownership, in a later hand, f. 1$^r$, is: icy commence le premier chapitre. Léopold Delisle, reprinting the 1706 sale-catalogue for the Bigot library's dispersal, suggested that its item 388, 'Julianae Anatoritae Revelationes, Anglice', is identical with P.[28] Since he informs us that with very few exceptions the Bigot manuscripts were acquired by the Bibliothèque du Roi, and are still preserved in the Bibliothèque Nationale,[29] since we know of no other Julian manuscript there, and since the sale-catalogue reproduces the misspelling of P, f. 174$^r$, *anatorite* (cf. 734.28), this is probable if not certain. The collection was begun in the first half of the seventeenth century at Rouen by Jean Bigot, and increased by his son Émeric until he died in 1689, when it was inherited by a cousin, after whose death it was sold.[30] If one of the Bigots did acquire P, it is interesting to speculate whether he recognized it for what it is, a product of his own age, or whether, like the catalogue of the Bibliothèque Nationale in the nineteenth century, he took it for some one hundred and fifty years older. There can be no question of P's being a 'forgery' — for that it is much too clumsy and inept — but its antique appearance may have recommended it to an undiscerning bibliophile.

Perforce the readings of P have wherever possible been retained, since, lacking any earlier exemplar of the long text, apart from the fragments in W (less possibly those in U), we have no certain criteria for emendation. But many of P's spellings and 'forms' seem to be no more

[28] *Bibliotheca Bigotiana*, 92.
[29] Ibid., iii.
[30] Ibid., iv-xix.

than an amateurish, Chatterton-like attempt to give the manuscript an appearance of antiquity by capricious departures from the norms of even the seventeenth century.

## 4 S1: London, MS British Museum Sloane 2499[31]

Ff. 57, 229 × 369 mm, paper, of poor quality. Recent binding. A sprawling and unattractive but regular hand of c. 1650, which closely resembles that of Mother Clementina Cary, ob. 1671, foundress of the English Benedictine nunnery at Paris, and daughter of Elizabeth, Lady Falkland, to whom, the year before Clementina's death, Cressy was to dedicate his edition. Her copies of the *Constitutions* and of Blosius are now preserved at Colwich Abbey.[32] They both seem more practised and contrived than the Sloane manuscript, but, none the less, the resemblance is close enough to warrant the suggestion that, if the scribes are not identical, their hands were formed in the same school. C. 40 lines to the page. The first eight folios, particularly, can be read only with difficulty, since the ink of either surface obscures the reverse. On f. 1$^r$, '6 5' at the head of the page and '1B' in the right-hand margin may be press-marks earlier than those of the Sloane collection. Several hands have supplied marginal and interlinear corrections and glosses, and one which frequently appears has on f. 19$^v$ underlined 'lak' and 'lakid' (cf. 409.13) and written in the margin: 'not liked of, from ye dutch word lacken to dispraise, to blame, being the opposit to ye D word prysen to praise'.

The only contents are the long text of the Revelations, as also in S2.

## 5 S2: London, MS British Museum Sloane 3705

Ff. i + i, 153 × 194 mm, paper. Nineteenth-century binding with Sloane arms. C. 23 lines to the page; the margins but not the lines ruled. A regular, flowing, legible hand of the eighteenth century. In an unnumbered folio of the same fine paper, between ff. 87 and 90, are mounted two smaller paper slips, 57 × 84 mm, numbered 88 and 89. On what are now the versos are drawn (both in black) the ten of diamonds and the ace of spades; on the rectos are what seem to be household recipes, many words in code, in a different, contemporary hand. On

---

[31] The descriptions of S1 and S2 in Samuel Ayscough's 1782 catalogue do not merit reporting.

[32] Placid Spearritt drew our attention to this resemblance. For Clementina Cary, see Gillow, 1 417.

f. i^r, '111 B' may be an early press-mark. Some contemporary marginal corrections and comments.

## 6 U: MS St. Joseph's College, Upholland (Lancashire, England)[33]

Ff. 127, 100 × 155 mm, paper, unruled. The cover is a portion of a vellum leaf with verses of the Psalms with musical notation from a late mediaeval choir office book. Another such leaf is used to bind MS Colwich Abbey 18, which was copied by the English Benedictine nuns at Cambrai c. 1650; and it is beyond any doubt that this Upholland manuscript was written there about the same time. Hywel Owen wrote: 'The manuscript is in four seventeenth-century hands. One of the hands is undoubtedly that of Dame Barbara Constable, the daughter of Sir Philip Constable of Evringham, Yorkshire. Born in 1617, she was professed in 1640 at the abbey of Our Lady of Consolation at Cambrai ... and died there in 1684. Since her hand occurs in the first seven and the last three folios (as well as intermittently between) this gives us a dating of 1640-1684 for the manuscript, and indicates that it was copied at Cambrai'.[34]

It is unnecessary here to repeat Hywell Owen's careful identifications of the contents of this manuscript. It is an anthology of Augustine Baker's Englishings, primarily for the benefit of the Cambrai nuns, of a wide selection from mediaeval and post-Reformation spiritual classics, and its chief importance is that it indicates the probability that we must thank Baker, as will be shown below, for the preservation of a complete long text of Julian and for its study in the seventeenth century, culminating in the 1670 printed text edited by his successor among the English Benedictines, Serenus Cressy. Whether Baker acquired his copy, now lost, of the Julian text, as he did that of *The Cloud of Unknowing,* from his fellow-countryman, also living in exile, Benet Canfield,[35] we do not know.

## 7 W: London, Westminster Archdiocesan Archives MS[36]

Ff. 112, 106 × 156 mm, vellum. A highly legible, somewhat characterless hand of c. 1500. Nineteenth-century binding. Annotated

---

[33] Cf. Hywel Wynn Owen: 'Another Augustine Baker Manuscript.'

[34] Ibid., 270.

[35] Placid Spearritt is at work on Augustine Baker, Kent Emery on Benet Canfield, and both scholars promise us studies of the contribution of Baker and Canfield to the revival among seventeenth-century English Catholics of study of the mediaeval mystics.

[36] Cf. James Walsh and Edmund Colledge: *Of the Knowledge of Ourselves and of God,* and Betty Foucard: 'A Cathedral Manuscript'; and see also N. R. Ker: *Medieval Manuscripts in British Libraries* 1, 418-419.

throughout in hands of the seventeenth century; and some of these notes suggest that, c. 1700, the manuscript was in Catholic hands and was then carefully studied.

Gatherings of eight, indicated by catchwords on ff. 8$^v$, 16$^v$, etc. An older set of folio-numbers mostly lost by cropping; if there were any signatures to the gatherings, these also have been totally lost.

F. 1$^r$ inc.: He that wonyth in þe helpe of the hyeste ...

f. 25$^r$ exp.: ... I shall loue hym and I shall shewe me vnto hym.[37]
  inc.: It is good to shryue to *our* lord god ...

f. 35$^v$ exp.: ... wysely and godly in all thyngis.[38]
  inc.: Hit nedyth to a soule þ*at* wold haue knowyng of goostly thyng*es* ...

f. 72$^r$ exp.: ... oþer sothfastenes of þe blessed trinite p*er*teynyng to þis mater þe whiche is ope*n*.[39] (The rest of the page blank.)

f. 72$^v$ inc.: Oure gracious *and* goode lorde god shewed me in party ...

f. 112$^v$ exp.: ... in this blessed beholdyng as often as we may *and* as long.[40]

Reference to the critical apparatus of the long text will show how this last item, a series of short extracts from Julian, is composed.

## II SCRIBES AND OWNERS OF MANUSCRIPTS AND OF THE PRINTED TEXT

### 1 A

It has already been stated that all that we know certainly about the ownership of A is that it bears the monogram of James Grenehalgh, and that this does not necessarily mean that A was in the Sheen monastic library or privately owned there. There is some slight evidence that Grenehalgh may at one time have been resident in the London monastery; after his removal from Sheen he was first at Coventry and thereafter at Hull, and there are surviving printed and manuscript books which he destined for Syon (though A lacks their distinguishing mark, a 'J.S.' or 'J.G.S.' monogram in his hand to draw some passage to the attention of his Syon confidante, Joanna Sewell).[41] But many of

---

[37] Cf. B. Wallner: *An Exposition,* 2-50.

[38] Cf. Wallner, 51-92. Wallner's edition appeared before the existence and contents of W were announced. He edited the two texts from five manuscripts, all probably earlier than W. These commentaries on *Qui habitat* and *Bonum est* have been attributed to Walter Hilton, but there is no manuscript tradition to support this.

[39] A compilation from Hilton's *Scale of Perfection*

[40] The compilation from Julian's *Revelations.*

[41] James Walsh and Edmund Colledge have had at press for a number of years with

the contents suggest that this anthology was edited by the Carthusians; the English *Mirror of Simple Souls* and what there is of an English Ruysbroek canon can be shown to owe their existence to them.

The presence in A but in no other known manuscript of Julian's short text suggests that after the long text was composed and put into circulation the earlier version was either suppressed or forgotten. As do other texts in A, this indicates an editor with an eye for rarities in the literature of contemplation.

The first post-Reformation indication of ownership is the inscription, f. 1ʳ, 'Vincit Winge his Booke'. The only Vincent Wings mentioned in DNB are the astronomer (1619-1668), his father, of North Luffenham, Rutland, and his son.

In the mid-eighteenth century, A was in the possession of Francis Peck, rector of Godeby by Melton in Leicestershire and author of *Academia tertia anglicana*. The preface to this work shows Peck to have been an indefatigable collector of mediaeval documents, so that he can compare himself with Eumnestes in *The Faerie Queene*:

> Whose chamber all was hang'd about with Rolls,
> Some made in Books, some in long Parchment Scrolls,
> That were all worm-eaten and full of Cankerholes.

Francis Blomefield, in the second volume of his *Norfolk*, describing St. Julian's Church in Norwich, wrote:

> In the East Part of this Church-yard stood an *Anchorage*, in which an *Ankeress* or *Recluse* dwelt 'till the Dissolution, when the House was demolished, tho' the Foundations may still be seen: In 1393, Lady *Julian* the *Ankeress* here, was a strict *Recluse,* and had 2 Servants to attend her in her old Age, Aº 1443. This Woman in those Days, was esteemed one of the greatest Holynesse. The Rev. Mr. *Francis Peck,* Author of the Antiquities of *Stanford,* had an old Vellum Mss. 36 4ᵗᵒ Pages of which, contain'd an Account of the Visions &c. of this Woman, which begins thus, 'Here es a Vision schewed be the Goodenes of God, to a devoute Woman, and hir name is Julian, that is *Recluse* atte Norwyche, and yitt ys on Life, Anno Domini M. CCCC. XLII. In the whilke Vision er fulle many comfortabyll Wordes & greatly styrrande to alle they that desyres to be Crystes Looverse'. [42]

---

the *Archivio italiano per la storia della pietà* their edition of MS Pembroke College Cambridge 221, Richard Methley's Latin translations of *The Cloud of Unknowing* and *The Mirror of Simple Souls* which contain much editorial work by Grenehalgh; Edmund Colledge and Michael Sargent are preparing an account of MS Douai Bibliothèque Municipale 396, also considerably edited by Grenehalgh; Michael Sargent is at work on a comprehensive study of the printed and manuscript books owned and edited by Grenehalgh.

[42] *Norfolk* 2 546.

Blomefield's '36 4$^{to}$ Pages' corresponds with the numeration of the Julian text in A, ff. 97$^r$-115$^r$; and the close agreement of his transcript of the opening lines with those in A, preserving spellings such as 'styrrande', 'looverse' and the form 'to alle they', cannot be fortuitous. It will be observed that whoever made the transcript has correctly interpreted the ambiguous first coloured initial as giving 'Here'. It is true that the date is wrong by forty years, but that is merely because the transcriber substituted 'l' for 'i', a very common source of error.

Blomefield published his second *Norfolk* volume in 1745, two years after Peck's death. We learn from Thomas Secombe[43] that Peck's widow retired to Harlaxton in Lincolnshire, where she died about 1758, in which year Peck's books were sold by auction.[44] From an older binding is still preserved the bookplate of William Constable. How A came into his possession is unknown. Joseph Gillow indicates that it was his father, Cuthbert Constable, 'the Catholic Mæcenas of his age', who formed the Burton Constable collection of books and manuscripts.[45] Cuthbert died in 1748, and was succeeded by William, who died without issue. That this Julian manuscript should have come to be owned by the Constable family, some of whose daughters had been distinguished members of the Cambrai and Paris English Benedictine communities,[46] so active in the preservation and dissemination of the long text, is a remarkable accident; but it seems to be no more than that.

### 2 C: Serenus Cressy[47]

Hugh Paulinus Cressy (who later took the religious name 'Serenus') was born in 1603 or 1605, probably at Wakefield in the West Riding of Yorkshire, where he was baptized, the son of Hugh Cressy, a barrister of Lincoln's Inn, and of Margery, daughter of Thomas d'Oylie. He was

---

[43] 'Peck, Francis (1692-1743)' (DNB).

[44] John Nichols: *Literary Anecdotes*, 3 655.

[45] *Biographical Dictionary*, 1 548-549.

[46] Dame Barbara Constable was professed at Cambrai in 1640; Dame Mary Joseph Constable was professed at Paris after 1695 and died there in 1767. When the Paris community was released from imprisonment in April, 1795, and returned to England, one of their number was Dame Frances Sheldom, a connexion of William Constable. We owe this information to Dame Eanswith Edwards of Stanbrook Abbey and Dame Edith Street of Colwich Abbey.

[47] The whole of this information concerning Cressy has been generously furnished by Placid Spearritt. See also his valuable article, 'The Survival of Mediaeval Spirituality among the Exiled English Black Monks'.

educated at Wakefield Grammar School and at Oxford, where he graduated B.A. in 1623, M.A. in 1627. He was elected at Merton College as a probationer in 1625 and as a fellow in 1627. At an unknown date he received Anglican orders, and was thereafter, on the recommendation of Archbishop Laud, made chaplain to Thomas, Lord Wentworth, later earl of Strafford. Some years before Strafford's fall, he had become chaplain to Lucius Cary, Lord Falkland, whom he accompanied to Ireland. There he was appointed successively prebendary of St. Patrick's and Christ Church, Dublin, and dean of Leighlin; but in 1639 he returned to England, where he became in 1642 a canon of Windsor. It would seem that he enjoyed the benefits of few or none of these preferments because of the Civil War.

Falkland had a house at Burford near Oxford, where Cressy often stayed, and where he became acquainted with Cuthbert Fursden, O.S.B., a disciple of Augustine Baker, whom Falkland's mother Elizabeth, who had been reconciled to the Catholic Church, maintained as a chaplain. All her four daughters, including Dame Clementia Cary, became nuns at Cambrai. After Falkland's death at the battle of Newbury and the rapid decline of Royalist fortunes, Cressy's High Church principles forced him to leave the country. About 1645 he went abroad on the grand tour as tutor to Charles Berkely, later Lord Falmouth. In the next year he was publicly converted to Catholicism in Rome. Thereafter he studied at the Sorbonne. In 1647 he published in Paris his *Exomologesis,* a justification of his reconciliation. At first he wanted to join the French Carthusians and to separate himself altogether from English speakers; however, it was to the exiled English Carthusians at Nieuport, 'Sheen Anglorum', that he first went. He was discouraged from pursuing their vocation because of his marked literary abilities. Instead, in 1648 he joined the English Benedictines at Douai, where he was professed in 1649, ordained in 1651, and in that year or the next sent as chaplain to the newly-founded house of English Benedictine nuns in Paris. In 1652 he went as subprior to St. Lawrence's, Dieulouard; from 1653 to 1660 he was again at Douai, where he wrote ascetical, historical and polemical works. In 1660 he joined the mission in England, and was established at Somerset House as a chaplain to Charles II's queen, Catherine of Braganza. In 1669 he received honorary appointment as titular prior of Rochester; and he spent his last years in the house of Richard Caryll at West Grinstead, where he died on 10 August, 1674.

Although Cressy's sojourn with the nuns in Paris was so brief, it is virtually certain that it was there that he began work on his Julian edition, as we shall see when what is known of the provenance and ownership of P, S1, S2 and U is summarized.

The prefatory epistle 'To the Reader' in the Cressy 1670 edition states that it has been produced at the expense of 'a more Venerable Abbot of our Nation'; and there is a marginal note to this, 'The V(ery) R(everend) F(ather) Jo(hn) Guscoyn L(ord) Abbot of Lambspring'. This was John Placid Gascoigne (1599-1681), a younger son of John Gascoigne, a Yorkshire Catholic created a Nova-Scotian baronet in 1635, and of Anne, daughter of John Ingleby. John Placid's third sister, Catherine, became abbess of Cambrai, and his sixth sister, Justina, was prioress of Paris when she died in 1690. His eldest brother, Thomas, and his wife, Anne, daughter of John Symeon, had among their children Catherine, who became prioress of Paris, and Frances, a nun at Cambrai.

MS Ampleforth 165, Peter Allanson's *Biography of the English Benedictines,* has some unenthusiastic things to say about Abbot Placid. He ruled over Lambspring for more than thirty years, and was best remembered for his implacable opposition to all the efforts of the English Congregation to make his office, like all their others, tenable for four years only. Allanson writes that he 'was much given to Literature himself, but was no ways solicitous in promoting learning among his subjects, and is handed down as being regardless of learning in those whom he admitted to their Profession', and he castigates the abbot's 'inactivity and apathy'.

This being so, it is probably not unjust to suspect that it was his family ties at Cambrai and Paris which won the abbot's help for the Cressy printed edition.

For two centuries after its appearance, Cressy's printed text was the only source of information for scholars, Blomefield and his report of A excepted. Cressy's work was known to some European theologians. The Protestant Pierre Poiret, who had detailed knowledge of Augustine Baker, Benet Canfield and Gertrude More, has, in his 'Catalogus Auctorum Mysticorum', an entry *'Julianae,* Matris Anachoretae, Revelationes de amore Dei. *Anglice.* Theodidactae, profundae, estaticae'.[48] Gerhard Tersteegen, whose spiritual reading as a young man had been guided by Poiret's works,[49] assures us that Poiret knew of Julian through Cressy,[50] who is the source also of Tersteegen's well-

[48] *Bibliotheca mysticorum,* 336.
[49] 'Tersteegen, Gerhard,' (*Allgemeine Deutsche Biographie* 37, 577).
[50] *Auserlesene Lebensbeschreibungen* 3, 252 note a.

informed and perceptive account of her.[51] He shows how highly he esteemed her in his artless verses:

Von scharfer Reinigung und hohem Gott-Beschauen
　　A Cruce weisslich redt;
Mechtild und Julian vom kindlichen Vertrauen,
　　Theresa vom Gebet;[52]

and the success of his translated extracts may be judged by this one quotation:

Es sagte unser guter Herr zu mir, fragende: Bist du wohl damit zufrieden, dass ich für dich gelitten habe? Ich sagte: Ja, guter Herr, ich sage dir Dank davor; ja, guter Herr, gesegnet müssest du seyn. Darnach sagte Jesus, unser guter Herr: Wann du zufrieden bist, dann bin ich auch zufrieden: es ist mir eine Freude, eine Glückseligkeit, und ein unendliches Wohlgefallen, dass ich mein Leiden für dich ausgestanden habe. Und wenn ich mehr hätte leiden mögen, ich würde mehr gelitten haben.[53]

Cressy's text was reprinted in 1843 by G. H. Parker, and again in 1902 with a preface by George Tyrrell; but original work on Julian began only in 1877, when H. Collins published his modernization of S1. This was followed in 1901 by Grace Warrack's version of S1, published with an excellent introduction which has well stood the test of time, and has been used (not, invariably, with due acknowledgment) by many later writers. When she first wrote, A, of the existence of which she knew from Blomefield, was thought to be lost; but in 1911, two years after it had been acquired by the British Museum, Dundas Harford's modernized version of the short text appeared. Many other such versions have since been published; as the celebrations in Norwich in 1973 to commemorate the six hundredth anniversary of her revelations demonstrated, Julian's popularity does not diminish.

3　Seventeenth-Century Copies of the Long Text

C, P, S1 and U are, all four, roughly contemporary; even U could have been written after C's appearance in 1670, since Barbara Constable, one of its scribes, lived for another fourteen years. Hywel Owen has shown conclusively that it was written at Cambrai; how it journeyed from there to Upholland we do not know. We cannot assign S1

---

[51] Ibid. 3, 251-274.
[52] Ibid. 3, 6.
[53] Ibid. 3, 257; cf. 382.3-383.8.

to any one house, but the variety of hands correcting and commenting on it suggest that it was written in a religious community and thereafter much used; and the note, already described in I 4, on f. 19ᵛ, correctly glossing the noun and verb 'lack', suggesting (as does NED) that the word in Middle English may have been borrowed from Middle Dutch, and adducing as antonyms Dutch 'laaken' and 'prijsen', must have been written by someone concerned to make the language of a mediaeval English spiritual writer comprehensible, and competent enough in Dutch to make this most accurate observation. Very clearly, this points to the circle of Augustine Baker and his successors, living and working in the border-towns between France and the Low Countries with their mixed French and Dutch-speaking populations. The inscription on f. 1ʳ of P suggests that it came to the Bibliothèque Nationale from private French ownership; it may be that it was before in the conventual library of either Cambrai or Paris. The close affinities of the texts of S1 and S2 suggest that S2 originated in the same house as S1.

In several places we have indications that P was copied from a manuscript in which words thought archaic had been glossed, and that the P scribe could not distinguish between archaism and modern-ization. 432.5-6, P reads: *for I was nott tho taught in thys tyme,* 'for I was not then taught at this time'. C, SS omit 'tho', nor is the word found in A (252.15-16); but we may conjecture that the ancestor of the long-text manuscripts read 'for I was nott tho taught', and that 'in thys tyme' was later supplied as a gloss to 'tho'. That the corresponding short text agrees with C, SS suggests that the gloss was supplied from it. P seems to have copied the whole blindly, and it was probably a later hand which cancelled 'tho'. So too with 464.42, 43, *interly inwardly* (cf. note) ; and in this case there has been no subsequent cancellation.

We have some evidence to show that the nuns' libraries in Cambrai and Paris did possess such copies of Julian. What is now MS Colwich Abbey 18, copied at Cambrai about 1650, bound in a piece of the same office book as supplied the cover for U, reads, p. 155: 'Thou hast saide, O Lorde, to a deere childe of thine, Lette me alone, my deare worthy childe, intende (or attende) to me, I am inough to thee, reioice in thy Sauiour and Saluation (this was spoken to Iulian the Ankress of[54] norw(ich), as appeareth by the booke of her reuelations)'. This is found in 'Gascoigne B', a work composed by Dame Margaret Gascoigne, born 1608, professed at Cambrai 1629, died 1637;[55] and it establishes that there was a text of the *Revelations* at Cambrai some time before 1637,

---

[54] Ms: or.
[55] Cf. Gillow, 'Records of the English Benedictine Nuns at Cambrai', 43.

earlier (in the present editors' opinion) than the writing of P, and certainly earlier than S1. If it was under Baker's guidance that Margaret Gascoigne was introduced to the text (that is, before he left Cambrai for Douai in 1633), it is very probable that he himself made a modernized, easily readable version, as he had done with the *Cloud* and the writings of William Flete and Walter Hilton.[56] In the quotation (from chapter 36 — cf. 439.47), the informative comment in parentheses much resembles Baker's editorial style. As Hywel Owen has observed, 'If a Baker modernization of the *Revelations* is found in the treatise of a Cambrai nun before 1637, then it follows that the version in U, itself a Cambrai manuscript, is more than likely to be from the same Baker modernization, since the possibility of there being two such versions, independent of each other, is very remote'.[57]

But a glance at the present edition of P will show that it is no such modernization. It is the work of a not especially gifted antiquarian, more concerned, we may suspect, with appearance and form than meaning. This at once absolves Augustine Baker of having any hand in its preparation or circulation. MS Mazarine 4058, quoted below, specifies that the Julian manuscript in its catalogue is not by him.

It will be seen from the long text's critical apparatus that in a number of places (notably 302.36, 303.43, 311.13, 333.81, 334.91, 335.95, 364.48, 411.27, 411.31, 474.65, 477.23, 509.44, 520.82, 521.98, 561.9, 570.9, 572.20, 576.7, 589.4, 615.13, 619.6) P's readings have been emended by correctors. One of them, it seems, collated P after the appearance of C with the printed text, others with a text of the type of S1 and S2.

There is independent evidence[58] that in Paris Julian's writings were available to the sisters. MS Mazarine 4058 (unfoliated) is entitled 'A Catalogue of the Manuscript bookes belonging to the Liberary of the English Benedictine Nunnes of our B. Lady of Good Hope in paris'. Among 'The Maniscripts which belongs not to the venerable Father Augustine Bakers Workes' is listed 'The Reuelations of Sainte Julian'. Placid Spearritt points out that in deciding whether this could be P, S1 or S2, 'one criterion would be the presence of the usual ownership formula on the fly-leaf: This Booke belongs to ye English Benedictine Nunnes ...; but none of the three manuscripts has such a mark. MS Mazarine 4057, a catalogue of the nuns' library dated 1702, has, under

---

[56] Cf. Hywel Owen, 'Another Augustine Baker Manuscript', 275-279.
[57] Ibid., 280.
[58] First brought to our notice by Placid Spearritt.

press-mark 12. M. 27, 'Mo: Juliana XVI Revelations publish'd by F. S. Cressy 1670'.

Doubtless other records would show that most Benedictine libraries, overseas and then, after the French Revolution, in England, possessed copies of Cressy. It was Benedictine devotion to Julian which preserved knowledge of her work (a few antiquarians such as Peck and Blomefield apart), and it was they who awarded her the 'beatificatio aequipollens', calling her 'Saint' and 'Blessed'. There may well be an unconscious reminiscence of her *Revelations* recorded in an anecdote concerning the deathbed of William Bernard Ullathorne, first archbishop of Birmingham, sixty-six years after he had first entered Downside, where he had been professed and ordained. A witness reported: 'When the prayers of the dying were being recited, at the words "From the snares of the devil deliver him, O Lord", he interjected "The devil's an ass"';[59] Julian's story (cf. 228.41 e.s., 346.24 e.s.) of how knowledge of the devil's impotence made her laugh aloud, so that all who thought that they were assisting at her last moments laughed with her, is surely too singular and too close to this for mere coincidence. Furthermore, we have direct evidence that Ullathorne had studied some of the mediaeval English mystics. The Benedictine Robert Ephram Guy tells us in his preface to his modernization of *The Scale of Perfection* that Ullathorne, when shown a specimen of it, expressed his approval both of Guy's choice of text: '... the Ladder of Perfection ... is perhaps the clearest, best balanced, and best adapted for wide circulation of any of them ('our old ascetic works')', and of his style, which the archbishop found more faithful to the original than Cressy's.[60] And the Oscott copy of the Worde 1519 *Scale* (a considerable rarity, not found in Pollard and Redgrave or the BM Catalogue) was given to the college library by Ullathorne.[61]

### III Relations Between the Short and Long Texts

The biographical information in the first lines of the short text seems to have been supplied by another hand and to witness to the editing to which the short text, no less than the long, was subjected. Julian herself gives us the following chronology: the revelations were received on May 13, 1373 (285.3), when she was thirty and a half years old (207.1, 289.2),

---

[59] Cuthbert Butler; *The Life and Times of Bishop Ullathorne*, 2 295.
[60] *The Scale (or Ladder) of Perfection*, xlvii.
[61] Ibid., xxxix; Dorothy Jones, *Minor Works*, xxvi-xxvii.

after which she meditated upon them for fifteen years or more (732.14), before producing her second version. We may suppose, though we cannot prove, that the short text was recorded soon after the event. There seems no reason for her to attach special importance to the year 1413, or for us to assume that it was only later, more than forty years afterwards, that the long text was first recorded. Rather, the preface in A suggests a scribe with local knowledge producing copies as they were required; and that he was free still to copy the short text also suggests that he was not working under Julian's own direction.

We have no guarantee that in A there is a descendant of Julian's own first account of her visions, recorded without any comparison with the second, longer version. [62] There is one place where the evidence seems irrefrangible that before A was copied there had been collation of the two versions. Where A reads

> ... þat sche behelde hyre god, that ys hir makere, mervelande with grete reuerence that he wolde be borne of hir that was a sympille creature of his makynge. For this was hir mervelynge, that he that was hir makere walde be borne of hir that was a sympille creature of his makynge. And this wysdome of trowthe ...

the text has been emended (cf. 214.30), since the second sentence is obviously the result of dittography, the careless repetition of what had already been written. But the same mistake is found in C, P and W (though not in SS; cf. 297.34). Whether this result of scribal error was introduced into the long text from the short or vice versa we cannot say; but manifestly there has been 'lateral contamination', and the evidence of W shows that it took place in the fifteenth century. That the defective reading is not found in SS is probably because of the S1 scribe's intelligent perception.

Within the manuscripts of the long text, S1 (and this will apply also to S2, which seems to be a discreetly modernized transcript of S1) is independent of P and also of C. This can be demonstrated from cruces where the editors have had recourse to S1 to restore to P the sense of the original. In the present text, *yerning* (302.36), *geyn (makyng)* (330.55), *foreseing* (337.9) all make notable improvement upon P; and in *clongyn* (357.10) we have the only witness (not excluding A) which has not reduced what Julian must have written to nonsense. It has already been suggested that Cressy for his version, close though it usually is to P, may

---

[62] The suggestion that there may be 'long text' readings in A, never to our knowledge previously made, was first advanced to us by Frances Beer.

have consulted a now lost modernization by Baker ; but S1 preserves many archaisms which such a modernization might replace ; e.g. *vnderfongyn* (287.23), *tempests* (287.28), *vnyd* (300.20), *sweeme* (319.31). S1 and P may well derive, though not immediately, from the same pre-Dissolution manuscript of the long text, but neither derives from the other.

Beyond this, the editors find it as impossible as Hywel Owen did [63] to pronounce on the inter-relations between the witnesses of the long text, except that with the obvious exception of W they all, somehow, seem to derive from Cambrai or Paris.

In the short text we can perceive the rudiments of the structure which Julian would evolve more completely for the long. She has clearly in mind what was the sequence of the revelations, and their distinctions. But, except for two passing references to 'this fyrste schewynge' (217.4) and 'the fyrst syght' (218.18), there is no indication that the sequence was numbered, as is that of the chapters in the long text. But in twenty-five places in A the scribe indicates a new section by beginning a new line and leaving space for a coloured initial, which the limner, not always correctly, supplies. When we observe that in twelve instances these incipits correspond with those of new revelations or chapters in the long text (i = 2, ii = 3, viii = III 11, x = VIII 16, xii = 22, xiii = X 24, xiv = 29, xv = 31, xix = XIV 41, xxii = 68, xxiii = 69, xxv = 74), we are left with little doubt that the A scribe is preserving an arrangement originally devised by Julian; and accordingly the editors have supplied these short-text 'chapters' with small Roman numeration. There can be no doubt that in the long text the division into sixteen 'showings' is Julian's work, whilst she was so carefully scrutinizing and revising what she had first written. So long as she adheres to the sequence and the subject-matter of the short text, she does not employ cross-references; it is significant how many of such cross-references (e.g. 331.64, 419.30, 427.9, 466.54, 566.11, 572.19, 580.52, 632.4, 692.32-33) occur in passages which have no correspondence with the first version. We may judge that it is not merely the greater length of the second version which accounts for the system which she employs in it. Such a passage as:

> Plentuously, fully and swetely was this shewde; and it is spoken of in the furst, wher it seyde we be all in hym beclosyd, and he is beclosyd in vs. And that is spoken of in the xvi shewyng, where he seyth he syttyth in oure soule ... (580.51),

---

[63] 'Another Augustine Baker Manuscript', 276-278.

testifies to the meditative processes which had endowed Julian with her perception of the unity of the revelations and the relevance of each to the others, so that finally she can write of the last that it is 'conclusyon and confirmation to all the xv' (632.4). To demonstrate this, she needed to number them, so that she could make such references as:

> and that shewde he in the ix<sup>th</sup>, where he sayth: It is a joy, a blysse, an end-lesse lykyng to me that evyr I sufferd passion for the. And this is the blysse of Cristes werkes, and thus he menyth ther he seyth in the same shewyng: We be his blysse ... (419.30)

and, where necessary, anticipate — 'in the xvi shewyng, as I shall sey' (572.19 and note).

One aspect of the relations between the two texts must be considered, four major discrepancies between the two differently-presented narratives.

The first of these dislocations occurs in chapter 4 of the long text or in the corresponding portion of the short:

> *and than I sayde: Benedicite dominus ... and agaynes alle gostelye enmyes* (210.16-211.27)

corresponds with

> *In this same tyme that I saw this sight ... that is made betweene my god and me* (299.2-300.22).

> *In this god brought oure ladye ... botte the blyssede manhede of Criste* (213.24-214.36)

corresponds with

> *In this he brought our ladie ... but the blessed manhood of Christ, as to my sight* (297.28-298.40).

> *This lytille thynge that es made ... me thought it myght hafe fallene for litille* (214.36-39)

corresponds with

> *This little thing that is made, me thought it might haue fallen to nought for littlenes* (300.23).

It will be seen that in the short text the 'bodily sight' of the hazel nut comes first, and is followed by the 'ghostly and bodily sight' of Mary; Julian says that she saw that Mary is greater than the rest of creation, Christ's humanity alone excepted, she implies that creation is symbolized by the hazel-nut she had been shown, and she repeats that it was so small that it could have perished. In the long text, however, the vision of Mary comes first; there is no allusion there to the hazel-nut, the vision of which comes second, so that the remark that it was so small that it could have perished appears only once.

So far as sense and doctrine are concerned, either text is acceptable. Stylistically, the longer text seems superior. It will be seen that in the account of the vision of Mary in both texts occurs the repetition through dittography already remarked. If some scribe-editor, engaged in the preparation of a revision (whether of the long text or the short), committed this error, and if his work thereafter was regarded as so authoritative that the other text must be made to conform to it, that would account for the mistake's appearance in either text.

The second dislocation affects the text of chapters 8 and 9 of the long text and of the corresponding portion of the short.

> *Alle this blyssede techynge of oure lorde god ... than I can or maye telle it zowe* (224. 1-7).

corresponds with

> *All this ... then I can or may tell it* (323. 29-34).

> *And in alle this I was mekylle styrrede ... and nathynge in specyalle* (224. 8-11)

corresponds with

> *In alle this I was much steryde ... was shewde in generalle* (319. 22-24).

> *Of alle that I sawe ... and syekernes in saule* (224. 12-14)

corresponds with

> *and of all the syght that I saw ... and syckernes in soule* (313. 31-34).

> *Than sayde I to the folke ... to hafe dyed* (224. 14-225. 20)

corresponds with

> *Than sayde I to them ... to haue dyed* (319. 25-30).

> *And aftyr this ... me nedyd na lyght botte hym* (225. 21-29)

corresponds with

> *And after this ... thou nedyth none but him* (324. 3-325. 14).

All that has happened here is that in one text or the other several brief reflections on the nature or the teachings of the revelations have been differently but quite harmlessly redistributed, doing no violence to the narrative.

The third dislocation, of a single passage only, affecting chapter 20 of the long text and its equivalent in the short, is as follows:

> *And thus sawe I my lorde Jhesu ... fullyest noghthede and witterlyest dyspyside* (237. 6-238. 15)

corresponds with

> *And thus saw I oure lorde Jhesu ... foulest condempnyd and vtterly dyspysed* (374. 2-375. 9).

> *Botte the loue ... and evere schalle be with owtynn any ende* (238.15-19)

corresponds with

> *The loue ... and shall be without ende* (386.46-387.49).

> *And sodaynlye ... And I was fulle merye* (239.1-5)

corresponds with

> *sodenly ... And I was fulle mery* (379.6-11).

Since the long text's additions in chapter 20 are as closely concerned with the Passion and its fruits as is the corresponding short text, the reflection on the topic in 238.15-19, 386.46-387.49 is as relevant in one place as in the other.

The fourth dislocation affects three widely separate places in the long text, chapters 40, 47 and 64.

> *he is so vnmyghttye ... for he sees nought* (262.64-66)

corresponds with

> *He is vnmyghty ... for he seeth not* (496.17-20).

> *and thann wenes he ... that þou erte commen* (262.68-75)

corresponds with

> *then we wene ... thou arte come* (454.5-455.13).

> *Before this tyme ... it schalle be nouȝt* (263.1-264.25)

corresponds with

> *Afore this tyme ... shall be nought* (619.5-622.30).

Again, this reflection is as congruent in its long-text context as in the other, and we are in no position to judge whether Julian herself may not have been responsible for its later transposition. But, whoever carried it out, plainly this and the three other cases considered (they are by no means the only instances of such transpositions, but their length and their content allow them best to be evaluated) are not the result of carelessness or mishap. Two manuscripts of *The Chastising of God's Children* have a curious dislocation which can be clearly seen to result from one leaf in a now lost ancestor having been excised from its gathering and replaced out of order. The consequence is two long dislocations of the text; but they are of equal length, and there are junctures of word-groups which give no sense.[64] Neither circumstance obtains in these cases; whoever made these changes did so with deliberation.

What has so far been considered seems to result from later scribes' manipulations of their copy-texts; but there is clear internal evidence that Julian herself rewrote her second version at least once, and that the process of revision followed illumination which she received about the meaning and congruence of showings which she for long had not understood, and mention of which she had therefore suppressed in the short text and also in her first draft of the long. She tells us that what we now have as the long text was not begun before 1388 (732.14). Comparison of the two texts shows, as the annotations indicate at the relevant places, how much was added to the short text, usually in the form of theological reflections; but there are certain additions which amplify her original account of what had been shown to her. The most notable of these additions is chapter 51, the allegory of the lord and the servant; and this cannot have been composed before March, 1393:

> For twenty yere after the tyme of the shewyng saue thre monthys I had techyng inwardly as I shall sey: It longyth to the to take hede to alle þe propertes and the condescions that were shewed in the example, though þe thyngke that it be mysty and indefferent to thy syght. I assentyd wylfully with grett desyer, seeing inwardly with avysement all the poyntes and the propertes that were shewed in the same tyme, as ferforth as my wytt and my vnderstandyng wylle serve, begynnyng my beholdyng at the lorde and at þe servannt (520.86).

This indicates plainly why the allegory does not appear in the short text: when that was written, she did not understand the *example,* which was *mysty,* and therefore thought that it could be treated as *indefferent,* that it could be omitted and forgotten. But this was not what happened. She has just before written of the 'three properties' of her showings: the first, that from their very reception she had had from them 'the beginning of teaching', the second, that she continued to receive further enlightenment, the third that *alle the hole revelation fro˜the begynnyng to the ende ... oure lorde god of his goodnes bryngyth oftymes frely to the syght of my vnderstondyng* (520.78). Later it will be observed how closely this accords with other definitions, regarded as authoritative, of what are the marks of authentic private divine revelation; and one sign will be that such revelations are integral.

---

[64] *Chastising,* 18-19.

We may deduce that the years 1388-1393 were spent in the composition of the long text's 'first edition', which now had to be revised
and converted into the second, to present the revelations in their en-
tirety, from a further piece of evidence. Chapter 1 of the long text is a
summary, revelation by revelation, of the contents. In the annotations
to this chapter the editors have shown the criteria, theological and
stylistic, which have led them to the opinion that this is Julian's own
work. But when in that chapter she describes Revelation XIV, all that
we read is:

> The xiiii is that our lord god is grownd of our beseking. Heer in was seen
> two fayer properties. That one is rightfull preaier; that other is verie trust,
> which he will both be one lyke large. And thus our praier liketh him, and
> he of his goodnes fullfillyth it (284.43).

This is the only summary in chapter 1 in which each revelation's notable
visions and locutions are not alluded to; this deals only with the matter
of the meditative chapters 41-43, and with none of the rest of
Revelation XIV as we now have it. The editors conclude from this that
when chapter 1 was composed, Julian had before her the 'first edition',
and that it contained neither the lord-and-servant allegory nor the long
following exposition of her understanding of the doctrine of 'God our
Mother'. Later it will be shown how logically in her thinking the
allegory led to the exposition in this, which is surely Julian's final account of her revelations, the long text's second edition.

It remains to be said that A, no less than the copies of the long text,
offers us abundant evidence of the care which Julian herself and her
scribe-editors spent on the presentation of her work. It is true that of
all the major Middle English spiritual treatises the *Revelations* seems to
have been least circulated, least popular; but, against that, it has been
preserved for us in manuscript versions of an exceptional accuracy and
purity.

## IV RELATIONS BETWEEN THE LONG TEXT WITNESSES

By the time all the witnesses had been collated, the editors had come
to see that in choosing their copy-text, they needed to concern themselves with only two manuscripts, P and S1. Although P evidently was
not written with the intention that it should be so used (plainly, it was
designed as a companion in a library for mediaeval devotional
manuals), none the less C was taken directly from it; and U probably
was taken from C. Just as plainly, S2 derives directly from S1, though

the S2 scribe seems to have collated with C as the work progressed. Thus we have only two independent witnesses.

P and S1 exhibit separate characteristics, and cannot be descended from any immediate common ancestor. This can best be shown by the confusion about where Revelation XV, chapter 64 should begin. It seems that both manuscripts derive from one in which the title showing this had accidentally been omitted, so that later scribes, remarking the failure, had to make their own decisions. One such, the ancestor of P or P itself, ended his chapter 63 at 618.47: *that alle manner thyng shall be welle*. Another, S1's ancestor or S1, ended at 619.4: *shulde be brougt agayne in to hym by grace*. The editors, it will be seen (619.1 e.s.) consider that both choices are wrong. Other instances of such textual crises differently solved will be found at 362.21, 371.22, 379.1-2, 449.4, 461.19, 547.14.

Frequently it has been possible to emend, where P is evidently mistaken in a reading, in the light of S1's superior transmission. Examples of this are at 302.36, 331.66, 335.95, 357.10, 474.68 (= 669.40), 497.29, 544.315, 549.40 (= 640.10, 709.17), 552.77, 556.22, 575.54, 659.1. Only rarely, in such conflicts, is P demonstrably superior — e.g. 348.22, 440.49, 622.32. At 473.58, 689.7, both manuscripts are patently wrong.

But in very many cases P and S1 offer differing readings equally acceptable; and in almost every such instance P has not been emended. There was never any serious question but that P must be chosen as the basic text. It is the work of a not very intelligent copyist, anxious to transcribe faithfully what was before him. (For convention's sake, and in the lack of positive evidence, we call the P and SS scribes 'he', though it is highly probable that they, as certainly were the four scribes of U, were nuns at Cambrai or Paris). S1 was written on quite different principles; it is an eclectic mixture of preserved archaic forms and modernizations, most of them well-informed and perceptive (although a few archaisms defeated the scribe — e.g. 289.7, 319.31), and it — and, consequently, S2 — are marred throughout by the persistent omission of words and phrases which the scribe — or his copy — had deemed superfluous to the sense, but which destroys Julian's rhetorical figures, which are integral to her thought.

Accordingly, this critical edition has been based on P; and in presenting it, the editors have perforce been guided by a conservative policy. One of the chief difficulties offered by P is its orthography, which is eccentric and erratic. Partly, this seems to have been because of a desire to make the finished product appear as 'mediaeval' as possible, but, even more, because of uncertainty as to how English of any epoch should be written. (If our guess as to the scribe's identity were correct, we might speculate whether she had not when young been sent abroad with little or no schooling, and, thereafter, had received insufficient formal instruction in writing). Had it been decided to emend P's work, it would have been virtually impossible to establish canons for such emendations; and the result would have been a text with scarcely an unemended line. Instead, it was judged better to transmit P, wherever possible, as it is, and, when its state is likely to present readers with serious difficulties, to give them the help, in the apparatus, of the C and SS spellings, or, in the last resort, of editorial comment in the annotations.

Here C is above all useful, for without question we have in Cressy's text a highly literate and intelligent man's presentation of what P had written (or, occasionally, what he thought P had written — 312.25, 313.34, 339.34, 354.9, 355.12, 674.27 are all nonsense-readings of his). The frequency with which he copies P's errors is alone guarantee that it was P and no other which served as his copy-text; e.g. 495.2, 585.30, 633.17, 640.10 ( = 640.11), 653.35, 678.3, 680.19, 684.8, 693.39, 698.17. Often this involves him in P's disagreements with SS; of this, *awne/geyn* (330.55) is the clearest example. Sometimes C has achieved a reading superior to P's by independent criticism; e.g. 356.28, 542.302, 558.37, 720.29.

The fidelity of the text of S2 to that of S1 leaves no doubt that the younger manuscript was copied from the older; and this is clearly shown at 684.1 in S1, where the scribe had omitted the chapter heading and number, which S2's scribe has supplied in the elegant capital Roman numerals which appear throughout S2. Many of S1's archaisms have been modernized; and it would seem that, linguistically, the S2 scribe was something of a purist (e.g. 310.2, 315.56).

W, the only pre-Dissolution witness of the long text, offers little help towards criticism; textually and linguistically it is colourless, but none the less it is clear that it derives from an ancestor which it shares with SS but not with P; e.g. 305.22, 307.45, 384.24-385.25.

Even more colourless is U, which may well have been made not from a manuscript but from C (e.g. 411.35, 414.6-7, 415.12). Chronologically, this is not impossible; the chief scribe of U, Barbara Constable, it has been seen, lived for fourteen years after the publication of C.

In editing both the short and long texts, wherever possible emendation has been avoided. even though this does make greater demands upon the perspicacity of readers. The great temptation, in looking at past ages' transmission of texts, is to deny to the scribes, so much closer than we to what they were copying, the dignity and credibility to which they are entitled. Once we begin establishing an 'ideal text', we unconsciously arrogate to ourselves the conviction that we know better than they what they were writing about. Julian shared with such contemporaries as the author of *Piers Plowman* a reverence for the word of Scripture, and it is only in reference to that word that either writer can be evaluated. Their 'ideal text' was the sacred text; and both writers were seeking to interpret that text, so as to make it reflect the situation of their own age, and also to affirm the entire message of Christian hope which they had learned from the Gospel. There is no one scribe of the Julian manuscripts who did not know this, who did not approach the task with his or her own reverence for the text, and the editors have sought, in evaluating their work, to show them a like reverence.

Two other matters concerning the interrelations between the texts are worth comment. There is some evidence that S1 (or an ancestor) had been in places accomodated to the readings of a manuscript of the short text; e.g. 649.14 and note. And, in examining the SS variants, it is remarkable how often NED states that individual words, found in SS but not in P, survived into the sixteenth and seventeenth centuries only in the Northern and Scottish dialects (cf. 358.14, 441.66, notes). Placid Spearritt, when we enquired of him, informed us that in the second half of the seventeenth century at Cambrai there was one Scottish woman, Melchiora Campbell, daughter of an earl of Argyll, and no less than eight Northumbrians, with names such as Shafto, Fenwick and Errington, all those of well-known local recusant families.

Although U had singularly little to offer in the preparation of the text, the certainty with which its hands have been identified makes it of quite exceptional value as evidence of the probability that we must thank Augustine Baker, and the spiritual school which he founded,[65] for the survival of the long text in any complete form.

## V Linguistic Characteristics of the Manuscripts

### 1 The Language of A

The dialect of the short text as it is preserved in A shows us that this copy must be several removes at least from what Julian wrote, if she spoke and composed in the North-East Midland dialect of Norwich, as

---

[65] See Spearritt's article, 'The Survival of Mediaeval Spirituality'.

we must suppose in the lack of contrary evidence. The dialect is a mixed one, with sounds, inflexions and vocabulary both Northern (which, for general purposes, means 'north of the river Humber') and non-Northern. This dialect mixture is in itself insufficient to support the theory that Julian was a Yorkshirewoman; those who have sought to support it with linguistic evidence seem in the first place to have been attracted to it by a belief that her devotion to St. John of Beverley could so be explained; but, as will be shown elsewhere, she could have learned of his legend in many parts of England.

What follows is a selection only of the dialect characteristics of the short text:[66]

1. Developments of OE ā:

   *abade, awe, awne, bathe* (3×) *bothe* (1×), *clothes, fra, gaste, gaste(lye)* (25×), *gostelye* (2×), *hale* (1×), *hole* (2×), *halye* (20×), *holye* (1×), *hamly* (5×), *homely* (1×), *hate, knawe, lathe* (1×), *lothe* (1×), *loo, mare* (46×), *more* (4×), *maste* (10×), *moste* (5×), *othere* (< OE *āwþer*), *sare, sawlle, s(w)a* (3×), *so* (4×), *takyns, tha, tho, twa* (5×), *two* (5×), *wa* (5×), *woo* (2×), *wate* (4×), *woote* (1×), *wha, whamm.*

2. OE ā + nasal:

   *ane* (27×), *one* (4×), *anly* (4×), *onlye* (1×), *aneȝ, aned, anyng, banes, na* (4×), *nane* (9×), *none* (3×), *nothere, nathynge* (9×), *nothynge* (2×), *nouȝt, ta.*

3. OE -ald-:

   *alde, behalde, behaldynge, calde, halde.*

4. OE ō:

   *goodenes, othere.*

5. 'To be':

   Present indicative 1: *am*;
                         2: *erte* (4×), *arte, ert, er*;
                         3: *is* (166×), *es* (87×), *ys* (28×);
                    Pl: *ere* (18×), *er* (17×), *are* (2×), *ar* (2×);
   Present subjunctive (singular and Pl): *be*;
   Preterite indicative 1 and 3: *was*;
                         Pl: *ware* (10×), *were* (2×);
   Preterite subjunctive 1 and 3: *ware* (18×), *were* (2×);
                         Pl: *ware* (4×), *were*;

---

[66] The criteria considered are those employed by Joyce Bazire: 'The Dialect of the Manuscripts of *The Chastising of God's Children*'.

Infinitive: *be*;
Past Participle: *bene*.

6. 'To have':

Present indicative   1: *hafe* (6×), *haffe* (2×);
                      2: *hase*;
                      3: *has* (21×), *hase* (11×), *hath* (2×), *hafes*;
                Pl: *hafe*;
Present subjunctive 2, 3 and Pl: *hafe*;
Preterite indicative 1: *hadde*
                   3: *hadde* (6×), *had* (2×);
Preterite subjunctive Pl: *had*.
Infinitive: *hafe* (14×), *haue*.

7. OE *witan*:

Present indicative 1: *wate* ;
                      2: *woote*;
Present subjunctive Pl: *witte*;
Preterite indicative 1: *wiste*;
Infinitive: *witte*;
Singular imperative: *witte*.

8. Inflexional endings of other verbs:

Present indicative   1: *-e* (24×), *-es* (3×);
                      2: *-es*;
                      3: *-es* (129×), *-ys* (11×), *-is* (3×), *-the*;
                Pl: *-es* (21×), *-e* (17×), *-s* (2×), zero (4×), *-ys*;
Present subjunctive 1, 2, 3 and Pl: *-e* or zero;
Present participle: *-ande* (53×), *-ynge* (1×).

9. OE *cyrice*:

*kyrke*.

10. OE *dēaþ*:

*dede, dedlye*.

11. 'She':

*scho* (7×), *sche* (2×).

12. OE *tō*, ON *til*:

(of time) *til* (2×), *to* (3×);
(of place, intention, etc.) *til* (1×), *to* (14×);
(with infinitive) *tylle* (1×), otherwise *to*.

13. OE *hwilc*:

*whilke.*

14. 'Would':

*walde* (21 ×), *wolde* (12 ×).

This shows that the vowels examined are predominantly Northern, but with a strong non-Northern element, and that there are no instances of the most markedly Northern developments, such as *ai, ei* < OE *ā; ui, oi* < OE *ō*. The verbal inflexions are not so consistently Northern; particularly, there is a smaller proportion of *-es* to *-e* present indicative plural forms than we might expect in a text originally recorded to the north of the Midland areas. But the whole evidence hardly justifies more than the conclusion that we may wholly exclude the Southern, Western and Kentish areas of ME; the solitary present indicative 3 form in *-the* evidently is sporadic. As we have it, the language of A may be the result of a more careful translation from North-East Midland into Northern, or of a less careful translation in the opposite direction.

We may profitably compare this examination with the results of applying some of the same criteria to that other unique text contained in A, *The Treatise of Perfection*:

1. *fro, goo* (9 ×), *gase* (1 ×), *goste, gostelye, holy* (< OE *hālig*; 8 ×), *haly* (2 ×), *holye* (< OE *hāllice*), *knowe* (13 ×), *knawe* (1 ×), *knawliche* (1 ×), *knawyn* (3 ×), *loo, moste, no, owe* (2 ×), *owne* (1 ×), *awe* (2 ×), *awne* (2 ×), *awȝt* (1 ×), *owthere, saule, so, þoo, who, whome.*

2. *none* (1 ×), *one* (29 ×), *oned* (22 ×), *onlye* (15 ×), *ane* (3 ×), *anely* (1 ×), *stone.*

3. *fourefawlde, manyfolde, holde* (8 ×), *halde* (6 ×), *behowdynge* (1 ×).

5. Present indicative    1: *am;*
                         3: *is* (213 ×), *es* (11 ×), *ys* (6 ×);
                     Pl : *are* (48 ×), *be* (20 ×), *bene* (3 ×), *ar* (1 ×), *arre* (1 ×);
  Present subjunctive singular and Pl: *be;*
  Preterite indicative 3: *was;*
  Preterite subjunctive singular: *ware;*
  Past participle: *bene;*
  Infinitive: *be.*

8. Present indicative Pl: *-e* (31 ×), *-es* (13 ×), *-ys* (5 ×), *-eth* (1 ×), zero
                       (5 ×);
  Present participle: *-ande* (1 ×), otherwise *-ynge.*

9. *chirche.*

11. *sche.*

Here also we have a Northern and non-Northern mixture, but of very different proportions. OE *ā* is more often represented by ME *ō*, in 'to be' the OE *bēo-* stem is not represented in the infinitive only, *scho, kyrke* and *til* are not found, in the present indicative plural there are many more *-e* and zero than *-es, -ys* forms, and there is one sporadic *-ande* present participle to compare with the one *-ynge* form in Julian. It is more probable even than with the Julian text that here we have a not very careful translation into Northern; but the one certain conclusion we may draw from the linguistic disparities of the two texts is that their translation was not executed by the same man, not by the scribe of A or of any ancestor of A. But the linguistic evidence will not tell us where A was copied, or even owned. By the directions of the general chapter at the Grande Chartreuse, James Grenehalgh was in the early 1500s literally sent to Coventry and forbidden to return to Sheen; and he spent his last years at Hull.[67] He could as well have inscribed his monogram in A at either of the two other houses as at Sheen. It has been shown (cf. I 1 A) that the corrector who wrote in plummet has, elsewhere in the manuscript, emended 'drawis' to 'drinkyth', showing that his dialect was non-Northern; but we cannot tell whether he was living and working in his native region.

## 2 The Language of the Long-Text Copies

The difficulties in the assessment of this have in part been indicated. The extracts in U and W are too brief and neutral to repay analysis. Of the others, P and S1 have many clear marks of derivation from an ancestor or ancestors earlier than the Dissolution — to select only one example, the preservation in S1 of *-and* present participle forms converted in P to *-ing* — but P's clumsy vagaries and the smooth regularity of S1's spelling-modernizations alike would make it unprofitable to subject either text to linguistic examination. But though such schematic treatment would be unrewarding, the editors have treated, in the annotations and the glossary, with the various problems, etymological, dialectal, lexical and grammatical, raised by individual readings in the long-text witnesses. As examples only of their discussions, they would now draw attention to the following words: abone (621.16), agreffe (380.17), a newyd (529.183), aneynst (418.22), assey (603.25), astynten (668.31: S1), befallen (368.29: S1), beflowyth (343.19: S1), behalseth (661.26: S2), beholdinges (492.17), be holdyng (349.32), boystours

---

[67] This information derives from the collections made from Carthusian records by Palémon Bastin and Anselm Stoelen, now preserved at Parkminster.

(362.22), brosyng (515.23), clongyn (357.10), cloose (438.29), colleth (661.26), contynuant (498.38), contrarioust (499.41: S1), daming (372.23: S1), druste (412.5), duryngly (483.3), ell (511.20: SS), flamand (527.156: SS), forthing (490.9: S1), fynde (596.28), gaveth (356.28), hayth (656.22), hyng (324.4), irkenes (354.9), lakid (409.13: S1), lefte (340.52), lowed (409.13: C), mightifully (355.14: C), myrre (623.33), noble (517.43), noblyest (314.48), noblyth (310.6: SS), one (328.39), onsparably (362.28: S1), passyng (377.31: S1), pertie (313.39: S1), pesid (424.31: S1), petovous (360.2: S1), portie (313.39: S2), rasyng (361.12), ronkyllid (363.36: S1), savyd (488.29), scoryd (635.7), slyppe (558.43: SS), soule (306.35), strenghyng (441.69), sweeme (319.31: S1), sweppys (541.289: SS), swylge (622.32), token (629.24: S1), vnderstand (295.15), vndertak (463.36), vnlothfull (516.36), vnpeas (508.41), werkyng (581.56), willy (458.44: S1), wote (321.4: S1), wordle (326.27), wrake (326.23), youngith (289.7: SS).

## VI Julian: Biographical Data

The texts of the *Revelations* furnish us with the following biographical information. Julian was thirty and a half years old at the time of her sickness (207.1), which culminated in the visions which she received on 13 May, 1373 (285.3), so that she must have been born about New Year, 1343. She devoted more than fifteen years to prayerful enquiry into the visions' total meaning (732.14), but her prayers were not fully answered until twenty years all but three months had passed, that is, until February, 1393 (520.86). The author of the preface to the short text states that in the year 1413 she is still alive (201.3), and living in Norwich as an anchoress.

This information can be supplemented from other sources. Roger Reed, rector of St. Michael's, Coslany in Norwich, on 20 March, 1393/4, bequeathed two shillings to 'Julian' anakorite'. In the will of Thomas Emund, a chantry priest of Ayslesham in Norfolk, proved in 1404, there is a bequest of one shilling to 'Juliane anchorite apud St. Juliane in Norwice'.[68] John Plumpton, citizen of Norwich, made his will on 24 November, 1415, and it was proved four days later; in it he bequeathes forty pence to 'le ankeres in ecclesia sancti Juliani de Conesford in Nor-

---

[68] Norwich Consistory Court, Reg. Harsyk, f. 194ᵛ; Lambeth Palace, register of Thomas Arundel I, f. 540ᵈ. The reference in Reed's will was found by Norman Tanner, that in Emund's by Aelred Watkin and communicated by him to Sr. Anna Maria Reynolds, then, later and independently, by Tanner, who kindly pointed this also out to the editors.

wice', and twelve pence each to her serving-maid and to Alice, her for-mer maid.[69] This shows at least that Plumpton knew that at this time the anchorhold was occupied by a woman; and his knowledge of the identity of her former servant may indicate a closer personal acquain-tance with Julian, who must be the anchoress concerned, as the count-ess of Suffolk's bequest will show. If Aelred Watkin's guess is right, and the chalice listed in the inventory of St. Giles, Norwich, 'ex dono Alicie hermyte', was given by the same woman,[70] that she had the means for such a gift suggests that she had served Julian out of devotion, not necessity; and 'Alice the Hermit' could be a friendly nickname given in her days of service, or it could show that after she left Julian she herself embraced some form of solitary living.

The fourth such will is that of Isabel Ufford, daughter of Thomas Beauchamp, earl of Warwick, who had married first John Lestrange of Blackmere, and then William Ufford, second earl of Suffolk, by whom she had no children. Shortly after he died in 1382 she entered the house of Augustinian canonesses at Campsey Ash in Suffolk, where she remained until her death in 1416, when she was buried in the con-ventual church beside her second husband.[71] She may have been professed there, but if so she must have been permitted to retain at least some of her goods and income, as had been done in 1347, when Margaret, countess of Ulster, took the habit at Campsey.[72] At the time of Isabel's death her sister-in-law Maud was a nun there, to whom, as to the prioress and to every other sister, she made bequests. There are legacies to various other religious houses, and, 'pur le graunt busogne qe je me soute avez des preiers come de mese chaunter', to every house of the four mendicant orders in Suffolk and Norfolk; but the only recluse mentioned is 'Item jeo devyse a Julian recluz a Norwich 20s'.[73]

In the case of John Plumpton's bequest and that of Lady Suffolk, we must allow for the possibility, recently indicated by R. M. Wilson,[74] that between 1413 and 1415 (or 1416) Julian had died and had been suc-ceeded in the cell by another recluse who had also taken the name of the church's patron saint. But if we can rely on the authenticity of the short text's prologue, Emund's bequest must be to Julian; and it

---

[69] E. F. Jacob: *The Register of Henry Chichele,* 3 413.

[70] *Inventory of Church Goods,* 1 18, 2 161.

[71] T. F. Tout, art.: 'Ufford, William de, second earl of Suffolk of his house' (DNB).

[72] Eileen Power: *Medieval English Nunneries,* 39.

[73] E. F. Jacob: *The Register of Henry Chichele,* 2 94-97.

[74] Reviewing Robert K. Stone: *Middle English Prose Style: Margery Kempe and Julian of Norwich,* in MÆ 42, 1973, 183-184.

therefore confirms the tradition, which hitherto had relied solely on Blomefield's statement, made three hundred years and more after the event, that it was in the anchorhold at St. Julian's that she lived. Hope Allen in her unpublished papers shows unwonted scepticism concerning such biographical data; and she justly observed how much confusion there has been of the author of the *Revelations* with her namesake, Juliana Lampit, who seems to have been enclosed in nearby Carrow nunnery for the greater part of the fifteenth century, and who is often mentioned in wills. But Miss Allen's doubts should have been silenced by her own major discovery, *The Book of Margery Kempe*.

More significant than these sporadic records of bequests, which undoubtedly show reliance on the intercessory prayers of enclosed women, and, possibly, veneration for Julian herself as an intercessor, but which tell us nothing of personal contacts between her and her benefactors, is the account which Margery Kempe has left of her 'holy dalyawns' with the anchoress. In what she presents as a series of connected episodes, she tells us that she was divinely directed to go to Norwich and seek the counsel of 'þe vykary of Seynt Stefenys' about the private vow of chastity which she wished to take whilst she was still bearing children and had recently given birth to one,[75] that she was then commanded to seek out the Norwich Carmelite friar William Southfield,[76] and that thereafter she was led to ask the advice of Julian with regard to the special grace which God had accorded her, 'for þe ankres was expert in swech thyngys and good cownsel cowd ȝeuyn'.[77] Dundas Harford had demonstrated that Richard Caister became vicar of St. Stephen's on 20 May, 1402;[78] and Sandford Meech showed, conclusively, it would seem, that the private agreement between Margery and her husband to live chastely was made on 23 June, 1413,[79] so that, if these consultations of Caister, Southfield and Julian all took place, as Margery seems to suggest, during the same visit to Norwich, this must have been earlier than 1415, when a later stay in the city can be established.[80]

Julian's advice to Margery, as it is reported, is a model of prudence and expertise; and it accords well, sometimes with remarkable exact-

---

[75] *The Book of Margery Kempe*, 38.
[76] Ibid., 41.
[77] Ibid., 42.
[78] Ibid., 276.
[79] Ibid., 269.
[80] Ibid., xlix, 308.

ness, with what we know of her thought and doctrine from the *Revelations*. She told Margery 'to be obedient to the will of our Lord God, and to carry out with all her powers whatever he might put into her soul, if it were not contrary to his glory and the profit of her fellow Christians, for if it were it could not be the prompting of a good spirit ... The Holy Spirit never inspires anything contrary to love, for if he did he would be in opposition to his own self, for he is all love'.[81] In the *Revelations* she tells us that when she expected to die, she willingly accepted this if her life could no longer be to the glory of God (290.14); and she insists that the revelations were given to her not for her own merits but so that they might be 'for the profytte of many oder' (220.17-18).

As in the *Revelations*, her counselling to Margery frequently alludes to Scripture. The Spirit 'inspires a soul to perfect chastity, for chaste livers are called the temple of the Holy Spirit',[82] which is quoting directly I Corinthians 6.19. The Spirit makes a soul steadfast in true faith, but 'a man who is double in soul is always unstable and unsteadfast in all his ways',[83] again a direct quotation, of James 1.8. Anyone must believe firmly that the Spirit dwells in his soul who has received such 'tokens'. Hope Allen, editing Margery's *Book*, pointed out how often mediaeval writers on 'discretion', 'discernment of spirits', call such manifestations of special grace *signa*; and Julian uses the same terminology when she writes that she was divinely assured that though her visions were transient, the increase of faith they brought would persist, outlasting any such *signa*, 'for he lefte with me neyther sygne ne tokyn where by I myght know it' (652.19-20).

More than this, 'when God visits a creature with tears of contrition, devotion or compassion, the creature must and should believe that the Holy Spirit is in his soul'. It can hardly be fortuitous that Margery's reporting here of Julian's words, '... þe grace þat God put in hir sowle of compunccyon, contricyon, swetnesse and deuocyn, compassyon wyth holy meditacyon ...'[84] repeats so closely the language of the first chapter of *The Chastising of God's Children* (where the author interpolates into his translation of Suso's *Horologium sapientiae* the following phrases from Bonaventure's *Evangelii sancti Lucae expositio in cap. x*): 'Þanne comen so many mery meditacions, wiþ plente of teeris: teeris of contricion, teeris

---

[81] Ibid., 42.
[82] Ibid., 42, 278.
[83] Ibid., 43, 279.
[84] Ibid., 43, 279.

of compunccion, teeris of compassion, teris of loue and deuocion ...',[85] when the present writers have in several places (e.g. 321.2, 343.10, 346.6, 353.30) indicated the probability that Julian, before she came to write her second version, had become familiar with the *Chastising*.

Equally close is the parallel between Julian's reported counsel, that the devil has no power over a man's soul, for Holy Writ says that the soul of a just man is the throne of God, and the sentence in the English prose *Qui habitat* (sometimes, though with small probability, ascribed to Walter Hilton): 'For þe wyse mon seiþ þat þe soule of a righwys mon is heuene and þe sege of vr lord'.[86] Though Hope Allen suggested that there is no Scriptural authority for Julian's citation, it is probably a conflation of Proverbs 25.5: 'Take away wickedness from the face of the king, and his throne shall be established with justice', Ezechiel 37.27-28; 'And my tabernacle shall be with them, and I will be their God ... when my sanctuary shall be in the midst of them forever', II Corinthians 6.16: 'For you are the temple of the living God', and Apocalypse 21.3: 'Behold the tabernacle of God with men, and he will dwell with them'. Again, in several places (e.g. 411.31-32, 425.43-44) it has been suggested that Julian may have known the English prose *Qui habitat* and *Bonum est,* and Margery's reporting seems to confirm this. The *Revelations* offer further evidence that when Julian uses Scripture she relies largely on her memory. In chapter 15 of the long text, on one of the occasions when she quotes the actual words of the New Testament, she is not at all concerned with chapter and verse. The citation from St. Paul, 'Nothynge shalle departe me fro the charyte of Crist,' is a conflation of Romans 8.35 and 39; and when she says with St. Peter, 'Lorde, saue me' (Matthew 14.30), she adds 'I peryssch', the cry of the apostles in the storm (Matthew 8.25). In one place, Margery too suggests that Julian had in mind this same narrative, where she recounts that she said: 'He þat is euyr dowtyng is lyke to þe flood of þe see, þe whech is mevyd and born abowte wyth þe wynd, and þat man is not lyche to receyuen þe ȝyftys of God'.[87] The analogy is common and ancient. In *The Book of Privy Counselling*[88] and *An Epistle of Discretion of Stirrings*[89] the author of *The Cloud of Unknowing* compares the soul and its trials with a boat on a stormy sea; and far more illuminating than Owst's somewhat banal account of the

---

[85] *Chastising*, 100, 265.

[86] Wallner, 37.

[87] *The Book of Margery Kempe,* 42.

[88] Hodgson, *Cloud,* 167-168.

[89] Hodgson, *Deonise,* 64.

simile's English history is the series of patristic authorities, cited by Cornelius a Lapide, who make the stormy sea of Matthew 8.23 e.s. signify temptation, doubt and fears, Christ asleep in the boat the soul which relies solely on God.

In her interview with Margery, Julian gives other interesting evidence of her knowledge of such spiritual classics. 'St. Paul says that the Spirit asks for us with indescribable lamentations and weepings' — this is Romans 8.26 — 'and if we respond to this our tears cannot be numbered ... No evil spirit can give these tokens, for Jerome says that tears torment the devil more than the pains of hell'. Here Hope Allen argued with great ingenuity that we have a conflation (probably Julian's own) of two sources cited in the English *Speculum Christiani*: '*Jerome*: Prayers please God but tears constrain him ... *Bernard*: Tears of a sinner torment the devil more than every kind of torture'.[90]

Julian's closing words are of encouragement and optimism. '"I pray that God may grant you perseverance. Put all your trust in God and do not fear what the world may say, for the more sorrow and shame and reproof that you receive in the world" (plainly, Julian here is recalling such Gospel texts as Luke 6.22-23, and John 15.18) "the more is your merit in the sight of God. You need patience, for in that you will preserve your soul" (which is Luke 21.19)'.

Only a perversely captious critic would deny authenticity to this account. It is filled, like all her *Book*, with Margery's morbid self-engrossment; it is evident that the many days of their 'holy dalliance' were occupied in talk about Margery and her favours, not about Julian. But this itself shows precisely what the *Revelations* tell us, that Julian regarded herself as no more than a humble, anonymous, unworthy recipient of unmerited favours. The story reveals all Margery's knowing judgment of others; she had recourse to Julian as an acknowledged expert (and here we have the testimony of Thomas Emund's will that as early as 1404 her fame was spreading); and she can hardly have been disappointed. She shows us Julian as skilled in Scripture, in spiritual theology and in the literature of 'discernment'. Faced with Margery's babblings, Julian reiterates some of her cardinal teachings, the impotence of the devil, the indwelling in man of his loving Lord; and she returns the classic answer of *probatio*: 'By your fruits they will know you'. She tells Margery what the other, indeed, seems to have learned well: 'Do you want to know what is our Lord's meaning? Love is his meaning'.

[90] *The Book of Margery Kempe*, 43, 279.

## VII Norwich in Julian's Age

In Julian's day, Norwich was second only to London in population
and wealth, and, of the provincial centres, only Lincoln possibly had
more parish churches.[91] There were three colleges of secular priests, St.
Mary in the Fields, only one hundred yards from St. Peter Mancroft,
owners of the hospital's advowson, whose parishioners were to rebuild
it so splendidly in the mid-fifteenth century, St. Giles' Hospital and the
Carnary College. At the end of the fifteenth century, St. Mary's had a
community of fourteen priests, St. Gile's a master, five fellows and
three stipendiary priests, Carnary College a master and probably three
other priests. The cathedral was a Benedictine priory; there, as in such
other great monastery-cathedrals as Canterbury and Durham, con-
ventual life was supported by exceptional prestige and opulence, and
the Norwich library was one of the finest in late mediaeval England,
considerably enriched by Adam Easton's bequest of his own collection,
brought there from Rome in six great barrels in 1407.[92] Adam had died
as a Roman curial cardinal, but when Julian was a girl he was one of
two young Norwich monks whose preaching campaigns were being
promoted by the priory,[93] the other, also dividing his time between
Norwich and his studies in Oxford, being Thomas Brinton, later to
become one of Rochester's celebrated Benedictine preacher-bishops.[94]
All four orders of friars had been attracted to the city by its wealth and
the opportunities it offered for pastoral work. It is worth remarking
that the handsome house of the Austin Friars stood in Conisford across
the lane from St. Julian's anchorhold. There, too, must have been a
fine library, to house which in the fifteenth century a rich devotee,
widow of a Norwich mayor, provided a new building.[95] In this house
the Augustinian theologian Roger Twiford, 'said to have flourished c.
1390', lived and worked.[96] The rules promulgated by the prior general
of the Augustinians on 3 February, 1456, for the administration of the
London Austin Friars library, also recently rebuilt, which may be taken
as normative, provide that books, 'especially those of a speculative

---

[91] Much of the information in this section is derived from Norman Tanner's valuable
study, *Popular Religion in Norwich ... 1370-1532.*

[92] Ibid., 75.

[93] W. A. Pantin: *English Black Monks,* 3 28-29.

[94] Sr. Mary Aquinas Devlin: *The Sermons of Thomas Brinton.*

[95] F. Roth: *English Austin Friars,* 1 374-375.

[96] B. Hackett: 'Spiritual Life', 452-455.

kind', are not to be taken from the library unless they are duplicates. This suggests that Julian might have been able to borrow from her neighbours a spare copy of, say, Chaucer's *Boethius*, or of *Piers Plowman*. George Kane in his edition of that work furnished evidence of monastic owners of its manuscripts, to which A. I. Doyle was able to add;[97] and Chaucer too was read in monasteries. One of the two known copies of *Disce Mori* is MS Jesus College, Oxford 39, written for Dorothy Slyghe, a Birgettine nun of Syon; on p. 623, where the text is dealing with 'impediments in the love of God and contemplation' and compares guilty lovers to 'a þeef to a þeef and dronken of þis sweet poison', a contemporary hand has annotated:

> of which poison, if ye lust more to rede,
> seeþ þe storie of Troilus, Creseide and Diomede.[98]

The intellectual life of the local Franciscans benefited greatly from the establishment in their convent by Benedict XII of one of the Order's seven English *studia generalia*, to which promising students could be sent from many parts of Europe. Nicholas of Assisi's notes of lectures and disputations which he heard there c. 1337 still survive, and in 1406 and 1407 the Franciscans John of Westphalia, John of Austria and Theodoric of Saxony were ordained in the city.[99] C. 1370, Peter of Candia was at the Norwich *studium* before he went on to Oxford. He ended his days as the short-lived Alexander V, known for his learning and piety;[100] and some of his devotional poems are known.[101] Though their modern editor has no high opinion of them, 'Fratres peramabiles, ob amorem Christi / Comedamus pariter sine vultu tristi' is a charming example of the 'sancta hilaritas' which marks the verses which, in Peter's age, Franciscan poets in England were composing in Latin, French and English. Among the Norwich Carmelites there was William Southfield, to whom Margery Kempe went for direction — she calls him 'a good man and a holy leuer';[102] and John Bale (who had himself been a Carmelite friar in the city) wrote 'Homo simplex erat, sed incredibile devotione preditus'[103] — Walter Diss, called 'one of the most famous Cambridge doctors of his age', a royal confessor and a great preacher

---

[97] Reviewing Kane in *English Studies* 43 (1962), 55-58.
[98] This information was kindly supplied by Michael Sargent.
[99] Tanner, 57, 74.
[100] Ibid., 74.
[101] W. Lampen: 'Prosae seu Poemata Petri de Candia'.
[102] *The Book of Margery Kempe*, 41.
[103] Ibid., 374.

against heresy, who died in 1404 and was buried among his Norwich brethren,[104] Thomas Bradley alias Scrope, whose eccentric pieties and evangelism as early as the 1420s had provoked his provincial, Thomas Netter of Walden, (Bradley thereafter lived at the Norwich friary as an anchorite, later becoming bishop of Dromore and a papal legate),[105] and John Thorpe, 'sacre theologie doctor', 'maistre en divinitie',[106] whom John Bale called 'doctor ingeniosus' and credited with Scriptural and other writings.[107] Though the city's Dominicans seem to have lacked the numbers, and, it may be, the distinction of the other three friaries, there were among them men such as John Somerton,[108] author of a series of sermons *per annum*.

It is easy to perceive how men of such attainments must have contributed to the spiritual and intellectual life of the place, and the links which they could provide with thought and letters in the capital and the universities, in England and abroad. Tanner's analysis of Norwich wills shows us the bequest of such books as Augustine's *Confessions*, Bernard's 'Meditations', 'Sermones Bonaventure de sanctis', Boethius, an 'English St. Bridget' (a lay bequest), *Dieta salutis*,[109] 'Le Doctrine of the Herte',[110] 'evangelia' (both these lay bequests), *Formula noviciorum*,[111] Gregory's Dialogues, Hugh of St. Victor's *De claustro anime*, 'Liber vocatum Hylton' (a lay bequest), Petrarch's *De remediis utriusque fortune*,[112] and 'Liber vocatus a vangeler'.[113] Julian, we can be certain, lived in a society in which spiritual books were prized and read.

But because there were others concerned with the life of the spirit in such propinquity, we must not assume that she knew them, consulted with them, received books from them. It is very evident that she was a learned woman, but we do not know how or from whom she acquired her learning. Of her historicity, it has been shown, there can be no doubt; but none the less, she remains an enigmatic figure. Her parentage, birth, education, the circumstances under which she was enclosed,

---

[104] Bale, *Anglorum Heliades* (MS BM Harley 3838), f. 86ᵛ; Emden, *Cambridge,* 188.

[105] MS BM Harley 211 (a valuable Norwich Carmelite collection of pastoral and devotional material), f.191ᵛ; Eubel, 2 146; J. Tait: 'Scrope, Thomas' (DNB).

[106] E. F. Jacob: *The Register of Henry Chichele,* 2 143, 149, two Norwich wills of 1 May and 2 June, 1477, kindly pointed out by Keith Egan.

[107] Emden, *Cambridge,* 586.

[108] Blomefield: *Norfolk,* 2 728.

[109] Among surviving manuscripts are Lambeth Palace 457 and 483.

[110] Cf. Sr. Mary Patrick Candon, ed.: *The Doctrine of the Hert.*

[111] P. Jolliffe: *Check-List,* items D.5, E.14, H.2, I.4, O.4, O.6, O.10.

[112] Ibid., J.9.

[113] Tanner, 329-330.

her associates and directors thereafter, the date of her death — none of
this is known to us. She resembles Hilton and the author of the *Cloud*;
and we may be content that this is so. Were we furnished with the
plethora of biographical information which exists for Rolle, that might
have served, in her case as it has in his, as an obstacle between us and
all that she set store by, the showings in which God revealed to her
secrets of his being.

That Julian wore her learning so lightly, that she is so insistent
(especially in her first edition) on her untutored simplicity, suggests,
certainly, that she knew that it would be impolitic to set herself up as a
bluestocking, but also that she herself had little use for bluestockings.
One of the present editors some years ago provoked irate criticism
when he adverted to Margery Kempe's story,[114] of her meeting with
Richard Caister, the saintly parish priest of St. Stephen's, Norwich, who
said, according to Margery, 'God bless my soul — what could a woman
find to say about our Lord's love that would take an hour or two?' The
observation, 'those who indulge in the kind of speculation which forms
so much of the scholarship of Hope Allen and her school, assuming that
because A and B both lived in C one of them must have "influenced"
the other, would do well to ponder Richard's evident indifference to
the *Frauenbewegung* of which Julian and Margery are held to be such
outstanding English members',[115] was not well received.[116] But Caister's
will, made on 27 March, 1420,[117] confirms the impression we may form
from Margery's story. He appoints three Norwich priests as his
executors. Ten pounds are left for two antiphoners for his own church,
and the rest of his goods are for the poor, those of his own parish to be
preferred. Drily he remarks that canon law defines that 'the goods of
the Church are the goods of the poor'. There are no bequests to
solitaries, Julian or anyone else, or to their servants, nothing for the
religious orders, no careful provisions for prayers for his own soul, no
treasured devotional manuals or pious books to be passed on. Caister,
we may surmise, would have been the same holy man had he lived on a
mountain top instead of in the Norwich of his days. Nor can we be sure
that every man and woman dedicated to the solitary life would edify

---

[114] *The Book of Margery Kempe,* 38 e.s.

[115] E. Colledge: 'Margery Kempe' (in *Pre-Reformation English Spirituality*, ed. J. Walsh,
221).

[116] By E. I. Watkin, reviewing *Pre-Reformation English Spirituality* (*Downside Review* 84,
1966, 99-102).

[117] Norfolk and Norwich Records Office REG/ 4 Liber 8, f. 135ʳ. We are indebted to
Frank Sayer for identifying Caister's will and having it copied for us.

others as we have seen that Julian did. According to Tanner's evidence, there was after her time a marked increase in their numbers in Norwich. 'At any given time between the 1420s and the 1470s there were probably at least eight hermits and anchorites'. [118] This may have been through her example; but we must not deduce too much. Some such persons seemed only to batten on the vapidities of 'enthusiasm'. Elsewhere the editors have already described how St. John of Bridlington — who died six years after Julian's revelations — once visited an anchoress near Richmond in Yorkshire, hoping for spiritual consolation from her, but cut the conversation short and left, saying that he had come to talk with her of the grace and goodness of God, when she began to tell him of her 'vision' of an eagle bearing in his beak a scroll written with 'Jhesus est amor meus' (a device beloved of many such enthusiasts), and that John himself was her eagle. Such women evidently did little more than trade in pious flattery. We may be sure that they would receive from Richard Caister, and, indeed, from Julian too, as short shrift as John of Bridlington gave his illuminata. [119]

## VIII Julian's Intellectual Formation

In considering this matter, we must begin with her knowledge of Scripture. Elsewhere[120] the editors have already described the enquiries they instituted and the expert advice they received, through which they were led to the inescapable conclusion that before she began to compose the short text, Julian already knew all the Vulgate; especially, she can be seen to be deeply familiar with all four gospels, the Pauline and Johannine epistles and Hebrews, the Psalms, the sapiential books and Deutero-Isaias. We can only make conjectures about how she acquired her Latin and her learning, for she is as reticent about this as over every other part of her external life; but of such conjectures, the most probable (at which she seems herself in several places to hint) is that when young — that is, in her teens — she entered a religious house, and that she was still there after February, 1393, when she was in her fiftieth year. Only after the completion of the long text, we believe, did she occupy the anchorhold at St. Julian's church and embrace the solitary, enclosed life[121] to which, Roger Reed's will shows, she was vowed in the following year. If Julian had been a nun before her enclosure, she was

---

[118] Tanner, 117.
[119] E. Colledge and J. Walsh: *Following the Saints,* 3 769.
[120] 'Editing Julian of Norwich's *Revelations*'.
[121] For a fuller statement of our reasons for this conjecture, see the same article.

not the only one in the locality living so. In the administration of the
goods of Katherine Samson, 18 July, 1417, she is described as 'monialis
ordinis sancti Bernardi recluse apud ecclesiam omnium sanctorum in
parochia de Sowth Ienne', that is Lynn All Saints in the Norwich arch-
deaconry;[122] and MS Bodley 73, f. 51ᵛ, in a list of Carmelites buried at
Norwich, has: Domina Emma carmelita reclusa et soror in religione
obiit anno domini 1422 2ᵃ decembris,[123] although this probably means,
like John Bale's reports in *Anglorum Heliades*[124] of Thomas Netter's
proselytizing activities, no more than that such women as Emma, before
or after enclosure as anchoresses, took the Order's habit and vows.[125]

An objection which has often been made to the possibility that Julian
was a nun at the time of her sickness is that she describes how she was
ministered to, when she was thought to be dying, by a secular priest.
But it was by no means the rule that nuns and anchoresses were invariably served as chaplains by religious priests; for many isolated nunneries and anchorholds, such a rule would have been impractical.
Aelred counsels his enclosed sister to choose as confessor either a
religious or a secular, provided he be of suitable age and disposition.[126]
The Benedictine women's abbeys at Shaftesbury, Wherwell, Wilton and
Winchester supported each four prebendary canons; and Eileen Power
considered that 'these prebends were doubtless originally intended for
the maintenance of resident chaplains'.[127] The Prioress in the Canterbury Tales was accompanied by three priests;[128] and when the Host
addresses one of them as 'Sir John',[129] he indicates that this was no
religious.

Where Julian had been a nun we have no means of knowing. It has
often been suggested that this was at Carrow, the house of Benedictine
nuns just outside the Norwich walls which was the patron of the St.
Julian's living. This may be so, but it is uncertain. What is however
beyond any doubt is that when young Julian had received an exceptionally good grounding in Latin, in Scripture and in the liberal arts,
and that thereafter she was able and permitted to read widely in Latin
and vernacular spiritual classics. Reference to the annotations to the

[122] A. Watkin: *Inventory of Church Goods*, 2 208.
[123] This information was kindly communicated by Keith Egan.
[124] MS BM Harley 3838, f. 37.
[125] J. Smet, art.: 'Carmelites — (Sisters) (NCE 3 121).
[126] *De institutione inclusarum* 6 (A. Hoste and C. H. Talbot, ed.: *Aelredi Rievallensis opera omnia*, 1 642).
[127] *Medieval English Nunneries*, 144.
[128] F. N. Robinson, ed.: *Complete Works of Chaucer*, 21.
[129] Ibid., 237.

short and long texts will show the evidence on which this opinion is based. She shows knowledge of such great masters as Augustine and Gregory; and she seems to have become deeply influenced, as she composed the 'second edition' of the long text, by William of St. Thierry, not only through his *Golden Epistle*, but also by other of his works, in her day known only in learned circles. Furthermore, her writing, in the long text especially, constantly displays remarkable congruity of both thought and language with contemporary English writings: notably *The Treatise of Perfection of the Sons of God, The Cloud of Unknowing* and *The Scale of Perfection* and their ancillary treatises, and Chaucer's *Boethius*. When we add to this the evidence, exhibited in detail in the annotations, that she was a highly accomplished rhetorician who could employ with ease the terms and concepts of the philosophers, only one deduction is possible: she must, early in life, have attracted the benevolent attention of some scholar or scholars who perceived her spiritual and intellectual gifts, and passed on to her the learning of the schools.

She is at some pains, in the short text particularly, to present us with a misleading picture of herself as a simple and unlearned woman, the humble recipient of unmerited graces. Partly this was dictated by true Christian humility, partly by an exceptionally sound theology of grace, partly by a wholly comprehensible wish not unnecessarily to antagonize her critics by any parade of erudition. But she does not conceal from readers who will pay her the attention she deserves that the *sancta simplicitas* which was indeed hers in no way is incompatible with the intellectual profundity and subtlety which informs all that she writes. Her book is a great monument to the Western monastic traditions of *lectio divina* of which she was heiress; and the learning she had inherited began and continued in the loving, prayerful study and memorization of sacred Scripture.

In many places, the annotations show, she is making her own translations direct from the Vulgate; and sometimes she furnishes a reference. Thus, it has already been demonstrated,[130] when in the short text she writes: *Swilke paynes I sawe that alle es to litelle þat y can telle or saye, for itt maye nouȝte be tolde, botte ylke saule aftere the sayinge of saynte Pawle schulde feele in hym þat in Criste Jhesu* (234.23), she is providing an exact reproduction of the Latin syntax of Philippians 2.5: Hoc enim sentite in vobis quod et in Christo Iesu. But even when no such reference is provided, some of her uses of Scripture are instantly recognizable.

130 E. Colledge and J. Walsh: 'Editing Julian of Norwich's *Revelations*'.

When she writes: *And as to thys* (her inability to accept that 'all manner of thing shall be well') *I had no other answere in shewyng of oure lorde but thys: That þat is vnpossible to the is nott vnpossible to me* (425.48), she expects her readers to discern that what she is reporting is no locution spoken to her individually, but her recollection of the applicability to her problem of Luke 18.26-27. In chapter 51 of the long text, writing: *alle is the manhode of Cryst, for he is the heed, and we be his membris, to whych membris the day and þe tyme is vnknowyn whan every passyng wo and sorow shall haue an eende, and the everlastyng joy and blysse shall be fulfyllyd, whych day and tyme for to see, all the company of hevyn longyth* (537.256), she is constructing a mosaic of New Testament allusions which begins with a direct borrowing from I Corinthians 12.12. A little further on, reflecting on 'kind made' and 'substantial kind unmade', when she observes: *whan god shulde make mannes body, he toke the slyme of the erth, whych is a mater medelyd and gaderyd of alle bodely thynges, and therof he made mannes body* (558.42), she is combining the Genesis account of the creation of Adam with the lore of the mediaeval physiologists.

Some of her many conflations of several different Scriptural texts seem to be carefully contrived. In chapter 15, *And in the tyme of joy I myght haue seyde with seynt Paule: Nothyng shalle departe me fro the charyte of Crist; and in the payne I myght haue seyd with seynt Peter: Lorde, saue me, I peryssch* (355.18, a *compar* taken over with little rewriting from the short text; cf. 231.33) appears knowingly to combine Matthew's account of Peter's rescue from drowning with the story in all the synoptic gospels of the disciples' appeal to the sleeping Jesus. But, naturally, Julian depended for her knowledge of the Bible on texts which were often faulty. In chapter 50 we have the *exclamatio*: *Goode lorde, I see the that thou arte very truth, and I know truly þat we syn grevously all day and be moch blame wurthy* (510.7), a plain allusion to the conflation of Proverbs 24.16, 'Septies enim cadet iustus', with Psalm 118.164: 'Septies in die laudem dixi tibi,' an error common in mediaeval Bible-manuscripts.

Once we have come to rely on the authority with which she uses Scripture, we can elucidate passages where her teaching can have been clear only to those who shared her knowledge. She writes, in chapter 12, of the Precious Blood: *For it is most plentuous, as it is most precious, and that by the vertu of the blessyd godhead* (343.17). The annotation calls this 'another example of the way in which Julian brings together popular devotion and her own Scriptural and theological learning', as she alludes to I John 5.6-8. In chapter 51 we read: *and within hym an hey ward long and brode, all full of endlesse hevynlynes* (523.125), but the meaning here has escaped those who did not perceive the allusion to such places in Scripture as 'susceptor meus et refugium meum' (Psalm 58.17), 'elevator meus et refugium meum' (II Kings 22.3). And in one of her many references to the 'Harrowing of Hell', when she writes: *and whan he was ther, than he reysyd vppe the grett root oute of the depe depnesse, whych ryghtfully was knyt to hym in hey hevyn* (542.300), there is a deft and complex evocation of the numerous texts in both Testaments which celebrate the Redeemer as the 'flos de radice Jesse'. If the author of the carol, 'O of Jesse thow holy rote', cited in the annotation, ever read or heard this passage from Julian's book, he would at once have understood its import, because he also had inherited the same monastic traditions. Without some knowledge of them, her book will remain closed.

It has already been suggested that one obstacle to acceptance of Julian as a proficient scholar has been a too willing credence in her own account of herself as 'a woman that could no letter'. If those who have sought to represent her in this light had been more familiar with the conventions of rhetoric, and, especially, with the rhetoricians' employment of *captatio benevolentiae*,[131] they might not have been so easily deceived. But when critics have attempted to use such a sentence as *I conseyvede treulye and myghttyllye that itt was hym selfe that schewyd it me with owtyn any meenn ; and than I sayde: Benedicite dominus* (210.15) as a demonstration that its writer knew no Latin grammar, they have betrayed their own lack of it. In truth we are still sadly ill-informed, largely for want of evidence, about the higher education of women in later mediaeval England:[132] but for the fourteenth century the *Revelations* are proof that it was possible for one woman to master the learning of past ages, and to acquire their skills, to present her thought in modes traditionally acceptable and comprehensible.

Reference to the Appendix will show that this is so. There the editors have described each of the rhetorical figures which Julian employs, giving first its definition, from *Ad Herennium* or from some other ancient or modern authority, and then supplying examples, from the *Revelations* and, usually, from the Vulgate and from Chaucer's *Boethius*. Had Julian known no other books than these, they would have sufficed; and if the suggestion that an enclosed nun or anchoress might have read Chaucer be regarded as frivolous, the evidence, already mentioned, that the nuns

---

[131] See E. Colledge and J. Walsh: 'Julienne de Norwich.'

[132] N. Orme, in *English Schools in the Middle Ages,* has been unable to add more than a little to Eileen Power's treatment of this topic. It tells us much of the material he has found that he subdivides his first chapter as: 'The clergy', 'Kings and princes', 'Nobility and gentry', 'Administrators and lawyers', 'Merchants, craftsmen, artisans', 'Villeins', 'Women'.

of Syon Abbey were familiar with *Troilus and Criseyde* should be considered.

It is by no means suggested that as a rhetorician Julian was either pioneer or innovator. If she read with perception such treatises as the *Ancrene Riwle*,[133] as she seems to have done, or *A Talking of the Love of God*,[134] as she may have done,[135] if she listened with attention, as she must have done, to 'men of Holy Church' embellishing their sermons with *colores* (long before the friars first arrived, Eadmer had written in admiration of Anselm's preaching skills: 'And when we say that he admonished, or instructed, or taught these things, he did it not as others are wont to teach, but far differently; he set forth each point with familiar examples in daily life, supporting them with the evidence of solid reason, and leaving them in the minds of his hearers, stripped of all ambiguity'[136]), if, presently, she read Chaucer's translation[137] with understanding for its techniques, she would know that what she was attempting in her presentation of the showings would take its due place in an already honourable tradition.

The experts tell us that Chaucer was at work on his translation of Boethius c. 1380, that is, at the time when Julian may be presumed to have been considering the problems which she must solve in the composition of her long text (if, that is, the short text itself were already published, which we do not know). Chaucer's problems were not dissimilar. Either writer was called upon to render into contemporary English matter which might seem intractable: in Chaucer's case, Boethius' haunting and evocative rhythms and metres, in Julian's, the *processe* of her visions and locutions, and her own given insights, often of a profundity which, she tells us, seemed as if it would defeat her powers of language. They were both rescued from their dilemma by rhetoric, Chaucer more easily than Julian, since he was turning into English another man's *colores,* whereas she was adapting to her own ends literary devices few of which anyone before Chaucer had attempted to employ in her native language. We can see at once how deeply the problem had engaged her when we observe how often she anglicizes the rhetoricians' technical vocabulary, as the author of the *Riwle* before her had begun

---

[133] For a discussion of rhetoric in the *Riwle,* see G. Shepherd: *Ancrene Wisse,* lxv-lxxiii.

[134] See Lois K. Smedick: 'Cursus in Middle English'.

[135] Cf. 469.16, 470.34, notes.

[136] R. W. Southern: *The Life of St. Anselm,* 56. Shepherd's admirable introduction to the *Wisse* drew our attention to this.

[137] There is a somewhat perfunctory consideration of Chaucer's use in Boethius of rhetoric by Margaret Schlauch: 'The Art of Chaucer's Prose' (in D. S. Brewer, ed.: *Chaucer and Chaucerians,* 14-163).

to do.[138] She shows that she knows the logical purpose of *concessio* when she writes: ... *me behovede nedes grawnte* (226.7 and note). She understands precisely the function of *exemplum*, which she calls *example* (313.35, 513.3 and notes). She variously designates *oppositio contrariorum* as *contrarytes* (372.25), *contraryousnes* (501.12), *contrarys* (550.55, 659.4), *contrarious* (687.23). A *propositio* she names *profyr* (370.6, and cf. 385.35); and *ratiocinatio* is called a *resonn* (263.17, and cf. 325.12, 365.58, 461.19). The theological-rhetorical 'appropriation' gives her the past participle *propred* (593.40) and the abstract noun *propyrte* (493.34).

It is evident from the short text that Julian's study of rhetoric and her familiarity with its *colores*, as she had observed them in the Vulgate and elsewhere, had begun long before she wrote down her first account of her visions. There she employs two figures (211.24, 259.17 and notes) which she reproduces unaltered in the long text; and she uses *adnominatio* (259.17), *chiasmus* (238.15, 276.20), *complexio* (213.16, 249.2), *conduplicatio* (211.24), *continuatio* (247.18), *conversio* (204.43, 220.25, 235.39, 244.56, 248.28, 271.26, 272.42, 274.19), *exclamatio* (271.26), *gradatio* (238.15), *membrum* (268.4), *oppositio* (214.29, 222.50, 224.11, 231.33, 238.15, 239.14, 254.10, 256.43, 263.12, 268.4, 272.45), *ratiocinatio* (212.10), *repetitio*, initial (206.52, 211.24, 220.25, 221.32, 221.38, 239.14, 240.24, 248.28, 249.5, 252.3, 263.11, 263.12, 265.51) and medial (204.43, 216.49, 220.25, 221.32), *similiter cadens* (257.14), *tautologia* (268.14), and *traductio* (217.8, 244.56, 251.31, 254.10, 259.17). She is skilled in the construction of *compares*, as can be seen throughout.

If it is thought that the editors are attributing to Julian skills which she did not possess, because of their own subjective interpretations of her texts (Lois Smedick recently defended herself with ability against such a contention), heed should be paid to the opening of chapter xv in the first version, where she writes:

> And thus oure goode lorde answerde to alle the questyons and doutes that I myght make, sayande fulle comfortabelye on this wyse: I wille make alle thynge wele, I schalle make alle thynge wele, I maye make alle thynge wele and I can make alle thynge wele; and þowe schalle se þat thy selfe, that alle thynge schalle be wele. There he says he maye, I vndyrstande for the fadere; and þere he says he can, I vndyrstande for the sonne; and þer he says: I wille, I vnderstande for the hali gaste; and þere he says: I schalle, I vndirstande for the vnyte of the blyssede trinyte, thre persones in a trewthe; and there he says: Thowe schalle se thy selfe, I vndyrstande the anynge of alle mankynde that schalle be sayfe in to the blysfulle trinyte (249.1; and cf. 417.2 e.s. and notes).

[138] See Shepherd's introduction.

In the long text this is preserved unaltered, except that there the auxiliary verbs are ordered in the first sentence as she probably wrote them. No more striking instance could be found of the conscious deliberation with which she uses such figures to give clarity to her theology as she expounds the revelations.

But when in this regard we contrast the composition of the short text and that of the long, we see that in the interval she had fully mastered not only a wider range of *colores* — *articulus, commoratio, commutatio, conclusio, conflatio, contentio, correctio, definitio, descriptio, disjunctio, dissolutio, distributio, inclusio, interpretatio, notatio, personificatio, sermocinatio, similitudo, transitio* — but the very essence of the rhetoricians' art, the ability to think and to feel in accordance with the classical models. She had become a complete mistress of *expolitio* and of the *argumentatio perfectissima*.

This is best shown in the long text's chapter 38. In the short text she had written:

> Also god schewed me that syn is na schame, bot wirschippe to mann (255.17),

and all that she had offered there as demonstration of this paradox were her reflections on the 'great penitents', David and the others. Now, in the long text, she sees the need better to establish the truth of the statement, and she has acquired the theological and philosophical equipment to do this. She uses her remark as a *propositio*:

> And god schewed that synne shalle be no shame, but wurshype to man,

and proceeds with consummate ability to construct the rest of the *argumentatio*. The *ratio* follows:

> for ryght as to every synne is answeryng a payne by truth / ryght so for every synne to the same soule is gevyn a blysse by loue,

using *repetitio*, initial (*for ryght ... ryght so*) and medial (*to every synne ... for every synne*), and *oppositio* (*a payne by truth ... a blysse by loue*). The *rationis confirmatio* is:

> Ryght as dyuerse synnes be ponysschyd with dyuers paynes /
> after that it be greuous /
> ryght so shalle they be rewardyd with dyvers joyes in hevyn /
> for theyr victories /
> after as the synne haue ben paynfulle and sorowfulle to the soule in erth,

continuing the *repetitio* (*Ryght as ... ryght so*) and elaborating the *oppositio* (*dyuers synnes ... dyuers paynes ... dyuers joyes in hevyn ... in erth*). Next is the *exornatio*:

> For the soule that shalle come to hevyn /
> is so precyous to god and the place so wurshypfulle /
> that the goodnes of god sufferyth nevyr /
> that soule to synne fynally þat shalle come ther;

and the *complexio* concludes:

> But what synners they are that so shalbe rewarded /
> is made knowen in holy church in erth and also in heaven /
> by over passyng worshypes (445. 2-446. 12),

in which the allusion to the *ecclesia militans* and *ecclesia triumphans* shows the force of the *oppositio* which recurs throughout the figure, and perfects the *argumentatio* by its demonstration that the Church on earth venerates David and other repentant sinners of the Old Testament, and has raised to its altars such men and women as Mary Magdalene, Peter, Paul, Thomas, John of Beverley. The Church does not conceal their former sinfulness; *Alle is turned them to worshyppe*. The greatness of their sins is the measure of their contrition and of their glory.

In both versions Julian is careful to insist that this illumination was a part of the showing: *for in this sight mynn vnderstandynge was lyftyd vp in to hevenn* (255. 18, repeated verbatim 446. 12); but in the long text the mention of John of Beverley (suppressed, we must assume, in the short text, for when she writes *god callyd hym seynt Johnn of Beverley, pleynly as we do, and þat with a fulle glade and swet chere*, 447. 24, she must mean that a part of the revelation was the rehearsing of the penitents' names) leads her to a typical homespun *exemplum* with which to extend and clinch the *argumentatio*, that what she is teaching, 'that sin shall be no shame but honour to a repentant sinner', is proved in John's case by the miracles which God constantly performs at his shrine. In Julian's age all England was awed by his cult, which would reach its height when Henry V attributed the victory at Agincourt to his intercessions; but her purpose in alluding to it is theological.

This account of Julian as rhetorician in no way exhausts the catalogue of her literary abilities. Her use of alliteration (e.g. 541.289, 615.20) and of rhyme (e.g. 437.21-22) has often been remarked on;[139] and one should also observe the ease with which in places (e.g. 387.49 and note, 729.11 and note) she raises the emotional level of her writing by employing markedly metrical structures. Nowhere do we find that she subordinates sense to sound; and her willingness to jettison one of

---

[139] The most recent examination of such matters is that by R. K. Stone. Cf. note 74, supra.

the most striking figures in her short text (271.26-36) as no longer fully corresponding with her insights has already been remarked. In this respect as in so many others, she shows that she had wholly freed herself of the influence of Richard Rolle and his school. But, born six years before he died, spending her childhood in the aftermath of the Black Death, in a land ringing with prophecies of woe and doom, in the intellectual and moral ferment so vividly and painfully described for us in *Piers Plowman,* she would be remarkable if not eccentric if her book did not show some traces of all this; and they are to be found.

They are shown by her opening words: *I desyrede thre graces be the gyfte of god. The fyrst was to have mynde of Cryste es passionn. The seconnde was bodelye syeknes, and the thryd was to haue of goddys gyfte thre wonndys* (201.6). In the annotations to this and comparable passages, the editors have shown how close Julian is to the temper of such devotional writings as the *Stimulus amoris,* Suso's *Horologium,* the *Fifteen Oes* (and many other anonymous, frequently still unpublished prayers and meditations in Latin, English and French), and to the immensely popular recension, *The Privity of the Passion,* of the *Meditationes vitae Christi* spuriously attributed to Bonaventure.[140] Elsewhere[141] they have pointed out how close Julian is, describing these early aspirations to take an active part in the Passion of her Lord, to some of Bonaventure's genuine writings, and to that whole body of meditative prose and verse, Latin and vernacular, spread all over Western Christendom, which we may call 'Franciscan'. (So to describe it is not to ignore the impetus given to discursive meditation on the life and death of Christ by writings earlier than Francis himself, such as the genuine and spurious works circulating under Anselm's name, or the contributions to such literature made by writers such as Richard Rolle and Henry Suso, who were not friars minor.)

A recent critic has also remarked[142] how deeply susceptible Julian is to the influence of pious art-objects; and the editors have described[143] the evidence which shows how richly furnished were the Norwich churches with such objects. Douglas Gray and Rosemary Woolf[144] have made important contributions to our understanding of how 'Franciscan' such visual art was, as also was the popular literature it inspired,

---

[140] Cf. e.g. 201.6, 201.12-202.13, 202.23, 205.51 and notes.
[141] In 'Editing Julian of Norwich's *Revelations*'.
[142] Douglas Gray: *Themes and Images.*
[143] In 'Editing Julian of Norwich's *Revelations*'.
[144] *The English Religious Lyric in the Middle Ages* (Oxford, 1968).

even though some of its outstanding surviving examples, such as the (to us) gruesomely illustrated Carthusian MS BM Add. 37049, were not produced by or for Francis's followers. It is in this tradition that Julian is writing:

> Me thought I wolde haue bene that tyme with Mary Mawdeleyne and with othere that were Crystes loverse, that I myght have sene bodylye the passionn of oure lorde that he sufferede for me, that I myght have suf- ferede with hym as othere dyd that lovyd hym, not withstandynge that I leevyd sadlye alle the peynes of Cryste as halye kyrke schewys and techys, and also the payntyngys of crycyfexes that er made be the grace of god af- tere the techynge of haly kyrke to the lyknes of Crystes passyonn, als far- furthe as man ys witte maye reche (201.11).

In the annotations to this passage it is observed that the reason for the suppression in the long text (cf. 286.12) of its conclusion, the ob- servation on the utility of devotional art, may be that the Lollard con- troversy about this, active when Julian was first writing, had by the 1390s abated. We can see that her position in this matter is that of moderation. In contrast to Margery Kempe's hysterical outpourings in a Norwich church at the sight of a *pietà*[145] — the image, and Margery's reaction to it, evidently resembled closely those described in *De arte lacrimandi*[146] — Julian makes the important reservation, *als farfurthe as man ys witte maye reche*; and the editors have observed that here she makes the *Ancrene Riwle*'s distinction, as elucidated by G. V. Smithers, between object and imitation or representation. This is an important witness to her own self-knowledge. She has asked for the grace of suf- fering, and for a vision of the Passion, so that she might in some form share in it, but not to increase her faith that Christ did suffer. Her faith is founded on the Church's teachings, and her imaginative awareness has been formed by such art objects, inadequate though she knows them to be.

One object which evidently had deeply and lastingly impressed her in her early years was the Vernicle, which, according to the legend as it had developed by her time,[147] was the kerchief with which the com- passionate 'Veronica' had wiped the face of the suffering Saviour on the Via Dolorosa, which had miraculously received the impression of his

---

[145] *The Book of Margery Kempe,* 145.

[146] Ed. R. E. Garrett. Cf. Rosemary Woolf, *The English Religious Lyric,* 258-259.

[147] For discussions and bibliographies, cf. K. Pearson: *Die Fronica;* E. von Dobschütz: *Christusbilder;* J. R. Hulbert: 'Some Medieval Advertisements of Rome'; E. Breitenbach: 'Israhel van Meckenem's *Man of Sorrows*'.

pitiful countenance, and which was now preserved in St. Peter's at Rome, where the faithful venerating it could gain indulgence, three thousand years to the natives of the city, nine thousand to cisalpine and twelve thousand to transalpine pilgrims. The Augustinian John Waldeby had enlivened his sermons with accounts of this relic after he returned from Rome in 1354.[148] Hulbert calls *The Stacyons of Rome* no more than a versified *liber indulgentiarum*; and from the early printed text of such a *liber* which he quotes, and which carefully specifies the days in the year when the relic is displayed and the indulgence may be gained,[149] it is very evident that Waldeby's confrère of the next century, John Capgrave, however much he may have been praised for the accuracy of his observations and transcriptions when he too visited the city, is in his *Solace of Pilgrims* merely translating or copying from another such *liber*.[150] Hulbert describes such literature as 'Part of an organized propaganda to attract pilgrims to Rome', and argues very persuasively that the Church and the city suffered throughout the fourteenth century, when the popes' absence in Avignon attracted fewer of the faithful to Rome. However disparate the origins (seemingly for the most part Byzantine) of the legend and of the various traits of the *vera ikon* may be, it seems to have been in Rome that they coalesced;[151] and by Julian's time, in England as throughout the West, the image and its accompanying texts were appearing in pious manuals. In MS Fitzwilliam 55, f. 122$^v$, there is a very fine miniature of the Vernicle followed by:

| | |
|---|---|
| Salue sancta facies | nostri redemptoris |
| in qua nitet species | diuini splendoris |
| inpressa panniculo | (n)iuei cando-(f. 123$^r$)ris |
| dataque Veronice | signum ob amoris ...[152] |

and the same hymn is incorporated in the 'Office of the Vernicle'.[153] In MS BM Royal 17 A xxvii (a composite, the devotional section c. 1400), there is, f. 72$^v$, a drawing of two angels displaying the extended Vernicle, with:

---

[148] Margaret J. Morrin: 'John Waldeby, O.S.A. (ca. 1315-1372)', 21.
[149] 'Some Medieval Advertisements', 403-405.
[150] C. A. Mills, ed.: *Ye Solace of Pilgrimes*, 63.
[151] *Die Fronica,* 9.
[152] Cf. Chevalier, *Repertorium,* no. 18189. A similar miniature and text are in MS Harley 211, f. 141$^r$.
[153] Cf. C. Wordsworth: *Horae Eboracenses,* 174-175.

O vernacule I honoure hi*m and* the
þat þe made þorow his preuite. / (f. 73ʳ)
Þo cloth he set to his face
þe prent laft þere þorow his grace.
His moth his nose his ine to,
his berd his here did al so.
Schulde me for al þat in my liue
I haue singud with wittis fiue;
namlich with mout of sclaunduring,
fals othus *and* bakbiting,
and made loste with toung al so.
Of su*n*nus þat I haue do,
lord of heuen for ȝeue it me
þorow syht of þe figur þat I here se. [154]

Whether Julian had learned from such manuals of the legend and its representation, or from such sources as the 'Legend of Pope Gregory'[155] or the 'Arma Christi',[156] it is clear that she knew the essentials and ignored what was irrelevant.

Her account of her visions of the face of the suffering Saviour begins where she tells, in chapter ii of the short text, how the priest brought with him a crucifix and urged her to look on it. However reluctantly, she did as he said, and set her eyes on the face of the image. Everything except the crucifix grew dark and ugly, 'as if it had been much occupied with fiends' (208.23-209.37, with which the long text agrees). It is suggested that this last detail is a reminiscence of mediaeval crucifixion iconography, or of apocryphal accounts of the devil assailing the crucified Christ. In chapter iii she describes how blood suddenly began to flow from under the crown of thorns; she does not say here that this does not refer to the crucifix brought by the priest, and in her later account of her conversation with the religious who visited her (266.9, and cf. 633.17), she specifies that it was *the crosse that stode atte my bedde feete*. We may recall the frequency in Julian's age of legends of crucifixes which spoke, moved, bled. [157] In chapter v she

---

[154] Cf. Brown and Robbins: *Index,* no. 2577, which lists fifteen manuscripts. Robbins and Cutler, *Supplement,* add two more.

[155] See Breitenbach, 25 and note 13, for the statement that this legend was propagated in the late fourteenth century, along with the identification of Santa Croce in Gerusalemme as the scene of the miracle, by the Carthusians, trying to raise funds for their new Charterhouse there.

[156] See R. Berliner: 'Arma Christi', with its lavish notes and bibliography.

[157] See E. Colledge, 'The Legend of St. Thomas Aquinas' (in A. Maurer, ed.: *St. Thomas Aquinas*), 24-25.

states that for so long as the 'ghostly sights' she has just described lasted, the bleeding persisted. She repeats this in chapter 7 of the long text; but the repetition is followed by a considerable addition (311.14-313.31), containing a minute description of the size, the changing colour and the persistence of the drops of blood, and the vividness and horror of the sight. Towards the end of the short text's chapter vii she implies that the sight had ceased and now has returned. She again states specifically that this was *the face of the crucifixe that hange before me,* but that this conveyed some of the afflictions, physical and mental, of the Passion to her (225.21-29, and cf. 324.3, again a more detailed account). Chapter x begins with yet another vision of Christ's face (not, this time, associated with the crucifix in her room), and of its discoloration as he died (233.1-10). This corresponds with the long text's chapter 16; but the rest of that chapter is concerned with details of the Passion not recounted in the short text.

It is only in the long text that these visions are associated with the Vernicle, in chapter 10, parts of which correspond with chapter vii of the short text, as already noted. As there, she describes how she wished that the Holy Face were not so darkly shown, and was answered *If god will shew thee more, he shal be thy light; thou nedyth none but him* (325.12). This leads her to reflect on our blindness as we seek God; and this is followed by the passage, already described, deriving from Ecclesiasticus and Psalm 138, concerning the 'drowned soul'. Then she writes that all this second revelation was 'so low and so little and so simple' that she doubted, until, later, she received divine assurance, whether it could be from God. Then, with what reads like abrupt transition, she continues: *It was a fygur and a lyknes of our fowle blacke dede, which that our feyre bryght blessed lord bare for our synne* (327.36). 'It' here can only refer to the revelation's beginning, the vision of the Holy Face; and Julian shows that this is so by continuing:

> It made me to thynke of the holie vernacle of Rome, which he portrude with his one blessed face, when he was in his hard passion, wilfully goyng to his death, and often chaungyng of coloure, of the brownhead and the blackhead, rewlyhead and leenhead. Of this ymage many marveyled how that myght be stanndyng that he portrude it with his blessed face, which is the feyerest of heauyn, flower of earth and the frute of the maydens wombe. Then how myght this ymage be so dyscolouryde and so farre from feyerhead? I desyre to say, as I haue vnderstonde, by the grace of god (328.38).

We see from this that she had received the Vernicle legend in its most modern form: that she believes that Christ's image was miraculously transferred to the kerchief as he went towards Calvary, that it is now preserved in Rome, and that it is there the object of great veneration. She suggests that her visions may be compared with it, in that she has been filled with the same reverent compassion. To all else, to the Vernicle's wonder-working properties and the indulgences, she seems quite indifferent.

She seems to suggest that the Vernicle itself exhibits what she saw in her vision, *often chaungyng of coloure*, and that one reason why those who see it displayed in Rome are astonished is because they expect a *vera ikon* to show Christ as the nonpareil of human beauty, as tradition, supported by Scripture, asserts him to be, whereas the Vernicle depicts him *so dyscolouryde and so farre from feyerhead*. It is this implication which has encouraged the editors to emend an evidently corrupt passage, later in the chapter, to read:

> And ther it seyeth of the vernacle of Rome, it meuyth by dyverse chan-ngyng of coloure and chere, somtyme more comfortable and lyuely, and some tyme more rewfull and deadly, as it may be seen (331.65);

and they have pointed out in their annotation how exactly this corresponds with what the art historians tell us of the two conflicting iconographic traditions, 'the first creating a Saviour with noble features, the second a Jesus more dead than alive, crowned with thorns, hair dishevilled and blood-spattered face'.

Julian's devotion to the Sacred Heart, and how the literature and iconography of the devotion seem to have influenced her, is less problematical, chiefly because both iconography and literature are much more clearly documented. Despite the popular opinion that the devotion was initiated by Margaret Mary Alacoque, it is found in England as early as Bede, it was well known to Bernard and to the author of the *Ancrene Riwle*, and was flourishing in Julian's time, as many surviving prayers and pictures testify.[158] In chapter xiii of the short text she had written:

> Fulle merelye and gladlye oure lorde lokyd in to his syde and behelde and sayde this worde: Loo how I lovyd the, as ȝyf he hadde sayde: My childe, ȝif thow kan nought loke in my godhede, see heere how I lette opyn my syde and my herte be clovene in twa and lette oute blude and watere, alle þat was thare yn; and this lykes me and so wille I that it do the (242.1).

---

[158] See E. Colledge, *The Mediaeval Mystics of England*, 11-13, and the authorities there cited, notably Ignazio Bonetti: *Le stimate della Passione*.

In chapter 24 of the long text this becomes:

> Wyth a good chere oure good lorde lokyd in to hys syde and behelde with joy, and with hys swete lokyng he led forth the vnderstandyng of hys creature by the same wound in to hys syd with in; and ther he shewyd a feyer and delectable place, and large jnow for alle mankynde that shalle be savyd and rest in pees and in loue. And ther with he brought to mynde hys dere worthy blode and hys precious water whych he lett poure out for loue. And with the swete beholdyng he shewyd hys blessyd hart clovyn on two, and with hys enjoyeng he shewyd to my vnderstandyng in part the blyssydfulle godhede as farforth as he wolde that tyme, strengthyng the pour soule for to vnderstande as it may be sayde, that is to mene the endlesse loue that was without begynnyng and is and shal be evyr (394.3).

The notable addition here is the allusion to the wounded Sacred Heart as 'a fair and delectable place, and large enough for all mankind'; and the editors have pointed out how this echoes such devotions as the *Anima Christi* and the *Fifteen Oes*. Rosemary Woolf has described and illustrated for us the extremes, sometimes horrific, sometimes mawkish, to which the cult could be taken by writers and limners of inferior taste; that this is a judgment not merely of our own age is shown by Julian's perfect restraint.

Those who read the more violent and intemperate products of the Richard Rolle school only with considerable reservations (and Walter Hilton and the *Cloud*-author are to be numbered among such critics) will find Julian as a devotional writer much more to their taste. She was not prepared to trust her own emotions, until *probatio* counselled her that they would lead her where God wished, to where God was to be found. She understood, as must anyone who seeks for spiritual progress, the need for knowledge: self-knowledge, and knowledge of the traditions established by those who before us have sought for knowledge of God. Her whole book, if it is read aright, shows how she had laboured for such knowledge, and how modestly and unaffectedly she used it when it was given. Very many historians of literature and spirituality have lauded her for the famous conclusion:

> What, woldest thou wytt thy lordes menyng in this thyng? Wytt it wele, loue was his menyng. Who shewyth it the? Loue. What shewid he the? Love. Wherfore shewyth he it the? For loue. Holde the therin, thou shalt wytt more in the same. But thou schalt nevyr witt therin other withoutyn ende (732.15).

When, however, we observe the subtlety with which the *colores* of the rhetoricians are here fused with the techniques of the philosophers and the schoolmen's teachings,[159] we must revere her even more. She ends as she has persisted: this is 'her Lord's meaning', and she knows it because she 'was answered in ghostly understanding'. We may learn to esteem her gifts, but she asks us only to esteem what, she truly believed, was given to her from on high.

## IX THEOLOGICAL CONTENT OF THE *REVELATIONS*

### 1 The Short and Long Texts Compared

In III it has been shown that there had been 'lateral contamination' between the two versions before in the mid-fifteenth century A was copied. None the less, the distinctions of content in either remain plain.

In their annotations to chapter 1, the editors have given their reasons for thinking that this *capitulatura* was composed by Julian herself (unlike the introductory paragraph of the short text), but before the compilation of the long text's revision, the 'second edition'. That and chapters 2 and 3 serve as prologue, and they correspond with the short text, omitting, however, its reflections on the utility and inadequacies of devotional art-objects, and the allusion to what she had heard 'a man ... of Holy Church' tell of the legend of St. Cecilia.

Revelation I, chapters 4-9 in the long text, dealt with three 'sights': the first is the crown of thorns and the streaming blood, which Julian calls a 'bodily sight'. In chapter 4, she writes that the vision of the blood flowing from under the crown inspired her to rejoice in the Trinity, *for wher Jhesu appireth the blessed trinitie is vnderstand*; this reflection (294.9-296.16) is not in the short text. There, the first paragraph of chapter iv, describing the *gastelye sight of his hamly lovynge* (212.2-7), the understanding of the all-embracing love of God, is reworked and transferred to the long text's chapter 5 (299.2-8); and in the two texts the accounts of the contemplation of the hazel nut and of Mary are transposed. They are otherwise substantially unchanged, although it is suggested (300.18 note) that *But what behyld I ther in?* is of the P scribe's own making as a variant to *Botte whate is that to me?* (213.17), with which SS and W agree. But the conclusion of chapter 5, *And also our good lord ...* (301.34-303.46), with the prayer, *God of thy goodnes geue me thy selfe ...*, and the meditation on how his goodness fulfils all creation, is not found in the short text; chapter 6, showing how our prayer is better directed to that goodness than to intermediaries, and how goodness totally encompasses us, is original to the long text, as is the opening of chapter 7, which ob-

---

[159] See the analysis of this passage, 732.15-17 note.

serves the relevance of this contemplation of divine goodness to the vision of Mary's spiritual greatness. Chapter 7 continues with an account of the bleeding caused by the crown of thorns. This begins (311.12) as does chapter v in the short text (217.1); but what is there merely two clauses has been in the long text expanded to occupy the rest of the chapter: the vivid description of the drops of blood, leading to the meditation upon God's 'marvellous homeliness'. Chapter 8 resumes the short text's account of the 'six things' which reflection on the first showing had revealed to Julian. In the annotations to chapter v, it is pointed out how these topics have been reordered in the long text according to their modes: 'bodily sights', 'ghostly in bodily likeness', and 'ghostly sights'. The rest of chapter 8, her remark to those at her bedside that this was Doomsday for her, her explanation of the remark, and her application of her entire narrative to the spiritual situation of every Christian, follows, with some reworking, the short text. Chapter 9 begins with the observation found in the short text, chapter v, 'For the showing I am not good unless I love God the better' (220.11, 321.2), but whereas in the short text this is followed by a reiteration that these revelations are for the profit of all, in the long text this is turned into an address *to you that be symple*. In either text there follows the statement that Julian does not claim for herself more love from God *than the lest soule that is in grace*, and her appeal to the unity of charity. Then, in the short text, there follows a passage, *And thus wille I love ... Jhesu that ys techare of alle* (221.33-222.52), her expostulation that she is an ignorant woman who is not teaching but merely repeating what has been revealed to her of divine love, not found in the long text. The significance of this omission has been remarked on (222.40 note). But both texts then continue with her affirmation of faith in the teachings of Holy Church (222.52-223.56, 323.20-28), after which chapter vii begins, Revelation I ends with her description of the 'three parts' in which the revelations were received, and of the inadequacy of her accounts of the 'ghostly sights'. The matter which then follows in the short text, her application of the revelations to all Christians (224.8-11), and her saying that this day was to be her judgment day (224.14-225.20), has, it has been seen, been moved forward in the long text to chapter 8.

Chapter vii of the short text ends and Revelation II, chapter 10, begins with the 'bodily sight' of the crucifix, relating its dolorous aspect. Julian could see this only with difficulty and asked for more light, and she was answered: 'If God wishes to show you more, he will be your light' (225.28, 325.12). Then, in the long text only, there follows a lengthy passage (325.14-335.96), the rest of Revelation II, containing her meditation on 'our common working in this life', seeing and seeking God, having him and wanting him, her account of the 'drowned soul' finding safety in God's keeping, the description of her perplexity over the seemingly commonplace nature of such showings, and the assurance she later received that they were divinely revealed. With this assurance she then interprets the vision of the crucified Christ with which Revelation II began as 'a figure and likeness of our foul black death ...', which, she says, made her think of the Vernicle at Rome, which astonishes those who venerate it by the lack of physical beauty in the Man of Sorrows. This leads her to another meditation on man as the image of the Trinity, and the Son of Man taking on him that image as man had befouled it. She refers to a coming passage in which she will write more of Christ's likeness, and she seems to assert that the Vernicle itself changes colour and appearance as did the Lord in her vision. Such fluctuations typify for her the 'seeing and seeking, having and wanting', all of which is according to God's will. We must wholly resign ourselves to that will; all of us must seek, joyfully, patiently, trustfully.

Revelation III, chapter 10, begins with her account of how she saw God *in a poynte*, how she saw him as omnipotent but failed to discern the nature of sin. This corresponds with the opening of chapter viii in the short text; but what is there concerning divine providence and prescience (226.5-7) has been expanded (337.8-16), in a passage which may owe something to Chaucer's *Boethius*, attributing to human ignorance or blindness any denial of providence. Similarly, the next sentence in the short text, *Whare fore me behovede nedes grawnte that alle thynge that es done es wele done, and I was sekyr that god dose na synne* (226.7), has been augmented: *Thus I vnderstonde in this shewyng of loue, for well I wott in the syght of our lord god is no happe ne aventure; wherfore me behovyd nedes to grannt that alle thynges that is done is welle done, for our lord god doth all. For in this tyme the workyng of creatures was nott shewde, but of our lord god in the creatures; for he is in the myd poynt of all thynges, and all he doth. And I was sewer that he doth no synne; and here I saw verely that synne is no dede, for in alle thys, synne was nott shewde* (337.16). Nothing in the short text has been deleted, but the reference to divine omnipotence has been added, she points out that the revelation is not concerned with human acts but with divine action upon humanity (which is why she could write in the short text that *synne is nouȝt*, here carefully rephrased as *synne is no dede*), and so leads with greater cogency to the demonstration that *he doth no synne*. Then in the long text comes the etymologizing remark on the 'two fair properties' of *ryghtfulnes,* after which both texts promise an ac-

count of a further revelation in which sin will be described. The rest of
Revelation III, her fuller reflections on divine prescience and
beneficence, and the affirmation of this by *repetitio, See, I am god ...*
(340.51 e.s.) are not found in the short text.

It next describes her vision of the Flagellation (227.14). This is recounted in even more painful detail at the beginning of Revelation IV,
chapter 12 (342.3-343.12). Both texts pass immediately to the
meditation on the plentiful waters created for our service, and on the
Precious Blood (227.20-24, 343.13-19), where the long text's rewriting
bears witness to Julian's now heightened literary skills. The further
meditation on the Precious Blood which is the rest of Revelation IV is
not found in the short text.

Revelation V, chapter 13, corresponds with the rest of chapter viii in
the short text, apart from the closing sentence there; but there are important additions. Both texts have the locution, *Here with ys the feende
ouer commynn* (227.28, 346.7), and the assurance that the devil is
powerless and that he sorrows on that account. But in the long text
Julian continues: *But in god may be no wrath ... and do against goddes wyll*
(347.18-348.23). In both texts we have the same account of Julian's
laughter as she sees God despising the impotent fiend, but the long text
omits her wish that all Christians might see and laugh as she did, and,
after the statement that she did not see Christ laugh, it adds that her
laughter was solely for the sight, and qualifies what she had written of
*scornyng*, lest it seem to contradict what she had written of there being
no anger in God, with *And ther I sawe ... which is durable* (349.31-35). The
account of 'game, scorn and earnest' follows in either text, but, again,
in the long text *scornyd* is given a further explanation.

Chapter viii of the short text concludes with the locution: *I thanke the
of thy seruyce and of thy trauayle, and namly in þi ȝough* (229.53), which is the
opening in the long text of Revelation VI, chapter 14 (351.3); but what
there follows, *And in thys my vnderstondyng ... fulfyllyth alle hevyn of ioy and
blysse,* is a new addition. Thereafter the beginning of chapter ix and
what follows in the long text agree, though the 'exsample', *A kyng ... is
mech incresyd* (352.24-26), and *For I saw ... all her lyfe* (353.32-36) are also
additions.

Revelation VII, chapter 15, quite unlike any of the first six, telling
only of the alternation of spiritual joy and depression, and seeming to
describe her state of soul at this point in the sequence of revelations,
corresponds with 230.18-233.10 in the short text. The variants between
the two are minimal.

Revelation VIII, consisting, as it has been edited, of chapters 16-20, has much more matter than any before; it opens, as does chapter x, with a showing of the Holy Face and all the sufferings of the Passion which that conveys. But soon Julian begins to rewrite. A long passage, *and the swete body ... so longe sufferde he* (357.11-358.24) is introduced, as also the sentence *And ther I say ... contynually dyeng* (359.26). Thereafter chapter 17 takes up the course of the short text again with the meditation on 'I thirst'; but the entire passage *for I vnderstode that for tendyrnes* (360.9) ... *and that other slow with clyngyng and dryeng* (364.45) is new. There is omitted from the short text the allusion to Philippians 2.5, and the narrative of how her mother made to close Julian's eyes, thinking her dead. The rest of the chapter follows the short text. Chapter 18 begins with the same announcement as in the short text (235.43) of the vision of Mary, this time as the Mother of Sorrows; but it adds the remarks about the 'kind love most fulsomely shown in his sweet mother' (366.6), and the sentence *For ever the hygher ... that he lovyd* (366.8). The sentence *Here saw I ... sufferyd with hym* (367.14) is from the short text (235.49); but the rest of chapter 18 is original. The narrative concerning 'Denis of France' probably derives from reading undertaken after the short text's completion. In chapter 19, the account of how she was commanded (she does not say by whom) 'Look up to heaven to his Father', and of how she was taught *to chese Jhesu only to my hevyn in wele and in woe* (370.2-371.20) follows the short text (236.57-237.6); but the rest of the chapter is new. The beginning of chapter 20, *And thus saw I ... and vtterly dyspysed* (374.2-375.9) is from the short text (237.6-238.15); but the rest of this chapter and the beginning of Revelation IX, chapter 21 (as it is edited) are original.

With *sodenly I beholdyng* (379.6), correspondence with the short text (239.1) resumes; but the meditation, beginning *I vnderstode that we be now in our lordes menyng ...* (379.11), and the rest of chapter 21 are not found in the short text. The opening of chapter 22, from *Then seide oure good lorde askyng* (382.2) to *in his properte and in hys wurkyng* (383.13), corresponds with the short text, chapter xii (239.6-17), and, after one interpolated sentence, *That is to sey, I saw in Crist that the father is,* the correspondence continues (239.17-240.25; 383.14-384.23). The next sentence in the long text, *And this was a syngular marveyle ...* (384.22) is new; what follows corresponds again (240.26; 384.24-385.28), but the rest of that paragraph (385.28-31) is new. The first sentence of the next paragraph follows without omission the short text (240.31-33; 385.32-33). Again, new matter is introduced (385.34-386.46). Then *The loue that made hym ... shall be without ende* (386.46-387.49) introduces what came earlier in chapter xi (238.15-19). The conclusion of the chapter, beginning *If I myght suffer more* (387.50), corresponds with 240.34-40. The beginning of chapter 23, *And in these thre wordes ... the holy gost lykyth* (389.2-6) continues the short text without break (240.40-241.45); but 389.6-391.24 are a new reflection. Then the short text is taken up again without omission, but what there begins as a statement, *Jhesu wille ...,* becomes in the long text an apostrophe, *A, Jhesu ...* (241.45; 391.25). The rest of the chapter, apart from a few lines indicated in the annotations, is new.

Revelation X, chapter 24, takes the opening sentence of chapter xiii, *Fulle merelye ... that it do the* (242.1-6), and uses most of the chapter as a frame for a new meditation on the vision of the Sacred Heart. The central idea of the short version, *zif thow kan nought loke in my godhede, see heere how I lette opyn my syde,* is suppressed, since Julian now has a different reflection; instead the pierced and wounded heart becomes *a feyer and delectable place, and large jnow for alle mankynde that shalle be savyd* (394.6). There is allusion to the earlier meditation on the Precious Blood, and this leads to Julian's statement that the vision of the Sacred Heart and of the Saviour's joy in it gave her 'understanding in part of his divinity', as much as then Christ wished to give. The locution, *Lo how I loue the* (in the short text, 242.2, we read *lovyd*), inspires new passages to replace *zif thow kan nought loke ...: my darlyng ... enioye with me* (395.16-19), and *behold and see ... and blysse with me* (396.21-28).

Revelation XI, chapter 25, uses the same technique of commenting on a locution by attributing speech in the first person (that it is such a comment and not a locution always carefully specified). It continues the short text narrative (242.7-10) without break, reporting the locution *Willt thou see her?* (398.5); and then Julian gives her own exegesis of this, *as yf he had seyd ...* (398.6-399.22). Then comes narrative from the short text (242.11-18; 400.24-31), Julian's answer to the locution, and her statement that although she had expected to see Mary in bodily likeness (A's reading, 242.12, is probably superior to P's *lykyng,* 400.26, or the SS variant), in fact she saw her in apotheosis. Then comes, in the long text, the *exsample,* 400.32-34, not found in the short, after which the rest of the chapter follows the short text (242.18-243.24; 400.35-401.41) without omission.

Revelation XII, chapter 26, very brief, reports the 'I it am' locution when Christ showed himself 'more glorified' (243.25-36), closely following the elaborate rhetorical structure, but drawing from it a markedly different conclusion (cf. 243.28, 402.4 and notes).

Revelation XIII comprises chapters 27-40. Chapter 27, 404.3-405.13, follows exactly the short text, 243.37-244.43, with its statement that

Julian in her folly had previously thought that if God had prevented sin, *alle schulde hafe bene wele,* which is preparing the ground for one of the most celebrated locutions. Then the long text telescopes a passage from the short, *But Jhesu that in this vysyon enformyd me of alle that me nedyd answeryd by thys worde and seyde: Synne is behouely* (405.11-13; cf. 244.46-52), and introduces for the first time the locution itself: *but alle shalle be wele, and alle shalle be wele, and alle maner of thynge shalle be wele,* not found at this place in the short text. What follows: *In þis nakyd worde: Synne ... whych be nott very good* (405.14-406.21), there is further omission of short-text matter (cf. 244.53-245.60). The rest of the chapter follows the short text, 406.22-407.38, 245.61-246.75 (as it has been edited), though the final paragraph, *And in theyse same wordes ...* (407.39-42) is original. Chapter 28's opening, *Thus I saw ... alle my evyn cristen* (408.2-5), is from the short text (246.77-80), but, except for *And than saw I ... Crist in hym* (246.80-83), the rest of this chapter is new. The whole of chapter 29 (412.2-413.17) corresponds with the short text, 247.1-16. Chapter 30, 414.2-416.26, reproduces the short text, 247.17-248.41. Chapter 31 begins (417.2-418.20) by following the short text, chapter xv, 249.1-250.18; but the rest of the chapter, *For we know in oure feyth ...* (418.21 e.s.) is original, except for the concluding phrases (421.50-53; 250.19-22). The next sentence in the short text, *And in thies ... ere for to comme* (250.22-25), is reproduced in the middle of the long chapter 31 (423.20-22), but with that exception the chapter is new. Chapter 32 omits what follows immediately in the short text, *for ryght ... nought wele* (250.25-27), but repeats the following sentence, *It is goddys wille ... alle that he schalle do* (250.27-28), towards the end of chapter 33, which otherwise is original. So is the first paragraph of chapter 34 (430.2-431.14); but the rest follows the opening of chapter xvi (252.1-12), omitting the conclusion of chapter xv (250.29-251.35). The first paragraph of chapter 35, the anecdote of Julian's overanxiety for *a serteyn creature* (432.2-433.14), repeats the short text (252.13-253.23), though the long text has been edited to conceal that the 'creature' was a woman (cf. 432.4 note). The rest of chapter 35 is new, as is the whole of chapter 36. Chapter 37 takes up again the short text without omission, supplying, however, its own minor interpolations. The first clause of chapter 38 follows the short text (255.17-18) without a break; but the treatment of the theme of the famous penitents whose examples show that 'sin is no shame, but worship' (254.9-256.25; 445.2-448.36) has been drastically re-edited for the long text, and the 'example' of John of Beverley is new. The opening of chapter 39 (449.2-450.13) reproduces the short text (256.25-256.36) without omissions and with only minimal rewording; but the meditation on humility which follows (450.13-452.29) is an addition. This leads to the passage *For by theyse medycins ... to worschyppe and to joy* (452.30-453.40), which follows the short text without omission (256.36-45) and with little re-editing; the conclusion of chapter 39 (453.40-48) is not in the short text. The first three paragraphs of chapter 40 (454.2-456.24), though they reproduce odd phrases from the short text (454.6, 455.12 notes) are new; the rest, 457.33-459.54, is an expansion of what immediately follows the last borrowing from there (256.45-47).

Revelation XIV, pp. 460-618, comprises chapters 41-63, and constitutes one third of the entire long text. The opening of chapter 41 (460.3-4, 5-462.20) continues without omission to follow the short text (258.1-2, 259.13-260.29); but the rest of the chapter in the long text, with its analysis of the locution, and its exhortations to have trust in praying, is new. Chapter 42, a continuation of this theme, is wholly new. Chapter 43, also concerned with prayer, has some borrowing from the short text (258.4-261.53 = 475.2-476.17; 261.59-262.64 = 478.28-479.33), but much new matter has been added. Chapters 44, 45 and 46 are original, as is chapter 47, apart from one phrase (262.64-67; 496.16, 17, 496.19-20); and the whole of the rest of this revelation is not found in the short text. Elsewhere in this Introduction the basic unity of the entire revelation, which is its concern to comprehend and expound divine compassion, is suggested; and the editors have there attempted to demonstrate that this wealth of fresh material includes the showing of the lord and the servant, received along with the others but suppressed in the short text, because Julian could not reconcile her convictions about God's love with her age's preoccupation with his anger and what she had been shown — and not shown — about sin, and that this leads to her teachings on 'God our Mother', and on the unity of all mankind which will be saved, as her final resolution of the theological and emotional problems which had prevented her from writing the short text in accordance with what, she was told, was God's will for it.

Revelation XV is constituted of chapters 64 and 65. In accordance with her new insights, Julian omits the passage in the short text dealing with the quenching of God's wrath (262.69-78), and begins chapter 64 with a new sentence: *Thus I vnderstode that all his blessyd chyldren whych be come out of hym by kynd shulde be brougt agayne in to hym by grace* (619.3-4). Then the second, third and fourth paragraphs follow (619.5-622.30), with little re-editing, chapter xx of the short text (263.1-264.25). Next there is the account of the *swylge stynkyng myrre* (622.31-625.60), and its application to the theme of 'merciful compassion', at the end of which

Julian introduces, re-arranged from the short text, *What shuld it than a greuyd* ... (625.59-626.67; cf. 265.57-58, 264.27-33). Chapter 65 is original to the long text.

Revelation XVI comprises the remaining chapters, 66-86. The beginning of chapter 66, 632.3-9, serves as preface to the whole revelation, and it is new. The rest of the paragraph, *and soone I feelt ... gostly and bodely* (632.10-15) paraphrases and expands the opening of chapter xxi (266.1-6). Then there follows, 632.16-634.35, the account of her conversation with the 'religious person' (cf. 266.7-267.25). Chapter 67 describes the nocturnal phantasm which assailed her sleeping, with much more vivid detail than in the short text (cf. 267.26-40). Chapter 68 follows the short text, chapter xxii, 268.1-269.27, but with an addition (641.17-643.36). Between chapters 68 and 69 the long text omits 269.28-42. Chapters 69 and part of 70 follow the short text's account of the second diabolic visitation (270.1-25), but with considerable re-editing; the two devils, for example, are reduced to one. But at the end of this account, chapter 70 continues (651.17-653.40) with a general reflection on the revelations' authenticity, and on Julian's pusillanimity in this regard, whereas the short text's rhetorical apostrophe to sin (271.26-36) is omitted, for reasons elsewhere suggested, as is the reflection on *wrecchednesse* (271.37-272.56). Chapters 71 and 72 are original. Chapter 73 begins (666.2-11) by following the short text (272.57-274.8). There follows a long new passage (667.16-669.38); and the chapter ends with two separated excerpts (669.39-673.19, 674.27-675.33), which together form the last quotation from the short text (275.25-277.23). The rest of the chapter, and of Revelation XVI, is original.

## 2 Criteria of Analysis

The problem facing the psychologist and the theologian concerning the relations between Julian's vision, her sickness and alleged cure have been canvassed too often for them to need detailed rehearsal here. Molinari has carefully catalogued the various possibilities, from the only evidence available; her text, her apparent good health for at least forty years afterwards, and Margery Kempe's testimony that she was active as a spiritual counsellor at the age of sixty or thereabouts, and, most significantly, had a reputation for discerning truth from falsehood in the matter of visions and revelations. Molinari's criticisms of past judgments are well reasoned.[160] In the preceding section of this In-

---

[160] *Julian of Norwich*, 22-31.

troduction, and, frequently, in their annotations, the editors have remarked the scrupulous care with which Julian, in revising her short text, scrutinizes all that she had written about her state of mind and body at the time of the showings, and her passionate regard for objective truth about herself. The long text is more than sufficient testimony to the many hours of prayer and exacting study demanded by the editorial task she had undertaken.

Two points have perhaps escaped the notice of previous critics. The more important is the clinical precision with which she describes the progress of her sickness, and especially her symptoms when *in extremis*:

> And when I was xxx[th] yere old and a halfe, god sent me a bodily sicknes in the which I lay iij daies and iij nyghtes; and on the iiij nyght I toke all my rightes of holie church, and went not to haue leuen tyll day (289.2).

It must first be noticed that *all my rightes of holie church* refers principally to the sacrament of the sick, or extreme unction, as it is officially entitled in the list of seven sacraments 'held and taught by the holy Roman Church' composed at the Second Council of Lyons in 1274.[161] By the middle of the twelfth century, the custom was to postpone the anointing until the sick person was near death, and it appears to have been Peter Lombard who first called it the sacrament of 'extreme unction'.[162] After him, the great scholastics taught that the purpose of the sacrament was to prepare the soul for death and for immediate entrance into heaven. Duns Scotus, for example, insisted that the anointing be administered only to those who are so close to death as to be incapable of further sin.[163] The view of Thomas Aquinas became general: extreme unction frees the soul from the debt of temporal punishment, so that when it departs from the body, nothing can prevent its entrance into glory.[164] It is thus clear that in the common estimation of those who were with Julian, and of whatever medical competence was available, she was 'in danger of death by sickness'. It was on the third night, after she had received the sacraments, when she *weenied often tymes to haue passed, and so wenyd thei that were with me* (289.6); and she writes:

> I vnderstode by my reason and by the feelyng of my paynes that I should die ... Thus I indured till day, and by then was my bodie dead from the miedes downward, as to my feeling. Then was I holpen to be set vpright ... vndersett with helpe ... My curate was sent for to be at my ending, and

---

[161] Denzinger-Schönmetzer, no. 860.
[162] *Sententiarum libri quatuor* IV dist. ii 1; PL 192 841.
[163] *Quaestiones in IV librum sententiarum* IV dist. xxiii (Paris, V ii 9).
[164] *Contra gentiles* IV cap. lxxii (Rome, 1934, 537-538).

before he cam I had set vp my eyen and might not speake ... After this the over part of my bodie began to die so farforth that vnneth I had anie feeling. My most payne was shortnes of breth and faielyng of life. Then went I verily to haue passed (pp. 290.14-292.35).

Specialists in diseases of the heart whom the editors have consulted accept the description of the extreme difficulty of speech, the loss of vision, the painful effort of breathing as that of an exceptionally observant and articulate lay-person reporting the symptoms of severe cardiac failure.

Secondly, Julian treats her cure as miraculous, in the strict theological sense, by applying the criteria demanded, then as now, in causes of canonization:[165] it was so sudden as to be outside the natural processes of recovery; it was not a medicinal cure; and it was complete:

> And in this sodenly all my paine was taken from me, and I was as hole, and namely in þe over parte of my bodie, as ever I was befor. I merveiled of this sodeyn change, for my thought that it was a previe working of god, and not of kynd (292.35, and cf. 292.35 note).

The agnostics (and there have been several during this last century of continually awakening popular interest in fourteenth-century English spirituality) amongst Julian's critics, since they cannot accept the possibility of miracle, have naturally tended to overlook her careful and (to the unprejudiced) objective descriptions of her experiences of suffering. Finally, if one finds oneself out of sympathy with her theological world, attempts to explain her visions as hallucinations, showing an abnormal mental state,[166] or even 'acute neurosis induced perhaps by an over-enthusiastic life of penance and solitude'[167] are ultimately inevitable. In any discussion of the nature and meaning of her revelations, there are no criteria except those of Catholic theology as it reflects over the centuries on the Christian faith as contained in Scripture and authentic ecclesial tradition. This theology affirms that God can reveal himself (in the strict sense of verbal revelation) to an individual person; and he can give to the recipient a sufficient certitude of the divine origin of this personal experience by internal or external criteria. Such revelations are called 'private', not because they are in-

---

[165] The best historical survey of the evolution of the processes is probably still that of Prospero Lambertini, Benedict XIV; and they can be observed at work in Julian's day in Isak Collijn's sumptuous edition of the documents dealing with Bridget of Sweden's first canonization. See E. Colledge: *'Epistola solitarii ad reges'.*

[166] R. H. Thouless: *The Lady Julian*, 25.

[167] C. Pepler: *The English Religious Heritage*, 312.

tended simply for the spiritual benefit of an individual, but because they are addressed through the beneficiary to the whole Church or to an important part of the Church. [168] Furthermore, the immediate beneficiary, at the very least, can have the right and even the duty of adhering to the content of such revelations by an act of faith, even though such revelations do not belong to the deposit of faith, the public revelation, which was completed with the death of the last of the twelve apostles. [169] But it does not follow that the authentic private revelation is merely an affirmation of what is already known (or can be known) by faith and theology, a kind of heavenly repetition of public revelation. Its essential character is imperative; it is a specific command, a manifestation of the divine will inspired in a member of the Church which is to affect the conduct of the Church, or of some of its other members, in a concrete situation. [170] That Julian is constantly aware of this theology of revelation is evident throughout her showings, and in both texts. What gives her courage to publish her short text, despite the opposition which she is convinced that the publication will arouse, is her assurance that *this that I saye, I hafe it of the schewynge of hym that es souerayne techare* (222.42); and she goes on:

> Botte for I am a womann, schulde I therfore leve that I schulde nouȝt telle ȝowe the goodenes of god, syne that I sawe in that same tyme that is his wille, that it be knawenn? (222.46).

That she is acutely conscious of her right and duty to believe without wavering that God has revealed himself and his love to her is shown in the distress she is still capable of communicating to us when she writes, more than twenty years afterwards, of her recklessness in doubting this even for a moment:

> I waxsyd full grettly ashamyd, and wolde a bene shryvyn. But I cowlde telle it to no prest, for I thought, how shulde a preste belieue me when I by seaying I ravid I shewed my selfe nott to belyue oure lorde god? Nott withstanding I beleft him truly for the tyme þat I saw hym; and so was than my wylle and my menyng ever for to do without end. But as a fole I lett it passe oute of my mynde. A, loo how wrechyd I was! This was a grett synne and a grett vnkyndnesse (633.23).

It is hardly necessary to cite examples showing how totally she takes it for granted that the showings and the Christian faith must coincide. She is a simple child of God because she is a simple child of her mother, Holy Church (cf. 494.49):

[168] K. Rahner: 'Les révélations privées', 506.
[169] Ibid., 512-513.
[170] Ibid., 513.

> Here may we see that we be all bounde to god for kynd, and we be bounde to god for grace. Her may we see that vs nedyth nott gretly to seke ferre out to know sondry kyndys, but to holy church into oure moders brest, that is to sey in to oure owne soule, wher oure lord dwellyth. And ther shulde we fynde alle, now in feyth and in vnderstandyng, and after verely in hym selfe clerely in blysse (612.22).

Julian knows well enough the part of the Church for which her revelations are intended. First, it is her fellow-Christians in England, for whom she writes so carefully in their mother tongue, translating and opening for them the Scriptures in the light of her showings and her experience, and sharing with them all that she has learned of contemplative life and prayer from the great monastic teachers of the West. She makes further specifications: *alle men and womenn that myghttelye and mekelye and wyrschipfullye takes the prechynge and the techynge of haly kyrke* (252.1); *what man or woman wylfully chosyth god in this lyfe for loue* (627.2); *swylke menn and womenn that for goddess love hates synne and dysposes thamm to do goddes wille* (274.6). The author of the prologue in A puts it succinctly: ... *in the whilke visyonn er fulle many comfortabylle wordes and gretly styrrande to alle thaye that desires to be Crystes looverse* (201.3), as does the colophon to S2:

> Here end the sublime and wonderful revelations of þe unutterable loue of God in Jesus Christ, vouchsafed to a dear lover of his, and in her to all his dear friends and lovers whose hearts like hers do flame in þe loue of our dearest Jesu (734.29 note).

## 3 Revelation I

In the summary of the sixteen showings which the editors believe to have been composed, by Julian herself, before she made the final redaction of the long text (cf. the annotations to chapter 1), at the beginning of the first chapter, it is stated that here *all the shewynges that foloweth be groundide and ioyned* (281.7). For purposes of illustration, one might say that Revelation I stands to the other fifteen in their final version as the Prologue stands to the rest of St. John's Gospel. The analogy is not so far-fetched as it may seem: the first showing concerns 'himself, God and man', God the everlasting lover, who comes down to us, to the lowest part of our need, born to her who was a simple creature of his making, dwelling in us, filling full all his creatures. Julian, like so many contemplatives of the Western Church before and after her, would know the Prologue by heart, as the final prayer of the daily Mass, associated with the blessing, and read indeed as a blessing in exorcisms and over newly baptized children and the sick. [171] Like the apostle, she is vividly aware that the Word was spoken to her — she saw his glory. But the purpose of her revelation could never be other than the purpose of the Gospel, spoken, shown, written that we 'may believe that Jesus is the Christ, the Son of God, and, believing, have life in his name' (John 20.31). *It is goddes wylle that ʒe take it with as grete ioy and lykyng, as Jhesu hath shewde it to yow* (320.39). From the first she is anxious to efface herself as much as possible. She is aware that the one who *is more then all that god made beneth her in wordines ... but the blessed manhood of Christ* (298.38) saw herself *so lytylle and so lowe, so symple and so poer in regard of hyr god* (311.8). But now, as Julian writes her long text, conscious of her gifts and developed talents, she begins by recalling that when she received the revelation, she had comparatively little learning (285.2), and that she was naive enough to ask for graces which, later, seemed to overwhelm her. *Yff I had wyst what payne it had be, I had be loth to haue prayde it* (371.21).

The editors have remarked on the 'Franciscan' influences in Julian's early piety, and particularly that of popular devotions to Christ's Passion, as evidenced, for instance, by her obvious acquaintance with such well-known works as the *Stimulus amoris* and the pseudo-Bonaventure *Meditationes*. Though we have no means of knowing how long before her thirtieth birthday she had asked for the three gifts, including the three 'wounds', she obviously considers the interval between her petitions and her sickness to have been significant enough for her to write: *This sicknes I desyred in my jowth, that I might haue it when I ware xxx*th *yeare olde* (288.38, and note), a youth during which, it is believed, she was already serving God in the religious state (cf. 351.3 e.s.) But she is of sufficient spiritual maturity to distinguish her first two desires from the third:

> These twey desyers of the passion and of the sicknes that I desyred of him was with a condicion; for me thought this was not the commune vse of prayer (287.34).

More than this, however, as will be seen in the analysis of Revelation XIII, the 'three wounds', of true contrition, kind compassion and wilful longing to God, are a concise description of the grace of compunction, integral to contemplative life and prayer in the Benedictine tradition, according to the teaching of Gregory the Great, the 'doctor of desire'. [172]

---

[171] R. E. Brown: *The Gospel according to John*, 1 18.
[172] J. Leclercq: *The Love of Learning*, 39.

- The first two gifts she sees as means to the third: the sickness is for passive purification (*And this ment I for I would be purgied by the mercie of god*: 287.29), the sight is for illumination (*wher in I might haue more knowledge of the bodily paynes of our sauiour ... the more true mynd in the passion of Christ*; 286.12-20), and the purgation and illumination, the fruits of her own sufferings and of her suffering with Christ, were to lead to union and to the fulfilment of her longing (*For I desyred to haue ben soone with my god and maker*; 287.32). It is perhaps unlikely that she saw so clearly, when she first conceived her 'mighty desire', which, she states, 'dwelt continually' in her consciousness, that she was longing and praying for a life totally given over to contemplation according to the classic triad. It is in the long text that she tells us that the desire was conceived not only by grace but also by the teaching of Holy Church (288.40), in this case of the great masters of monastic living and contemplative prayer. What one is certain of is the mature quality of her life and prayer at the time of her sickness; her mind and heart were ready to receive the revelations. For Julian, the first showing properly begins, not (as the SS editors have unfortunately indicated) with the third but with the second chapter of the long text; she believes her sickness to be the direct answer to her previous prayer for purification. 'God sent me' is not merely pious jargon, as the *ratiocinatio* indicates:

> For my thought all that tyme that I had leued heer so litle and so shorte in regard of that endlesse blesse, I thought: Good lorde, may my leuyng no longer be to thy worshippe? And I vnderstode by my reason and by the feelyng of my paynes that I should die (290.12).

In this chapter also, she makes it clear that her miraculous cure (which has already been discussed) was, unknown to her, God's immediate preparation for her to receive the showing. In fact, the word 'suddenly' introduces a series of three graces, of which the cure is the first (292.35) and the bodily showing (294.3) the third. The second is what she clearly considers to be a divine impulse to pray for the second wound:

> Then cam sodenly to my mynd that I should desyer the second wound of our lordes gifte and of his grace, that my bodie might be fulfilled with mynd and feeling of his blessed passion, as I had before praied, for I would that his paynes were my paynes, with compassion and afterward langyng to god (292.43).

This is really a prayer for and a description of the first gift (cf. 285.5 e.s.), but without a bodily sight, as well as the second wound; and it explains clearly what she understands by 'compassion'. This prayer is answered, first by the bodily sight, and then by all that she sees and understands in the entire first showing and beyond it, in particular, in the great showing of the Lord's compassion, Revelation XIII (cf., for example, 443.13-15).

It is noteworthy that her first description of the first bodily sight in chapter 4 (there is close correspondence with the short text) is very austere, by contrast with, in particular, Revelations II and VIII. The reason for this becomes clear in the long text, where she writes that the Trinity suddenly filled her heart with utmost joy (294.9). There is no reference, throughout this revelation, to the dolours of the Passion. The stress is on the consolation; and she tells us what was her first reaction to the sight of Christ, glorified and exalted, yet on his cross:

> Thus I toke it for that tyme that our lord Jhesu of his curteys loue would shewe me comfort before the tyme of my temptation; for me thought it might well be that I should by the sufferance of god and with his keping be tempted of fiendes before I should die (296.20).

The Trinitarian showing, which is apparently a 'touch' as well as a sight, has no place in the short text. This may be because initially she attributed her joy to a response of faith, and only perceived later that it was an earnest of the joy of heaven. *Wher Jhesu appireth the blessed trinitie is vnderstand* (295.15). This is for her a truth of faith; she does not see it as belonging to the showing of the suffering Jesus until in the parable of the lord and the servant she understands how it is that the dolorous Passion and the joy of the Resurrection co-exist. The same is probably true of the clear *oppositio contrariorum* which she introduces into the long text with the phrase *so reuerent and so dreadfull* (296.18, and note to line 16).

After the bodily sight of the bleeding head, and the wonder she experiences in her contemplation of it, in the short text she next records 'the ghostly sight of his homely loving' (212.2 e.s.); whereas in the long text there follow, first, the vision of Mary, seen 'ghostly in bodily likeness' (297.28 e.s.), which in the short text is placed after the showing of 'all that is made' (213.25 e.s.). It would appear that in neither text is Julian intending to record the various elements of the whole of Revelation I in chronological order. The 'bodily sight', she tells us in the long text, *contynued tylle many thynges were sene and vnderstondyd* (311.19); and this occurs after she has referred a second time to the showing of Mary (310.2 e.s.), a passage which has no correspondent in the short text. Here in Revelation I, though she will conclude (in both texts) by telling us that

> All this was shewde by thre partes, that is to sey by bodyly syght and by worde formyde in my vnderstondyng, and by goostely syght (323.29; cf. 224.1).

and although she also offers us six headings under which she arranges its total content, none of this refers to chronological succession. It seems probable, however, that she has deliberately arranged the showing of Mary to follow that of Christ, man and God, not merely for the theological reason *that she is more then all that god made beneth her in word-ines and in fullhead; for aboue her is nothing that is made but the blessed manhood of Christ, as to my sight* (298.38), and therefore takes precedence of all else which is made, but also because of the movement in the showing from 'ghostly in bodily likeness' to vision of a higher sort. As Molinari has pointed out in his classification of the sights, this term occurs elsewhere only in chapter 51, where it is used in conjunction with another term, 'more ghostly without bodily likeness',[173] also to describe the dynamic progress from a lower to a higher kind of 'ghostly sight'. It could well be that in chapter 51 Julian, seeing clearly for the first time the distinction, was then able to find language to express it. But the vision of Mary seems to have been clarified fully for her before that of the lord and the servant, in chapter 44, where she can tell us as she saw (cf. p. 483), so that she has no need to make the sort of distinctions for the sake of clarity which she draws in chapter 51.

It has been noted that at the end of Revelation I Julian writes of three modes of manifestation, one of which is 'words formed in my understanding'. In both texts, Julian may be observed using *ratiocinatio* in various ways to communicate her assimilation and understanding of what she saw. This she never considers as a kind of negative exercise, arguing or reasoning with herself. The three answers in chapter 5 concerning the little thing, the size of a hazel nut, *It is all that is made* (300.12), *It lasteth and ever shall, for god loueth it; and so hath all thing being by the loue of god* (300.15), *Verely, the maker, the keper, the louer* (300.19), are formed in her understanding. That the locutions, too, are of different kinds has frequently been noticed.[174] Here Julian's own reflection on what she is shown produces the questions; but she is convinced that she cannot of herself find the answers.

Molinari argues with reason that here we have an intermediate type of locution, corresponding with the type of sight called 'ghostly in bodily likenesse',[175] different from the dialogue between the Lord and Julian, at the beginning of chapter 22, for example, which Molinari sees as analogous to the bodily sight, which he understands as an

---

[173] Molinari, 42.
[174] Ibid., 67-69.
[175] Ibid., 69.

imaginative, not a bodily vision.[176] However, Julian affirms again in chapter 73:

> Alle this blessyd techyng of oure lorde god was shewde by thre partys, that is to sey by bodely syght, and by worde formyd in myne vnderstondyng, and by gostely syghte (666.2);

and she adds:

> ... for þe words, I haue seyde them ryght as oure lorde shewde them me (666.5).

Thus we must conclude that in whatever form they were cast by Julian, she did not wish to differentiate one locution from another by applying to them the terms 'bodily' and 'ghostly'. She seems also to imply, not only here but in several other places, as will presently be considered, that often enough she sees the words themselves in the same way that she sees a ghostly sight, though not a bodily one. A clear example occurs in Revelation XI, chapter 25:

> Wylte thou see her? I answeryd and seyde: 3e good lorde, grannt mercy, ye good lorde, yf it be thy wylle. Often tymes I preyde this, and I went to haue seen her in bodely lykyng; but I saw her nott so. And Jhesu in that worde shewyd me a goostly syght of her (400.24).

Just as with the bodily sights, she tells us as she sees, *as truly as I can* (666.5); and yet she can also say that these sights in the first showing are *tokyns of the blessydfulle passion*. So the words formed in her understanding, in so far as they are of human speech, are tokens of what God wills to communicate to her. Teresa of Avila, in so many respects a woman of calibre like Julian's, has much to write on these interior words: they are very distinctly formed,[177] much more clearly understood than if heard by the ear,[178] of themselves convincing that they come from God,[179] carrying authority,[180] producing sudden change in the soul,[181] persisting in the memory.[182] All these are indeed Julian's convictions about the words formed in her understanding.

At this point in the short text, after the showing of Mary (pp. 213-14), Julian, writing of contemplative purification, observes:

---

[176] Ibid., 68.
[177] *Autobiography*, xxv 2.
[178] Ibid., xxv 6.
[179] *Interior Castle*, 'Sixth Mansion', III 12.
[180] *Autobiography*, xxv 12.
[181] Ibid., xxv 5.
[182] *Interior Castle*, 'Sixth Mansion..', III 11.

> Of this nedes ilke man and woman to hafe knawynge that desyres to lyeve contemplatyfelye, that hym lyke to nouȝt alle thynge that es made for to hafe the love of god that es vn made (215.41).

The editors have suggested in their annotation to this that Julian in the long text edited out the pericope because she did not wish to restrict what she had to say to *ex professo* contemplatives. In addition, the passage is part of a comparison which might appear to be universally condemnatory off all 'actives'; Julian had no wish to criticize or to offer merely negative advice. On the other hand, in the text as she has re-arranged it, her purpose remains unchanged: she is writing of a basic disposition for union with God which is offered to all Christians. In fact, the whole of Revelation I in the long text can be said to serve as an introduction to contemplative prayer and the way of thinking conducive to it. She tells us first, in chapter 4, of the God who communicates himself to us, by associating the great names of the Trinity (295.11 e.s.) with his 'homeliness' and 'courtesy'. Next she shows Mary as the model of that reverent beholding in wisdom and truth (297.31), which is contemplation. Chapter 5 begins with an image of 'homely loving' compounded from Scripture: the Psalmist, speaking of the universe clad in the majesty of the transcendent God, united to the detail from Luke of the swaddling clothes of the manger at Bethlehem; and the showing of the little thing like a hazel nut has its purpose, to explain that the God who seeks us, and he alone, has and is what can fulfil us. The chapter ends with her own petitionary prayer for this unitive life, the expression of this natural yearning of the soul which is itself a response to the inspiration of the Spirit of God. If and when the devout Christian has learned this lesson, that:

> he is the endlesshead and he made vs only to him selfe and restored vs by his precious passion, and ever kepeth vs in his blessed loue; and all this is of his goodnes (303.44),

he will wish to examine his customary habits of prayer, to see how adequate his response is to the manifold expressions of this goodness. To help him here, Julian describes her own devotional life; and we can see how closely she must have followed the patterns prescribed and recommended in the *Ancrene Riwle*. [183] She writes: *We praie to god for his*

---

[183] In what follows here, and in the annotations to the text, quotations are wherever possible taken from the still unpublished *Riwle* text in the Vernon MS, since it, though retaining a spelling system by its time archaic, in many places has a modernized vocabulary closer than that of any earlier *Riwle* version to the speech of Julian's contemporaries.

*holie flesh*; the *Riwle* has: In þe masse hwon þe prest halt vp godes bodi, siggeþ þis vers ...: Ecce salus mundi, verbum patris, hostia vera, viua caro, deitas integra, verus homo. [184] Compare also: *for his precious bloud*: þencheþ on godes flesch and on his derworþe blod þat is aboue þe heiʒe weued; [185] *his holie passion*: Tuam crucem adoramus domine, tuam gloriosam recolimus passionem;[186] *his dere worthy death*: Ladi seinte Marie, for þat ilke muchele blisse þat þou haddest þo þou seʒe þi dere derworþe sone aftir his deore deþ arysen; [187] *and worshipful woundes*: Jhesu for myne sunnes was honged on rode, for þat ilke fiue wounden þat þou on hire bleddest;[188] *for all the blessed kyndnes*: And at þis word Nascendo formam sumpseris cusseþ þe erþe;[189] *of speciall sainctes*: Halewen þat ʒe louen best, in heore worschupe siggeþ oþer les oþer mo;[190] *and the endlesse life that we haue*: Tu esto nostrum gaudium qui es futurus premium. Sit nostra in te gloria per cunta semper secula;[191] *for his sweete mothers loue*: Ladi seinte Marie, for þat ilke muchele blisse þat þou haddest in with þe in þat ilke tyme þat Jhesu god, godes sone, after þe angels gretinge nom flesch and blod in þe;[192] *for his holie crosse*: Adoramus te Christe et benedicimus tibi quia per sanctam crucem tuam redemisti mundum.[193] Such devotions were integral to the life of prayer as she knew it (cf. 304.4 note); and she goes on to state explicitly that, so long as we understand and know that God is the goodness of all, *it pleaseth him that we seke him and worshippe him by meanes* (305.27).

The rest of chapter 6 is one of her finest descriptive passages, which will be given theological definition when she expounds the doctrine of the Trinity as *natura creatrix*. Here she presents us with the images of mother, father and nurse as symbolizing divine goodness; it is the fulness of what God has to give and longs to give which *the soule sekyth and ever schalle, tylle we knowe oure god verely, that hath vs all in hym selfe*

---

[184] F. 373[a]; cf. Day, 13.
[185] F. 340 (recte 372)[b]; Day, 7.
[186] F. 340 (373)[c]; Day, 7.
[187] F. 373[b]; Day, 17.
[188] F. 340 (372)[b]; Day, 11.
[189] F. 340 (373)[c]; Day, 8.
[190] F. 340 (372)[d]; Day, 12.
[191] F. 340 (373)[c]; Day, 7.
[192] F. 373[b]; Day, 16.
[193] F. 340 (373)[c]; Day, 7. It will be observed that whereas such *Riwle* manuscripts as Nero and Corpus present these Latin tags so much abbreviated that they can only have served as a guide to some book of devotions where the prayers will be found written out in full, these in Vernon can be read as they stand; this makes more interesting the suggestion offered to us by Nita S. Baugh, that Vernon was written for a woman.

*beclosyde* (306.32) All true prayer, she concludes here, is consummately unitive; it is the expression of a mutual giving which God has made possible for us, and has demonstrated to us in the incarnate Jesus.

> For oure kyndely wille is to haue god, and the good wylle of god is to haue vs, and we may never sesse of wyllyng ne of louyng tylle we haue hym in fulhede of ioy (308.57).

In chapter 7 she returns again to the showing of Mary, because in her Julian has seen that this unitive prayer of petition is the asking and receiving, in the one movement, of divine wisdom, truth and love. It is Mary of the Visitation as well as of the Annunciation whose love and reverent fear will express themselves in an abundant charity towards Christ's brethren (309.64). But this contemplation of Mary, as Julian will show with greater precision in Revelation XI, is not an end in itself, but a sight *wher by I am leernyd to know my self, and reuerently drede my god* (399.21). So Julian naturally adverts again to the sight of the head bleeding, which now in the long text she sees as expressing for her the paradox of Crucifixion and Resurrection, life and death, joy and suffering (312.29 e.s.). But, as throughout this revelation, it is consolation which dominates; and she moves to a final manifestation of the 'homely loving'. This particular showing, which she calls an 'example', adding that it was shown bodily, she did not record in the short text. It is an allegory of the condescension displayed by a king or a noble to a poor servant, which will give the servant greater joy than rich gifts offered in a distant manner (313.35-314.45), which is followed by her gloss, 314.46-316.67. This gloss, significantly, concludes with her observation about the application of the rule of faith, hope and love to the contemplative life. A *shewyng* (316.60) is an operation of divine love; the insights it gives into mysteries is a grace freely given. But when the time of the revelation is past and what was seen has disappeared, its fruits are preserved by the grace of the Holy Spirit to the end of life. We need not doubt that she is here writing, in 1395 or later, of how there have been preserved for her the showings and their fruits which she had been given twenty years or more ago. The example is deceptively simple. As has been observed (313.35 note), it is common in contemporary literature. But for Julian it *was shewde so hygh that thys mannes hart myght be rauyssched and almost foryet hym selfe for ioy of thys grette homelynesse* (314.43). It is clear that she is now seeing it in the light of the great parable of the lord and the servant.

The importance which Julian attaches, in the long text, to this first revelation has already been remarked. The point is made again when

we notice how carefully she has reorganized and rewritten, in chapters
9 and 10, what she had set down in chapters v, vi and vii of her first version. To begin with, she adds immediately to her own brief analysis of
the contents of the showing that a movement of the heart in love
towards all her brethren accompanied the entire revelation, and is integral to her evaluation of it. It is therefore logical that she should go
on to provide an example of this movement of the heart; and her
remark to those at her bedside, *It is this daye domys day with me* (319.25), is
precisely that: *This I sayde for I wolde they schulde loue god the better, for to
make them to haue mynde that this lyfe is short, as they myʒt se in exsample*
(319.28). She therefore inserts these two passages, with which she
originally closed the revelation in the short text (224.8), here into chapter 8. She also recalls an experience which she seems to have forgotten
when she was writing the short text: the wonder and perplexity which
she felt at this point. She was convinced that she was going to die, and
yet the purpose of the whole revelation was not, as she had previously
thought, to comfort her in the moment of death (296.20 e.s.), if, as now
appeared, it *was schewde for them that shuld lyue* (319.32). The pericope
neatly introduces the next section (which had been the beginning of
chapter v in the short text), and gives added weight to the apologia, *leue
the beholdyng of a wrech . . .* (320.36) (as though she were saying, 'What
more useless vehicle of God's love and goodness could there be than
one who was at the point of death?'), and illustrates the claim that it is
as though Jesus had showed it directly to all whom he loves (320.40
e.s.). The same theme dominates chapter 9. What is remarkable here is
that although she still uses much of what she wrote in her short text
(chapter vi, 219.1-223.56), the whole tone and temper have changed.
Previously she conveyed a certain apprehension in her humility, as
though her readers might not believe her when she proclaimed her un-
worthiness:

> I praye ʒowe alle for goddys sake, and cownsayles ʒowe for ʒowre awne
> profyt, that ʒe leve the behaldynge of the wrechid worme, synfulle
> creature, that it was schewyd vnto (219.3),

and also a fear that if she protests too much her revelations might not be
received at all. Now, however, she is serene, balanced and at peace with
herself; and even the most captious must believe her as she allies herself
with *yow that be symple, for ease and comfort; for we be alle one in loue* (321.4).
She no longer needs to protest, as she seems to do in the first version
(220.11), that *For the schewynge I am not goode but ʒif y love god the better*; she
can state it quite straightforwardly, and round it off with a deceptive

rhetorical simplicity and with quiet conviction: *and in as much as ʒe loue god the better, it is more to ʒow than to me* (321.2 and notes). With deft touches, such as the insertion of *I hope* (322.10; cf. 220.21), *for god* (322.14; cf. 221.32), and the omissions of *he is safe* and the clause which follows (322.16; cf. 221.33), she is able to avoid possible theological inaccuracies and misinterpretations, as that she is claiming absolutely to be in a state of grace and confirmed in that state. Finally, she sees that any apologia about the publication of private revelations demands, not only for prudence's sake, but for theological assessment, a clear and lucid profession of faith. This she supplies in the long text, where, in a sense, she goes beyond it. She tells us that the faith *stode contynually in my syghte* (323.24) throughout the showing, which informs us that in spite of the sickness, she was in full possession of her faculties. But it also tells us that she came to her revelations with a constant mental background to all that she saw or heard furnished by her previous deep meditation and contemplation on the truths of her faith.

4 Revelation II

Chapter 10 of the long text, Julian's account of Revelation II, well illustrates her reflective and meditative processes at work on the subject matter of the showings. It begins with her account of what she saw in the face of the crucified Christ (324.3-325.14). There is substantial verbal agreement with the short text (225.21-29), but the detail added — that she saw, first, half of the face covered with dried blood, and then the other half — seems to be a recollected imaginative observation, owed, at least partially, to the reflection on seeking and seeing (325.14-326.10), which in its turn seems to be prompted by her desire for more light with which to see clearly what is happening to the crucifix.

Her inability to do so distresses her; but she is calmed, not by any emotional consolation, but by a *ratiocinatio* in the form of a hypothesis: *If god will shew thee more, he shal be thy light* (325.12). From this point on, the rest of chapter 10 is not found in the short text.

Her mind seems to be engaged by a succession of images and ideas, derived from her reading and meditation, presented afresh to her as lights from God. She imagines herself on the sea-bed, and knows herself as safe there as anywhere else in the universe, in the presence of God. Again, this is presented to her reason: *I vnderstode thus* (326.23). It brings consolation: *Mor solace and comforte then all this wordle may or can tell* (326.26); but it appeals to her faith, the dogmatic fact that it is in God that we live and move. She reverts to her longing to see, her trouble that she could see so little, and she resolves it by faith: *For he will that we beleue that we see hym contynually, thow that vs thynke that it be but litle* (326.27).

The recollection of the 'bodily sight' of the Crucifixion presents itself to her mind again and again, and she contrasts her first perturbation, *mornyng, dredfull and longyng* (327.33), that it was so unremarkable, and her consequent fear that it was perhaps not sent by God, with the increase of sight which he gave her as the vision was represented to her mind, as she came to perceive its true significance. When she writes: *And then dyuerse tymes our lord gafe me more syght* (327.35), plainly she is describing not the first reception of the vision but the insights which she has received since it happened, and, perhaps, since she wrote the short text. The vision was given to make her see how Christ who is God suffered death, which came into the world by man (I Corinthians 15.21). Characteristically, she makes her point by a visual contrast: ... *our fowle blacke dede, which that our feyre bryght blessed lord bare for our synne* (328.37); and she continues without interruption: *It made me to thynke of the holie vernacle of Rome.* She knows of the Vernicle's reputation (328.42 e.s.), but that is of no interest to her; she wants to penetrate the representation of Christ's suffering humanity, to perceive its spiritual significance (329.44 e.s.).

To do this she has recourse to fundamentals of the Christian faith: that the Trinity made man in their image and likeness (Genesis 1.27), and that only man's Creator could restore fallen man. Using the same image again (330.59 e.s.), she contrasts the foul blackness of our mortality with Christ's radiant beauty. Not only does Julian herself affirm the ancient belief that Christ upon earth was as he now is in heaven, the perfection of human loveliness, but also she thinks that everyone else should believe this (330.61 e.s.). But it is important to observe that her motive for wishing that this were generally accepted is not sentimental *Brautmystik,* but because of the theological insights it has given her, as it could to others, into the mystery of the Redemption. She refers her readers to what she will write on this topic in chapter 18 (a clear indication of how carefully the long text was drafted).

Then follows a third and final exposition of the theme of 'seeking and seeing', itself an important introduction to her extended teaching on prayer in chapters 41-43. The vision of the Crucifixion has illumined her understanding. The soul can do no more than *seke, suffer and trust* (332.70); and the more that she does this, the more is she pleasing to God. Ordinary grace is needed for this to be begun; for it to be perfected in *the clernesse of fyndyng* (332.71) is of the special grace of the Holy

Spirit, which is his free gift. Seeking pleases God, finding pleases the soul; and therefore *was I lernyd to my vnderstandyng that sekyng is as good as beholdyng* (332.74). When the work is completed, God will have contributed his grace and his guidance, the soul its disposition from the humility given to it (333.78). But whether the soul seeks or sees, the greatest honour it can pay to God is to surrender itself to him (333.81). Seeking is *comyn,* and every soul is given the grace for this (334.84). Grace must form in us three dispositions: zeal and joy (334.87), perseverance and resignation (334.90), and perfect trust.

The authority with which her thinking develops, the clarity and precision of her language, and the ease and subtlety with which this complex of inspirations and the associations which they suggest to Julian is resolved, make this chapter a truly remarkable and wholly professional performance.

## 5 Revelation III

At the end of Revelation II, in the long text, Julian wrote:

> For his workyng is prevy, and he wille be perceyved, and his aperyng shalle be swethe. sodeyn (335.94).

Now, at the beginning of Revelation III, she writes: *And after this I saw god in a poynte* (336.3). It is important for her transition here from II to III that she stress the sudden nature of this sight of God, and for two reasons: this is a ghostly sight, following one which was bodily and repulsive, the image of the face of Christ after he had been crowned with thorns and mocked by the soldiery — *dyspyte, spyttyng, solewyng and buffetyng, and manie languryng paynes, mo than I can tell* (324.5). It was only after she had received enlightenment 'diverse times' (327.35) that this bodily sight became *a lernyng to my vnderstandyng* (332.68) on seeking and finding God, so that eventually she learns that the finding will be as sudden as it is blissful (335.93). Thus this ghostly sight with which chapter 12 begins is precisely the finding of God; and she sees him 'in a point', *in puncto, in ictu oculi,* as the Latin Vulgate text of I Corinthians 15.52 writes of the resurrection of the body (cf. 226.1 note). Secondly, in the short text this ghostly sight is made the immediate answer to her prayer for more light, for she is told, in the long-text version of the *ratiocinatio*: *he shal be thy light; thou nedyth none but him* (325.13).

In this intellectual vision ('I saw ... in my understanding'), Julian unobtrusively shows her acquaintance with scholastic metaphysics. 'God', writes Thomas Aquinas, quoting the *Glossa ordinaria,* 'is in all things by his presence, his power and his substance', and he briefly explains this: 'He is in all things by his power, because all things are within his power, and by his presence, because all things are open to his sight, and by his substance he is present in all things as the cause of their being'.[194] Julian's purpose is not, however, philosophical argument about the divine attributes, but to express her contemplative awareness of the reality of his presence. The same 'unknowing of love' which drives the fearful to pray to God as if he were a pagan deity (cf. 304.4) is also responsible for the ascendancy, in the secular literature of Julian's day, of the ancient Roman cult of the Goddess of Fortune and the personification of 'Saeva Necessitas'; nothing could be more detrimental to contemplative life and prayer, which demands keen awareness that the rational creature is at the centre of the divine concern of a God who is ever at work in his creation:

> This vision was shewyd to my vnderstandyng, for our lord wylle haue the sowle turned truly in to the beholdyng of hym, and generally of all his workes (339.31).

In the previous chapter, in the example of the 'drowned soul' (326.21 e.s.), Julian touches upon a cause of unease in contemplatives, the feeling of insecurity which the awareness of evil, and especially of personal sin, can bring. It is true that the Christian must learn to live with this insecurity; but he can only do this with the help of prayer proceeding from faith informed by a sound theology; and to this purpose, to impart this theology, Julian bends her considerable skills and erudition, whether this be her knowledge of the sapiential books, her sympathetic understanding of Chaucer's insights into *De consolatione philosophiae*, or her grasp of the teaching of John and Paul on the mysteries of faith, the Trinity and the Incarnation. All this finds striking expression in the final summary of this revelation, which shows the triune God speaking of his active presence in creatures and in events, reasoning with Julian in ἐξετασμός of the classical rhetoricians, and evoking from her the loving response which she knows is his heart's desire:

> ... Thus myghtly, wysely and louyngly was the sowle examynyd in this vision. Than saw I verely that my behovyth nedys to assent with great reverence and joy in god (341.56).

---

[194] *Summa theologiae* I.8.3 *in corp.*

## 6 Revelation IV

The fourth, fifth and sixth revelations seem to form a group in themselves; the first of them, chapter 12, recounts a bodily sight, the next, chapter 13, is a locution, 'words formed in my understanding', the last, chapter 14, another locution, 'I thank thee for thy service ...', and Julian's meditations upon heavenly rewards. The bodily sight of chapter 12 constitutes the third way in which *oure curteyse lorde shewyd his passyon to me* (389.8); it is the only one in which she is shown any other mystery of the Passion beside the crucified Christ in his last moments. (Though she writes of the crown of thorns in Revelation I, and, in Revelation II, of the results of the soldiers' ill-usage, she does not mention the actual crowning.) There is possibly here an unusual discrepancy between the short and long texts. The long text reads:

> And after this I saw beholdyng the body plentuous bledyng in semyng of the scoregyng (342.3);

but the short text has:

> And aftyr this I sawe be haldande the bodye plenetvouslye bledande, hate and freschlye·and lyfelye ... And this was schewyd me in the semes of scowrgynge (227.14).

The short text clearly refers to the furrows made by the scourges; she is not seeing in the vision the scourging itself. However, *in semyng of the scoregyng* would appear to mean that she was granted an imaginative and not a bodily vision of the actual flagellation at the pillar. As is noted at 342.3, *semyng* could be interpreted as 'furrowing', but this is rather less likely. More probably, we have in *semyng* editorial tampering in a long-text common ancestor with Julian's *semes*, preserved in the short text.

It may be thought that here she departs from her customary moderation in describing the physical details of the Passion, when she continues:

> The feyer skynne was broken full depe in to the tendyr flessch, with sharpe smytynges all a bout the sweete body. The hote blode ranne out so plentuously that ther was neyther seen skynne ne wounde, but as it were all blode (342.4).

We need, however, to recall the early application in the West[195] to Christ in his Passion of Psalm 128, and the established variant, 'supra cervicem

---

[195] E.g. Hilary of Poitiers on the Psalms, ed. A. Zingerle, 637-647.

meam arabant arantes' (introduced into many manuscripts of Roman and Gallican psalters, but originating in Jerome's *Juxta Hebraeos* translation[196] of its verse 3: 'supra dorsum meum fabricaverunt peccatores', applied to the scourging in particular. None the less, this description of Christ bleeding from the scourging reflects more contemporary enthusiasm for meditating in detail, often gruesome, on the physical sufferings of Christ than do her other descriptions of the 'pains of the Passion'. In addition, the extended reflection in the long text on the Precious Blood, itself at first sight a departure from her customary sober approach, might suggest some acquaintance with the visions and teachings of Catherine of Siena. Chronology (even though some of Catherine's dates have been hotly controverted) suggests however that this could not have been the case. The Bollandists dated Raymond of Capua's *Legend* as 1390,[197] and in 1931 I. Taurisano wrote of it as 'pubblicato nel 1398'.[198] In any case, it would be as misguided and misleading to seek to represent Catherine as an innovator or popularizer of devotion to the Precious Blood as have been the attempts to associate Margaret Mary Alacoque with Sacred Heart devotions more closely than is warranted by the facts. If proof of this be needed, it is found in the *Fifteen Oes* (inevitably, falsely attributed, usually to Bridget of Sweden), circulating throughout the Western Church in the fourteenth century, recorded both in Latin and English (cf. 201.6 note) in Julian's day:

> O Jhesu veritatis speculum, vnitatis signum, caritatis vinculum, memento innumerabilium tuorum vulnerum quibis a summo capitis usque ad ymum pedis vulneratus fuisti et ab impijs Iudeis laceratus fuisti et sacratissimo sanguine tuo rubricatus fuisti, quam magnitudinem doloris in virginea carne tua pertulisti pro nobis. Pie Jhesu, quid ultra debuisti facere quod non fecisti? Scribe queso pie Jhesu omnia vulnera tua in corde meo precioso sanguine tuo, ut in illis legam tuum dolorem et amorem, ut in graciarum accione usque in finem vite mee iugiter perseuerem. Amen.[199]

Furthermore, a careful examination of this passage in Julian (343.13-345.31) in the light of Pauline soteriology, as expressed in Romans chapters 5 and 6 and reflected in Hebrews chapters 8 to 10, leaves us in

---

[196] PL 28 1293.
[197] *ASS* April III, 861.
[198] *Enciclopedia Italiana* 9, art., 'Caterina da Siena, santa'.
[199] MS Cambridge Fitzwilliam Museum 55, f. 119.

little doubt as to the primary source of Julian's reflection (cf. 344.24 note). As to the language in which the reflection is couched, there are many analogues in contemporary versions of the *Meditationes vitae Christi* and the *Stimulus amoris* (cf. the annotations to 342.4-7, 344.21-22).

What is most remarkable about this bodily sight, and surely an argument in favour of its authenticity, is the clarity with which Julian distinguishes between a bodily and an imaginative vision; and this is no hindsight, but an account of the vision itself:

> ... and this ranne so plenteuouslye to my syght that me thought, ʒyf itt hadde bene so in kynde, for þat tyme itt schulde hafe made the bedde alle on blode and hafe passede onn abowte (227.16, and cf. 342.9).

It follows from this observation that her other sights of the bleeding and dying Christ were likewise imaginative.[200] We are reminded of the description of 'a spiritual vision or imaginative' in the *Chastising*,[201] and of the doubts expressed by the *Cloud*-author that Martin and Stephen 'saw such things with their bodily eyes'.[202]

## 7 Revelation V

In her contemplation of the suffering Christ, bleeding so freely from the scourging, Julian had remarked upon the redeeming power of his sacrifice, signified by the shedding of the blood:

> For it is most plentuous, as it is most precious, and that by the vertu of the blessyd godhead. And it is our owne kynde, and blessydfully ovyr flowyth vs by the vertu of his precious loue (343.17).

Another visionary, the seer of Patmos, had beheld the blood of the Lamb which washes clean and ascends to heaven (cf. 344.24 e.s.). And here, in Revelation V, as she is still pondering what she sees, the words which she hears: *Here with is the feende ovyr come* (346.7), echo another text from the Apocalypse: 'and that great dragon was cast out, that old serpent who is called the devil and Satan, who seduces the whole world ... and they overcame him by the blood of the Lamb' (Apocalypse 12.9-11). In the showing which follows, *for he shewed that the passion of hym is the ovyrcomyng of the feende* (347.9), Julian laughs, as the valiant woman who 'will laugh at the latter day' (Proverbs 31.25),

[200] For another view, see E. I. Watkin: *Poets and Mystics*, 78.
[201] Bazire and Colledge, 169, 170-171.
[202] Hodgson, 106-107.

because *he schalle be scornyde at domys day generally of all that schal be savyd*
(350.44). She sees with God that *all sowles of saluacion eskape hym wor-
shyppfully by the vertue of his precious passion* (347.13). With Scripture as her
foundation, she synthesizes briefly the teaching of the Western fathers
on the impotence of the devil, though the striking phrase, *hys myght is alle
lokked in gods hande* (347.18), is surely her own. He can do no harm at
all, unless man permits him, because Christ the true David has trium-
phed through the Cross over the hellish Goliath.[203] She also holds with
Aquinas that the devil's attacks proceed from his malice and envy,[204]
and that all this will redound to the glory of the elect by the divine
will:[205] *for all that god sufferyth hym to do turnyth vs to joy and hym to shame
and payne* (347.15).

A notable addition to the short text is her penetrating theological
reflection on how God regards the reprobate, which anticipates the answer, conveyed through the parable of the lord and the servant (cf.
511.16 e.s.), to her conundrum, how does God see us in our sin? So she
first states that even though there can be no wrath in God, *with myght
and ryght he withstondyth the reprovyd, the which of malyce and of shrewdnes
besye them to contrary and do against goddes wyll* (348.21). This is the first
part of her explanation of what she means by the word 'scorn' when
she attributes it to God. She then develops the thought by elucidating
what *withstondyth* signifies in the context. The passage (349. e.s), which
is evidently corrupt, might be rendered into modern English as follows:
'Where I saw him scorn his malice, this was by the fixing of my understanding on our Lord; that is to say, it was an inward showing of his
constancy — there was no change of expression. For as I see it, this immutability of God is a worshipful attribute'. She seems to be conveying
the opinion that God 'looks right through' the reproved, who no longer
exist for him, but are, in the Old Testament phrase, 'blotted out of the
book of the living' (Psalm 68.29).

## 8 Revelation VI

Implicit in the locution in Revelation V, 'Herewith is the fiend overcome', is the classical teaching of monasticism, which in the West has its
origin in Athanasius's *Vita Sancti Antonii*,[206] that the Christian life is a

---

[203] Caesarius of Arles (the attribution to Augustine is now regarded as spurious;
Dekkers, no. 368), *Sermo CXXI*, ed. Morin, 1 504-509.
[204] *Summa theologiae* I.114.1 *in corp.*
[205] Ibid. ad 3.
[206] See F. Vandenbrouke, 'Démon en occident'.

spiritual combat against the world, the flesh and, particularly, the devil, because to oppose the devil is to share Christ's own battles in the service of his Father. Consequently, the Scriptural theme of Revelation VI is the Pauline hymn, 'If we endure with him, we shall also reign with him' (II Timothy 2.10-13), when the devil *shall see that all the woo and tribulacion that he hath done them shalle be turned in to encrese of ther ioy without ende* (350.46); and it is largely concerned with a special insight into God's 'homely loving', his gratitude for man's service, and particularly that of dedicated contemplatives. The revelation begins with a locution common to both texts, which, as we learn from Julian's editing, is a lifting up of her understanding (351.4). All God's servants are to be the recipients of his everlasting thanks for their patient endurance, but especially those who have made to him the gift of their youth. This ghostly sight is first conveyed by an example, which, it seems, was suppressed in the short text because it so resembles the parable of the lord and the servant, which at that time she did not intend to record. It may itself be a 'ghostly sight in bodily likeness'; at all events, it greatly resembles in form those several instances (e.g. 323.20 e.s.) of Julian's highly individual method of *lectio divina,* where her recollection of Scripture and her power of imagination rapidly work together, as she contemplates a showing, to construct an illustrative and imaginative 'sight'.

The three aspects of heavenly bliss which are described are common to both texts (230.2-8, 352.13-20; 230.8-11, 352.21-23; 230.11-17, 353.27-32). What she sees as she continues to look at the whole is the applicability of another Pauline text, Romans 8.15-22, where the apostle expresses his confidence that though we are groaning and in travail now, the sufferings of this time are not to be compared with the glory to be revealed in us; and this is because we are co-heirs with Christ. But in the long text particularly, Julian is pre-occupied with the Lord's courtesy. She gives the example of a lord rewarding his servant to show the first degree of bliss; and for the second she offers another curial example:

> A kyng, yf he thanke hys subiettes, it is a grett wurschyppe to them; and yf he make it knowen to all the realme, then ther wurschypp is mech incresyd (352.24).

But it is the addition in the long text to the account of the third degree which is most significant. Though the length of service of those who, as she, we believe, had done, have freely dedicated themselves to the contemplative life in their youth will receive a wonderful reward, it remains true that a single day spent in the divine will receives the same gift, the same measure of bliss. This precisely is the teaching of the parable of the labourers in the vineyard, so feelingly and tellingly expounded by Julian's contemporary, the *Pearl* poet. For though God thanks her with the gift of himself, and shares his knowledge and gratitude with all the blessed, the gift still is unmerited, a *curtesy* (353.35). The very term recalls Pecham's 'dilexit, inquam, curialiter' (see 392.37 note); and the vision of this courteous love increases her desire to serve him all her life.

## 9 Revelation VII

Though the subject-matter of this revelation — the alternation of spiritual consolation and desolation, the various reasons for the withdrawal of special grace, and how the contemplative is to conduct himself in times of dereliction — is commonplace in late patristic and mediaeval reflection on contemplative life and prayer, it has its importance in the evolution of Julian's practical experience and later theological reflection. First, it reveals what is her response when she is enabled to contemplate the joys of heaven, and that she understands this response to correspond to the fact in faith of her loving union with *the endlesse lykyng that is god* (356.34). It also associates the heaviness of spiritual desolation with the pains of Christ's Passion, so serving as an introduction to Revelation VIII, with its emphasis on the contemplative prayer of darkness, which assimilates the soul to Christ in his suffering mystical body, his 'ghostly thirst'. Then, too, it begins to prepare the way for her exposition of the mystery of the Incarnation and its effects on the life and prayer of the Christian (chapter 55 e.s.), where she concludes that *we may nevyr come to the full knowyng of god tylle we knowe furst clerely oure owne soule* (573.32).

It has already been observed that the variation in this chapter between the short and long texts is minimal. There are seven certain variants, none of them consisting of more than a few words. Yet each change is theologically significant. First of all, Julian had in the short text described this vision of God's union with the soul as *myghtlye festnede with owtyn any drede* (230.20). Now she adds the adjective *paynefulle* (354.5), precisely because she has come to perceive that there is a fear which belongs to the unitive life, in heaven as on earth, and that is 'reverent dread':

> Loue and drede are bredryn, and they are rotyd in vs by the goodnesse of oure maker, and they shall nevyr be taken from vs without end (673.20).

As she will explain, in the same chapter 74, all other fears, even those which are profitable, are painful. The two words which she most commonly employs to describe her experience of God's dealing with the soul are 'mind' and 'feeling'. In the short text, she had written of the 'sovereign ghostly liking': *This felynge was so gladde to me and so goodly* (230. 20). But in editing this, she seems to have thought it too subjective, and not clearly distinguishing from natural feelings of well-being; and so she writes: *This felyng was so glad and so goostely* (354. 5). As her life of prayer developed after the revelations, she received the grace of a progressively deeper contemplative penetration into the mysteries of the Trinity, to such an extent that, in chapter 51, she can paraphrase the text 'Philip, he who sees me sees the Father' (John 14.9) as follows:

> But man is blyndyd in this life, and therefore we may nott se oure fader god as he is. And what tyme that he of hys goodnesse wyll shew hym to man, he shewyth hym homely as man, not with stondyng that I saw verely we ought to know and beleue that the fader is nott man (525.140).

So here, where she is attempting to convey her experience of the union of love which is human as well as divine, she substitutes the more personal 'our blessed Lord', which is no pious cliché, but 'said for reverence', for the less personal 'God'.

Margery Kempe's testimony about Julian's expertise in spiritual guidance is constantly confirmed by the long text; and there is evidence of it here. Julian had written, of the state of spiritual desolation:

> ... it es nedefulle to ylke mann to feele on this wyse ... And sum tyme for the profytte of his saule a man es lefte to hymselfe; and to whethere synne es nought the cause (231.37).

Now she has come to see that universal statements about the divine action in bestowing or withdrawing contemplative graces are imprudent; 'the Spirit breathes where he will' (John 3.8). So she qualifies:

> ... it is spedfulle to some soules to feele on thys wyse ... all thogh hys synne is nott evyr the cause (355. 21).

The additions, *to some soules, evyr,* are important; and she also gives her reason for the last statement. In the short text it has been:

> For in this tyme I synnede nought wherefore I schulde be lefte to my selfe (231.43);

but in the long text we read:

> For in this tyme I synned nott were for I shulde be left to my selfe, for it was so sodeyne (356. 26),

where *for it was so sodeyne* is not only the observation of common sense —
she had not had the time even for a sinful thought — but also the application of an important canon of spiritual discernment. One way of
distinguishing the peace of the Lord and his gladness from natural joie
de vivre, or human depression from spiritual desolation, is to look for
possible natural causes or occasions of a state of mind before attributing it to the divine action.

In her reflections at the end of this revelation on the wonderful alternation of *wo and wele, blysse and payne,* she is solicitous to find the
balance, which is hope, between despair and presumption. So she adds,
to her earlier observation that pain will be brought to nothing, the
qualifying phrase which has so much meaning for her: *to them that shall
be savyd* (356.32 and note).

## 10 Revelation VIII

The eighth revelation is longer and considerably more complex than
those which precede it, apart from the first; and for that Julian
provided a recapitulation of the contents (317.4 e.s.). Here she is
equally aware that her readers may require help, particularly with the
expanded version in the long text. So she concludes the final chapter of
this revelation with another such summary:

> It is gods wylle, as to my vnderstandyng, that we haue iij maner of
> beholdyng of his blessyd passion. The furst is the harde payne that he suf-
> feryd (this is the first *maner*), with a contriccion (the second *maner*) and
> compassion (the third); and that shewde oure lorde in this tyme, and gaue
> me myght and grace to see it (377.33).

The 'beholding of the hard pain' — *a parte of hys passyon nere his dyeng*
(357.3) — the beginning of this showing, is a bodily sight, no detail of
which does Julian spare us. There appear to be two reasons for this intense concentration upon the physical sufferings of the Passion. First,
she wishes to show how completely her first prayer, to have recollection
of the Passion, was answered:

> Me thought I woulde haue ben that tyme with Magdaleyne and with
> other that were Christus louers, that I might haue seen bodilie the passion
> that our lord suffered for me, that I might haue suffered with him, as
> other did that loved him. And therfore I desyred a bodely sight, wher in I
> might haue more knowledge of the bodily paynes of our sauiour, and of
> the compassion of our lady and of all his true louers that were lyuyng that
> tyme and saw his paynes; for I would haue be one of them and haue suf-
> fered with them (285.8).

The second reason is contained in the sentence which, according to the scribe of P, closes chapter 20:

> And I lokyd after the departyng with alle my myghtes, and wende to haue seen the body alle deed (379.3).

This, and the allusion to her 'doomsday' in chapter 8, seem to suggest that she thought that the moment of her own death might coincide with her sight of Christ's. She had already complained of her failing eyesight (291.28 e.s.), and the concentration which this demanded from her enabled her to retain (and, apparently, when she came to write the long text, to recall) a wealth of detail, much of which will cause discomfort to a modern reader, which she would otherwise have missed or forgotten. She sees the effects of Christ's suffering, in chapter 16, especially in his head (357.4 e.s.); and the rest of the bodily sight (357.11 e.s.) is concerned with what she calls Christ's greatest bodily pain, the 'deep drying'. She interrupts this only to promise us, later, her reflections on his other, spiritual thirst (360.6; cf. 418.14 e.s.).

The equivalent 'ghostly sight' which follows this description of Christ's pain is that she begins herself to feel his sufferings, *as I had before desyerde* (364.52). The long text here may seem to lose some of the clarity and force which the short text has when it cites from the Christological hymn in chapter 2 of Philippians (cf. 234.25 and note). Perhaps she or a later scribe removed this rare direct Scriptural quotation, with its source adduced, because of the contemporary controversies which culminated in the 1408 Oxford condemnation and prohibition of such translation without episcopal licence.[207] But she may have decided that Paul's words were not so apposite as she had once thought. He is inviting the Philippians to imitate Christ's humility and obedience, not to experience directly his bodily sufferings. Doubtless she also found it inappropriate to exhort others to share this experience, as she had done in the short text: *ylke saule ... schulde feele in hym þat in Criste Jhesu* (234.25), especially since she discovers that she herself can hardly tolerate her participation in his pains.

It is at this point that she becomes aware that her prayer for contrition (cf. 286.20) is being answered in an unforeseen way. She finds herself repenting her one-time aspiration to suffer the same pains as Christ and those who stood by his cross (364.50 e.s.). But she is enabled, through *ratiocinatio*, to understand that this pain of Christ which

---

[207] M. Deanesly: *The Lollard Bible*, 294-297.

she is now sharing is the purification which she had asked for (cf.
286.21 e.s.); it is truly redemptive, because it proceeds from her love
for him (364.56 e.s.).

The third 'manner of beholding', 'with compassion', now begins.
First she is shown the quality of Mary's compassion for Christ: *she was so
onyd in loue that the grettnes of her loue was cause of the grettnes of her peyne*
(366.3); and then how those others who were close to him shared in this
compassion. She sees this suffering extended to all creatures capable of
experiencing pain, because of the *grett onyng betwene Crist and vs* (367.14).
All of them suffered at the time of the Crucifixion, each in his own
fashion, including the pagans, Pilate and Denis 'of France'; and she concludes chapter 18 with the reflection:

> Thus was oure lord Jhesu payned for us; and we stonde alle in this maner
> of payne with hym, and shalle do tylle that we come to his blysse (369.36).

These sights and the accompanying meditation enable her deliberately
to choose the crucified and suffering Saviour as the only fulfilment she
desires:

> for I had levyr a bene in that payne tylle domys day than haue come to
> hevyn other wyse than by hym (371.12).

This deliberate choice enables her to put into psychological and
theological perspective her previous feelings of reluctance to share his
sufferings. The temptation to reject them was no more than *grugyng and
dawnger of the flessch without assent of the soule* (372.23). In her experience
of such *oppositio* between 'repenting and wilful choice', she appears to
have in mind Christ's own struggle in the garden: 'Father, if it be
possible, let this chalice pass' (Matthew 26.38 e.s.), and that of Paul:
'Who will deliver me from the body of this death?' (Romans 7.24).
Here, too, she makes for the first time the distinction between the two
parts of the soul, a teaching of Augustinian psychology which she finds
helpful in the elucidation of the parable of the lord and the servant and
of its attendant problems (372.24 e.s.). Further, she is shown that the
inward and outward parts are destined, in and through Christ, to be
united in eternal blessedness (372.33 e.s.).

With Christ's sufferings still the focus for her continued reflections
on contrition and compassion, Julian considers anew, in the last chapter
of this revelation (374.2 e.s.), Christ's own compassion. She expounds
the common theological opinion of her day, that the *vnyng of the godhed
gaue strenght to the manhed ... to suffer more than alle man myght* (cf. 374.2
note); and she explains, in a significant addition to the short text, that
the purpose of contemplating the Passion is *to thynke and to know ... what*

*he sufferyd, and ... for whom that he sufferyd* (375.10). An important point here, she believes, is to consider the mutual compassion between Christ and Mary (376.21), because this illumines the ineffable quality of his compassion for all who will be saved. Her contemplation is not merely recollection of an historical event. She has observed earlier, with theological precision, *I wyste welle he suffyryde but onys* (364.50); here she adds that although *now he is vppe resyn and no more passibylle, yett he sufferyth with vs as I shalle sey after* (376.24), promising the treatment of the divine compassion which will follow in Revelation XIII. In these last lines of Revelation VIII, she intimates that this contemplation of passion and compassion demands the presence and action of the Holy Spirit — *And I beholdyng alle this by hys grace* (377.26) — and that what is true for her is true for all:

> For the soule that beholdyth thus whan it is touchyd by grace, he shalle verely see that tho paynes of Cristes passion passe all paynes; that is to sey, whych paynes shal be turned in to everlastyng joy by the vertu of Cristes passion (377.28).

This analysis necessitates a departure from the division of all the manuscripts into revelations, a departure which is warranted by their lack of agreement (cf. the critical apparatus to 360.2, 378.36, 379.6 and 382.1). First, P and C indicate that Revelation IX begins with chapter 17 (360.1), though they add to the confusion by repeating the rubric at the beginning of chapter 22 (382.1). But at 360.1 SS do not announce a new revelation, merely a new chapter (which S1 erroneously calls 'xviij'). The next confusion concerns the division of chapters 20 and 21. SS begin chapter 21 at 377.33, but P and C at 379.6. The editors consider that both families are wrong, that Julian intended chapter 20 to end with her recapitulatory remarks on the three manners of beholding (377.33-36), and chapter 21 to begin with her discussion of a new topic, when she adverts to the bodily sight, and writes that although she had expected to see Christ dead, the revelation did not follow this course, because *sodenly I beholdyng in the same crosse he channgyd in blessydfulle chere* (379.6). The introductory remark cannot be separated from the account of the suddenness of this change in Christ's appearance and Julian's mood without doing violence to the sense; and, accordingly, chapter 21 has been made to begin at 379.3. And this has also been made the beginning of Revelation IX, rather than 360.2 (P, C) or 382.2 (P, C, SS). There can be no doubt that Julian intended to convey that with the sudden change, a new revelation began.

Firstly, when she is describing the five manners in which our Lord showed her his Passion (the first three of which are related in Revelations I, II and IV respectively), she writes:

> the iiij^th is the depe drying — theyse iiij as it is before seyde for the paynes of the passion — and the fyfte is thys that was shewyth for the joy and the blysse of the passion (390.11).

We should note here not only that she does not begin to describe the joy and bliss of the Passion until the 'changing of cheer' in chapter 21, but also that she continues to describe the 'deep drying' throughout chapter 17 (360-364).

Secondly, in her theological discussion of substance and sensuality in chapter 55, she remarks that these two 'parts' are in the incarnate Christ, and that the lower part, the sensuality, suffered for the salvation of mankind. Then she adds:

> And theyse two pertyes were seene and felte in the viij shewyng, in whych my body was fulfyllyd of felyng and mynd of Cristes passion and his dyeng. And ferthermore with this was a suttell felyng and a prevy inwarde syghte of þe hye partys, and that was shewed in the same tyme, wher I myȝte nott for the mene profer loke vp in to hevyn (569.52).

This passage must refer in its totality to Revelation VIII, since she refers both 'parts' to that showing. It follows then that for Julian the eighth revelation continued to at least the end of chapter 19, where the two parts are first discussed (372.33 e.s.).

Thirdly, we have argued that this revelation is summarized in the *iij maner of beholdyng of his blessyd passion* towards the end of P's chapter 20 (377.33-378.36), and that the summary forms the natural end of the eighth revelation. In the short text, the beginning of chapter xii, which corresponds with the opening of Revelation IX, is very clear:

> And sodaynlye, me behaldande in the same crosse, he channchede in to blysfulle chere (239.1);

and the addition prefixed to this in the long text:

> And I lokyd after the departyng with alle my myghtes, and wende to haue seen the body alle deed; butt I saw him nott so. And right in the same tyme that me thought by semyng that the lyfe myght no lenger last … (379.3)

emphasizes the suddenness of the change; at one moment she is expecting his last breath, in the next Christ shows himself full of life and gladness, and she stresses this again by her repetition of the word 'suddenly'.

The scribe of S1 appears to have had in his copy a chapter-division approaching that which the editors propose. But the difficulty with that is that S1's division interrupts the smooth transition from the first four manners, shown for the pains of the Passion, to 'the fifth ... that was shown for the joy and the bliss of the Passion' (390.13). What signals the beginning of the new revelation is neither the summary of what has gone before (SS 377.31) nor the locution at the opening of chapter 22 in P (382.3), but the new bodily sight, introduced by the key word *sodeynly*. These discrepancies are best explained by the hypothesis that all the witnesses derive from a common ancestor in which the 'Revelation IX' rubric had been omitted, so that later scribes had to use their own judgment about where it should be inserted; and the editors have proposed that this ninth revelation as Julian wrote it in all probability began thus:

> And I lokyd after the departyng with alle my myghtes, and wende to haue seen the body alle deed; butt I saw him nott so. And right in the same tyme that me thought by semyng that the lyfe myght no lenger last, and the shewyng of the ende behovyd nydes to be nye, sodenly I beholdyng in the same crosse he channgyd in blessydfulle chere ... (379.3)

## 11 Revelation IX

As has already been noticed, Revelation IX (chapters 21-23) is briefly described by Julian herself as 'shown for the joy and the bliss of the Passion' (390.13). The sudden change from suffering to joy in chapter 21 reveals to her not only our solidarity with Christ in his own human condition during his Passion, but the immediate connexion between the joy and glory of the risen Christ and the glorified Church in heaven. In Revelation VIII, her thought was centring on the first part of the Christological hymn of Philippians 2: 'Let that mind be in you ... He humbled himself, becoming obedient to death, death on a cross'. Here she has the second part of the hymn in recollection: 'For this reason God has exalted him', with its corollary in the other hymn in Paul's second letter to Timothy (2.12): 'If we endure with him, then we shall also reign with him'.

In chapter 22, following on the bodily sight, the locution: *Arte thou well apayd that I sufferyd for thee?* (382.2), is Julian's way of expressing and communicating what appears to be a singular infused grace affecting alike her will and her intellect. *In thys felyng my vnderstandyng was leftyd vppe in to hevyn* (382.7). This seems to describe a 'rapture' in the traditional sense, judged both by its language and by what she has previously described. She had been in the severest bodily and mental anguish (cf. 360-364), and suddenly she is taken out of herself.[208] This appears to have been one of the occasions when the bodily sight persisted, unlike her account of the first revelation, when she writes: *And the bodyly syght styntyd, and the gastely syght dwellyd in myne vnderstandynge* (218.19), because it was in Christ's manhood that she saw the Father (383.12, an addition to the short text), and the bliss of heaven (or of the three persons of the Trinity), graces which belong to the *manyfolde joyes that folowen of the passion of Crist* (393.47).

In the long text, as a result of protracted meditation 'with great diligence' on the locution: *If I myght suffer more, I wolde suffer more* (387.50), with Hebrews 10.10 constantly in mind (cf. 385.34 note), she is able to communicate the fact in faith that God's love for the world, the proof of which is the sacrificial death of his Son, is as sure and active and manifest now as it was at the time of Christ's passion and death. Every day a glorified Redeemer *is redy to the same, yf it myght be* (385.35). Modern exegetes can write, on the text of the Apocalypse: 'I died, and behold I am alive for evermore', in the same vein:

> All the mysteries of Jesus's earthly history, from the cradle to the grave, have been mysteriously endowed in his glorified humanity with a totally new and enduring actuality;[209]

but they say less than Julian does, as she begins, her understanding of word, of sight and of her own experience unfolded, to develop the insight she receives into the mystery of the Trinity and the divine relationship, in her own person, with all who are to be saved in Christ. She is at one with John, in chapter 15 of his gospel, and with Hebrews chapter 10, in seeing the revelation and operation of the Trinity as focused particularly on the Passion, death and Resurrection of the incarnate Christ. In this suffering all mankind is involved; it is the preparation for the fulness of salvation. It is *a noble precious and wurschypfulle dede done in a tyme by the workyng of loue* (386.47), and yet this love is the eternal providential love of the triune God, of his power, wisdom and goodness. *The cause why that he sufferyth is for he wylle of hys goodnes make vs the eyers with hym in hys blysse* (381.23). Because the sight of Christ in his now glorified manhood is constantly before her inward eye, and his words in her recollection, she is able to write firmly and lucidly, using the ideas and the vocabulary with which Scripture provided her in abundance.

---

[208] For a discussion of such phenomena, see C. Butler: *Western Mysticism*, especially 71-78.

[209] D. Stanley: 'Contemplation of the Gospels', 430.

So the sudden change recalls not only the Transfiguration (cf. 379.6 note), but also Paul's prophecy of the resurrection of the body (cf. 380.14, 15 notes), and of our transformation, even in this life, through contemplation (cf. 380.18, 20 notes). With John, as well as with Paul, she can link Passion and Resurrection, earth and heaven in the glory and exaltation of Christ in which we are called to share: *Betwene that one and that other shalle alle be one tyme; and than shall alle be brought in to joy* (380.15).

She begins here, too, to develop her teaching on the Holy Spirit, and, as does John himself, she identifies the Spirit with that love which comforts and strengthens (390.15 e.s.). Finally, at the end of the revelation, she offers us a short example which summarizes all the teaching contained:

> And in this he brought to my mynd the propyrte of a gladde geauer. Evyr a glade geauer takyth but lytylle hede at the thyng that he geavyth, but alle hys desyr and alle hys intent is to plese hym and solace hym to whome he geavyth it. And yf the receyver take the gyft gladly and thankefully, than the curtesse gevyr settyth at nought alle hys cost and alle hys traveyle, for joy and deleyght that he hath for he hath plesyd and solacyd hym that he lovyth (392.37),

a method in which, in the long text, she proves herself so adept. She has stressed the work of the Father and his joy in giving mankind as a gift; he is the glad giver, and the Son, who receives the gift along with that of his own manhood, is he who pays little heed to the value of the gift ('he did not consider equality with God a prize to be coveted' — Philippians 2.6). He receives from the Father, but becomes a courteous giver to the Father, and the Holy Spirit is in the gift, for he is the joy and delight of Father for Son, of Father and Son in us and for us.

## 12 Revelation X

As the footnotes to the text indicate, the 'bodily sight' of Revelation X (394.3 e.s., and cf. 242.1 e.s.) has much in common with contemporary representations of the Sacred Heart. Julian's susceptibility to such iconography has been remarked on in Section VII. But we may here ask why in the long text she insists that this be introduced as a separate revelation, and what is the reason for the very significant change in the account there from that in the short text.

First, there is a marked difference in tone between Revelation X and much of the devotional writing of her own age. (As an example, see the French prayer, recorded in England, quoted in 394.3 note). Julian was shown not the Man of Sorrows but a joyful, glorified Christ (an aspect of the Sacred Heart devotion which almost disappeared in the post-Tridentine Church, largely through the impetus of the revelations to Margaret Mary Alacoque). Secondly, in the long text Julian has decided to introduce the image of the heart as 'a fair and delectable place', which will find an echo in the parabolic vision of the lord and the servant: *Now is the spouse, goddys son, in pees with his lovyd wyfe* (545. 326); *Now sittyth nott þe lorde on erthe in wyldernesse, but he syttyth on hys ryche and noblest seet, whych he made in hevyn* (543. 312). Thirdly, in the short text she had glossed the locution, *Loo how I lovyd the*, as follows:

> ... as ȝyf he hadde sayde: My childe, ȝif thow kan nought loke in my godhede, see heere how I lette opyn my syde and my herte be clovene in twa (242. 2).

Since then there had been shown *to my vnderstandyng in part* — that she writes 'in part' is surely significant — *the blyssydfulle godhede as farforth as he wolde that tyme* (395. 11). In other words, since she has received new understanding, of which chapter 51 is the foremost example, she has been enabled, in some of the more complex showings, to identify assuredly revelation which is intermediate between 'bodily sight' and 'ghostly sight', that is, 'ghostly in bodily likeness' (514. 6). The love of which the pierced heart of Jesus, now glorified but still displaying the marks of his Passion (cf. John 20. 19-20, 27), is the sign which she now understands as meaning *the endlesse loue that was without begynnyng and is and shal be evyr* (395. 13); and yet in this love of the Godhead he remains her brother and her Saviour, who has died and risen for her, and she his darling and his child.

This insight into the mystery of the Incarnation, particularly as a corrective of the deficiencies of contemporary devotion, too often betraying its writers and its devotees as morbid, neurotic, hysterical, is of sufficient importance to Julian to merit isolation as a separate and integral revelation.

## 13 Revelation XI

In the closing sight of the 'hard pains' of Christ's sufferings, Julian was shown the compassion of Mary, which the S1 scribe, writing in the seventeenth century, calls her 'spiritual martyrdom': *she was so onyd in loue that the grettnes of her loue was cause of the grettnes of her peyne* (366. 3). It is thus logical that the sight of the exalted and glorified yet crucified Christ — 'the joy and bliss of the Passion' — should end with a showing of Mary sharing her Son's joy. So in Revelation XI, chapter 25, the bodily sight seems to be extended to include the mother who is standing by the cross (John 19.25). But Julian has already insisted in the short text that this was an intellectual vision:

> Ofte tymes I prayed it, and wened to haffe sene here in bodely lykenes; botte I sawe hir nought soo. And Jhesu in þat worde schewed me a gastelye syght of hire (242.11).

Here in the long text she tells why she 'saw her not so': it is far more expedient to see

> the vertuse of her blyssydfulle soule, her truth, her wysdom, her cheryte, wher by I am leernyd to know my self, and reuerently drede my god (399.20).

Julian has no use for sentimentality in her devotion. As she will tell us further on, what Mary exemplifies par excellence is that

> a mans soule is a creature in god whych hath the same propertes made ... endlesse souereyne truth, endelesse souereyne wysdom, endelesse souereyne loue (484.13, 11),

so that it can do what it was made for, perceive God, contemplate him and love him.

In this same revelation, in chapter 25, we have another instance of Julian introducing an 'example' which does not appear in the short version, and, apparently, for the same reason as before, its connection with the parable of the lord and the servant. Indeed, this 'example' seems to be no more than a reference back to the matter of chapter 14. There she wrote:

> ... thys exsample was shewd. A kyng, yf he thanke hys subiettes, it is a grett wurschyppe to them; and yf he make it knowen to all the realme, then ther wurschypp is mech incresyd (352.23).

Julian does not now state specifically that this was a part of the revelation introduced by the locution 'Wilt thou see her?', or that the example was shown, as she had written in chapter 14, 'in this time' (352.23); and it seems that she is here doing no more than indicating the relevance of an earlier insight also to this revelation.

## 14 Revelation XII

When Julian had recapitulated, for purposes of reconstruction, her first great showing (in the long text, chapters 4-9, 294-323), there are

three points which she made with all possible emphasis; that the goodness of God is all (318.15, 322.12), that he is true rest, and that there is
no rest except in union with him (301.25), and that this showing, like all
the revelations, is given to her for the benefit of all who persevere in the
knowledge and love of God (319.23, 319.33, 321.2).

These are the themes to which she returns in Revelation XII, which
concludes the first part of her book. The first eleven revelations
manifest a progressively deeper insight into the Pauline prayer, '... ut
Christum lucrifaciam et inveniar in illo ... ad cognoscendum illum et
virtutem resurrectionis eius et societatem passionum illius, configuratus
morti eius; si quo modo occuram ad resurrectionem quae est ex mor-
tuis' (Philippians 3.8-11). So Revelation XII was given as a bodily sight
in ghostly likeness, when *oure lord shewyd hym more gloryfyed as to my syght
than I saw hym before* (402.3). The point is of significance for her. In the
short text, she had taken the showing in conjunction with that of Mary
(243.25 e.s.), because of the very important observation she makes concerning contemplative graces; now she omits this observation (probably
because her revelations are not to be restricted to *ex professo* contemplatives), and she stresses the new application of the sight of the
glorified Christ as Lord and God who is portrayed to her in the intellectual vision, 'I it am'. And it is as Lord and God that he shows himself as he did in the first revelation, *full of joye, homely and curteys and
blessydfulle and very lyfe* (402.5; cf. 314.46). But now it is in and through
the bodily sight in ghostly likeness of the exalted crucified Christ that
she sees afresh and comprehends more deeply that 'where Jesus appears, the blessed Trinity is understood' (295.15). ... *I it am that is alie. I
it am that holy church prechyth the and techeyth thee. I it am that shewde me
before to the* (402.10). But she has still more to see and to learn about the
relations of the Trinity and the *operationes ad extra*. She does not yet
know what is comprehended in the word of the triune God, 'I it am' (cf.
403.11, 15 notes). So she ends the revelation, as she had done in the
short text, by recalling that her only purpose for writing at all is so that
everyone who will be saved, *evyry man, aftyr the grace that god gevyth hym in
vnder standyng and lovyng* (403.16), may receive the locution according to
Christ's meaning in it.

## 15 Revelation XIII

During her exposition of the parable of the lord and the servant in
chapter 51, Julian informs us that she was granted three ways of
knowing the secrets of all that was shown to her, which became so

united in her understanding that she was unable to distinguish them:

> The furst is the begynnyng of techyng that I vnderstode ther in in the
> same tyme. The secunde is the inwarde lernyng that I haue vnderstonde
> there in sythen. The thyrd is alle the hole revelation fro the begynnyng to
> the ende whych oure lorde god of his goodnes bryngyth oftymes frely to
> the syght of my vnderstondyng (519.76).

It is here, in the long Revelation XIII, which occupies chapters 27 to 40
in the long text, that she begins in earnest to give us the fruit of this
knowledge, as a comparison with the corresponding sections of the
short text (243.37-257.23) soon reveals.

The opening sentence, identical in either text: *And aftyr thys oure lorde
brought to my mynde the longyng that I had to hym before* (404.3, and cf.
243.37), is so muted that one is hardly aware that this announces a
separate revelation, until, after her indiscreet reflection (identical with
one of the *Piers Plowman* poet's) that if sin had never been all would
have been well (cf. 404.6 and note), she tells us that this is indeed a
vision; and it is followed immediately, according to the normal pattern
of the revelations, by a locution, which here she emphasizes by calling
it, in the long text, *þis nakyd worde: Synne* (405.14).

Thus the vision consists of two sights: her longing for God (cf.
288.40), and the *oygly syȝte* (406.26) of all that is not good. This second
sight includes her experience of Christ's sufferings, as she has already
beheld and pondered them, and the sufferings of his followers, which
she associates with the kenosis of the incarnate Word (405.15 e.s.). It is
not that she sees sin itself (she makes the precise theological observation
that *it had no maner of substannce* — 406.27 and notes); she sees all the
pain that sin occasioned Christ, and still occasions all who will be
saved. In the long text this is stressed by a repetition of the original
locution (405.13) in another form: *It is tru that synne is cause of alle thys
payne, but alle shalle be wele* (407.33).

So far, her experience of this double showing resembles that of
Revelation VII (354.2 e.s.), with its alternation of consolation and
desolation; but here she is anxious to indicate how the desolation
which accompanies the sight and experience of pain occasioned by sin
*redely passyd ovyr in to comfort* (406.24); and the chapter ends, in the long
text, with her first reference to what will become the focal point of this
revelation, the *hygh mervelous prevyte hyd in god, whych pryuyte he shalle
opynly make and shalle be knowen to vs in hevyn* (407.39).

Chapter 28 shows her reflecting on the comfort which our Lord has
just afforded her, the experience of his compassionate love for all men,
that is, for his own body, the Church. His joy is born of compassion for

the tribulations of his servants, the chastisement which is to bring them to the bliss of everlasting union with God. Here again, it will be in the parable of the lord and the servant that we shall find, in the long text, the clarification of her deep understanding of the divine compassion in the mystery of the incarnate Christ, *the rewth and the pytty of the fader* over *the fallyng of Adam* (524.134), *the joy and the blysse* for *the fallyng of his deerwurthy son* (524.135), the Father's permitting *his owne son wylfully in the manhed to suffer all mans payne* (541.287). And here she begins to explain how the longing for God with which the vision begins is shown in Christ's compassion, which we are called to share (410.21 e.s.).

At the beginning of chapter 29, she seems to be telling us that the alternation of consolation and desolation afforded by the experience, now of divine compassion, now of the pain and harm of sin, has been with her whenever she reflects on the 'ugly sight'; and it would appear from the complete agreement at this point of both texts that she is satisfied with the answer her question invited — it is one of the Lord's 'homely courtesies' that he reasons, in the strict philosophical sense, with her (cf. 247.3 note) — an answer which is a summary of the contemporary theology of atonement, theology which Shakespeare in his turn would paraphrase:

> Why, all the souls that were were forfeit once,
> And he that might the vantage best have took
> Found out the remedy. [210]

In chapter 30, Julian's sight of the divine compassion becomes the sight of Jesus himself, crucified and glorified, in his mystical union with the Church; and, as she noted at the outset of the long text, *wher Jhesu appireth the blessed trinitie is vnderstand, as to my sight* (295.15). When she recorded her first version, she was already sufficiently advanced in theology to state clearly that the whole of divine revelation, both the canonical Scriptures and the Church's magisterial tradition, concerns the unity and trinity of God, and the *operationes ad extra* of this same Trinity, revealed and performed in Jesus Christ the incarnate Word (248.26-41); so that any authentic private revelation will do no more than cast a brighter light on this, the constant and exclusive object of divinely-inspired Christian contemplation, *oure saviour and oure saluacyon* (414.2). There is nothing else here on earth that the heart of man can profitably conceive of *oure lordes prevy conncelle*, which is the teaching of Paul (cf. 415.13 and note). Nor does Julian see any reason for altering a

---

[210] *Measure for Measure*, Act II Scene 2.

word of this in the final text of her revelations. Here is indeed the whole content of her world; whatever is outside its scope cannot be the proper object of contemplation, and will thus militate against the building up of the body of Christ. Her sight at the beginning of this revelation (404.3) was of her own longing for God. Now, in chapter 31, through the reformulation of the locution 'All shall be well' in an explicitly Trinitarian context, common to both versions (cf. 249.1 e.s.), she perceives that this longing is a participation in Christ's own longing; and she now gives us the reflection which she had promised on his 'ghostly thirst' (cf. 418.14 note). She begins with a sight of its fulfilment, everlasting rest and peace, which resembles in doctrine and language the celebrated hymn of Peter Abelard:[211]

> O quanta qualia sunt illa sabbata ...
> quae fessis requies, quae merces fortibus
> cum erit omnia deus in omnibus.

It may well be that this meditation on the love-longing (419.26-421.49) was omitted from the short text because it depends on her then still undeveloped understanding of the Trinitarian locution in Revelation XII, 'I it am ...' (cf. 403.15 and note), and of the relationship between Christ and all mankind who will be saved, as this emerges later in the parable of the lord and the servant.

In the examination (in the long text, in chapter 32) of the two forms of the locution of this revelation: *Alle maner a thyng shalle be wele ... Thou shalt se thy selfe that alle maner of thyng shalle be wele* (422.2; and cf. 244.52, 249.5), what Julian sees and understands belongs to the showing of the compassion which will cease in the fulness of unitive love in heaven (cf. 421.50). The last great work of the Trinity on Judgment Day is not now the proper object of contemplation; that is the compassion which is shown in the hiding of that work for our present peace and joy. It is at this point, when her mind is again occupied by the contraries inducing that disquiet and perturbation of mind which are the hall-marks of spiritual desolation, that she wishes to show that 'reasoning' on God's word (422.9 e.s.) is a form of meditative prayer, which can lead the soul back into God's comfort. The desolation, however, continues to oppress her, here and in the succeeding chapter 33. The 'great deed' may not be the proper object of contemplation until it is done in the fulfilment of the Lord's compassion, when *thou shalt se thy selfe that alle*

---

[211] Cf. Chevalier, *Repertorium,* no. 13560.

*manner thyng shall be wele* (423.17), but the doctrines of the faith are:

> And one poynt of oure feyth is that many creatures shall be dampnyd, as
> angelis that felle ouȝt of hevyn for pride, whych be now fendys, and meny
> in erth that dyeth out of the feyth of holy chyrch (425.40).

Here is a contrary which reasoning cannot resolve (426.49 e.s.). Thus
she is emboldened to ask for a sight of hell and purgatory (427.2 e.s.).
But this is a prayer which is not answered, and she must, following the
advice which she gives herself and us in the showing on prayer, await a
better time, a greater grace or a better gift (469.27). She recalls that in
all of her visions of Christ's Passion she saw none of the reproved, except only the devil himself; and this accords exactly with the Church's
teaching, which, in affirming eternal damnation, has never defined that
anyone is in hell, except only the devil.[212] She takes this occasion to offer another, far more reasonable theological opinion than that current
among the scholastics which Hilton repeats (cf. 427.2 note):

> In whych syȝt I vnderstond þat alle the creatures þat be of the devylles
> condiscion in thys lyfe and ther in endyng, ther is no more mencyon made
> of them before god and alle his holyn then of the devylle, notwyth-
> stondyng that they be of mankynde, wheder they haue be cristend or
> nought (427.10).

In chapter 34 Julian further clarifies the distinction which she has
already made (414.2 e.s.) between matters which belong to our
salvation and matters which do not. She accepts that there are *de facto*
secrets which it is profitable for us to know in this life, but which our
ignorance and sinfulness prevent us from seeing. Such privities are
revealed, both in her showings and in the Church's teachings, and to
know these is to be consoled by God's compassionate love. But curiosity
about matters belonging to the great mysteries, such as predestination
and reprobation, can only bring disquiet and a troubled conscience.
This is her introduction to the general solution of the apparent contradiction: that since God is Holy Church, its teachings cannot be opposed to authentic revelation (430.5 e.s.).

At this point in the short text (252.13 e.s.) Julian had written that the
consideration of this revelation of God's immense goodness and compassion prompted her to ask the question, on behalf of a friend, which
is at the root of so much Christian fear and preoccupation: shall I persevere to the end in the grace and love of God? The stock spiritual an-

---

[212] E.g. Lateran IV (Denzinger-Schönmetzer 801).

swer to this in contemplative writings is that this is a false question, in that it draws a person away from God's own view of his creatures, and is thus an obstacle to contemplative prayer (cf. 432.5 and 252.15, notes). In the short text Julian seems to have accepted this, for she writes: *and in þis desyre I lettyd my selfe* (252.15). In the long text, however, she qualifies this: *and in this syngular desyer it semyd that I lettyd my selfe* (432.5), because she has learnt that the contemplative is being drawn to see and feel the divine compassion in a way which cannot possibly exclude the particular case (440.49 e.s.), though it remains true that any overriding anxiety is itself a hidden lack of trust in God's love, and is thus a cause of desolation. So in this chapter 35, she is led again to reflect on what she has already seen in Revelation III: the whole Trinity working in all things to bring the divine love to fulfilment in every creature (433.15 e.s.), and that this is possible because of the nature of the divine attribute of rightfulness, which not only is not contradicted by his mercy and compassion, but is complementary to it, in bringing good out of evil (435.34 e.s.). It is also subordinated to it, since, when all are made perfect in love, and the ghostly thirst has an end, the working of divine compassion will cease.

Chapter 36 begins with a locution in reported speech, a grammatical device not often used by Julian (cf. 436.4, 438.35, notes) which was a cause of confusion to the scribes. The locution represents a more penetrating insight into the Lord's compassion. It is a sight of the promise of God's fulfilment, consequent on his gift to his creature of the longing for himself, which follows naturally on the contemplation in the previous chapter of righteousness and mercy; and the end is the rest and peace of the eternal Sabbath. Julian explains clearly, again in the context of the 'great deed', that man can do nothing in the order of his salvation which is pleasing to God without prevenient and concomitant grace. This was the teaching of the Council of Orange (A.D. 529) against the heresy later to be called 'semi-Pelagianism'; the seventh canon there defined states: Si quis per naturae vigorem bonum aliquid, quod ad salutem pertinet vitae aeternae cogitare ut expedit aut eligere, sive salutari, id est evangelicae praedicationi consentire posse confirmat absque illuminatione et inspiratione spiritus sancti ... haeretico fallitur spiritu; and it goes on to quote II Corinthians 3.5: Not that we are sufficient to think anything by ourselves, as of ourselves; but our sufficiency is from God. [213] Here is the meaning of Julian's phrase, startling to ears less theologically attuned, *and man shall do ryght nought but synne*

---

[213] Denzinger-Schönmetzer no. 377.

(438.38). The firm confidence of her theology here is in marked contrast to the view that the saints in heaven will rejoice in the sufferings of the damned (extended by Hilton, as we have seen, to those who in this life are raised to the higher stages of contemplative prayer); and it is rooted in her own contemplative experience of purification, active and passive, illumination and union. All this she specifies as she describes the Lord's compassionate dealings with one who longs for him:

> ... here hast thou mattyr of mekenesse, here hast thou mattyr of loue, here hast thou matter of knowyng thy selfe, here hast thou mattyr of enjoyyng in me. And for my love enjoy in me (439.41),

where *mekenesse* and *nowten* (the SS variant, probably superior, to *knowyng*) describe active purification, *loue* and *enjoyyng* passive purification;

> And as long as we be in this lyfe, what tyme that we by oure foly turne vs to the beholdyng of the reprovyd, tendyrly oure lorde towchyth vs and blysydfully callyth vs (439.44),

describing the impulse of grace, drawing the soul towards union;

> seyeng in oure soule: Lett me aloone, my derwurdy chylde, intende to me. I am inogh to þe, and enjoy in thy sauiour and in thy saluation (439.46),

describing the soul's illumination. This whole passage is reminiscent of one of the most beautiful images of the divine compassion in sacred Scripture, Isaias 66.12-13, which will again be present in her mind when she writes in chapter 60 of the 'forthspreading' of God's motherhood (594.2 e.s.). Her immediate comment on this locution: *The soule that is perced therwith by grace shalle se it and fele it* (440.49), illumines this entire revelation. She is writing of compunction of heart, which, according to Jean Leclercq, is primary in Gregory the Great's conception of Christian life and prayer:

> Compunction becomes pain of the spirit, a suffering resulting simultaneously from two causes: the existence of sin and our own tendency towards sin — *compunctio paenitentiae, timoris, formidinis* — and the existence of our desire for God and even our very possession of God. St. Gregory, more than others, accentuated this last aspect: an obscure possession, awareness of which does not last and consequently gives rise to regret at seeing it disappear and to a desire to find it again. The 'compunction of the heart', 'of the soul' — *compunctio cordis, animi* — always tends to become a 'compunction of love', 'of delectation' and 'of contemplation' — *compunctio amoris, dilectionis, contemplationis*. Compunction is

an act of God in us, an act by which God awakens us, a shock, a blow, a 'sting', a sort of burn. God goads us as if with a spear; he 'presses' us with insistence (*cum-pungere*), as if to pierce us ... How is this action of God accomplished in us? By what means, through what intermediaries, and on what occasions? By all kinds of trials: tribulation, the *flagella Dei,* the thousandfold sufferings of life, sin itself ... The ultimate role of compunction is to bring to the soul a longing for heaven. [214]

Here and elsewhere in Revelation XIII, as she recounts it in the long text, Julian is expanding Gregory's doctrine of compunction from her own experience of sights, sickness, and, it would seem, the infused graces which followed the showings. Much of the account (433.15-441.73) is an addition to the short text, inserted, it would appear, not so much because it depends for its clarity on the parable, but because it is integral to all that she has seen, heard and felt since she first recorded her showings. This seems particularly true of the special understanding she has received concerning miracles (440.59-441.73), itself a corroboration of what she has formulated concerning the great deed which will not be known until it is done (cf. 440.57 and note). Just as the angel instanced the miracle of the opening of Elizabeth's womb as corroboration of the miracle of the Incarnation — 'No word will be impossible with God' (Luke 1.37) — so here for Julian *That pat is vn-possible to the is nott vnpossible to me* (426.49). The gospel miracles are pre-eminently signs of God's compassion (healing, feeding, stilling the storm, raising the dead), of the consolation which follows trouble, anguish, desolation (440.60).

As Julian explains in chapter 37, the greatest sign of the Lord's compassion is that he loves us whilst we are in sin. This is a truth which she finds hard to grasp; and she expects this to be hard also for her fellow-Christians. Thus she is anxious to communicate it to them, even though, in this final draft of the long text, she knows that it will not become clear — as it did not become clear to her — except in the light of the parable (cf. 442.5 and note). Once again, she points out that Revelation XIII consisted in two 'sights', the first of the mystery of the divine compassion, the second of the mystery of sin. At this juncture she had received special grace to attend more closely to the second sight; and the fear and desolation which came upon her were assuaged by the final locution of the original showing: *I kepe the fulle sekerly* (254.3).

Then there follows her first reference to the godly will. She has already defined sin as 'all that is not good'; and now she reflects on how it is possible for God to love that which is evil. She knows, from what

[214] *The Love of Learning*, 37-39.

she has learned of the 'ghostly thirst', that God loves to heal and to save, the well-spring of the divine compassion revealed in Christ crucified and glorified. She begins to write of the godly will as it is found in all those who are to form one soul with the heavenly host, and of their love for each other in Christ. It is this love which is the godly will, and it is incorruptible. The theologian whose thought and language appear closest to hers (and we must recall that this passage is common to short and to long texts) is William of St. Thierry, in his *Golden Epistle*; and, significantly, this is in the final section of his treatise on the interior life of the monastic solitary, the third or spiritual state of the religious man, when 'the memory has been transformed into wisdom' and 'the thinker's understanding becomes the lover's contemplation'.[215] So William writes:

> For love (*amor*) is a great will towards God, another love (*dilectio*) is a clinging to him or uniting to him, and a third love (*charitas*) is delight in him. Yet the unity of the spirit with God in a man who lifts up his heart towards God is the perfection of his will, when he not only wills God's will, he is not only drawn to God, but in that drawing he is so made perfect that he can will nothing but what God wills. For to will what God wills, this is to be like God; not to be able to will except what God wills, this is to be what God is, for whom willing and being are one and the same. So it is well said that 'we shall see plainly what he is, when we shall be like him' (I John 3.2); that is, we shall be what he himself is.[216]

This is the *godly wyll in the hygher party* (443.18) which 'constantly the Holy Spirit, the Spirit of life, himself pours in by the way of love',[217] *whych wylle is so good that it may nevyr wylle evylle, but evyr good. And therfore we be that he lovyth, and endlesly we do that he lykyth* (443.19). 'And likeness to God is perfection in man', William continues, 'but not to wish to be perfect is to fail'.[218] So Julian concludes the chapter in the long text: *but for feylyng of loue in oure party, therfore is alle oure traveyle* (444.25).

In the first sentence of chapter 38, which corresponds to the short text (255.17-18), Julian has made one small but significant change. Where, before, she had written: *god schewed me that syn is na schame, bot wirschippe to mann,* she now writes: *synne shalle be no shame, but wurshyppe to man* (445.2). This is indicative of her desire for theological precision; sin, at the time of its commision, and until it is forgiven, is the occasion

[215] PL 184 347.
[216] Ibid. 348.
[217] Ibid. 347.
[218] Ibid. 348.

of shame, just as the glorious wounds of the risen Christ were, at the
time of the Crucifixion, signs not of honour but of the world's sin and
shame. She writes similarly of her own sinfulness (cf. 633. 23 and note).
Here, in the long text, she sees the need to establish the truth of this
simple but paradoxical statement; and now she has the theological and
rhetorical equipment to do it. She constructs an *argumentatio perfectissima*, of which the opening statement becomes the *propositio*; and the
other steps of the argument follow.

> ... for ryght as to every synne is answeryng a payne by truth, ryght so for
> every synne to the same soule is gevyn a blysse by loue (445. 3).

is the *ratio,*

> Ryght as dyuerse synnes be ponysschyd with dyuers paynes after that it
> be greuous, ryght so shalle they be rewardyd with dyvers joyes in hevyn
> for theyr victories, after as the synne haue ben paynfulle and sorowfulle to
> the soule in erth (445. 4)

is the *rationis confirmatio,*

> For the soule that shalle come to hevyn is so precyous to god and the
> place so wurshypfulle that the goodnes of god sufferyth nevyr that soule
> to synne fynally ·þat shalle come ther (445. 8)

is the *exornatio*, and

> But what synners they are that so shalbe rewarded is made knowen in
> holy church in erth and also in heaven by over passyng worshypes (445. 10)

is the *complexio*. This remarkable dexterity is heightened by resuming,
with the next sentence, the short text: *for in this sight mynn vnderstandynge
was lyfted vp in to hevenn* (255. 18), in such a way — *and then god brought
merely to my mynde ...* (446. 13) — that the Lord himself provides her
with the rhetorical *exempla,* Magdalene and the others, which render her
reasoning 'clear, vivid, plausible'.[219] And, finally, the last section of the
chapter, where the Lord brings John of Beverley to her mind, becomes
a preacher's homely example, to drive home the point that the miracles
worked through the intercession of penitent-saints are pre-eminently
tokens of the working of the divine compassion, which in and through
Christ continues to bring joy and honour out of sin and shame.
   The sight of Christ bleeding from the scourging had been for Julian a
most deeply moving experience in the early showings, and itself a sign
of Christ's kinship with us, and the instrument of the divine com-

[219] F. Nims.

passion. Here in chapter 39, she sees sin as the scourge of those who will be saved; for it is in our sins that we have the most need of the divine compassion which we experience in our contemplation of the suffering Christ. The Pauline doctrine of reconciliation is clearly in her thought: ... He has reconciled us to himself by Christ ... for God was indeed in Christ reconciling the world to himself, not imputing to them their sins ... He made sin for us him who knew no sin, that we might be made in him the justice of God (II Corinthians 5.18-21). Here too, in another addition to the short text (451.14-452.29) we have a precise summary of the Western teaching on compunction of heart, which has already been described, in its presentation as the Lord's visitation with the three wounds with which she had prayed to be pierced:

> And also whom oure lord wylle he vysyteth of his specialle grace with so grett contricion, and also with compassion and tru longyng to god that they be sodeynly delyverde of synne and of payne, and taken vp to blysse and made evyn with seyntes. By contryscion we be made clene, by compassion we be made redy, and by tru longyng to god we be made wurthy. Theyse be thre menys, as I vnderstode, wher by that alle soules com to hevyn, that is to sey that haue ben synners in erth and shalle be savyd (451.21).

In a final addition (453.40-48), she once more anticipates the parable of the lord and the servant, alluding to the lord's compassion for the servant who is shown not only for Christ, but also for Adam and every soul who will be saved.

In chapter 40, the last of this revelation, Julian establishes a close link between the central locution of the divine compassion, 'I keep thee full surely', and Revelation XIV, on prayer, which will follow next in the long text. In the short text she had concluded her account of the showing 'for prayer' with a reflection on the sinful soul's unhappy state until God turns to look on her with compassionate love (262.67-76). This she has now carefully edited and expanded, so that it introduces and puts into the clear context of our need for prayer the *caveat* against the particular form of 'liberty of the spirit' (cf. 456.28 note) which she here makes her special concern:

> But now because of alle thys gostly comfort that is before seyde, if any man or woman be steryd by foly to sey or to thynke: if this be tru, than were it good for to synne to haue the more mede, or elles to charge the lesse to synne, beware of this steryng. For truly, if it come, it is vntrue and of the enemy (456.26; cf. 257.1).

Again, in the long text she edits by constructing another *argumentatio,* this time rebutting the *propositio* which she now explicitly stigmatizes as 'untrue'. On the contrary, sin is to be hated, because God's love teaches us so (457.31-32, the *ratio*). Her own contemplative experience confirms this: the more we see his courteous love, the more we reject sin and are ashamed of it (457.33-35, the *rationis confirmatio*). The argument is then embellished with a conditional syllogism and an appeal to her showing (457.35-458.39, the *exornatio*); and the conclusion is the *complexio*:

> ... for a kynd soule hatyth no payne but synne; for alle is good but syn, and nought is yvell but synne (458.40).

And the revelation itself ends with a gentle exhortation: the showing of God's compassion is intended to teach us to love ourselves and our brethren as he does. This is his endless comforting of us.

## 16 Revelation XIV

'This is eternal life: that they may know thee, the one true God, and Jesus Christ whom thou hast sent' (John 17.3). Julian's revelations are basically concerned aith two moments in the existence of the incarnate Word, his coming from God and his going to God (cf. John 13.3); for these two moments, of incarnation and of death and resurrection, express scripturally the purpose of the manifestation of the mystery of God and Christ, his plan of salvation for all who will receive him. To receive Christ is to enter into an intimate relationship with God, the relationship of children to a Father: 'as many as received him, to them he gave the power to become sons of God' (John 1.12), which power, here on earth, is the knowing and loving of him who is unseen. It is only in heaven that we shall see God face to face, writes Julian, echoing Paul:

> And ther shall we se god face to face, homely and fulsomly. The creature that is made shall see and endlesly beholde god whych is the maker; for thus may no man se god and leue aftyr, that is to sey in this dedely lyffe (481.53)

Julian has already made it clear, when she wrote of prayer in the context of Revelation I, that this knowing and loving will be the constant preoccupation of all those who, like herself, are committed to the contemplative life:

> ... for oure kyndely wille is to haue god, and the good wylle of god is to haue vs, and we may never sesse of wyllyng ne of louyng tylle we haue hym in fulhede of ioy. And than we may no more wylle, for he wylle that we be occupyed in knowyng and louyng tylle the tyme comyth that we shal be fulfyllede in hevyn (308.57).

This she understood to be the purpose of her revelations, *this lesson of loue*
(309.62); and it is in Revelation XIV, with its deceptively simple
opening, *Affter thys oure lorde shewed for prayer* (460.3), more than twenty
years after receiving her visions, that she is enabled to explain, with an
immense wealth of theological and spiritual detail, that prayer is a
living and growing relationship with the triune God in Christ Jesus,
such an assimilation to him as will reproduce his own 'coming from
God and going to God', to the extent that she ends her account of this
long and complex showing with the words:

> Thus I vnderstode that all his blessyd chyldren whych be come out of
> hym by kynd shulde be brougt agayne in to hym by grace (619.3).

Most commentators on the long text of the *Revelations* have taken it for
granted that this fourteenth showing on prayer occupies only three
chapters, 41-43, and that Julian then returns to her obsessive problem
about sin, damnation and the wrath of God, which is eventually solved
(to her satisfaction, if perhaps not to ours) through years of pondering
over the parable of the lord and the servant; and this is a view which
seems to be corroborated by the account of the same showing in chapter xix of the short text. The opinion of the present editors is, however,
that if the prayer relationship depends on the union of man's heart and
mind with his God, then, whenever God is wrathful with sinful man,
discord and alienation take the place of harmony and the divine
presence, and so the life of prayer ceases. Further, throughout her
revelations Julian never saw God at odds with his creature, man. It
seems important, therefore, before analysing this fourteenth revelation
chapter by chapter, to offer a brief summary of the showing's unity.
First of all, Julian defines the contemplative prayer of petition
('seeking'), and explains its conditions and what it involves. It is, in fact,
the creature's response to the creative, redemptive, unifying action of
God; and as soon as the creature begins to know in faith that his
seeking God is already answered, petition becomes thanksgiving, and he
begins to understand that the term of the divine action in him is the
beatific vision. Thus prayer is the knowledge of salvation, the mutual
expression of the covenant by which man and God are partners, for the
sake of man's ultimate fulfilment. Who, then, is this God who so unites
himself with man in contemplation (chapter 44)? He is the God whom
Mary contemplated in the moment of the Incarnation. Julian then
proceeds to consider the limitations of the human power of knowing
and loving in the contemplative process, the fluctuation in man's apprehension and judgment of himself and of God, as opposed to the
divine immutability (chapter 45). Though God is always at one with

man, man is very often at odds with himself; the contradiction will persist, so that there will be times when this unitive prayer will appear meaningless, until man truly sees himself and his God (chapter 46).

So it is essential that prayer be marked not only by wonder and reverence, but also by humility and the readiness to endure our own frailty and foolishness, an unlikeness to God in the human condition which demands submission to the workings of mercy and grace (chapter 47). From this it follows that contemplative prayer is very frequently and predominantly passive, demanding patient expectation, even when the soul experiences the Spirit's compassionate purification and loving illumination (chapter 48). Thus prayer involves our being moved from an awareness of sinfulness and alienation, through the divine illumination, to a measure of the sight and experience of the peace of God with man, which is permanent (chapter 49). So the problem arises that the truth of God seems to be incompatible with the Church's judgment on sinful man as blameworthy. If there were such incompatibility, contemplative prayer might be illusory. How can the soul's relationship in prayer with God which was described in chapter 41 exist together with sinfulness and consequent judgment (chapter 50)? What in the end the parable of the lord and the servant explains is precisely how the relationship between God and man persists through human inadequacy and frailty. It involves Julian in a careful doctrinal exposition of the mysteries of Incarnation, redemption and the interrelationships of the persons of the Trinity, as well as of the incorporation into Christ of every man who will be saved (chapter 51). What follows is that the contemplative relationship is Trinitarian: the Christian becomes, in Christ, the term of the divine creative activity across time into eternity (chapter 52). How this is so, how, that is, creation and redemption come together in Christ, the head of human nature, is then explained (chapter 53), as are its effects in all incorporated into Christ (chapter 54). The precise nature of this incorporation, in terms of Christ's relationship with his Father and the Spirit of them both, is then elucidated (chapter 55); and after this Julian is able to show how this knowledge in faith of God in Christ enables the creature to grow in understanding of its own nature, that is, in the context of union with the Trinity and the mutual indwelling, and the gifts which flow from that indwelling (chapters 56-57). This contemplative knowledge of Trinity and Incarnation, of the divine economy of creation is further developed (chapter 58); and contemplative prayer and Trinitarian theology compenetrate one another as Julian discourses on the Trinitarian 'perichoresis' and the *operationes ad extra* (chapter 59).

From the consideration of the divine *natura creatrix* in the Trinitarian context which she has established, Julian is able to illumine for us, better perhaps than her more illustrious forebears such as Augustine and Anselm, the traditional doctrine of the creating and redeeming activity of the second person of the Trinity, using the image of 'God our Mother' (chapters 59-62). She concludes the revelation by emphasising what, for her, is the sublimest expression of man's relationship with God in contemplative prayer: the acceptance of feebleness and failing of insight and understanding which comes from loving trust in God and which finds its truest human analogy in the authentic relationship of the child with its parents (chapter 63).

Though Julian had written, in her short-text account of this revelation: *thus makes prayere accorde betwix god and mannes saule* (261.53), it is there by no means obvious that prayer, for her, is consistently the petition for union. She seems rather to be writing of her own case, drawing the analogy between what was shown to her and infused contemplation (cf. 261.55 note); and under the one heading, 'prayer', she includes vocal prayer (258.9-10), and petitions for the spiritual well-being of her neighbours (258.10-259.13). In her final version, however, she begins from an entirely different viewpoint. She is now bringing to the matter of this revelation the principle laid down for her in the parable: *It longyth to the to take hede to alle þe propertes and the condescions that were shewed in the example* (520.87). Writing of the two conditions for prayer, she is more concerned about God's intention (460.3 e.s.) than with her own experience. So she can now sum up the first condition by using the epithet *ryghtfulle*, since she has already explained its meaning in chapter 36 (433.19-435.36); thus, the prayer which she is now describing is, in its term, the contemplation of God's righteousness and the participation in this 'blessed harmony' of all the souls that will be saved (cf. 435.33). She is, however, content to retain, verbatim, what she had written in the short text about the other condition, sure trust, because, to her lasting shame, she experienced a lack of this in the course of the revelations themselves (cf. chapter 66). Prayer is always the communication of God's wisdom and truth, his rightfulness; but man must enter into the relationship by accepting the gift of faith, hope and charity.

What then follows, in both texts, is the nucleus of the showing, the locution: *I am grounde of thy besekyng* (461.11; and cf. 259.20). But in the long text, the reflection upon the *ratiocinatio* which concludes the revelation itself develops in an entirely different way; no longer does Julian interpret the locution as *a sobere vndertakynge* (260.29) directed at her lack of trust. Instead, she tells us that the petition is for 'mercy and grace', and she argues from the question, *how schoulde it than be that thou shuldyst nott haue thy besekyng?* (461.13), that God's goodness is the cause of our prayer, in the sense in which she is now able to define the contemplative prayer of petition:

> Besechyng is a trew and gracious lestyng wylle of the soule, onyd and fastenyd in to the wylle of oure lorde by the swet prevy werkyng of the holy gost (463.30).

The Trinitarian character of this definition should be observed. It is the Father who by his righteousness fastens the will of the soul to the will of the incarnate Son, and this creative act *ab aeterno* is continued in time by the *werkyng,* the *missio ad extra* of the Holy Spirit. The glorified Christ is thus the immediate term of the soul's longing; and Julian rounds out the definition with a homely description of his office as mediator:

> he takyth it full thankefully, and hyghly enjoyeng he sendeth it vppe above (463.33).

*Prayer*

If the soul can only see that this prayer is the immediate effect of God's eternal and creative relationship with his creature, and that he himself seeks for our response — *he lokyth ther after, and he wyll haue it* (463.39) — any particular level of emotional experience will cease to be of any great importance in the inner life of the devout Christian, and his hope will be increased.

Julian associates herself firmly with the Western tradition, as she associates prayer without ceasing with good will. 'In ipsa ergo fide et spe et caritate', writes Augustine, 'continuato desiderio semper oramus'.[220] Equally, when Julian writes that thanksgiving belongs to this *prayeng contynually* (465.49), one must understand that she is referring not simply to private prayer, with its large dependence on what were called from early times 'ejaculations' ('... crebras ... orationes, sed eas tamen brevissimas et raptim, quodam modo iaculatas'),[221] but to the *laus perennis* of a contemplative community like the one to whom the *Ancrene Riwle* is addressed: the eucharistic liturgy and the divine office and the various devotions linked to this *opus Dei.*[222] What, perhaps, is special in Julian is the degree to which she sees petition and thanksgiving integrated in the one contemplative process. The contemplative effort is itself a response to the Spirit's working in

---

[220] *Epistola 130*, ed. Goldbacher, CSEL 3, 2 60.
[221] Ibid., 62.
[222] Cf. supra, IX 3.

us, moving us now to thanksgiving, now to a cry for mercy and grace (cf. 467.60 e.s.); and all is seen as dependent on the *lectio divina,* the power of the Lord's word, alive, penetrating and quickening (cf. Hebrews 4.12).

In chapter 42, Julian begins to explore the nature of this relationship, the true expression of which is contemplative prayer. To do so, she has recourse to the current philosophical doctrine on causality (as she will do again at the end of her book, as she ponders the reason of the revelations as a whole — cf. 732.15 note). Thus God is the efficient cause of the relationship, and of every true expression of it, *by hys good-nesse* (468.5); God is the highest good, and all desired perfections flow from him as from the first cause.[223] The form and the quality of our response is next stated: 'Man inheres in God', Thomas writes, 'in whom alone true happiness consists'.[224] Thirdly, the actuality of the relation ship is located in God as the final and exemplary cause, *to be onyd and lyke to oure lorde in althyng* (468.12). As Thomas expresses it, 'in homine invenitur aliqua Dei similitudo, quae deducitur a Deo, sicut ab exemplari';[225] 'secundum quod homo Deum actu cognoscit et amat perfecte, et sic attenditur imago secundum similitudinem gloriae'.[226] Finally, Julian again stresses that it is the triune God to whom man is united and assimilated:

> ... and he wylle helpe vs, and he shalle make it so, as he seyth hym selfe, blessyd mot he be (468.13),

where *helpe* is for the Holy Spirit, *make* is for the Father and *seyth* is for the Son made man.

Julian continues by considering in more detail the quality and shape of our response; because of faith and grace it can in some mysterious fashion be 'large' (469.16), matching to some degree the liberality and generosity of the divine lover, and though our sight of his gift of himself is often severely limited, he is the sure object of the prayer of hope. Her own trust is so 'large' that here she begins to catch a glimpse of the Lord who is visiting her with mercy and grace, communicating his very being to her.

> He wylle that we haue true knowyng in hym selfe that he is beyng; and in thys knowyng he wylle that oure vnderstandyng be groundyd with alle oure myghtes and alle oure intent and alle oure menyng (469.28).

---

[223] *Summa theologiae* I.6.2 *in corp.*
[224] Ibid. I.82.2 *in corp.*
[225] Ibid. I.93.4 *in corp.*
[226] Ibid. I.93.4 *in corp.*

She holds with St. Thomas that God's self-knowledge is his being,[227] and that in contemplation we are drawn to share in this knowing. So to respond evokes from us the concentration of all our mental and spiritual powers, given to us in *our noble and excelent makyng* (470.34), restored and enriched in us by his redemption, and supported and enlivened by all the rest of his creation. All the divine activity, or all of it which is revealed to us in Christ, has as its term this unitive relationship which is called prayer:

> Beholde and se that I haue done alle thys before thy prayer, and now thou arte and prayest me (471.37).

More than this, all that he is doing now belongs to the same relationship; and prayer, on our part, is the simple realization and acknowledgment that God is for us and that we are for God. But Julian still retains the monastic understanding inherited by Thomas Aquinas and all those who followed him that every human happiness is a participation in divine beatitude, and thus of its nature is both contemplative and eschatalogical. Thomas had written: '... quidquid est desiderabile ... totum eminentius in divina beatitudine praeexistit. De contemplativa enim felicitate habet continuam et certissimam contemplationem'.[228] So Julian offers us another definition of prayer:

> ... prayer is a ryȝtwys vnderstandyng of that fulhed of joy that is for to come, with tru longyng and very trust. Saworyng or seyng oure blysse that we be ordeyned to, kyndely makyth vs to longe; trew vnderstondyng and loue with swete menyng in oure savoure graciously makyth vs to trust (473.55).

This is a reminder that she is also no stranger to the doctrine of the spiritual senses, particularly the sense of taste, as developed by the Cistercian spiritual writers.[229] Julian's final description of prayer has much in common with William of St. Thierry's exegesis of John 17.3: 'Haec est, inquit, vita aeterna, ut cognoscant te' ... Beata scientia, in qua continetur vita aeterna. Vita ista ex illo gustu est, quia gustare, hoc est intelligere.[230]

Already in the first revelation, Julian had been at pains to stress that contemplative prayer means on our part to seek, suffer and trust under the prompting of the Holy Spirit (cf. 332.68). Here, in chapter 43, she amplifies this teaching. To pray is to acknowledge to God that we need

---

[227] Cf. *Summa theologiae* I.14.4.
[228] Ibid. I.26.4 *in corp.*
[229] Cf. J. Walsh: 'Guillaume de Saint-Thierry et les sens spirituels'.
[230] *De natura amoris*, X 31; PL 184 399.

him in order to attain to union with him in knowledge and love; but to
pray is also witnessing to God that, through his grace, we desire to have
him as he desires to have us. In the ninth revelation (382 e.s.) she had
seen not only the longing of Jesus to suffer for the whole of mankind
and for each individual, but also the joy of the Trinity in the salvific
achievement of Jesus (391.22-25). For Julian, as for Bernard, God is a
God who moves his creatures because he desires them: 'Deus movet
sicut desiderans';[231] and the movement brings peace and consolation —
… *comfortyth the conscience and ablyth man to grace* (475.5). Thus the prayer
of petition is an expression of mutuality in the relationship; we become
partners first in desire and then in fact. We share God's activity, and all
this is prayer:

> And thus he techyth vs to pray and myghtyly to trust that we shalle haue
> it; for he beholdyth vs in loue, and wylle make vs perteyner of his good
> wylle and dede (475.6).

Implicit in this understanding of God as *Deus desiderans* is Julian's
previous insight of herself at prayer: 'I saw him and I sought him; I had
him and I wanted him' (325.14). What frustrates his desire and our own
is the *vnablynes of oure selfe to Jhesu* (478.29). So prayer in times of
desolation is equally prayer for union and a response to grace, which itself implies the divine presence: *our lord god folowyth vs, helpyng our desyre*
(479.34). All of this, as has been noticed (cf. 477.19 note), belongs to
the contemplative exegesis of the Canticle of Canticles, which was Bernard's speciality,[232] and for him 'You would not seek me, had you not
already found me' is a principle of unitive prayer.

   The sight and the feeling of God which is the term of this prayer
(479.33-38) and also its purpose (477.21-26) is of the Trinity, working
the salvation, of all men, indeed, but in particular of the one who
receives the grace of contemplation, the *hygh myghty desyer to be alle onyd
in to hym* (480.42), itself an assurance of that fulness of sight and
possession which is the Beatific Vision. Here Julian again has recourse
to the doctrine of the spiritual senses, as taught especially by William of
St. Thierry in his *Expositio altera in Cantica*.[233]

---

[231] On the theme of 'Deus desiderans' in Bernard and other Cistercian spiritual
writers, cf. Dumontier: *S. Bernard et la Bible,* 40-43.

[232] Ibid. 43 note 2.

[233] For such passages as 'videndo claritatem tuam, sentiendo charitatem tuam,
illuminetur in te conscientia mea; … tractando quae proprie tua sunt, dulcius te sa-
piunt, suavius redolent, sapiat mihi gustus tuus, spiret odor', cf. J. Walsh, 'Guillaume
de Saint-Thierry et les sens spirituels', 34-35.

Now that Julian has shown, with all her spiritual learning and literary skills, the contemplative process as the consummate point of union attained in the immediacy, totality and mutuality of the relationship which is the divine presence, the variations to which it is subject here *in via,* and its final transcendence in the Beatific Vision, she can demonstrate how this happens in practice in the prayer of the Gospel prototype, *our lady sent Mary* (483.6). So chapter 44 begins with a proleptic allusion to man as the servant in the parable, the son who *werkyth evyr more his* (the Father's) *wylle and his wurschyppe duryngly without styntyng* (483.2), and how this 'working' (the force and content of the word will not be lost on any reader of the *Cloud*) is achieved. The task Julian sets herself is to describe the object of Mary's contemplation; and she sees this contemplation as an intellectual and affective 'sight' of the mutual presence and relationship of the divine persons in the soul of Mary, which she has seen 'in part' in the first revelation (cf. 297.28-298.40, 310.2-311.11). The truth which is the Father sees God who is the Son; and the wisdom which is the Son beholds God who is the Father; and the Spirit who is love is endlessly proceeding from this mutual contemplation. And yet, mysteriously, 'all is of God's making' (484.11), because the Son who is wisdom is at the same time a human being who beholds, is given the power to contemplate, as well as seeing divinely; his *soule is a creature in god* (484.13), possessing by participation these same properties of truth, wisdom and love. So Julian now beholds, in the contemplative prayer of Mary (of which the evangelist Luke writes repeatedly when he deals with Christ's infancy), the analogue of the divine processions and relationships, in which the creature truly knows himself as made and existing now for ever (*evyr more it doyth that it was made for,* 484.14), out of the divine creative love, but also for the love with which God loves him endlessly.

(It is worth remarking that Ludolph of Saxony, in his *Vita Christi,* offers the speculation that the angel came to Mary when she was 'tota abstracta in devotissima oratione, vel in continua contemplatione ... Rationabile enim videbitur quod quando sibi voluit uniri Verbum aeternum, tunc ipsi spiritualiter sibi fuerit unita in contemplationis actu'.)[234]

At the beginning of this fourteenth revelation which 'our Lord showed for prayer', Julian wrote of righteousness as prayer's true condition, by which she meant the participation in the divine peace and

[234] Ed. Rigollot, I.v.7.

harmony of all who will be saved, as they behold God:

> And the beholdyng of thys blessyd acord is full swete to the soule that
> seeth it by grace. Alle þe soules that shalle be savyd in hevyn withouȝt
> ende be made ryghtfulle in the syȝt of god and by hys awne goodnesse, in
> whych ryghtfullnes we be endlessly kepte and marvelously aboue all
> creatures (434.32).

In the chapters (41-43) which followed, Julian had explained that prayer
is the expression of the graced creature's cooperation in God's
righteousness, seen at its most perfect in Mary's contemplation of the
incarnate Word in the moment of his conception (chapter 44). All of
this flows from the truth that man, in his creation and his immortal
existence, is assimilated to God in his substance (cf. 475.2-3). It is,
however, equally true that *homo viator* 'is often unlike in condition by
sin' (475.3). Now, in chapter 45, she begins to reflect on the apparent
incompatibility of these two truths and their consequences in man's life
of prayer. God's knowledge and judgment of us is 'upon our kindly
substance'; that is, in our relationship to him as Father, through the
Son, in the Holy Spirit:

> A hye vnderstandyng it is inwardly to se and to know that god, whych is
> oure maker, dwellyth in oure soule, and a hygher vnderstandyng it is and
> more, inwardly to se and to know oure soule that is made dwellyth in god
> in substance, of whych substance by god we be that we be (562.12).

But there is another knowledge and judgment which is only partial, one
which does not see this unchangeable substance, except in so far as it is
reflected in man's visible actions, which involve his changeable sensuality. It is the work of God, of his mercy and grace, with our
cooperation (and this mutual activity is what she has called prayer) to
transform the sensuality, so that man becomes like to God in condition
as well as in substance. (It is this that Walter Hilton calls 'reforming in
feeling'.) However, throughout the whole revelations, all that Julian has
seen is God knowing and approving us in our substantial relationship
with him (which she will come to see, through the parable, as our
relationship in Christ, one perception and one knowledge, the divine
wisdom and the incarnate Word). However, the teaching Church which
proclaims Christ's perfection (as she will ultimately be shown: *I it am
that holy chyrch prechyth the and techyth the. That is to sey: All the helth and the
lyfe of sacramentys, alle þe vertu and þe grace of my worde, alle the goodnesse that
is ordeynyd in holy chyrch to the, I it am* (597.34)), is also the learning
Church, the body of Christ not yet completed (cf. 418.20), which must
acknowledge its own sinfulness; that is, in that condition it is incapable
of being incorporated into God's righteousness. It would seem that at

precisely this point Julian was shown the parable of the lord and the servant, which, when finally understood, would show her how God reconciles the apparently irreconcilable, and, what is more to the point, manifests that sinful man is called to contemplative prayer *by the swet prevy werkyng of the holy gost* (463.31). As yet, however, she cannot at all see its relevance; she can only reiterate that God's word and the Church's teaching alike must contain all that is relevant to salvation, the key to all Christian experience:

> ... the more knowyng and vnderstondyng by the gracious ledyng of the holy gost that we haue of these ij domes, the more we shalle see and know oure felynges (488.36).

When Julian writes, at the beginning of chapter 46, that

> whan we know and see verely and clerely what oure selfe is, than shalle we verely and clerly see and know oure lorde god in fulhed of joye (490.3),

she is not simply dealing with the eschatalogical character of all contemplative prayer, or giving voice to her own desire 'to be dissolved and to be with Christ' (Philippians 1.23); she is reflecting as a monastic theologian on the nature of man. He can only know and love himself truly in the fulness of his knowledge and love of the incarnate, glorified Christ. So William of St. Thierry teaches that the ultimate object of Christian contemplation is not simply God, nor is it the self. It is something else, a *tertium* or *medium quid,* which he calls the *beata conscientia*: ... cum in amplexu et osculo patris et filii medium quodammodo se invenit beata conscientia; cum modo ineffabili incogitabili fieri meretur homo dei non deus, sed tamen quod est deus, homo ex gratia, quod deus est ex natura.[235] However, Julian is here at pains to insist

---

[235] *Epistola ad fratres de Monte Dei,* ed. Davy, 146. The text here does not differ materially from that of Mabillon in PL 184 348; but the need for another critical edition is stressed by J.-M. Déchanet's articles in *Scriptorium* 6, 8 and 11. It is especially interesting, in view of the present editors' belief that Julian knew some of William's writings, to observe Déchanet's 'Anglo-Saxon' group among the manuscripts belonging to his 'Cistercian family', Antwerp, Plantin-Moretus Museum 103 (13th century, unknown origin, possession of William Warham, ob. 1532), London BM Royal 6 B xi (13th century, Germany, but owned by some dependency of Tewksbury Abbey), Bodleian Hatton 103 (SCN 4051; England, a composite of 13th and early 14th-century pieces belonging to the Hereford Franciscans), Bodleian Auct. D. 55 (SCN 27875; 13th century, England, unknown provenance). Shewring writes that this section of the *Letter* 'could fairly be described as a *précis* of the *Speculum fidei*', and adduces PL 180 394; and it is part of Déchanet's thesis that all of Part III and other material derives from William's 'Treatise', later Carthusianized by him to form the *Letter* requested by Mont-Dieu.

(and this is another insight which flows from her reflection on the parable) that through Christ and his Spirit there is interaction between substance and sensuality, which leads to the intensification of this contemplative knowledge of self:

> We may haue knowyng of oure selfe in this lyfe by contynuant helpe and vertu of oure hygh kynd, in which knowyng we may encrese and wax by fortheryng and spedyng of mercy and grace (490.7).

And if the woe and pain which sin brings constitute an obstacle in this life to the communication of wisdom and truth by the grace of contemplation, still this is communicated in the doctrines of Holy Church by the gift of faith. In this second kind of beholding of truth (which the showings constantly confirm as authentic), Julian seems to assert that there is room for error, at least so far as the conclusions to be drawn from such truth are concerned:

> And thus in alle this beholdyng me thought it behovyd nedys to se and to know that we be synners and do many evylles that we ouȝte to leue, and leue many good dedys vndone that we ouȝte to do, wherfore we deserve payne, blame and wrath (492.26).

where *me thought* advances this as no more than her own opinion, which she then proceeds to refute, notwithstanding, for example, the contrary view which the author of the *Ancrene Riwle* cites from Anselm (cf. 492.28 note). Her *propositio* is that the Lord never was nor never will be angry (493.30). Her *ratio* is that such a view is incompatible with all the divine attributes (493.31-32). As *confirmatio*, she lists the essential properties of the Trinity (493.32-35); and for *exornatio* she embellishes the argument with the statement that the term of the Trinitarian *operatio ad extra*, the divine goodness, leaves no room for either wrath or forgiveness (493.35-39). All the showings are the final proof, *complexio* of this. Julian therefore concludes that in her prayerful relationships with the Lord she needs to wait for him to express himself more clearly or (which is the same thing) to prepare her to receive his communication. Meanwhile, she exercises herself in both beholdings, the wonder of contemplation and the childlike submission to the truths of faith as proclaimed by the Church.

One of Julian's mature reflections on the mysterious parable of the lord and the servant deals with how easy it is for human frailty to be exposed in the contemplative situation. Consolation very quickly turns into desolation, if the soul allows itself to be overtaken by restlessness and agitation, when it cannot penetrate the divine mysteries, either because God himself hides them 'for love' (494.46), or because he has not yet made us worthy to see them (494.47). So at the beginning of chapter 47 she reminds us that wonder and reverence, which themselves lead to abiding consolation, and the patient endurance of this lack of knowing, itself involving the confident expectation that *we shalle in short tyme se clerely in hym selfe all that we desyer* (495.4), are elements integral to contemplative prayer, the way in which we should respond to grace. It is the failure to meet these obligations which she seems here to be indicating as the sin to which contemplatives are prone: yielding to the temptation to sorrow and woe because they cannot see clearly (496.19). The pattern of her thought in the short text had been that, in the time of such temptation and falling, man is moved by God's love to contrition and confession, so that he comes again to *fynde a reste in saule and softnesse in conscience; and than hym thynke þat god hase for gyffynn his synnes, and it es soth* (262.71). Now, however, she sees that, whether or no she was right in believing that *the forgevenesse of his wrath shulde be one of the pryncypall poyntes of his mercy* (495.11), it is certainly a very limited view of mercy and forgiveness. Thus she begins to tell us, as a preparation for her full account of the parable, against the background of twenty years of contemplative reflection on this 'showing for prayer' (cf. 460.3), how she *saw and vnderstode of the workyng of mercy* (496.13).

She begins with an examination of her own feelings and reactions in times of desolation, the course of which she perceives to be a failing of her sight of God. She couches her description of this desolation in terms of that *dissimilitudo* which is contrary to the Trinitarian appropriations, power, wisdom and goodness (cf. 496.16, 18 and notes). The powerlessness and unknowing, she observes, are in the self; but the will is 'overlaid'. So we see that she is writing not merely of her own experience of such desolation, but of all that she has seen and understood concerning the will of the servant (the *oone man* — 522.104) in his falling. Here, as there, it is the 'godly will' with which she deals:

> This man was hurte in his myghte and made fulle febyll, and he was stonyd in his vnderstandyng, for he was turnyd fro the beholdyng of his lorde, but his wylle was kepte in gods syght. For his wylle I saw oure lorde commende and aproue, but hym selfe was lettyd and blyndyd of the knowyng of this wyll (522.104).

In the desolation she also perceives the hidden working of this godly will, in *the grett desyer that the soule hath to se god* (497.25). She is thus able to identify, as spiritual writers so distinguished as Bernard and Richard of St. Victor before her had done, the various affections whence her interior reactions originate, and the quality of the discretion to which she has attained through her own experience, not merely of the alternation of consolation and desolation, of which all the great masters of Western spirituality write — a classical instance is the famous conclusion of Hugh of St. Victor's *De arrha animae*[236] — but of the co-existence of desolation and consolation, a theme much more rare.

This interior knowledge of *the contraryous that is in oure selfe* (499.41), the confrontation, that is, between rejoicing, desire and true hope, and mourning and dread (cf. 497.26-498.34) brings her to reflect, in the next chapter, 48, on the predominantly passive nature of contemplative prayer. There is no such *contraryous* in the good Lord whom she has seen as the initiator and also as the term of all human spiritual endeavour. We can no longer foist off our own inner contradictions on the God *whych is endlesse lyfe dwellyng in oure soule* (500.2). So she is able to describe human wrath, which the *Cloud*-author, following Bernard, denounces as 'þe foulist and þe worst filþe of alle',[237] as the substance of man's unlikeness to the Trinity:

> ... for wrath is not elles but a frowerdnes and a contraryousnes to pees and to loue. And eyther it comyth of feylyng of myght or of feylyng of wysdom or of feylyng of goodnesse, whych feylyng is nott in god, but it is in oure party (500.7).

Far from calling down divine anger, it merely invites that mercy which is

> a swete gracious werkyng in loue, medlyd with plentuous pytte, for mercy werkyth vs kepyng, and mercy werkyth turnyng to vs all thyng to good (501.17).

Julian has no wish, however, to minimize the pain of this contemplative experience. It involves her in the daily dying of which Paul writes in II Corinthians (cf. 501.20 note). Her adept use of the rhetorical *colores* to emphasize this point rivals that of the Latin Vulgate. None the less, with Julian as with Paul, an optimistic note predominates. Here she begins to treat of the Trinitarian processions, and of their interaction in the working out of man's total salvation. As the *Cloud*-author writes at the end of his treatise, perhaps echoing an aphorism of Anselm's, 'not what þou arte, ne what þou hast ben, beholdeþ god wiþ his mercyful iʒe, bot þat þou woldest be'.[238] Her reflection on this constant Trinitarian concern and care for the work of the divine hands leads her here (502.26 e.s.) to anticipate her teaching on motherhood as a divine

---

[236] PL 176 970 inc.: Hoc ultimum interrogationis meae ...
[237] *A Treatise of Discretion of Spirits;* Hodgson, *Deonise,* 85.
[238] Hodgson, *Cloud,* 132, and note, 204.

attribute, and to introduce for the first time her own coined word for
the highly technical περιχώρησις, *circumsessio: spredyng abrode* (cf. 502.28
note), as referring to the inter-relationship of Son and Spirit indwelling
in man:

> Mercy is a pyttefull properte, whych longyth to moderhode in tender
> loue; and grace is a wurshypfull properte, whych longyth to ryall lord-
> schyppe in the same loue. Mercy werkyth kypyng, sufferyng, quyckyng
> and helyng, and alle is of tendyrnesse of loue; and grace werkyth with
> mercy, reysyng, rewarding, endlesly ovyr passyng that oure lovyng and
> our traveyle deseruyth, spredyng abrode and shewyng the hye plen-
> tuousnesse, largesse of goddes ryall lordschyppe in his mervelouse curtesy
> (502.28-503.35; and cf. notes).

She will have much more to write, in the light of her coming exposition of the parable, on the Trinitarian mystery; but few theologians
of her time, and, it may be, since her time, have written with such
clarity and concision, such simplicity and courtesy of this high mystery.
No less a theologian than Karl Rahner has recently insisted that the
great theological trap, which by no means all the scholastics or their
precursors were able to avoid in writing on the Trinity, is to attempt to
speculate on the unity and distinction of the persons *in abstracto*, pre-
scinding, that is, from the data of revelation of the divine economy, the
triune God, concerned eternally with and for man's salvation, manifested in the existence of the incarnate Christ. What Rahner has written[239] emphasizes for Julian's readers that she was not so trapped, as she
writes of the

> properte of blessyd loue that we shalle know in god, whych we myght
> nevyr haue knowen withouȝte wo goyng before (503.46).

In chapter 49 she continues to share her reflections on the illumination which she has received concerning divine mercy, grace and love,
following her experience of purification; but here the prayer is not
purely passive — she is *with grett diligence beholdyng* (505.3). The first part
of the chapter consists of two syllogistic *argumentationes*, (505.2-507.22),
in which the major premiss (either the *propositio* or the *ratio*) is what she
saw or what she was shown; and the conclusions drawn are identical:
there is no wrath in God, but only endless goodness and friendship. The
immediate object of this consideration appears to be that the
illumination is inevitably leading to contemplative union; for she con-

---

[239] *The Trinity,* 19.

firms her statement that wrath in God is an impossibility by a reference to *the soule that of his speciall grace seeth so ferforth of the hye marvelous goodnesse of god, that we be endlesly onyd to hym in loue* (505.7); and the soul in question, manifestly, is herself. As is indicated in the annotations to this chapter, Julian is not merely reflecting on the Pauline and Johannine teaching on the loving union of God with every soul in grace; the divine goodness is present to her in the person of the risen and glorified Christ:

> I saw full truly that where oure lorde aperyth, pees is takyn and wrath hath no stede (506.13).

In the risen and glorified Christ are the Father and the Spirit, are endless might and endless goodness as well as endless wisdom. She develops here the traditional teaching that the God who is in some way consciously present to us in consolation, when we are aware of the Spirit producing in us his fruits (cf. 507.21 note), is equally present in the darkness of the contemplative's desolation, and that this is the experience of our sinful nature, a presence which is manifest as soon as we perceive our need for his forgiveness:

> that same endlesse goodnesse contynually tretyth in vs a pees agaynst oure wrath and our contraryouse fallyng, and makyth vs to see oure nede with a true drede, myghtely to seke vnto god to haue forgyvenesse with a gracious desyer of oure saluacyon (507.25).

Here she is reiterating, but with a much firmer and more assured comprehension of the Trinitarian mystery, all that she saw in the first revelation of God's goodness and his homely loving (cf. chapter 5, pp. 299.309). She is writing, too, of her own apparently frequent experience over twenty years of what she evaluates as faltering contemplative perseverance: tribulation, disquiet, woe, blindness and *pronyte*. She concludes by describing, now in the context of the Western tradition's anagogical interpretation of 'Jerusalem' as the symbol of everlasting peace, how the heavenly fulfilment will mean that we shall be as pleased with ourselves and our fellow-Christians as we shall be with God and with all his works.

Julian has already indicated, in the long series of contemplative insights and reflections upon them which are introduced in Revelation XIII by the locution *Synne is behouely* (405.13), that compunction of heart is a virtue which is essential to contemplative life and prayer. The constant tradition, in the East as in the West,[240] is that shame and sorrow

---

[240] Irenée Hausherr: *Penthos*.

for sin are linked with a proper fear of the divine retribution. Julian here writes, out of her considerable knowledge of the Western tradition, the precise truth that it is the common teaching of the Church and also the feeling of every true contemplative who treasures the tradition, *that the blame of oure synnes contynually hangyth vppon vs, fro þe furst man in to the tyme that we come vppe in to hevyn* (511.11). Yet it is equally true, not merely from what God has seen fit to show her but from her prayerful understanding of Scriptural texts such as that quoted in the annotation to 510.4, that God guards, watches over and protects his own, no matter what man's judgment may be. (The *Cloud*-author makes a like observation, when he writes of sinners who have become contemplatives.)[241] Yet the clarity with which she sees both 'dooms' only intensifies her anxiety; as she states her dilemma with the logic of the trained scholastic's *ratiocinatio, How may this be?* (511.10), she is not dismissing it, but merely sharpening its horns. It is, however, not simply a problem in logic, but a real cause of suffering to many a good and simple contemplative; and she is no longer, as in the short text, ex-pounding with lyrical intensity a philosophical conundrum — *A wriched synne, whate ert þou ...?* (271.26 e.s.). What she does here, after she has reflected on the nature of her longing for relief from her fear and per-plexity (which, again, her training leads her to set out as another *ratiocinatio*, in a dialogue with the Lord), is to formulate a simple petition, prefaced by an ejaculation:

> A, lorde Jhesu, kyng of blysse, how shall I be esyde, who shall tell me and tech me that me nedyth to wytt, if I may not at this tyme se it in the? (512.36)

When, of course, she protests that what she is asking for is a 'low — common — thing' (512.30), we may justly suspect her of art, of the rhetoricians' *captatio benevolentiae,* especially when we perceive how deeply complex is the Lord's simple-seeming *exemplum*. Were it not that for twenty years she persevered in prayer, and preserved her confident, child-like expectation that in the end divine help would be given to her, she might well have been hoist with her own petard. What emerges as wholly admirable is that she was able, despite her constant anxiety and lack of knowing, to make a coherent whole of the short text and yet in it to suppress any reference to her prayer for relief and to the showing, still at that time dark, mysterious, troubling, which had been given in answer to the prayer.

[241] Hodgson, *Cloud,* 64-65.

Though the editors have insisted that Revelation XIV in the long text, from chapter 41 to chapter 63, is a unified showing 'for prayer', they have sought to make it equally clear that the long text here differs radically from the short in every way except one: in both texts, Julian is at pains to reproduce faithfully the visions and locutions of her showings, and the order in which she received them, apart only from the suppression in the short text of all that has to do with the *wonderfull example of a lorde that hath a servannt* (513.3). The annotations to the two texts remark how dramatically her theological, literary, rhetorical and scholastic skills and the breadth of her reading developed during the period which passed (how long this was we have no means of knowing) between the publication of the short text and her final redaction of the long version. She also leaves it to her readers to discover for themselves the nature of these skills and how she may have acquired them; our almost complete lack of biographical information, and the benefits which such ignorance may bring to scholarship, have already been remarked. We know so little about Julian the woman in the first place because she herself plainly considered that curiosity about her personal history would be irrelevant to the purposes of her book. What she does undertake to describe, in chapter 51, succeeding with remarkable clarity, is her contemplative method, under the guidance of the Holy Spirit, with regard to the content of all the showings, and with particular application to the parable of the lord and the servant, since in this *mysty example the pryvytes of the reuelacyon be yet moch hyd* (519.71). She tells us that, even before she received, early in 1393, special additional insights into the parable, she had found that in her private prayer (which, naturally, had as its centre the content of her showings) she was able to distinguish three kinds of contemplative understanding, or rather three modes ('properties' is her word) of the one inner knowledge:

> The furst is the begynnyng of techyng that I vnderstode ther in in the same tyme. The secunde is the inwarde lernyng that I haue vnderstonde there in sythen. The thyrd is alle the hole revelation fro the begynnyng to the ende whych oure lorde god of his goodnes bryngyth oftymes frely to the syght of my vnderstondyng. And theyse thre be so onyd, as to my vnderstondyng, that I can nott nor may deperte them. And by theyse thre as one I haue techyng wherby I ow to beleue and truste in oure lorde god, that of the same goodnesse that he shewed it and for the same end, ryght so of the same goodnes and for the same end he shall declare it to vs when it is his wyll (519.76).

What she is writing here, and what follows until she recounts the locution which introduces Revelation XV (chapter 64, 620.13 e.s.), concern her prayer, how and with what gifts she applies herself to the traditional contemplative processes, reading, meditating, praying and contemplating:

> ... lectio ... meditatio, oratio, contemplatio. Haec est scala claustralium qua de terra in coelum sublevantur, gradibus quidem distincta paucis, immensae tamen et incredibilis magnitudinis, cujus extrema pars terrae innixa est, superior vero nubes penetrat et coelorum secreta rimatur.[242]

She enumerates what she has been given: 'the beginning of teaching' — the revelations themselves in their due order, the content of which is predominantly the word of God (as the annotations consistently show), spoken directly to her in the context of her own formation and sacred learning; this, for Julian, is 'lectio'. Then there is the 'inward learning' — her divinely-assisted reflection upon the 'lectio' over a period of twenty years, her *spiritualis intelligentia*. Finally, there is her gift of total recall of what she has seen or heard. Although Julian is quick to refer this ability entirely to immediate divine action, she takes no pains, as we might do, to distinguish between natural and supernatural gifts; the useful terms 'acquired' and 'infused' for describing two kinds of contemplative gifts and the modes of relationship between God and man in prayer are of a much later coinage (see the annotation to 519.76). As Jean Leclercq has pointed out, discussing the Biblical imagination:

> Another important factor explained by rumination and reminiscence is the power of imagination of the medieval man. Exuberant as this faculty is, it possesses on their part, however, a vigour and a preciseness which we find it difficult to understand. We are used to seeing, almost without looking at them unless with a distracted eye, printed or moving pictures. We are fond of abstract ideas. Our imagination having become lazy seldom allows us any longer to do anything but dream. But in the men of the Middle Ages it was vigorous and active. It permitted them to picture, to 'make present', to see beings with all the details provided by the texts: the colours and dimensions of things, the clothing, bearing and actions of the people, the complex environment in which they move. They liked to describe them and, so to speak, recreate them, giving very sharp relief to images and feelings. The words of the sacred text never failed to produce a strong impression on the mind. The Biblical words did not become trite; people never got used to them.[243]

[242] Colledge and Walsh, *Guigues II,* 84.
[243] *The Love of Learning,* 93.

Thus it is that when

> ... twenty yere after the tyme of the shewyng saue thre monthys I had techyng inwardly as I shall sey: It longyth to the to take hede to alle þe propertes and the condescions that were shewed in the example, though þe thyngke that it be mysty and indefferent to thy syght (520.86),

Julian was wholly capable of carrying out to the letter this direction, by making herself imaginatively present to the parabolic picture, in all its wealth of detail, drawn for her so many years before: the manner of the lord's sitting, the place where he sat, the colour and fashion of his garments, his facial expression; how the servant stood, where and how he went, how he was dressed and how he held himself. But this was an exercise not only of the imagination, but also of spiritual discernment. Just as the original showing of the parable was not merely an imaginative sight —

> Whych syght was shewed double in þe lorde, and the syght was shewed double in the servannt. That one perty was shewed gostly in bodely lycknesse. That other perty was shewed more gostly withoute bodely lycknes (514.4)

so here she understands that she is to 'behold' (that is, 'contemplate' — cf. 491.16 note) the lord's *nobley and his goodnes within* (521.95) and the servant's *inwarde goodnes and his vnlothfulnesse* (521.98). Again, the distinction of historical exegesis is implied between *historica interpretatio* and *spiritualis intelligentia*. The parable itself as Julian now recounts it, postulating these distinctions as her principles of contemplative investigation, leave us in no doubt that between 1373 and 1393 she had become thoroughly acquainted with, adept in the practice of 'mediaeval exegesis' in the technical sense in which this term has been used by every commentator since Henri de Lubac published his monumental work. [244] The evidence that for Julian the content of the revelations constituted *lectio divina* has already been observed; this is especially true of the parable-revelation, and it is stressed by the subsequent reflections. In the annotations to these passages, some one hundred and fifty Scriptural allusions have been identified, and, no doubt, if the editors knew their Vulgate as well as Julian did, they would have found even more. There may be those who will think that some of these identifications, and, indeed, the whole treatment which Julian has been given in this book as Scripture scholar, Latinist, rhetorician and theologian, reflect chiefly the editors' subjective responses to her work. Against this, they

---

[244] *Exégèse médiévale; les quatre sens de l'Ecriture.*

would appeal to the opinion of scholars of the eminence of de Lubac and Leclercq, the second of whom has written:

> This way of uniting reading, meditation and prayer, this 'meditative prayer', as William of St. Thierry calls it, had great influence on religious psychology. It occupies and engages the whole person in whom the Scriptures take root, later on to bear fruit. It is this deep impregnation with the words of Scripture that explains the extremely important phenomenon of reminiscence whereby the verbal echoes so excite the meaning that a mere allusion will spontaneously evoke whole quotations and, in turn, a Scriptural phrase will suggest quite naturally allusions elsewhere in the sacred books. Each word is like a hook, so to speak; it catches hold of one or several others which become linked together and make up the fabric of the exposé. [245]

The editors consider that the method which Julian employed and the structure which she achieved, throughout her work but especially in this Revelation XIV, are very precisely described by Leclercq; and that he could so delineate the characteristics of a writer with whom he is probably unacquainted, certainly not in her original language, can only point to the pervading influence in her of the great Western spiritual writers whose modes of thought and of writing he has devoted his scholarly life to examining.

As was indicated some years ago,[246] the servant in the parable is none other than the 'Suffering Servant of God', as he (and his Lord) are depicted in the 'servant-songs' of Isaias. Furthermore, Julian's first reflection upon this servant identifies him with Adam, with Adam's friendship with God and with his fall, though she hastens to add that the servant is not wholly identifiable with the historical Adam (cf. 519.67-70), that is, with the narrative of Genesis 1.27-28, 3.8, 17-23. All this accords well with a fundamental principle of mediaeval exegesis, that the Old Testament has to be 'opened', examined, so that the incarnate Word can be found. Thus the parable is offered in the form of a preacher's *exemplum*. The mediaeval preacher is pre-eminently an *expositor veteris testamenti*, so that he may truly be a *dispensator novi testamenti*.[247]

> Littera gesta docet, quid credas allegoria,
> Moralis quid agas, quo tendas anagogia.[248]

---

[245] *The Love of Learning*, 91.

[246] J. Walsh: *The Revelations of Divine Love*, 31-32; and cf. 513.3 note.

[247] *Exégèse médiévale* 2 673, citing Augustine, *Contra Faustinum*.

[248] Augustine of Dacia, O.P.; cf. Walther: *Proverbia sententiaeque*, no. 13899; and see H. de Lubac, *Exégèse médiévale* 1 23.

This distich, opening with the aplomb and the metre of a Martial epigram, even though the rest of it is doggerel, achieved epigrammatic status, and is an accepted mnemonic for the objects of a tradition ancient in the time of Cassian.[249] Julian's parable shows that in her times and environment the tradition still prevailed; this is particularly evident in the importance for her of Gregory the Great's teaching.[250] We may take it that for her the *res gestae* which build the foundation of the parable are contained in the first chapters of Genesis, but are also adumbrated in the Isaian prophecies. She is well aware, as she constructs chapter 51, that she is embarking on the use of Scriptural allegory, in which the *superficies verborum* is there to lead us to the *intima sententiarum*.[251] It cannot be accidental that in writing of the first showing of the parable, Julian should use the adverb *full mystely* (513.2; and cf. note), or that the later remark concerning the parable, *For twenty yere after the tyme of the shewyng saue thre monthys I had techyng inwardly* (520.86), should apply to it the epithets 'misty' and 'indifferent':

> It longyth to the to take hede to alle þe properties and the condescions that were shewed in the example, though þe thyngke that it be mysty and indefferent to thy syght (520.87).

It would seem from the contexts, especially of the second, the locution enjoining prayerful and studious acceptance of the entire revelation, where the showing's obscurity is stressed by the adjective *indefferent* (see 521.89 note), that Julian intends us to understand by these epithets what the exegetes called *allegorica, allegorice*. Gregory the Great writes of allegory as the *historia mystica* of the sacred text;[252] and the established synonyms for the word and the idea are *mysticus ordo, mystica interpretatio*.[253] One cannot, of course, use in these contexts the English word 'mystical' in the vague and wholly irresponsible fashion in which it has in modern times been employed; in this century, probably no one did more to popularize and to debase the term than Hope Allen. When one writes of mediaeval allegory as the 'mystical sense of Scripture', one is referring to the Pauline *Mysterium Christi,* the *sacramentum absconditum* (Ephesians 3.1-9), hidden in God from the beginning and now to be revealed in the apostolic preaching. So Julian writes, after the allegory's first showing:

---

[249] *Exégèse médiévale* 1 190-192.
[250] See supra, IX 15, Revelation XIII; and cf. *Exégèse médiévale* 1 187-190.
[251] Ibid. 2 483 note 1.
[252] Ibid. 2 493 e.s.
[253] H. de Lubac: "'Typologie" et "allégorisme'", 187.

... the full vnderstandyng of this mervelouse example was not gevyn me in that tyme. In whych mysty example the pryvytes of the reuelacyon be yet moch hyd (519.70).

The reality hidden in God is revealed to individual men at the moment when it is realized in Christ,[254] but only in so far as it is addressed to each individual man: 'Sunt enim quibus nondum natus est Christus'.[255] Elsewhere, Bernard had written: 'Semel locutus est deus, sed continua et perpetua locutio est'.[256] This mystery of Christ is inseparable also from the mystery of the Church. Augustine had written: 'Totum omnium scripturarum mysterium Christum et ecclesiam (confitetur)'.[257] Thus, as soon as Julian has understood that the lord of the parable is God, she also understands that the servant

> was shewed for Adam, that is to sey oone man was shewed that tyme and his fallyng to make there by to be vnderstonde how god beholdyth alle manne and his fallyng. For in the syghte of god alle man is oone man, and oone man is alle man (522.101),

'all mankind', as she will write later, 'that will be saved by the sweet Incarnation and the Passion of Christ' (537.254). Finally, allegory has a doctrinal quality. Since its central object is the divinity of the incarnate Word — and it is precisely thus that the parable in the end unfolds for Julian — it presupposes faith. This knowledge, *cognitio*, which is *mystica, occulta,* of the whole Christ can be revealed only to the internal eyes of the soul, the eyes of faith illumined by the Gospel.[258] Julian, through the constant contemplation of her revelations, is convinced that there is no discord between them and the common faith of the Church, and that

> I haue techyng wherby I ow to beleue and truste in oure lorde god, that of the same goodnesse that he shewed it and for the same end, ryght so of the same goodnes and for the same end he shall declare it to vs when it is his wyll (520.82).

As Gregory had written, allegory not only presupposes faith but builds it up.[259]

Julian, in her first reflections on what she was shown 'for prayer',

---

[254] *Exégèse médiévale* 2 397.

[255] Ibid. 2 566, citing Bernard, *Sermones de diversis* 44.

[256] Ibid. 2 567; *Sermones de diversis* 5.

[257] Ibid. 2 500; *Enarratio in Psalmum* 79.

[258] Ibid. 2 522-525.

[259] Ibid. 2 530, quoting *Homiliarum in Evangelia II,* Sermon 40, and many similar aphorisms.

began by considering how she (and we) should conduct ourselves in all
that concerns our relationship with God, in the life which is prayer (cf.
chapter 41, 460.3 e.s.). Here we have the parable's moral or
tropological sense (*Moralis quid agas*); the Word is always addressed to
us, and to how we live in its light. [260] In fact, every grace for which
Julian ever asked, including the bodily sickness, was so that she might
live more to God's glory (cf. 287.30). Through the tropological sense,
the mystery of Christ, prefigured by the allegory, is made real and actual in the Christian soul;[261] and this is an interiorization which takes
place in the present moment, 'moraliter, intrinsecus, quotidie, hodie'. [262]
So Julian from the start recounts the actions of the lord and the servant
in the present tense: *a lorde that hath a servannt ... the lorde syttyth ... the servannt stondyth ... goyth ... stertyth ... rynnyth ... fallyth.* Gregory had written
that the tropological sense is that which tends to the infusion of divine
love: (Mira atque ineffabilis sacri eloquii virtus agnoscitur cum
supremo amore animus penetratur). [263] So, after the enumeration of the
servant's *vij grett paynes* (515.22; the number seven, de Lubac observes,
exercises a special fascination for the mediaeval exegete),[264] Julian
remarks upon the servant's virtues, his meekness and endurance
(516.32), his good will and great desire (517.44), and upon the various
aspects of the lord's love for him (516.38). She is, of course, writing in
the tradition of the monastic or contemplative development of the
tropological sense, as she extracts the various virtues of the lord and the
servant from their general appearance and demeanour. Of the lord, for
example, she writes:

> The blewhed of the clothyng betokenyth his stedfastnesse, the brownhed
> of his feyer face with the semely blackhede of the eyen was most ac-
> cordyng to shew his holy sobyrnesse, the largnesse of his clothyng, whych
> was feyer flammyng about, betokenyth þat he hath beclosyd in hym all
> hevyns and all endlesse joy and blysse (526.153).

At the same time, as has been noticed more than once in the comparison
of the short and long texts, she avoids the tendency among monastic
exegetes to dismiss all other forms of spiritual living but their own
which de Lubac observes especially in the Cistercians and the Vic-

---

[260] Ibid. 2 551-552.
[261] Ibid. 2 557, quoting Origen: 'Vere impletur in nobis'.
[262] Ibid. 2 562-563, citing Adam the Scot and Gregory the Great.
[263] Ibid. 2 569, citing *In Ezechielem*.
[264] Ibid. 1 131.

torines. [265] In editing the long text she deliberately suppresses every indication in the short that she may be addressing herself only to those who are cloistered. What she is able to draw from the parable, in its allusion, for example, to Isaias 53.4-7 and to the comment of Paul to the whole Corinthian community, is that

> thus hath oure good lorde Jhesu taken vppon hym all oure blame; and therfore oure fader may nor wyll no more blame assigne to vs than to hys owne derwurthy son Jhesu Cryst (535.232, and cf. notes).

Though she understands well and appreciates that mystical tropology which is the renewed experience of the interiorized savour and joy of the allegory, she is never guilty of emphasizing a personal interior life to the detriment of the social and eschatological elements of Christian spirituality. In the last analysis, as the S2 scribe insists, these *revelations of þe unutterable loue of God in Jesus Christ* were *vouchsafed ... to all his dear friends and lovers* (734.29 app.), and not simply to cloistered contemplatives.

*Quo tendas anagogia*: Julian is very much at home with the anagogical sense of Scripture, which for so many of the Fathers expresses the whole of the Christian mystery, and, as such, absorbs the allegorical and tropological senses, and makes the synthesis of the *sensus spiritualis seu plenior*.[266] So much of her contemplation throughout the revelations (and signally in the first, which sets the tone and temper of the rest) is anagogical; it could with justice be described as the meeting place of her developing understanding of Scripture and of the infused contemplative graces bestowed on her. The word itself, ἀναγωγή — 'subvectio', 'elevatio', is one which she very often renders. She writes of *a ledyng of my vnderstandyng in to the lorde* (516.41), *my vnderstandyng was led in to the lorde* (527.158), *now was my vnderstandyng ledde ageyne in to the furst* (517.45), *oure good lorde ledde forth my vnderstandyng in syght and in shewyng* (518.62), all in this chapter; and much earlier, she writes of a *bodely exsample* very reminiscent of the lord-and-servant parable that it *was shewde so hygh that thys mannes hart myght be rauyssched and almost foryet hym selfe for ioy* (314.43).

Yet perhaps the most anagogical of all Julian's experiences was

---

[265] Ibid. 2 577-578, quoting, among others, Walter Daniel, writing of Aelred of Rievaulx 'qui me genuit per evangelium dei ad vitam S. Benedicti'; he is alluding to Aelred's own comparison of Benedict with Paul, applying to Benedict I Corinthians 4.15.

[266] Ibid. 2 631-633.

Revelation IX, when, like Paul (II Corinthians 12.2), her understanding was lifted up to where she saw three heavens (383.8). It is to this experience, and its link with her sight of the suffering Christ (382.3 e.s.) that she reverts as she contemplates the parable, an anagogy which is both doctrinal and contemplative,[267] one which echoes Gregory's classical statement, 'Et ipsa civitas, scilicet sancta ecclesia, quae regnatura in caelo, adhuc laborat in terra':[268]

> For all mankynde that shall be savyd by the swete incarnacion and the passion of Crist, alle is the manhode of Cryst. For he is the heed, and we be his membris, to whych membris the day and þe tyme is vnknowyn whan every passyng wo and sorow shall haue an eende, and the everlastyng joy and blysse shall be fulfyllyd, whych day and tyme for to see, all the company of hevyn longyth or desyreth. And all that be vnder hevyn, whych shall come theder, ther way is by longyng and desyeryng; whych desyeryng and longyng was shewed in the seruant stondyng before the lorde, or ellys thus in the son stondyng afore the fadyr in Adam kyrtyll. For the longyng and desyer of all mankynd that shall be safe aperyd in Jhesu (537.254).

Here we have an expression of the whole Christian mystery in which the anagogical sense embraces the allegorical and the tropological.[269] A similar *ascensio mentis* through the three spiritual senses is equally evident in her progressive consideration of the place where the lord sits and of the ravine where the servant lay after his fall. The ravine was *alang, harde and grevous* (516.30 and note). The lord was seated *symply on the erth, bareyn and deserte, aloone in wyldernesse* (523.120 and note). Later this landscape becomes the scene of the servant's toil as a gardener, *deluyng and dykyng and swetyng and turnyng the erth vp and down* (530.195 e.s. and notes), the place where is the treasure *whych the lorde lovyd* (529.185 e. s. and notes); and finally it becomes the city of God, the city of rest and peace which is at once man's soul, redeemed and perfected, and the New Jerusalem, the bride of Christ:

> Now is the spouse, goddys son, in pees with his lovyd wyfe, whych is the feyer maydyn of endlesse joy. Now syttyth the son, very god and very man, in his cytte in rest and in pees, whych his fader hath dyʒte to hym of endlesse purpose, and the fader in the son, and the holy gost in the fader and in þe son (545.326 e.s. and notes).

---

[267] Ibid. 2 624-625.
[268] Ibid. 2 627.
[269] Ibid. 2 631-633.

'Allegoria', Bede had written, 'est cum verbis sive rebus mysticis praesentia Christi et ecclesiae sacramenta signantur'.[270] Throughout her final investigation of the parable at the Lord's behest — *It longyth to the to take hede to alle þe propertes and the condescions that were shewed in the example* (520.87), she is seeking and finding, in its *res* and *verba*, the presence of the incarnate Word in his suffering past, 'in the days of his flesh' (Hebrews 5.7), in his glorified present, and in his mystical body, the Church: *he is the heed, and we be his membris* (537.256). What Julian has achieved in this chapter, through the contemplation of the parable against the background of the whole sequence of the revelations, is a unified spiritual exegesis in which the three senses, allegory, tropology and anagogy, are constantly and easily identifiable, but, none the less, inextricable. It is Paul who is the father of such exegesis, and it appears to be from her study of the Pauline letters in the Vulgate (there are at least thirty such allusions in chapter 51 alone) that she has chiefly acquired her exegetical skill, based on her understanding of revelation (whether this be Scripture and tradition or her own contemplative graces) and of the nature of Christ's Church. Her life of prayer is from first to last 'In aedificationem corporis Christi, donec occurramus omnes in unitatem fidei et cognitionis filii dei, in virum perfectum, in mensuram aetatis plenitudinis Christi' (Ephesians 4.12-13).

The opening paragraph of chapter 52,

> And thus I saw that god enjoyeth that he is our fader, and god enjoyeth that he is our moder, and god enjoyeth that he is our very spouse, and our soule his lovyd wyfe. And Crist enjoyeth þat he is our broder, and Jhesu enioyeth that he is our savyour (546.2),

appears to be the *culmen contemplationis* of the parable, her beholding and sharing in the joy of the Trinity in their own divine activity, which terminates in the incarnate Word, the glorified and risen Christ in his relationship with the Church in glory. This is a vision similar to that granted to John on Patmos of the heavenly liturgy: 'I saw a great multitude clothed in white garments standing before the throne and in the presence of the Lamb ... and they cried out with a loud voice ... 'Blessing and glory and praise and thanksgiving and honour and power to our God, for ever and ever'" (Apocalypse 7.9-12). But in addition, Julian's sight has comprehended the various aspects of God's relationship in Christ with mankind, the origins of her 'five joys': Father/Son, mother/child, husband/wife, brother/sister, Redeemer/redeemed.

---

[270] Ibid. 2 500, citing *De tabernaculo et vasis ejus* I 6.

The chapter proper begins with a renewed reflection on this last relationship of Christ with us as our Saviour. The working out of this salvation involves us (as it did him) in *a mervelous medelur both of wele and of woo* (546.9). Julian establishes this proposition by an *argumentatio perfectissima,* based on her understanding of the relations between the first Adam, as natural parent of the human race, and the second Adam, Christ, the race's spiritual parent, and of the participation of all the children in the life of both parents. In the *exornatio* of the argumentation (547.13-549.33), she makes it clear that we still have, as the chief object of our attention, unitive prayer: the mercy and grace which work in us, when God *of his goodnesse openyth the ey of oure vnderstanding* (547.18), demand from us *holy assent þat we assent to god when we fele hym, truly wyllyng to be with hym with all oure herte, with all oure soule and with all oure myghte* (548.24), a Trinitarian allusion which is also a tropological exegesis of the great commandment: 'You must love the Lord your God with your whole heart and your whole soul and with all your might' (Luke 10.27).

In what follows, Julian elaborates what she has stated to be the second condition for unitive prayer at the very beginning of this revelation, *seker trust* (460.5). The foundation of this trust is the doctrine of Christ's two natures and his consequently two-fold relationship with us, his presence to us in his divinity and iv his glorified humanity. The divine power manifested in the raising up of Adam (the 'Harrowing of Hell'), which, characteristically, she sees as manifestations of the Lord's ruth and pity (549.44), operates equally in all those who fell with Adam. They are even now being raised *by the vertu of the passyon and þe deth of his deerwurthy son* (549.45). Our falling with Adam, as she stressed earlier in the revelation, is real enough, dreadful, shameful, sorrowful (502.23 e.s.); but there she adds, from her contemplation of the Suffering Servant who was bruised for our sins (Isaias 53.5), what is the cause of our deepest sorrow: *for oure synne is cause of Cristes paynes* (550.51). It is the sorrow of the contemplative, which leads to that 'sweet touching of grace' which may readily be experienced in the sacrament of penance, when we *wylfully amend vs vpon techyng of holy chyrch* (551.62). Like Bede and many another before her, Julian is ever conscious, in her consideration of sinfulness, of the evils of Pelagianism, which so easily drive a man to despair by robbing him of his hope; we must

> mekely know oure febylnes, wyttyng that we may nott stonde a twynglyng of an ey but with kepyng of grace, and reverently cleue to god, in hym oonly trustyng (551.66).

The showing of the parable has also enabled her to reconcile the apparently contradictory 'dooms' which earlier she had seen as threatening a conflict between her revelations and the teaching of the Church (487.13 e.s.). The solution lies *in þe doubyll chere in whych the lorde behelde þe fallyng of hys lovyd servant* (552.72). What the Church teaches is that we should accuse ourselves, both sacramentally and in prayer, to a Lord who is loving and merciful. This she now sees *in þe doubyll chere ... shewde ouȝtward*, whereas before this she has been aware only of *that other of inwarde endlesse loue and ryght* (552.75). What is more, this second, outward 'doom', which *is þe meke accusyng that oure good lorde askyth of vs* (552.80), is itself a grace:

> hym selfe wurkyth there it is, and this is the lower party of mannys lyfe (553.81),

and *it comyth downe to vs of the kynde loue of the selfe by grace* (553.87), the grace which belongs to the one unitive love which is the working of the Trinity.

In chapter 37, at the beginning of Revelation XIII, dealing with the divine compassion, Julian, in associating her awareness of her own sinfulness and the pain and sorrow which accompanied it with that of her fellow-Christians, 'all that shall be saved', was already writing, in the last version of her long text, in the light of the parable. Dealing there with what she here calls the *godly wylle that nevyr assentyd to synne ne nevyr shall* (555.12), she had taken it for granted that her readers would be acquainted with the principles of Augustinian psychology,[271] at least in the simplified form in which they are found, for instance, in the *Cloud*-author's disquisition on the powers of the soul[272] or in Hilton's *Scale* II[273] — a psychology which is the point of departure for all her teaching on the Trinity in its *operationes ad extra*. Now, here in chapter 53, she can repeat with assurance, and verbatim, what she has already written about the godly will, and she can add that this is the partial answer to her question — how can God love us in our sin? What she has seen in the parable, what she is now contemplating, is the good will which is God's first gift in the creation of the human soul of his servant, Christ, who is every man who will be saved in Christ, a creation which is participation in the divine being. Furthermore, she now sees (and for this understanding she is certainly in the debt of the monastic theologians,

---

[271] See *De Trinitate*, XII.

[272] Ed. Hodgson, 115 e.s.

[273] Underhill, 272-273.

and particularly of William of St. Thierry) that this teaching is no
novelty in her showings, but belongs, of the Lord's will, to the faith and
belief of the Church:

> There fore oure lorde wylle we know it in the feyth and the beleue, and
> namly and truly that we haue all this blessyd wyll hoole and safe in oure
> lorde Jhesu Crist, for that ech kynde that hevyn shall be fulfyllyd with
> behovyd nedys of goddys ryghtfulnes so to be knytt and onyd in hym that
> there in were kepte a substannce whych myght nevyr nor shulde be partyd
> from hym, and that thorow his awne good wyll in his endlesse forseing
> purpose (555. 16).

(Her contemplation here is in the fullest sense anagogical; she is seeing
Christ not only in his fall into the maiden's womb and into the pains of
his Passion (cf. 534. 222, 541. 294 e.s.), but in his union with the blessed
in glory, now and to the end of time.)

It would seem that the lines which follow (556. 23 e.s.) are in paren-
thesis. They may explain why the parable is still only a partial answer
to her desire (555. 9). She does not tell us why, but simply states: *yett the
redempcion and the agayne byeng of mannekynde is nedfull* (556. 24). Be that
as it may, the passage which precedes this, *There fore oure lorde wylle we
know it ...,* just cited, is clearly the proposition of an *argumentatio perfectissima,* of which the *ratio* now follows: *For I saw that god began nevyr to
loue mankynde* (557. 26). The *exornatio* of the argument (the *rationis confirmatio* runs from 557. 27, *for ryghte the same that mankynd ...,* to 557. 30,
*... knowen and lovyd fro without begynnyng in his ryghtfull entent*) must be
counted as one of the finest examples of Julian's polished prose, one
which demonstrates vividly the powers and the uses of the rhetorician's
art. It is an equally fine example of theological writing at its best, ex-
plaining with a wealth of Trinitarian detail, firmly based on Scripture
and tradition, all of it purposefully designed to draw out the *complexio*
(itself an echo of the prologue to John's gospel): *And thus is mannys soule
made of god, and in the same poynte knyte to god* (558. 39). It also shows us
Julian at prayer; in the depths of her soul she is aware of the Father
speaking his purpose (*entent*), and of the Son responding (*assent*) in the
Spirit (*full acorde*) who, as she had already written, *is the evyn loue whych is
in them both* (533. 218), concerning the *operatio ad extra* which is at once
creation, Incarnation, Passion and Resurrection, recapitulating all
mankind who, in Christ, are to come from and return, like himself, to
the Father in the same Spirit. God loves us, she sees in his eternal ut-
terance, and as soon as we exist we participate in the response to his
love. This love-made is the made-love, and it is thus attributed to the
Spirit, with the power of the Father and the wisdom of the Son per-
meating it.

As Julian penetrates further into the mystery of the incarnate Christ, still pondering the parable, speculating about the origins, divine and human, of the servant — *I marveylyd from wens the seruant came* (532.210) — she is, as very often, close to Paul and his Trinitarian teaching in the eighth chapter of Romans. Though it suits Julian here to translate into her own English the language of the schools, when she describes God as 'substantial kind unmade', and insists with Bede (cf. 559.45 note) that when we speak of *creatio ex nihilo*, we mean the 'inspiring' of the soul, her point is ultimately Pauline: there is nothing between man's soul and God, because 'nothing can separate us, neither now nor in the time to come, from the love of God which is ours in Christ Jesus' (Romans 8.38-39):

> In whych endlesse loue we be ledde and kepte of god, and nevyr shalle be lost; for he wyll that we know that oure soule is a lyfe, whych lyfe of hys goodnesse and his grace shall last in hevyn withou3t ende, hym lovyng, hym thangkyng, hym praysyng (559.51).

As Julian continues her reflection on the parable, in chapter 54, she seems to be especially aware of Johannine teaching: 'The Word was with God from the beginning ... the Word was made flesh ... to every one who received him, he gave the power to be the children of God ... the only begotten Son who is in the mind and heart of the Father, he has made him plain ... of his fulness we have all received' (John 1.1-18). Again she is concerned, by means of the tropological and anagogical exegesis of Scripture which the Church's tradition has taught her, to insist on the unity between the Church's faith and belief and what she continues to see in her contemplation of her revelations. Like the apostle, she is telling of what she has seen, and his purpose is also hers: 'What we have seen and heard we are telling you, that you also may have this union (*societatem*) ... with the Father and with his Son Jesus Christ ... and we write this so that you may rejoice, and that your joy may be full' (I John 1.3-4). So she describes the mutual indwelling, not, as do so many of her contemporaries (see 562.17 note), with respect to transforming union, but by oblique reference to John chapter 17, where Christ is praying, with full confidence that the Father hears him, for all believers, 'that they may be one, as thou, Father, in me and I in thee, that they may be one in us'. The sight that accompanies this belief is indeed *full of prevytes* (539.271); and so, with a theologian's care, she insists that though

> I sawe no dyfference betwen God and oure substance, but as it were all god ... yett my vnderstandyng toke that oure substance is in god, that is to sey that god is god and oure substance is a creature in god (562.17).

But the truth of Scripture and tradition remains; Christ's place is the
Father and he is the Father's place (John 17.23-24), and we are the Son's
place, and his place is ours (cf. 563.23 note).

Aware, however, that those for whom she is writing may have too
limited a view of the faith of Holy Church in this Trinitarian doctrine,
she also stresses the tropological sense of all these Johannine texts; love
leads ('If any man love me ...'), and the gift of indwelling is equally the
gift of unitive love. But it is faith that gives understanding of this:

> for it is nouȝt eles but a ryght vnderstandyng with trew beleue and suer
> truste of oure beyng, þat we be in god and in vs, whych we se nott
> (564.30).

This is a power received when Christ becomes incarnate, when our sensual nature is linked with our substance, that substance in God which
becomes ours and becomes human when Christ becomes human by the
power of the Spirit in the womb of the virgin (cf. Luke 1.35). Early in
Revelation XIV, in chapter 43, she had written of the prayer of faith
which is itself a participation in God's rightfulness:

> thus he techyth vs to pray and myghtyly to trust that we shalle haue it;
> for he beholdyth vs in loue, and wylle make vs perteyner of his good wylle
> and dede (475.6).

This brings an awareness of ourselves as God's children which does not
come from normal human sight or understanding. So she sees faith as
the form of all man's knowing and loving, by means of which we
believe, hope and love what we do not see. This powerful presence has
for its sign baptism, which effects its initiation, that baptism by which
we become God's children and followers and members of the Mystical
Body.

So far, Julian has related the mutual indwelling which she has come
to see contemplatively in the relationship between the lord and the servant with the Trinitarian teaching of John and Paul, as interpreted
allegorically and tropologically by traditional exegesis. Now, in chapter
55, she turns again to Christ as she saw him in the ninth revelation (cf.
566.11 note), as leading us where we are to go (*quo tendas — anagogia*).
As is observed (565.4 note), there is allusion to a text of Paul's which
she must have known well, in Ephesians 5.25-32, where the Vulgate
makes him write of the 'sacramentum in Christo et in ecclesia'. Julian
writes of *Crist, vs alle havyng in hym that shall be savyd by hym* (565.3).
Gregory the Great had written: 'Christus et ecclesia una persona est',[274]

---

[274] *Moralia* XIV xlix 1; PL 75 1068.

the *persona* which Augustine had called 'duo in carne una';[275] and Julian writes: *Crist in his body myȝtely beryth vs vp in to hevyn* (565.2).

Hope is the virtue of anagogical contemplation, just as it is the prerequisite for Julian's unitive prayer. It is the virtue which flows from our incorporation into Christ, and it becomes operative in the first moment of our separate existence:

> And what tyme oure soule is enspyred in oure body, in whych we be made sensuall, as soone mercy and grace begynne to werke, havyng of vs cure and kepyng with pytte and loue, in whych werkyng the holy gost formyth in oure feyth hope that we shall come agayne vp abovyn to our substannce (566.16).

It is, however, an existence in Christ, as is seen in the sign of its inception, *as soone mercy and grace begynne to werke,* that baptism in which the formal cause is the Holy Spirit, *in whych werkyng the holy gost formyth in oure feyth hope.* She also sees Christ in relation to his Mystical Body as life ('I am ... the life', John 14.6), and suggests that the *poynt* of the divine presence is also the *poynt* of union between soul and body (where 'point' seems to indicate time — see 226.1 note — and place — see 338.20 note — together):

> for in the same poynt that oure soule is made sensuall, in the same poynt is the cytte of god, ordeyned to hym fro without begynnyng (567.25).

Again she reverts to the ecclesial implications in her contemplation of the lord and the servant, as she refers to the divine gift to man of growth and alludes to Christ's own human growth:

> all the gyftes that god may geue to the creature he hath gevyn to his son Jhesu for vs, whych gyftes he wonnyng in vs hath beclosyd in hym in to the tyme that we be waxyn and growyn, oure soule with oure body and oure body with oure soule (567.31).

It is here, as she reflects, with William of St. Thierry, on 'imago et similitudo' (cf. 568.40 note), that she offers us a definition of her contemplative understanding of this aspect of the parable, to which she had been led by God:

> Thys syght was fulle swete and mervelous to beholde, pesyble and restfull, suer and delectabyll (568.42).

It is perhaps in this reflection on the union of soul and body in Christ incarnate and in his brethren that she begins to see more clearly what

---

[275] *Enarrationes,* Psalm 140.3; CCSL 40 2027.

before she had simply stated as a fact, mankind's need of the redemptive activity of the whole Trinity in Christ. But she sees it first in the revelation of the person of Christ in his Incarnation, and only then as she regards the person suffering: *The lower perty, whych is sensualyte, sufferyd for the saluacion of mankynd* (569.51). This is not abstract theologizing; Julian has come to understand it through her own experience of desolation during the showings of the Passion.

In the parable, the final object of this showing which had seemed to her *mysty and indefferent* (521.89) is Christ and the Father in the unity of the Spirit working out man's salvation. Faith and knowledge, given her 'for prayer', led her to persevere in prayer here *in via*, and so she was given self-awareness. As chapter 56 begins: *For oure soule is so depe growndyd in god and so endlesly tresoryd* ..., she is thinking of Colossians 3.3 (see 570.3 and note). It is only when we are risen with Christ that we shall see ourselves in him. So she returns to her teaching on contemplation, to that desire for God which leads us to seek the hidden treasure which is the life of union with him. She accepts that we can only know the nature of body, soul and spirit and how they are kept together (570.3) in so far as we are shown *from wens the seruant came* (532.210). So she examines again the whole course of the parable: the servant's fall, his preparation of the treasure, the sitting and the standing (571.12 e.s.) In the sixteenth revelation she will write more of the process of assimilation to Christ, which is our becoming *holy in this holynesse* (560.64). Meanwhile, like Paul, we must share Christ's Passion (cf. 573.34 e.s., Philippians 3.10), if we are to enter the depths of his charity (cf. 576.8, Ephesians 3.18-19).

*I had in perty touchyng*, she writes (573.38). Here she reinforces what she has just been expounding about growth in the unitive life by this reference to her own contemplative experience. This divine activity, the dynamic relationships of the persons of the Trinity can be 'felt' in us when God wishes to 'touch' us, that is, to make us aware of such activity in a way which transcends our normal intellectual and affective processes, because of our existential participation in the divine life. We are in some way integral to God's substance by virtue of our creation *ex nihilo*. At the same time (Julian reiterates this teaching in a variety of images and concepts) this activity can be known and is known only because it is revealed in the mystery of the incarnate Word. She finds the English with which to convey the Trinitarian teaching of the Latin theologians. Mercy and grace (Son and Spirit), eternally flowing from substantial kindness (Father, and also the triune God) complete their *missio ad extra* (the Son is sent by the Father, the Spirit by both Father and Son) by returning man in Christ to his source:

> Of this substancyall kyndnesse mercy and grace spryngyth and spredyth
> in to vs, werkyng all thynges in fulfyllyng of oure joy (574.39).

She shows art and skill and she indicates her multiple triadic terminology by the singular pronoun 'it':

> It be thre propertes in one goodnes, and where that one werkyth alle
> werkyn in the thynges whych be now longyng to vs (574.44).

Her knowledge of the Trinitarian operations and attributes is
theological, but it is also contemplative, a beginning, growing
knowledge in love of the three persons:

> God wylle we vnderstande, desyeryng with all oure hart and alle oure
> strengh to haue knowyng of them evyr more and more in to the tyme that
> we be fulfyllyd; for fully to know them and clerely to se them is not elles
> but endles joy and blysse that we shall haue in hevyn, whych god wyll we
> begynne here in knowyng of his loue (574.47).

The 'touch', however, is not merely in our reason or the higher part of
our nature, though it has there its ground. It is in our sensuality, which
Christ, second person of the Trinity, has taken. The Incarnation, the
sending of the second person into human existence, and his
glorification through Passion and death, is not only the term of the
Trinitarian operations; it constitutes a second creation for mankind.
The Spirit, proceeding from Father and Son, was 'sent' into Christ's
human, sensual soul to join it to his human substance, spirit. All this
Julian sees as the manner and the order of human endowment, that is,
of all those who are destined for final fulfilment, by the working of the
Trinity, through *kynde, mercy and grace.*

In Revelation XVI Julian will show that the Trinity *made mannes soule
as feyer, as good, as precious as he myght make it a creature* (644.41). Here, in
chapter 57, she states why this is so: because our (that is, Christ's)
human substance is a participation in God's substance, the Father's will
is fulfilled in the will of his creature, Christ and all that will be saved in
him (the destiny of those who are not to be saved, if there be any such,
was never shown to her). This salvation, she insists, is the restoration
and the fulfilment of the sensual soul of man, which, by virtue of its
substance, participates in the endowment of his substantial spirit, but
through the operation of mercy and grace (Son and Spirit) out of
Christ's spiritual fulness, *by mesure* (576.6; cf. John 1.16).

Julian is repeating here something of what she has written in the
previous two chapters, because, it would seem, there is a mutuality

achieved between God and man in the eternal activity of the Trinity, a mutuality which itself is eternal, because the Son accepted to become man *ab aeterno* (cf. 557.30):

> for oure kynde, whych is the hyer party, is knytte to god in þe makyng, and god is knytt to oure kynde, whych is the lower party in oure flessch takyng (577.17).

Thus in Christ all the Trinitarian operations, of which the Father is the *principium originans*, are comprehended. The incarnate Word is the term of the divine activity; there is no other. So faith is described as our participation in and reception of the Word made flesh, who *for loue ... made mankynd, and for the same loue hym selfe wolde become man* (578.25), in his relationship, that is, with the triune God. Hence Julian can write that faith is grounded in us and we in it; the relationship, by gift, is instantaneously mutual. On our side, it is a knowledge which has its impact on the lower part of our life which Christ has assumed. In him, every mode of his human relationship with his Father is available to us — the reflection of God's life by human kind as he prepares it to receive the Son (the commandments of the Old Covenant, which Christ came to fulfil and not to destroy), the power which Christ as man receives from the Father and shares with his Church (the sacraments), that power in which we receive the Spirit. Again Julian is contemplating the servant's origins, *from wens he came,* so that her mind is logically led to that maiden who is the human origin by the power of the Spirit of Christ's sensual life; and she makes the point that this mode of his relationship, also, is available to us. She catches exactly the mystical tropology in monastic exegesis of the twelfth century, especially in the Mariological commentaries on the Canticle of Canticles. The union of the Word with all human nature was achieved in Mary's womb, so that she is to be found at the heart of the mystery of the Church, Mary in whom every Christian soul realises its perfection.[276] But Julian also takes the occasion here (following, apparently, Augustine — see 580.50 note) to observe that it is Christ who is Mary's spiritual mother, not Mary Christ's. The teaching on the spiritual motherhood of the divine and human Christ which she is about to develop at length has come through her renewed contemplation, after the showing of the parable, of the mutual relations between God and man in Christ, and of what she was shown in the first and the last of her revelations.

---

[276] *Exégèse médiévale,* 2 561 and notes.

In chapter 58 Julian presents us with a synthesis of all that she has learned in her contemplative reflection, not only on the parable but also on the first, ninth and eleventh revelations, as illumined by her understanding of the lord and the servant, about the mysteries of Trinity and Incarnation. She now sees mankind as a whole in its relationship to Christ; and this is the same view which all mediaeval exegetes who are in the authentic tradition of Origen and Gregory have of the union between Christ and his Church, seen at once as *militans et triumphans*. It is thus that in our making (*he made vs alle at onys* — 582.6 — in Christ) we are destined now and everlastingly to share in his own will, the *bona voluntas*, the divine goodness.

> this is the werkyng whych is wrought contynually in ech soule that shalle be savyd, whych is the godly wylle before seyde (582.10).

Again she rehearses the various characteristics of this relationship with God, one and three; but here she differs in emphasis from the Cistercian and Victorine spiritual writers and from such contemporaries as Hilton, the *Cloud*-author and the English translator of Suso's *Horologium sapientiae*. The Church, as she consistently understands it, all who will be saved, is for her the virginal wife of God the Trinity, in the Trinity's union with the incarnate Christ. We may, if we wish, follow other writers of the fourteenth century (cf. 582.14, 583.15, 16 notes) in applying this teaching to the relationship of Christ with the individual soul in the transforming union, the 'spiritual marriage'; but Julian, though her language closely resembles theirs (*I loue the and thou louyst me, and oure loue shall nevyr parte in two* — 583.17), never makes this application. The nearest she ever comes to it is in her account of the procession of penitent-saints in Paradise (chapter 38), in whom the godly will was never extinguished and whom God mercifully preserved in their falling.

Here, in writing of the creative activity of the Trinity, the *natura creatrix*, she carefully lays down the principles which she will follow when she comes to deal with the motherhood of God and the incarnate Christ (cf. 584.25 note, 586.44 note). To explain the matter as clearly as she herself had seen it in her contemplation, she constructs another *argumentatio*, the proposition of which is the showing she had received of Christ in his 'pre-existence': *he stondyth before the fader evyn ryghte* (544.315) ... *his stertyng was þe godhed* (539.278) ... *seyng in his menyng: Lo, my dere fader, I stonde before the* (536.248) ... *stondyng redy before the father in purpos tyll what tyme he wolde sende hym* (535.235), who *is now become oure moder sensuall* (585.39). Her *ratio* is that *we be doubell of gods makyng, that is to sey substannciall and sensuall* (585.39). After referring in the *confirmatio* to what she has seen of the divine *natura creatrix*, 'in our substancial making' and his working of mercy in accepting for his own our sensuality (585.40 e.s.), she embellishes her argument by rehearsing the way in which this mercy works through Passion, death and Resurrection, thus keeping our 'parts undeparted', and uniting us to our substance, the triune God. She goes on to summarize what she has seen in contemplative prayer concerning the operation of the Holy Spirit, the working of that grace which belongs to the royal lordship (cf. 502.26 e.s.), elucidating what she had there called 'rewarding' (503.32), by defining it here as *a gyfte of trust* (587.53 and note). And she ends the chapter with a characteristic anagogical contemplation: the purpose of the divine Trinitarian operation in the Incarnation of Christ is that all who are to be saved should be

> wurschypfully brought vp in to hevyn, and blyssydfully onyd to oure substannce, encresyd in rychesse and nobly by all the vertu of Crist and by the grace and werkyng of the holy gost (588.66).

As Cassiodorus had written of the Church's ultimate reality: 'collectio fidelium sanctorum omnium anima et cor unum, sponsa Christi, Jerusalem futuri saeculi'.[277]

Julian devotes the last chapters, 59 to 63, of Revelation XIV to setting out, in as clear and orderly a fashion as possible, the fruits of all that she has seen and heard concerning the second person of the Trinity, the 'mid person' who never appears to her understanding except in his relationship to Father and to Spirit:

> ... the trinitie is our endlesse ioy and our bleisse, by our lord Jesu Christ, and in our lord Jesu Christ. And this was shewed in the first syght and in all, for wher Jhesu appireth the blessed trinitie is vnderstand, as to my sight (295.13).

Twenty years of constant study and contemplative reflection on the parable of the lord and the servant, in which, she tells us, the mysteries and obscurities of all her showings were hidden (519.71), have enabled her to do this. There is now a serenity in her contemplative vision of Jesus. She sees in him every man who will be saved, enriched by his wisdom and knowledge, built up in him who is the firm hope of heavenly glory, for all the fullness of the divine substance is incorporated in his glorified humanity — 'in ipso inhabitat omnis plenitudo divinitatis corporaliter' (Colossians 2.9). Her mind and heart

---

[277] Ibid. 2 515 and note 5.

seem to be impregnated with the wealth of Paul's Christological insights. As he does, she sees Christ as God's principle and instrument of goodness, opposing all the evil and wickedness in the sinful world of man, '... delens quod adversus nos erat ... quod erat contrarium nobis, et ipsum tulit de medio ... expolians principatus et potestates, traduxit confidenter, palam triumphans illos in semetipso' (Colossians 2.14-15).

This is the starting point in chapter 59 for her magisterial teaching on the motherhood of God, teaching which stands as an unique theological achievement in the Church's spiritual traditions. The working of mercy and grace is the simple countering of evil by goodness; and this belongs to the feminine principle of the *natura creatrix*, the divine creative activity *where the ground of moderhed begynnyth* (589.10). Without this carefully developed Christology, her teaching on the Trinity, though it would still be remarkable from the pen of a woman of the fourteenth century, could be accounted nothing more than a skilful restatement of traditional monastic theology. She may have suppressed any mention in the short text of this doctrine of God's motherhood, not merely because its implications only became fully clear to her after the publication of that version, but also because she feared the reception which such a theological development might have from readers unaware that here, too, she has tradition on her side. John Gerson, writing only a few years after she completed the long version, with, it would seem, Catherine of Siena in mind, remarks that 'the female sex is forbidden on apostolic authority (he is alluding to I Timothy 2.12) to teach in public, that is either by word or by writing ... All women's teaching, particularly formal teaching by word and by writing, is to be held suspect unless it has been diligently examined, and much more fully than men's. The reason is clear: common law — and not any kind of common law, but that which comes from on high — forbids them. And why? Because they are easily seduced, and determined seducers; and because it is not proved that they are witnesses to (*cognitrices*) divine grace'.[278] This is the voice of authority sounding in a world made by men for men; it is well known how Christine de Pisan inveighed against such a world, and against that particular voice.

André Cabassut has remarked[279] that to find in certain mystical writings the title 'Mother' given to Christ would occasion no surprise in the thirteenth century or in the seventeenth, to the contemporaries of

[278] *De examinatione doctrinarum* Pars I Consideratio 2a, 3a; *Omnia opera*, ed. Ellies-Dupin, 1 14-16.
[279] 'Une dévotion médiévale', 236.

Francis of Assisi or of Benet Canfield; and, as the annotations to these chapters abundantly prove (see the notes to 597.32, 599.54, 606.48, 616.24), the devotion, if not the theological implications, was well established among Julian's immediate precursors such as the author of the *Ancrene Riwle*, Mechtild of Hackborn and the editor-translator of *The Chastising of God's Children*. Of particular importance here is the evidence that the devotion had found expression in popular preaching in England over a century and a half earlier, just as the lyric cited at 597.32 note shows that the devotion had won a place in popular piety. The homily entitled by Richard Morris *An Bispel*,[280] found in MS British Museum Cotton Vespasian A.22, contains the following:

> (God) is indeed a father; he gives us his earth to till, he gives us corn to sow ... But can we, in any way, call him a mother, we ask? Indeed we can. What does the mother do with her child? First she cheers[281] and rejoices over it as it sees the light, and then she supports it on her arm, or covers its head to send it to sleep and give it rest ... Moreover, he spoke a wonderful word to the soul by the prophet Isaias: 'Can a mother forget her babe and not have pity on the son of her womb?' (Isaias 49.15). If she does forget, yet shall I not forget you, says the Lord.[282]

The reference to Isaias is of particular interest. It occurred spontaneously (with the other Isaian texts, 49.1 and 66.12-13) in this context to Cabassut,[283] who did not know of the existence of *An Bispel*, just as the text Matthew 23.37 occurred to Anselm as he wrote, with affective devotion, first of Paul and then of Jesus as our mother:

> Sed et tu Iesu, bone domine, nonne et tu mater? An non est mater qui tamquam gallina congregat sub alas pullos suos? Vere, domine, et tu mater. Nam et quod alii parturierunt et pepererunt, a te acceperunt. Tu prius illos et quod pepererunt parturiendo mortuus es et moriendo peperisti ... Ambo ergo matres. Nam etsi patres, tamen et matres. Vos enim effecistis, tu per te, tu per illum, ut nati ad mortem renasceremur ad vitam. Patres igitur estis per effectum, matres per affectum ... Tu quoque anima, mortua per te ipsam, curre sub alas Iesu matris tuae et conquerere

---

[280] *Old English Homilies* 1, 233-235.

[281] For 'cheers' the manuscript reads *cheteð*, a hap. leg. which, MED suggests, should be emended to 'chereþ'. This is very probable; the author seems to be recalling John 16.20-21: Tristitia vestra vertetur in gaudium. Mulier cum parit tristitiam habet quia venit hora ejus; cum autem peperit puerum, jam non meminit propter gaudium, quia natus est homo in mundum.

[282] We owe our knowledge of this passage to Sr. Mary Arthur Knowlton: *The Influence of Richard Rolle and of Julian of Norwich*, 78 n.4.

[283] 'Une dévotion médiévale', 236-237.

sub pennis eius dolores tuos ... Christe mater, qui congregas sub alas pullos tuos, mortuus hic pullus tuus subicit se sub alas tuas.[284]

Cabassut remarks that this prayer seems to be the beginning of the devotion: 'Anselme parait être en effet l'initiateur de la dévotion à Jésus notre mère'.[285] This may well be true, so far as the devotion itself is concerned; but we must look elsewhere for possible sources of the Trinitarian theology which for Julian is the cause and the foundation of the devotion. In her *Revelations*, contemplation and theology are interdependent, whereas the Trinity can hardly be in Anselm's mind as he writes of Jesus and Paul as *ambo matres*.

Richard Rolle, perhaps, points us in the right direction, in his exposition on the first few verses of the Canticle of Canticles:

Unde et, allegorice loquendo, ad quemlibet sanctum potest dici illud quod mulier dixit in evangelio ad Christum: Beatus venter qui te portavit et ubera que suxisti (Luke 11.27). Quemadmodum namque antequam in mundum nascimur corporaliter in matris utero portamur, et priusquam ambulare vel currere vel aliquem cibum forte sumere possumus necessarie est ut lac ab uberibus matris capiamus; ita, spiritualiter, ante baptismum vel ante penitenciam, in utero Christi, id est in paciencia sua, ne vel abortivi suffocemur vel diversis sceleribus dampnati simus, gestamur. Cum vero per baptismum vel per penitenciam a carcere infidelitatis vel iniquitatis parturiente nos deo, extracti fuerimus, opus habemus ut lac quo nutriamur sugendo ad ubera pendamus. Unde apostolus: Quasimodo geniti lac concupiscite (I Peter 2.2).[286]

Rolle's commentary is in the tradition of that authentic mediaeval exegesis which in the previous century had begun to degenerate through an exaggerated attention to the tropological sense of Scripture as the privileged field of the ex professo contemplative. In the annotations to 596.22, 606.48, 608.64 will be found citations from the English translation, contemporary with Julian, of the *Liber specialis gratiae* of Mechtild of Hackborn which well illustrate this degeneration. However, another witness to the devotion to the motherhood of Christ, which we must consider as well-established by the end of the thirteenth century, Margaret d'Oyngt, shows a more balanced approach (see the annotations to 616.24 and 616.31).

It seems certain that the source of Anselm's devotion is Augustine's exegesis of Psalm 101.7, 'similis factus sum pelicano in deserto', since

---

[284] Ed. Schmitt, 'Oratio ad Sanctum Paulum', 3 40-41.
[285] 'Une dévotion médiévale', 238.
[286] Ed. Murray, 29-30.

there, having written that 'Christ exercises fatherly authority and maternal love', he adds 'just as Paul is also father and mother ... through his gospel-preaching' (cf. 599.57 note). Augustine here would expect his readers to refer the 'auctoritas paterna' to Christ precisely as revealing the Father, just as, in the *Confessiones*, where he writes, as Julian does, of the divine creative activity, which he sees operating in his own human parents (see 599.57 note), we know that he is addressing the triune God. Bede in his turn, as he expounds the text of Proverbs 31.1, reminds us of another strand of the tradition which Julian was to inherit, when he writes that the mother of Lamuel's vision is none other than divine grace or the spirit of Wisdom (cf. 598.45 note). This becomes, as we should expect, a mediaeval commonplace in traditional exegesis, especially among contemplative writers with their partiality for the sapiential books, where Wisdom is explicitly called the creative principle which is feminine. For example, in Ecclesiasticus she says of herself: 'I am the mother of fair love, of fear and knowledge and holy hope. In me is all the grace of the way and the truth ... all hope of life' (24.24). Yet even though these are titles which Christ applies to himself in the fourth gospel (cf. e.g. John 14.6), the tradition shows a persistent reluctance to make the connexion which is Julian's audacious starting-point: *And the depe wysdome of þe trynyte is our moder* (563.21). Cabassut observes how infrequently this title is given to Christ in Christian antiquity, and that when the apocryphal *Acts of Peter* were translated into Latin in the fifth century, the word 'mother', used of Christ in the context of Matthew 12.49-50, was suppressed.[287] It is worth noticing that the only other such example cited by Cabassut is that of John Chrysostom, citing the same text from Matthew. It could be argued that in neither case is any Trinitarian reference, direct or indirect, intended; and the Matthean text will not bear any such interpretation. Mediaeval Dionysians like Joannes Sarracenus and Thomas Gallus are prepared to transliterate Denis's invocation of Trinitarian Wisdom, ὑπερθέε, as *superdea*; although John Scotus Erigena had insisted on *super-deus*.[288] The *Cloud*-author translates as *sovereyn goddesse*,[289] which in the context is faintly ludicrous. Augustine, writing of Christ's descent into hell and his liberation there of Adam, cites Wisdom 10.1-2, which states that 'she (Sapientia) preserved Adam, brought him out of his sin and gave him lordship over all things' (cf. 554.4 note). But one suspects, in

---

[287] 'Une dévotion médiévale', 237-238.
[288] Chevallier, *Dionysiaca* 1 565, 709.
[289] Hodgson, *Deonise* 2.

Augustine, the same reluctance to assign to the eternal Son a feminine, creative role. We also know how early the theologians of the Western Church established the title 'Domina Mater Ecclesia' (cf. 607.57 note) and how totally the spiritual exegesis of this depends on the identification of Christ with the Church (for example, in Augustine; see 607.63 note). But it is strange to find (so far as de Lubac has been able to marshal the facts) that although the Church is Christ's 'flesh',[290] and the figure of Christ as husband and the Church (or the individual soul) as his beloved wife is wholly acceptable to every exegete from Origen onward,[291] as also is the concept of the 'daily birth of the Word',[292] there appears to be no attribution to the Son of motherhood before that of William of St. Thierry (cf. 582.12 note), and in him one detects a somewhat cautious use of language as he expands the notion of the *natura creatrix*. Indeed, one may perhaps state that the proliferation of Marian commentaries on the Canticle of Canticles from the twelfth century onwards,[293] reviving and pressing the earlier doctrine of Mary as the new Eve, may have prevented a more general and explicit development of the Trinitarian theology of motherhood, of which Julian remains the single forthright exponent in the Western mediaeval tradition.

For Julian, the most exalted of her revelations had been the twelfth, where our Lord had shown himself more glorified than she had seen him before (402-403). Accompanying this rarified intellectual vision of the heavenly Christ had been the locution 'I it am', which she often heard repeated. She implies there that her inability to comprehend the number of the words, which were 'in the highest', had to do with unity and Trinity (cf. 403.11, 15, notes). Now, through her understanding of the Trinitarian relationships in the light of the parable, she is able to offer a truly evangelical interpretation of the great revelation of the name of God, 'I am who am' (Exodus 3.14). If the qualities of human fatherhood are the vestiges in creation appropriated to the first person, as Paul had taught (see Ephesians 3.14-15), then equally the qualities of motherhood should be appropriated to the second person, whilst the fecundity of this knowledge and love in the *natura divina creatrix* is rightly appropriated to the third person.[294]

One of the profoundest New Testament statements on the eternal

---

[290] *Exégèse médiévale* 2 502.
[291] Ibid. 2 559 e.s.
[292] Ibid. 2 565.
[293] Ibid. 2 561 e.s.
[294] Cf. P. Pourrat: 'Attributs divins'.

relationship between Father and Son is that reported by Matthew: 'No one knows the Son except the Father, and no one knows the Father except the Son and those to whom the Son wishes to reveal the Father' (Matthew 11.27), that is, the children to whom, Christ has just said, those things will be revealed which the Father has hidden from the wise and prudent (ibid. 11.25). And Christ, who as Julian intimates here is within the Trinity *hyest, noblyest and wurschypfullest* (590.19), goes on in the gospel to say of himself to the children 'Come to me ... learn of me, for I am meek and humble of heart' (Matthew 11.29), just as Julian notes that this human soul of the incarnate Word is also *lowest, mekest and myldest* (590.20).

In her final version of the first revelation, Julian repeats several times that God is all that is good (cf. 299.3, 301.29, 303.42, 304.10, 306.28, 318.15, 322.12). So here she writes of the unity of God: *I it am, the hye souereyn goodnesse of all manner thyng* (590.16). This is 'the substantial ground' in which we participate by the eternal decree of the Trinity: the divine nature, his being, which is communicated to us in the second person who is first our mother, equal to the Father, and then in the Incarnation *oure very moder in grace by takyng of oure kynde made* (592.38); and finally he is our Saviour through his *moderhed in werkyng*, in which, in the Godhead, he is equal to the Spirit, who confirms the working of the motherhood (591.29). Here she reminds us that this entire revelation is still 'for prayer'. Our response to the knowledge of our existence and growth in the Trinity is

> to loue oure god in whome we haue oure beyng, hym reverently thankyng and praysyng of oure makyng, myghtly prayeng to oure moder of mercy and pytte, and to oure lorde þe holy gost of helpe and grace (592.30).

Here also, as has been observed (592.38, 40, notes) she mentions the godly (or, more probably, 'goodly') will for the last time:

> Alle the feyer werkyng and all the swete kyndly officis of dereworthy motherhed is in propred to þe seconde person, for in hym we haue this goodly wylle, hole and safe without ende, both in kynde and in grace, of his owne propyr goodnesse (592.38).

Her first reference to it was in similar terms, in Revelation I, again in the context of contemplative prayer:

> And therfore we may with hys grace and his helpe stande in gostly beholdyng, with euer lastyng marveylyng in this hygh ouerpassyng vnmesurable love that oure lorde hath to vs of his goodnes; and therfore we

may aske of oure louer with reuerence all that we wille, for oure kyndely
wille is to haue god, and the good wylle of god is to haue vs (308.53).

As one of the present editors indicated several years ago,[295] Dom Roger
Hudleston was right in linking Julian's teaching with that of William of
St. Thierry, but was wrong in dismissing it as unorthodox. Hudleston's
opinion continues to be repeated.[296] Her own visions and 'beholdings'
coincide with the teaching of William in his *Aenigma fidei*: it is in-
conceivable that in the predestined, those that will be saved, the good
will of God in Christ should be absent or extinguished; for that would
be a sign that they are among the reproved (and Julian saw none of
these except the devil himself — cf. 427.8 e.s.). It now appears likely,
in view of her closeness to William's teaching, and of such considered
statements as

> God is more nerer to vs than oure owne soule, for he is grounde in
> whome oure soule standyth, and he is mene that kepyth þe substannce and
> the sensualyte to geder, so that it shall nevyr departe (571.11)

that she was as well aware as was the *Cloud*-author in his teaching on the
sovereign point of the spirit[297] that, affectively as well as morally, the
*scintilla synderesis* will never be extinguished in the minds and hearts of
the predestined. And for Julian, as for monastic theologians in general,
the very movement towards repentance is the sign of his continuing and
permanent presence, *of his owne propyr goodnesse* (593.41). The text employed by both William of St. Thierry and Hugh of St. Victor,
discussing this matter, is I John 3.9: 'Whosoever is born of God does
not sin'.[298] To 'be born of' refers properly to the mother:

> ... it may not verely be seyde of none ne to none but of hym and to hym
> that is very mother of lyfe and of alle. To the properte of moderhede
> longyth kynd, loue, wysdom and knowyng, and it is god (598.46).          Ch.59

To conclude this chapter 59, Julian classifies the Trinitarian modes of
the divine motherhood as she has become aware of it in her contemplative prayer (cf. 593.43 note); and in this same context she again
uses the word which she had previously coined to translate the
technical term for the relationship within the Trinity, *circumsessio*, 'forth
spredyng', this time in the Pauline reference to the Christian's interior
knowledge of the expanding dimensions of the divine love in Christ

---

[295] J. Walsh: *The Revelations of Divine Love*, 37-40.
[296] See, e.g., C. Wolters: *Julian of Norwich*, Introduction, 37: 'This is wishful thinking
and not the teaching of the Church'.
[297] E.g. Hodgson, *Cloud*, 18.
[298] See J. Walsh: *The Revelations of Divine Love*, 39-40 and notes.

(Ephesians 3.18-19) in his own spirit. This is the working of the motherhood of God in creation, redemption and glorification, which is the content of these last four chapters of Revelation XIV.

Its first movement (cf. 594.7) is the moment of the Incarnation, as it was shown to her in the sight which she received in Revelation I of Mary in the mystery of the Annunciation (cf. 594.7 note). Julian's implication is that Mary's own contemplation of her God in her own acceptance (cf. Luke 1.38) of *the servyce and the officie of moderhode* (595.14) is a reflection of Christ's own service in the mystery of the Incarnation as this was shown to her in the parable of the lord and the servant. (It is perhaps worth noting here that Vatican Council II's Constitution on Divine Revelation explains tradition as that which has been handed on by the apostles 'sub assistentia Spiritus Sancti in Ecclesia', and affirms that the perception of tradition grows through the contemplation and investigation of believers who, like Mary — and Luke 2.19, 51 are cited — treasure these things in their heart).[299] He served thus when *he arayed hym and dyght hym ... in oure poure flessch* (595.12); and Julian goes on to show that the mothering which Christ received from Mary is derived from his own:

> The moders servyce is nerest, rediest and suerest; nerest for it is most of kynd, redyest for it is most of loue, and sekerest for it is most of trewth. This office ne myght nor coulde nevyr none done to þe full but he allone (595.14).

Here Julian has in mind both the Lucan description of Christ's Nativity (Luke 2. 6-7) and the image Christ uses in John 16.20-21 of the sufferings of a woman in labour and her joy in the birth of her son, so as to explain the impact of his death and Resurrection on his apostles and the Church: *Thus he susteyneth vs with in hym in loue and traveyle* (595.20).

> The moder may geue her chylde sucke hyr mylke, but oure precyous moder Jhesu, he may fede vs with hym selfe, and doth full curtesly and full tendyrly with the blessyd sacrament, that is precyous fode of very lyfe (596.29).

This image, as has been noted, is common enough among the mediaeval commentators, but elsewhere the emphasis is almost always on its pictorial and derivative qualities. Ludolph of Saxony is here typical, when he writes: '... ad ipsum pium patrem pauperum, tanquam parvulus ad matris gremium curre ... sicque recumbens super pectus Jesu suge ubera eius et in pace in idipsum dormies et requiesces'. But for Julian

---

[299] *The Documents of Vatican II*, ed. W. M. Abbott, 116.

the statement is a reasoned theological deduction from the nature of
the triune God as it has been revealed to her, and the term of God's
operation in the incarnate Word (cf. 596.29 note). So it is that in the
end she elucidates the 'I it am' locution by making the total identification between Holy Mother Church and Christ, God and man.

> I it am that holy chyrch prechyth the and techyth the. That is to sey: All
> the helth and the lyfe of sacramentyes, alle þe vertu and þe grace of my
> worde, alle the goodnesse that is ordeynyd in holy chyrch to the, I it am
> (597.34).

Thus, for one who accepts the word 'sweet' as indicative of the
anagogical sense of Scripture, the ascent of the spirit into God, and the
word 'kind' as indicative of the divine condescension into God's
creation, it follows that only the Christian notion of motherhood can
embrace together the mysteries of Trinity and Incarnation, and let them
grow in the life of faith, hope and charity (cf. 599.57 note).

*He is our moder in kynde*, Julian writes at the end of chapter 60, *by the
werkyng of grace in the lower perty* (599.58); and it is in this way that she is
found to be at one with so many of her contemporaries who share her
devotion to Christ the mother (without necessarily being capable of the
care with which she develops her theology). A characteristic example is
the analogy of the mother playfully hiding from her child, a theme, dear
to very many mediaeval spiritual writers, with its Scriptural origin in
Isaias 66.13: Quomodo si cui mater blandiatur, ita ego consolabor
vos. We find the theme in the *Ancrene Riwle*, and, as we have seen, in
Anselm's *Oratio X*. It appears in a version of the 'Vespasian Homily', in
Mechtild of Hackborn, in the *Stimulus amoris*, in William Flete, in
Bridget of Sweden and in Catherine of Siena. Julian could have derived
her imagery and her language from any one of these sources; but of all
these writers, she is the only one who bases her devotional expression
on a firm theological and contemplative understanding:

> He kyndelyth oure vnderstondyng, he prepareth oure weyes, he esyth
> oure consciens, he confortyth oure soule, he lyghteth oure harte and
> gevyth vs in party knowyng and louyng in his blessydfull godhede, with
> gracyous mynde in his swete manhode and his blessed passyon, with cur-
> tesse mervelyng in his hye ovyr passyng goodnesse, and makyth us to loue
> all that he louyth for his loue, and to be well apayde with hym and with
> alle his werkes. And whan we falle, hastely he reysyth vs by his louely
> beclepyng and his gracious touchyng (601.4).

It is only thus that Christ our mother *may suffer þe chylde to fall some tyme*
(604.35) but he *may nevyr suffer vs þat be his chyldren to peryssch* (605.39), for
that would contradict the very nature of the Godhead.

Here, too, Julian reinforces the teaching of this revelation on contemplative life and prayer. Hers is a spirituality of consolation: periods of dryness or desolation are not meant to be prolonged. The prayer of petition for union is readily heard, if we are prepared to *use the condicion of a chylde* (605.45). Our mourning and weeping (plainly, she was thinking of the *Salve Regina*) will be quickly answered by a mother's *ruth and pytte* (607.54). Again, her devotion is rooted in her understanding of Christ in his self-identification with his Church:

> ... he wylle þat we take vs myghtly to the feyth of holy chyrch, and fynd there oure deerworthy mother in solas and trew vnderstandyng with all þe blessyd comonn (607.57; and see 607.57, 59, notes).

There is great difference, in devotional tone and temper, between Julian, who can see how in the motherhood of Jesus the unity of the whole Church is necessarily preserved, so that she can draw the conclusion

> And therfore a suer thyng it is, a good and a gracious to wylle mekly and myghtly be fastenyd and onyd to oure moder holy church, that is Crist Jhesu (607.61),

and the language, say, of Aelred of Rievaulx, when he writes 'That a man may not succumb to carnal concupiscence, let him turn his whole affection to the attraction of the Lord's flesh'.[300] (Aelred is, of course, writing here for beginners. There is much in common between his allegorical vision of Christ in 'Adam's tunic' — we must remember how greatly daring he was to use what Talbot has called the 'fatal word',[301] in an age still scandalized by Peter Abelard's unacceptable solutions to the problems of the Hypostatic Union, whereas in Julian's time the controversy had become ancient history, so that she could safely write about the servant's *kyrtell* which is Adam's flesh — as he draws out the contemplative meaning of 'the Word was made flesh', and Julian's account of the parable of the lord and his servant.) Even as she writes of Jesus as 'nurse' and 'mother', notions which had joined the 'main stream of popular piety' more than a century before,[302] she is not reflecting, as that piety did, merely imaginative meditation about the Son's human nature; her thoughts on the topic show us that it had been granted to her to penetrate the mystery of the triune God in prolonged contemplation.

---

[300] A. Squire: *Aelred of Rievaulx*, 47, quoting the *Speculum caritatis*.
[301] C. H. Talbot: *Sermones inediti*, 22.
[302] A. Squire: *Aelred of Rievaulx*, 47.

In chapter 62, as she draws to the end of her final redaction of Revelation XIV, Julian returns, in a highly figured summary, to the three chief lessons of the parable. First, the servant was shown for Adam in his falling, *to make there by to be vnderstonde how god beholdyth alle manne and his fallyng* (522.102); secondly, the servant was shown for God's Son, with his power, wisdom and goodness (cf. 534.230, 537.254-256); and thirdly it was shown that Jesus is our keeper in our time of falling (547.11 e.s.). This summary reflection leads into another of wider scope. Behind the parable of the lord and the servant is the revelation of the being and working of God, one and three, the concept of all creation as emanation from and return to the divine being, *processus — reditus*, firmly based on Scripture, and the *reditus* is perceived as salvation through grace:

> And alle kyndes that he hath made to flowe out of hym to werke his wylle, it shulde be restoryd and brought agayne in to hym by saluacion of man throw the werkyng of grace (611.15).

Here she sees, it would seem, through the eyes of William of St. Thierry (himself indebted to Gregory of Nyssa) in his *De natura corporis et animae*. All created things find their integration in the creature man, whose royalty is a participation in the sovereign being of God: 'Omnipotentis enim naturae imaginem fieri, quid est alius quam continuo regalem conditam fuisse naturam?'[303] This man is, of course, Christ who is also God; to him we (that is, the Church in the anagogical sense) are all fastened by nature and grace: *we be all bounde to god for kynd, and we be bounde to god for grace* (612.22). This is the quality and extent of his motherhood; all is known in him, and he in us. It is one of Julian's extraordinary gifts that she is able to take up the phrase γνῶθι σεαυτόν, with all its mediaeval philosophical and theological implications, and express it in devotional language.

Julian had written early in the showing:

> Prayer onyth the soule to god, for though the soule be evyr lyke to god in kynde and in substannce restoryd by grace, it is ofte vnlike in condescion by synne of mannes perty (475.2).

Now in the last chapter, 63, she returns to the point of union and disunion, with a variation on the words she has used in chapter 59 to describe goodness (with mercy and grace) and wickedness as ad-

---

[303] PL 180 717, and see J.-M. Déchanet: *Aux sources de la spiritualité de Guillaume de Saint-Thierry*, 28.

versaries. Here the antagonists are *kynd* (which is *all good and feyer in it selfe* — 614.3) and *synne*. *Kynd* here stands for *alle kyndes that he hath made to flowe out of hym to werke his wylle* (611.15), and grace again is the restorative, now seen also as destructive of all that prevents the *reditus*, the return to God. She seems to be making the point that sin is not merely transgression of a divine commandment; its malice consists in its being against human nature:

> For it (sin) is contraryous to our feyer kynde; for as verely as synne is vnclene, as trewly synne is vnkynde (615.15).

But it is the loving soul that will see this malice; and it will tend to be overcome by its burden. Again Julian moves with dexterity from what appears to be abstract theological speculation into 'Franciscan' devotional language as she counsels us to have recourse in such a dilemma

> to oure derewurthy mother, and he shall all besprynkyl vs in his precious blode, and make oure soule full softe and fulle mylde (615.20).

Alternation between meditative reflection and devotion is the pattern of this chapter, in a last recapitulation of the motherhood in its Trinitarian relations and its Christological operation which is followed by a pictorial image of this theological statement: the chief virtue of a child is true trust, which is the golden mean between despair and presumption:

> ... kyndly the chylde dyspeyreth nott of the moders loue, kyndely the chylde presumyth nott of it selfe (617.38).

The chapter ends with the anagogical contemplation of this child with its parents in eternity:

> And than shalle þe blysse of oure moderheed in Crist be new to begynne in the joyes of oure fader god, whych new begynnyng shall last, without end new begynnyng (618.47).

## 17 Revelation XV

At the end of her account of this fifteenth showing in her short text, Julian had written *And here was ane ende of alle þat oure lorde schewed me that daye* (265.59). In this long text she is more exact in her recollection, telling us of the length of time which the showings occupied and when they began and ended:

> Of whych xv shewynges þe furst beganne erly in þe mornynge, aboute the oure of iiij, and it lastyd shewyng by processe, fulle feyer and soberly, eche folowyng other, tylle it was none of þe day or paste (631.37).

The statement is not without its psychological significance. Though she knew that she was the object of a direct supernatural intervention (as has been noticed, she offers us objective evidence for her statement that her sickness had brought her to the point of death, and tells us that she suddenly felt *as hole ... as ever I was befor* — 292.36; cf. 291.34, 292.35 notes, and Introduction, *supra*, IX 2, 'Criteria of Analysis'), it cannot be doubted that twelve hours of intense concentration, coupled with the alternation of spiritual consolation and desolation, culminating in the mental perplexity which accompanied the showing of the parable, must have greatly taxed her mentally and physically. All this appears to be part of *þe woo that is here* (619.6) to which she alludes at the beginning of this revelation. It is noteworthy, too, that when she reports the locution which is the substance of the long text,

> Sodeynly thou shalte be taken from all thy payne, from alle thy sycknesse, from alle thy dyseses and fro alle thy woo ... (620.14),

there is the phrase *from alle thy sycknesse* which is not found in the corresponding short text (cf. 263.10).

Her situation at this moment was very much that of Gregory the Great, as he describes it at the beginning of his *Dialogues*,[304] where he admits that he awaits his death with longing, as a blessed release which would deliver him from the pains of this exile and admit him to the joys for which he was created. This is the 'wound of desire' which characterizes the whole of Gregory's spiritual theology, the same wound for which Julian had in the past prayed with such fervour. The locution, which is an answer to her present prayer in which she experiences once again the mingling of joy and woe, is heavy with Scriptural allusions. The most significant among them is perhaps the implied reference to the vision of heaven in the Apocalypse, God's dwelling among men, when there will be no more weeping nor mourning. This is also the text which she seems to have had in mind as the account of the revelation begins and she writes of the 'new beginning without end'. The preponderant influence of Gregory through the tradition is evident in her reflection on this locution, although the form in which she couches it, the *ratiocinatio*, has become typically her own, as she draws out the quality of the patience which must be a part of the affective and effective desire for God. It is Gregory who teaches that 'if desire for God is ardent, it is also patient. It grows under the trial of time. One must learn to wait for God in order to love him more, and to take ad-

---

[304] Umberto Moricca: *Gregorii Magni dialogi libri IV*, 14-15.

vantage of the passage of time to become ever more open to his infinite plenitude'.[305] Leclercq has observed of Gregory: 'Everyone in fact had read him and lived by him'.[306] It is highly probable that this is true of Julian. But one would not wish to adduce this passage as evidence of that, or say more than that the lines which follow the locution,

> And also god wylle that whyle the soule is in the body, it seeme to it selfe þat it is evyr at þe poynte to be takyn (622.27),

are in themselves evidence that Julian had read the *Cloud*-author's *Epistle of Prayer*, which offers precisely the same counsel.[307]

Thus far in this revelation (619.5-622.30) there has been almost verbatim agreement with the short text (263.1-264.25). Now, however, Julian adds a short parabolic picture, which, though it is an *exemplum* in the strict sense, is introduced by the rubric *And in thys tyme I sawe* (622.31). In other words, this belongs to the objective content of the revelations, so that, once again, the question arises, why was it suppressed in the short text? Several reasons suggest themselves. Firstly, this vision of a body *whych ... shewde heuy and feerfulle and with oute shape and forme, as it were a swylge stynkyng myrre* forces Julian out of her normal delicacy and restraint, as she describes the miseries of the flesh (see 622.31 note). Secondly, her feeling about this is much the same as when in Revelation II she described the dreadful face of the dying Christ. There she had written:

> This secounde shewyng was so lowe and so little and so symple that my spirytes were in great traveyle in the beholdyng, mornyng, dredfull and longyng; for I was some tyme in a feer wheder it was a shewyng or none (327.32, and see note).

Considering this similar showing 'in bodily likeness', she may have wondered whether it was merely the product of an imagination affected by pain, sickness and desolation. Thirdly, as with her great *exemplum*, the parable of the lord and the servant, she may have been unsure, at the time when she wrote down the short text, of the techniques of Scriptural interpretation which she had needed another twenty years to master. So now she explains the details of this *exemplum*, and how it helps, by its sharpness of contraries, to lead to that contemplation of the evangelical promise of 'the glory that is to come', which reveals

---

[305] *Moralia* XXVI 34, PL 76 386, quoted by J. Leclercq, *The Love of Learning*, 32.
[306] *The Love of Learning*, 32.
[307] Hodgson, *Deonise*, 48.

once more the Lord's merciful compassion, in his preservation of us and his promises to us (cf. 624.40-42). De Lubac has written of the rupture which Dionysian influence tended to introduce into the tradition, a dissociation between the *invisibilia* and the *futura*, between the life of unitive prayer and meditation of the Scriptures. Julian, who here shows her familiarity with Dionysian terminology —

> It is goddys wylle that we sett þe poynt of oure thought in this blesfulle beholdyng (624.49) —

at the same time rejects the Dionysian anagogy which wishes to leave behind the order of visions, preferring that of 'pure contemplation'. For her, the grace of contemplation is related firmly to her vision. So she continues:

> ... as oftyme as we may and as long tyme kepe vs ther in with his grace, for this is a blesfulle contemplacion to the soule that is ladde of god, and fulle moch to his wurschyppe for the tyme þat it lastyth (625.50).

The similarity between the bodily sight in this revelation and the face of the dying Christ which reminded her of the Vernicle in Rome in Revelation II (cf. 327.36) has already been remarked. Nor does the resemblance cease there. She had also written in the long text of the

> two workynges that may be seen in this vision. That one is sekyng; the other is beholdyng (334.83),

and of this seeking she had added:

> It is gods wil that we haue iij thynges in our sekyng of his ȝefte. The furst is that we seke wyllfully and besyly withouȝte slowth, as it may be with his grace, gladly and merely without vnresonable hevynesse and veyne sorow; the seconde þat we abyde hym stedfastely for his loue, withouȝte gronyng and stryvyng agaynst hym, in to our lyvys ende, for it shall last but a whyle. The iij is that we truste in hym myghtely, of fulle and tru feyth, for it is his wille þat we know that he shall aper sodenly and blyssydefully to all his lovers (334.87).

When rightly understood, during the time that God wishes us to wait for his coming in hope, this is as good as contemplating. This teaching is now confirmed, in the long-text version of Revelation XV, by the locution and the vision of the example which accompanies it. The trust in his promise is the spiritual energy of contemplative reflection on the evangelical word: 'I am the resurrection and the life; he who believes in me, though he be dead, will live' (John 11.25), particularly in those times when, as the great spiritual masters of the West consistently teach (cf. 625.53 note), contemplative vision fades and the human frame feels the weight of its weakness:

> ... whan we falle agayne to oure selfe by hevynes and gostely blynesse and felynge of paynes gostely and bodely by oure fragylyte (625.53).

Her reflection continues in chapter 65 with a conclusion which is implicit in her aphorism 'Seeking is as good as beholding':

> For he wylle we kepe this trustly, þat we be as seker in hope of the blysse of hevyn whyle we are here as we shalle be in suerte when we ar there (627.4).

Her use of the words *here* and *there* is a clear indication of how much at home she feels herself in the contemplative tradition of the twelfth century.[308] Chatillon cites as a key text for the understanding of this vocabulary a passage from Caesarius of Arles, probably in Julian's time attributed to Augustine:[309] 'Salvator noster ... ascendit in caelum; non ergo turbemur in terra; ibi sit mens, et hic erit quies. Ascendamus cum Christo interim in corde. Cum dies eius promissus advenerit, sequemur et corpore'. All the other texts used by Chatillon to demonstrate the meaning of 'here' and 'there' and 'meanwhile', Augustine, Alcuin (via Thomas Aquinas), Bernard and William of St. Thierry, stress the various points made by Julian: joy in the Holy Spirit as one is mindful of the blessings to come, and the tolerance of present tribulation (Bernard); the persevering prayer of petition (Alcuin); the steadfast belief in the divine promise through the illumination of the Word (William); and, finally, the reference by Augustine to the Mystical Body': 'Membra mea estote, si ascendere vultis in caelum ... In hoc ergo ipsi interim roboremur, in hoc votis omnibus aestuemus'.[310] It is this last point which Julian develops in her own way, by referring back to her final statement on God's motherhood, on the contemplative disposition of a child of God, that total trust of which the elements are love, joy, reverence and humility.

> And euer the more likyng and joye þat we take in this sekernesse, with reverence and meeknes, the better lyketh him. For as it was shewed, this reverence þat I meane is a holy curious drede of our lorde to which meekenes is knyt; and that is that a creatur see þe lord meruelous great and her selfe mervelous litle (628.7).

---

[308] F. Chatillon: 'Hic, ibi, interim'.
[309] Ibid. 194, note 1.
[310] Sermo 263, *De ascensione Domini*, PL 38 1210.

Then, once again, she sees Mary as the type of the perfect contemplative
and the image of the Church at prayer (cf. 628.7 note). Here Julian
returns to the spiritual tropology initiated by Gregory: 'Omnipotens
Deus, qui nec in magnis tenditur nec in minimis angustatur, sic de tota
simul Ecclesia loquitur, ac si de una anima loquatur; Et saepe quod ab
eo de una anima dicitur, nil obstat si de tota simul Ecclesia in-
tellegatur'.[311] Thus she writes:

> It is gods wyll that I see my selfe as much bound to hym in loue as if he
> had done for me all þat he hath done; and thus shuld everie sowle thynke
> in regard of his louer. That is to say, the charyte of god makyth in vs such
> a vnitie that when it is truly seen, no man can parte them selfe from other.
> And thus ought ech sowle to thynke þat god hath done for hym all that he
> hath done (628.16).

All the revelations, like the whole of Scripture, *shewith he to make vs to loue
him, and likyn him* (629.22). Again, it is Gregory who writes: 'mira atque
ineffabilis sacri eloquii virtus agnoscitur, cum superno amore legentis
animus penetratur'.[312]

Now Julian, as she comes to the end of Revelation XV in the long
text, is looking both ahead and backwards to her experiential fear of
the evil one, and she is desirous, for her readers' sake as well as for her
own, to place the matter in perspective. There is only one true fear, as
she will tell us later, and that is the 'lovely dread' which dwells in
brotherhood with the divine love poured out in our hearts (cf. 673.20
e.s.) At this point, it may be, she wishes to prepare her readers to share
her own fearful experience. So she uses all her rhetorical skill to make
the point that all diabolic fears have a hallucinatory and transitory
quality about them, no matter how much they may move us and con-
fuse us. They are a part of our normal experience of inadequacy and
suffering, which *as soone as we may, passe we lightly over* (630.29).

So Julian concludes the first part of her showings; the first fifteen
revelations divide themselves, both chronologically and psychologically,
from the last vision. And here she reminds us that the assurance which
God's gift of hope confers is very much hers, as she reflects at this point
upon the contemplative graces of more than twenty years (cf. 631.35-
37).

---

[311] *In Hiezechihelem* II, 2, ed. M. Adriaen, 235.
[312] Ibid. I 7, ed. Adriaen, 88.

## 18 Revelation XVI

Julian had written that the first fifteen revelations lasted until after three o'clock in the afternoon, *tylle it was none of þe day or paste* (631.39 and note). Now, at the beginning of chapter 66, she tells us that *the goode lorde shewde the xvj revelation on the nyght folowyng* (632.3). She is careful to explain what happened in the interval. As soon as the long showings came to an end, although she felt certain that she was not now going to die, she was afflicted with a deep spiritual desolation, and also with the return of the physical pain which had accompanied her sickness, and with its concomitant mental anguish:

> And sodeynly all my body was fulfyllyd with sycknes lyke as it was before, and I was as baryn and as drye as I had nevyr had comfort but lytylle, and as a wrech mornyd hevyly for feelyng of my bodely paynes, and for fautyng of comforte gostly and bodely (632.11).

Whilst she was in this state, she was visited by a religious. Whether he was a priest or not she does not say; but the conjecture that he was would be fair, because, it seems, she thought of making her confession to him when she saw his reactions to her brief allusion to the imaginative vision of the bleeding crucifix, which vision, as she had just told him, she was at that moment inclined to consider a hallucination:

> And when I saw that he toke it so sadly and with so grete reverence, I waxsyd full grettly ashamyd, and wolde a bene shryvyn (633.22).

At all events, he must have been in her confidence for her to have mentioned the matter to him at all. His immediate tendency to take seriously her remark that it had seemed to her that the crucifix was covered in blood is also an indication that he knew her well and was prepared to give credence to what she might say: he *waxsed all sad, and merveylyd ... and I thought: this man takyth sadly the lest worde that I myght sey, that sawe no more therof* (633.19). Nor was he inclined to believe her when she said that she had lost her wits — *he lugh lowde and enterlye* (266.8). This disbelief overcame her only momentarily; almost as soon as she had spoken, she repented it, and she calls it *a grett synne and a grett vnkyndnesse,* even whilst she accepts the cause, *for foly of felyng of a lytylle bodely payne* (634.31). After this visit, the experience of contrition which followed it and her continuing prayer of trust in God's mercy, she fell asleep as night came on, which, at that time of the year, would be between nine and ten o'clock. In chapter 67 she relates how, during that night, she had the nightmare about the devil being on the point of choking her. This visitation is followed by *grete reste and peas;* and whilst she was lying there, *without sycknesse of body or drede of conscience* (638.25), the sixteenth revelation began, as she describes in chapter 68. As the revelation develops, it moves through all Julian's various classification of her sights, and it is succeeded by 'a showing of words'. At the end, when she 'saw no more', she experienced a further assault of diabolic temptation, which she endured for what was left of the night:

> And thus he occupied me alle that nyght and on þe morow tylle it was about pryme day (651.11 and note).

Julian had pondered well her own experiences, and the insights they had given her into the problems of demonology. She used her own knowledge of diabolic temptation and illusion, and her theological reflections on their impact upon the Christian life, particularly upon the life of contemplation, not only as a link between the first fifteen revelations and the last great showing on the mystery of divine indwelling. Margery Kempe reports Julian as saying:

> God and þe deuyl ben euyrmor contraryows, and þei xal neuyr dwellyn to gedyr in on place, and þe devyl hath no powyr in a mannys sowle.[313]

This is an obvious allusion to the sixteenth revelation, and to her subsequent contemplative insights. Here, in her narrative of the revelation, she employs those insights to bring together all the words which God had formed in her understanding (cf. 666.3). The locutions had been reported in a variety of forms and rhetorical figures, but the most direct and manifest seem to be on the two occasions when the Lord 'formed' words in her soul (cf. 227.27-28, 346.6-7) or 'showed words' (cf. 269.23-24, 645.53-55), 'without voice and without opening of lips'. Thus she writes, at the end of the sixteenth revelation:

> And ryght as in the furst worde þat oure good lorde shewde, menyng his blessyd passyon: Here with is the fende ovyr come, ryght so he seyde in the last worde with full tru feytfullnes, menyng vs alle: Thou shalt not be ovyr come (646.60; and cf. 269.29).

Julian was aware, just as was Margery Kempe in her own illiterate and enthusiastic fashion, that the evil spirit can occasion imaginary fantasies which might be mistaken for imaginative visions; but she had also grasped, whilst she was recording in her short text these two primary locutions to form an *inclusio*, the teaching, specifically Johannine, on the victory achieved by the sacrifice of the Passion in the struggle against

---

[313] *Book of Margery Kempe*, 43.

the principalities and powers of evil. 'Now', says Christ as he goes to the Passion, 'the prince of the world will be cast out' (John 12.31). 'Now the prince of this world comes ...' (ibid. 14.30). 'In this world you will have distress, but have confidence; I have overcome the world' (ibid. 16.33). This is Julian's precise point as she reflects on her final locution:

> He seyde nott: Thou shalt not be trobelyd, thou shalt not be traveyled, thou shalle not be dyssesyd; but he seyde: Thou shalt not be ovyrcom (647.68).

As Heinrich Schlier has noted,[314] the terms 'victory' and 'overcome' are peculiar to the Johannine writings, and are employed in three ways. First, the overcoming of the world of which Jesus speaks at the Last Supper is a victory over death, darkness and distress ($\theta\lambda\tilde{\iota}\psi\iota\varsigma$, *pressura*, which Julian properly renders as 'trybulacyons', 647.67), of which the fiend, the enemy, is the prince. Julian knows from John's Gospel, as well as from her revelations, that Jesus by his Passion has overcome this 'world' (346.7). Despite her lack of personal experience of so much that is evil, she is well aware through the writings of Paul and John that this struggle is of cosmic proportions. In the light of the parable of the lord and the servant she can write of this conflict, which she sees as the primaeval opposition, older even than Adam's sin:

> For wyckydnesse hath ben sufferyd to ryse contrary to þat goodnesse; and the goodnesse of mercy and grace contraryed agaynst that wyckydnesse and turnyd all to goodnesse and wurshyppe to all that shall be savyd (589.5).

She knows that from now until the end of time, God's chosen will have to endure the consequences of the struggle:

> Holy chyrch shalle be shakyd in sorow and anguyssch and trybulacion in this worlde as men shakyth a cloth in the wynde (408.6);

and she also knows that it will be only at the *parousia* that the victory will be final and all-embracing, when

> we shalle alle sey with one voyce: Lorde, blessyd mott thou be, for it is thus, it is wele (729.14).

Secondly, John teaches that those who have true faith in Jesus as Son of God participate in the power of his Passion, and overcome the world: 'This is the victory which overcomes the world, our faith' (I John

---

[314] *Principalities and Powers*, 63 note 58.

5.4). For Julian, those who will be saved possess this faith; they are born of God, who is their Father and mother:

> Oure feyth is a lyght, kyndly comyng of oure endlesse day that is oure fader, god, in whych lyght oure moder, Cryst, and oure good lorde the holy gost ledyth vs in this passyng lyfe (723.14).

This is why Julian anguishes so greatly over her momentary lapse of faith, and treats it with such seriousness. It is on the 'children of unbelief' that the 'prince of the power of the air' is at work (cf. Ephesians 2.2).

Finally, the verb 'to overcome' has a special application to those who overcome the devil by the supreme witness of their lives (cf. Apocalypse 5.5, 7.14, 12.11). So Julian, who had asked for the grace of suffering with the dying Christ and of a sickness which might seem as if mortal, desired to share this combat — 'all the dreads and temptations of fiends' (287.27).

In Revelation V, Julian had written that she was shown the devil's total impotence (cf. 346.8-347.10). Her language there, in chapter 13, resembles that of Paul in his letter to the Colossians: '... despoiling the principalities and powers, he has confidently exposed them in open showing, triumphing over them in himself' (that is, on the Cross — Colossians 2.15). And when she writes of the devil's malice and wrath and sore travail (347.10-18), she has in mind John's imagery: '... the devil has come down to you, having great wrath, knowing that he has but a short time' (Apocalypse 12.12). Schlier, as he reflects on New Testament teaching about the 'principalities and powers', writes of the sacrifices of Christians for the sake of truth, justice and peace, that struggle against the forces of evil which John calls 'the patience of the saints', who 'keep the commandments of God and the faith of Jesus' in the conflict with the great beast (Apocalypse 14.9-12). He goes on: 'The enemy is powerless against this sacrifice ... He is passed over in this sacrifice as though he no longer existed, and indeed, for the man who accepts sacrifice, he is no more'.[315] That appears to be exactly the point which Julian makes, as she reflects on this topic in chapter 33: *I vnderstond þat alle the creatures þat be of the devylles condiscion ... ther is no more mencyon made of them before god and alle his holyn then of the devylle* (428.11). Such souls may just as well not exist.

Thus, Julian's belief in the devil is firmly rooted in Scripture; and

---

[315] Ibid., 62.

when she insists that temptations against faith (cf. 637.20-638.23) and hope (cf. 687.30-688.41) come from him, she is merely echoing Paul and John in their cosmic visions of the struggle between death and life, light and darkness, good and evil. As Lefèvre has pointed out, Hebrews 2.9-14 provides us with a summary of New Testament teaching on Christ's victory over the devil: 'The power of evil is powerlessness. All the devil can do is only trickery and mirage ... death and sin are annihilated by the Cross and the Resurrection. It was by the grace of God that Jesus submitted himself to death; by his death he brought the devil to nothing'.[316] This is Julian's theological position, too, in all that she has to say of 'the fiend'. It was Christians of her calibre that Paul had in mind when he wrote: 'I would have you be wise in good and simple in evil; and may the God of peace speedily crush Satan under your feet' (Romans 16.19-20).

As she describes her nightmare (635.2-638.26) and the temptations which she endured after the sixteenth revelation (648.2-651.13), Julian can still betray the agitation which she then suffered; but, apart from this, all that she writes on the theology of the devil and temptation is a model of restraint, and is of impeccable orthodoxy. She shows none of the self-consciousness, so common in her time, of those who, considering themselves chosen souls, expect frequently to be harrassed by the fiend. There is nothing in Julian's experience which remotely resembles, for example, the pretensions of Mechtild of Hackborn, when she writes:

> The feende trauaylede fulle ofte this holye maydene ande goddes seruaunte with temptaciouns als he is wonte to greve ande noye alle thoo that be deuowte to God. Ande þan itt felle on a daye that God hadde gyffen here plenteuoslye his grace, ande that same daye when oure lorde hadde doone a grete benefete to here sowle, þan comme preuelye the feende to tempte here. Ande he putte in here herte suche a drede of hevynesse, and putte in here mynde to thenke that the gyfte whilke sche hadd come nought of god.[317]

On the contrary, Julian is concerned to minimize the role of demonic activity in the life of the contemplative. It is remarkable that although the revelations show her so concerned with the enigma of sin and damnation, no mention is made of the sin of the angels. She can personify

---

[316] 'Angel or Monster?' in *Satan,* ed. B. de Jésus-Marie, 66.
[317] Halligan, 345.

wrath (505.9) without mentioning, as does the *Cloud*-author,[318] the evil
spirit; and in her account of Adam's fall, in the parable (521.100), and
of the Harrowing of Hell (534.224), there is no mention of Satan or of
devils, whereas in every other contemporary treatment of these themes
they are the protagonists. Though in times of sickness or depression
fear of the fiend seems to have been prominent in her consciousness
(e.g. 291.31, 370.4, 687.29 e.s.), that fear is elsewhere merely
catalogued with all the other 'doubtful dreads' (629.23 e.s.); and she
can write with serenity that fear of ghostly enemies is profitable, along
with dread of pain and bodily death, as a point of entry into contrition:

> for man that is harde of slepe of synne, he is nott able for þe tyme to
> receyue þe softe comforte of the holy goste, tylle he hayth vndertaken this
> drede of payne of bodely deth and of gostly enemys. And this drede
> steryth vs to seke comfort and mercy of god; and thus this drede helpyth
> vs as an entre, and abyllyth vs to haue contrycion by þe blessydfulle
> touchyng of þe holy gost (671.7).

And in the long text she is content to suppress the short text's gloss on II
Corinthians 11, when she had proferred her advice on dealing with
'doubtful dread', presumably because she herself had never seen the
devil so disguised (cf. 276.16 e.s. and notes).

In their annotation to chapter 67, the editors have canvassed the
opinion that, writing some twenty years after the event, Julian may in
the long text have embellished out of her imagination the 'ugly showing
made while she slept'. The short text merely has:

> And in my slepe atte the begynnynge me thought the fende sette hym in
> my throte and walde hafe strangelede me, botte he myght nought. Than I
> woke out of my slepe (267.26).

It is possible, for example, that the detail, 'his hair was as red as rust',
originates in the remark in the *Ancrene Riwle* about 'the devil called
Rufinus who is Belial's brother';[319] in the contemporary *Seinte Marherete*
the demon in the likeness of a black man calls his dead brother
'Rufines', but refuses to tell his own name.[320] Given, however, Julian's
scrupulous care to record as exactly as she can all that she saw and no
more, and what seems to be her gift of total recall, we may think it
more probable that as she ponders again with compunction her lack of

---

[318] *A Treatise of Discretion of Spirits*; Hodgson, *Deonise*, 83.
[319] Salu, 108.
[320] Ed. Mack, 30.

faith, the dream, the consequence of her unbelief, returns to her in all its vividness. What she is describing is, according to Heinrich Spitta, in his work *Die Schlaf- und Traumzustände der menschlichen Seele,* the classic demon of nightmare:

> The apparition of a *kobold* or a monster, squatting on the chest of the sleeper, moving nearer and nearer to his throat and threatening to strangle him ... It is so clear and so evident that it causes great anguish ... The sleeper tries in vain to defend himself against this horrible apparition; he tries to cry out, but his voice is strangled in his throat, his limbs seem paralyzed, sweat pours from him, his hands are like ice. Suddenly he comes to with a cry, to fall back again on his bed, exhausted, but with the relieved feeling that he has just escaped from imminent danger of death. [321]

Whatever naivety we may see in the faith of Julian and her contemporaries in devils (we may recall, for example, the *Cloud*-author's credence in the stories of the 'disciples of necromancy'),[322] for the Catholic 'the existence of angels cannot be disputed in view of the conciliar declarations';[323] for instance, it was defined at Lateran IV that 'diabolus enim et alii daemones a Deo quidem natura creati sunt boni, sed ipsi per se facti sunt mali. Homo vero diaboli suggestione peccavit'.[324] For the rest, Julian shows herself to be singularly free from what François Vandenbroucke has called the 'fièvre satanique' from which he sees the Western Church suffering from c. 1300 for the next four centuries.[325] He singles out a description by Suso, in the *Horologium sapientiae,* of hell and the activities there of the demons, and comments: 'One perceives here a very lively imagination, and one may ask how much of this is true vision, how much pure literary fiction'.[326]

The additions in the long text — she there calls the dream a 'showing', and writes that *in all this tyme I trustyd to be savyd and kepte by þe mercy of god. And oure curtesse lorde gaue me grace to wake* (636.12) — indicate that Julian ascribes a preternatural quality to the nightmare. It is in the order of an imaginative vision. So is the smoke, accompanied by the great heat and the foul stench, perceptible to her alone, just as the

---

[321] Quoted by Yolande Jacobi in 'Dream Demons', *Satan,* 268. When she wrote, Dr. Jacobi was assistant to C. G. Jung.

[322] Hodgson, *Cloud,* 103.

[323] K. Rahner, 'Angel', in *Sacramentum mundi* I, 32.

[324] Denzinger-Schönmetzer, 800.

[325] 'Démon en Occident', DSp 3 225 e.s.

[326] Ibid., 226.

'bodily talking' (648.4) is in the order of a locution. In describing all this, Julian has confidence that her readers will believe that her senses were physically assailed by these phenomena, which were part of the diabolical temptation:

> The stynch was so vyle and so paynfulle, and bodely heet also dredfull and traveylous (648.3).

The vividness of her description of the 'bodily talking' —

> ... semyng to me as they scornyd byddyng of bedys whych are seyde boystosly with moch faylyng devout intendyng and wyse diligence, the whych we owe to god in oure prayer (648.8) —

makes the same demands on our credence. Here again, Julian is not simply relying on the canonized fables known to monastic tradition (abundant examples of which are cited in the annotations to these chapters); she can appeal to reputable theological opinion, such as that of Thomas Aquinas, who cites Augustine as answering with a vigorous affirmative his question: 'Utrum daemones possint homines seducere per aliqua miracula?'[327] Aquinas observes: '... daemon potest mutare phantasiam hominis, et etiam sensus corporeos, ut aliquid videatur aliter quam sit'; and he goes on to refer to *De civitate Dei*, and to Augustine's opinion there that the devil '... phantasticum hominis, quod etiam in cogitando, sive somniando per rerum innumerabilium genera variatur, velut corporatum in alicuius animalis effigie sensibus apparet alienis ... quia daemon, qui in phantasia unius hominis format aliquam speciem, ipse etiam potest similem speciem alterius sensibus offerre'.[328]

When, however, all this is said, we must recall that in the more informed of the popular devotions of her time, it was held that such demonic illusions, whether of the night-time or of the noon-day devil, were temptations primarily against faith, and called for the sort of prayers which are found, for example, in MS Ushaw 10:

> Ex omnipotencia patris:
> O swytte blyssyd lade, as thow arte moste myght nexte god in hewyn and in herthe, I beseke þe so, be present and defende me fro my gostely enmys in the howre of my dethe.
> Aue Maria.
> Ex sapiencia filij:
> O glorius lady, as thow arte moste wytty nexte god in hewyn and in her-

---

[327] *Summa theologiae* I.114.4.
[328] Ibid., ad 2.

> the, I beseke þe so, be present and kype me in þe ryghte fathe of holy
> kyrke in þe owre of my dethe.
> Aue Maria.

And in MS Cambridge University Library Ff.6.8, on an originally blank
leaf there is an addition in a hand of the fifteenth century:

> O thou blessyd virgyne Mary, Cristes moder dere and glor(i)ose me-
> diatrice betwyx god and man, ... atte that tyme that my syght shal be
> agrevyd with the blak howuyng of deth, that I shal not mowe meve my
> tonge to clepe after helpe, and my harte quake for drede of enemyes of
> helle, and al my body ful of angwysshe of peyne of deth ... vouchesafe
> þan to have pety on me, with praying to thi son that my acousours have
> noo powere ouer me ...

So it was that Julian's experience of diabolic temptations had its desired
effect: she was able to place all her revelations upon the ground of her
faith:

> But wytt it now, that is to seye, now thou seest it. This was seyde nott
> onely for the same tyme, but also to sett there vpon the grounde of my
> feyth, where he seyeth anone folowyng: But take it, and lerne it, and kepe
> thee ther in, and comfort the ther with, and trust therto, and thou shalt
> nott be ovyr com (653.36).

Revelation XVI, Julian tells us, *was conclusyon and confirmation to all the
xv* (632.4); and it is also the climax of what may be called her mystical
experience. She indicates clearly that it *was shewde ... by gostely syghte*
(666.2) when she writes: *And then oure good lorde opynnyd my gostely eye and
shewde me my soule ...* (639.2). At first glance the revelation appears to be
simply a bodily sight, an imaginative vision of Jesus dressed as a king
and seated on a throne, closely resembling (as Molinari has noted[329])
Teresa of Avila's celebrated meditation on the mystery of the divine
indwelling:

> And now let us imagine that we have within us a palace of priceless
> worth, built entirely of gold and precious stones — a palace, in short, fit for so
> great a Lord. Imagine that it is partly your doing that this palace should be
> what it is — and this is really true, for there is no building so beautiful as a
> soul that is pure and full of virtues, and, the greater these virtues are, the more
> brilliantly do the stones shine. Imagine that within the palace dwells this great
> king, who has vouchsafed to become your father, and who is seated upon a
> throne of supreme price, namely, your heart.[330]

[329] *Julian of Norwich,* 162.
[330] Ibid., citing the E. Allison Peers translation.

Julian, however, is trying to find words and images to express what for her is ineffable: *And for the gostely syghte, I haue seyde some dele, but I may nevyr fulle telle it* (666.6). So she uses the phrase 'as it were', and writes of Jesus as *clothyd solemply in wurschyppes* (640.8). She also substitutes in the long text *I vnderstode þat it is a wurschypfulle cytte* for the short text's *me thought it was a wirschipfulle cite* (268.4), presumably in order to make it plain that she is seeking to describe the special insight into the mystery which was granted to her.

In chapter 52 of the long text she has already neatly summarized, as she began to draw out her Trinitarian reflections concerning the allegory of the lord and the servant, what her revelations and the faith of the Church (Scripture and tradition) teach her about the divine presence, that relationship which must find its human expression in unitive prayer:

> ... he wyll we trust that he is lastyngly with vs, and that in thre manner. He is with vs in hevyn, very man in his owne person, vs vpdrawyng; and that was shewd in þe gostely thyrst. And he is with vs in erth, vs ledyng; and that was shewde in þe thyrde, wher I saw god in a poynt. And he is with vs in oure soule, endlesly wonnyng, rewlyng and gemyng vs; and that was shewde in the xvi, as I shalle sey (549.34).

It is with this third mode of presence that this final revelation concerns itself. It is indeed a 'conclusion and confirmation', in that it depends for its understanding upon her careful and informed elaboration of the mysteries of the Trinity and the Incarnation. It has recently been observed that the richest context for theological reflection on the mystery of the indwelling is the doctrine of the Trinity, particularly with regard to 'missions' and 'processions':

> The Trinitarian context ... illumines better the mystery of man in his immediate relation with the Trinitarian mystery, and it makes more evident the unity of our theological knowledge, as it refers spiritual theology to the revelation of the deepest mystery of God. [331]

This is why the sixteenth revelation, in the long text, changes character dramatically, to show Julian contemplating the delight of the Trinity as the Word is made flesh, its *homelyest home and ... endlesse dwellyng* (641.16). This is surely an echo of Wisdom's words: I was with him forming all things, and was delighted every day ... and my delights were to be with the children of men' (Proverbs 8.30-31). *In this,* Julian writes, *he shewde the lykyng that he hath of the makyng of mannes soule; for as wele as the*

---

[331] Roberto Moretti: 'Inhabitation', DSp 7 1745.

*fader myght make a creature, and as wele as þe son myght make a creature, so wele wolde þe holy gost that mannys soule were made, and so it was done* (641.17). Plainly, just as the prologue to John's gospel is full of allusion to the Genesis creation-narrative, so here Julian, treating ostensibly of the creation on the sixth day of human kind, is developing and relating three themes: man's creation, God's delight in his creation, and the Trinity's delight in the Incarnation, as she alludes to Genesis, to the sapiential books and to the Johannine prologue. *And so it was done ... et factum est ita ... et verbum caro factum est.* This echo presents Julian with an *inclusio* which is deeply theological. As Moretti has written: 'The Biblical vision of the relations between God and man finds, in the Trinitarian indwelling, its most perfect expression'.[332] The same author remarks that in the New Testament, the mystery of divine indwelling is presented under two distinct though closely-connected aspects: one is static, the other dynamic. In the static aspect, the mystery is considered as union, in the fulfilment of knowledge and love. But it is also viewed dynamically; there is concern for the process of sanctification, of assimilation, where the action of the Holy Spirit receives close attention. In the short text, Julian seems to have restricted herself to the first consideration, again presumably because the activity of the Trinity, and especially the appropriation to the Holy Spirit of the 'working of grace', only became clear to her through her later understanding of the parable. Now, as well as expressing her delight in all that is static in the revelation —

> And this was a singulere ioye and a blis to me that I sawe hym sitte, for the behaldynge of this sittynge schewed to me sikernes of his endelesse dwellynge (268.19) —

she is able to use an *exemplum* which was provided at the time of the showing, but was suppressed in the short text. It belongs to the group which seem to derive from the great *exemplum* of the lord and the servant (cf. e.g. 313.35 e.s., and note), but it serves her here to recall the activity of the Holy Spirit (the 'lordship') in detaching us from the things of earth and bringing us up above. *And he wylle that oure hartes be myghtly reysed aboue þe depnesse of þe erth and alle veyne sorowes, and enjoye in hym* (644.43).

The context also of the mirror-image:

> And the saule that thus behaldys, it makys it lyke to hym that is behaldene, and anes in reste and in pees (268.17),

---

[332] Ibid. 1744.

is significantly different in the long text. There, Julian adds *by hys grace* (645.50). The vision has become anagogical contemplation in the technical sense. Though the text which appears to be foremost in Julian's mind is Pauline (cf. 644.49 note), she is contemplating, under the impulse of the grace she receives as she recalls the showing, the *otium quietis* which is the bliss of heaven,[333] and in this experiencing a foretaste of God's own endless joy: 'We shall be like to him, because we shall see him as he is' (I John 3.2). The grace is also one of enlightenment:

> he ȝawe me knowyng truly þat it was he þat shewde me alle before (645.51);

whereas in the short text she had simply written *I knewe sothfastly* (268.21).

Thus the locution which follows becomes a confirmation of all that faith and grace have taught her in the twenty years which she devoted to the love of learning, and to the desire for that God who has revealed himself in Christ to all will be saved, saved from all harm and for all bliss, through Christ:

> ... ryght so he seyde in the last worde with full tru feytfullnes, menyng vs alle: Thou shalt not be ovyr come (646.62).

The short text at this point shows her still in the sort of trouble and distress which, the locution had indicated, might be her lot:

> He sayde nought: Þou salle not be tempestyd, thowe schalle not be trauayled, þou schalle not be desesed; bot he sayde: Þou schalle nouȝt be ouercommen (269.37).

There, she apostrophized sin because, like the *Cloud*-author, she was experiencing the sorrow of the contemplative,[334] the heavy burden of herself, but also because the revelations are at an end, and she has not yet seen *this truth in the, whych arte my god, my maker in whom I desyer to se alle truth* (512.27). So she had ended the apostrophe with an ejaculatory prayer against the evil one: *God schelde vs alle fra the. Amen pour charyte* (271.35). Now her life of prayer and study enables her to see matters quite differently. She is well content that the sight should have passed; faith has sought and brought understanding of the living truth: *whych blessyd shewyng the feyth kepyth with his owne good wylle and his grace* (652.18). So, in the long text, she recalls that with the final locution which

---

[333] J. Leclercq, *The Love of Learning*, 84.
[334] Hodgson, *Cloud*, 157.

followed her lapse of faith and her first temptations, *he shewde hyt all ageene within my soule, with more fullehed with the blessyd lyght of his precyous loue* (653.31). God in his mystery has become the light of her life; and this is faith, as she will write when she brings her book to a close:

> Oure feyth is a lyght, kyndly comyng of oure endlesse day that is oure fader, god, in whych lyght oure moder, Cryst, and oure good lorde the holy gost ledyth vs in this passyng lyfe (723.14).

In chapter 71 of the long text, Julian continues her protracted reflection on the final locution, and on what the saying teaches about the relationship between the showings and the faith. By faith, here she means both the power of understanding God's word, the *spiritualis intelligentia,* and all that the word expresses, the mysteries of the faith. The power is weakened and the content of faith is obscured, not only because we see now only 'through a glass in a dark manner ... in part' (I Corinthians 13.12, a text which is clearly in her mind), but also by the hostile presence of evil in ourselves and in our world, *oure gostely enemys within and withoute* 654.7). She goes on to add:

> And there fore oure precyous louer helpyth vs with goostely lyghte and tru techyng on dyuerse manner within and withoute, where by þat we may know hym (654.7).

The ghostly enemies at least include wicked spirits (she seems indifferent about the use of singular or plural when she refers to the devil) but she has nothing to say of the activities of good spirits; as she will tell us later, *I beleue and vnderstonde the mynystracion of holy angelys, as clarkes telle, but it was not shewde me* (710.22). *I it am, the trynyte* (590.16). *I it am that holy chyrch prechyth the and techyth the* (597.34). So it is that for the contemplative, faith and vision reflect one another, until faith receives the reward it deserves (cf. 656.16).

This working of faith and grace she now connects with God's three ways of looking at his creature, always 'wiþ his mercyful iȝe'.[335] So she can chart the progress of her revelations: of the incarnate Word suffering and dying (Revelations I, II, V and VIII); of the lord, the Father, looking on the servant, the Son, in his falling, in which servant are all who will be saved — *pitte and ruth and compassion, and this shewyth he to all his louers with sekernesse of kepyng that hath nede to his mercy* (657.28); and, finally, the joyful face of Christ glorified, which she first saw in the ninth revelation (cf. 382.3 e.s.), but which *was oftenest shewyd and longeste*

---

[335] Ibid., 132, where the author is quoting Gregory; ibid., 204.

*contynuyd* (657.31). The first two in this life are *comyn cherys* (657.36); the third is known only through infused contemplative grace, *by gracyous touchyng of swete lyghtenyng of goostly lyfe* (658.38). This is what the *Cloud*-author calls the higher part of contemplative life,[336] and what Hilton means by 'reforming in feeling'.

In chapter 72, having concluded her reflections on the final locution, Julian appears to be reviewing what she had written at this point in the short text, the apostrophe to sin. She now feels able to confront the problem:

> ... in what manner that I saw synne deedly in the creatures whych shulde nott dye for synne, but lyue in the joye of god with oute ende (659.2).

She is of course in the first place writing of the penitent-saints whom she had seen in the great revelation of the divine compassion (chapter 38), of all the predestined to salvation, and also of those who are his lovers and trust in his promises. With regard to these last, she speaks in the language of William of St. Thierry and the author of the *Cloud* (cf. 660.15 note), and she has in mind the text 'The souls of the just are in the hands of the Lord, and the torments of death will not touch them ... they seemed to die ... but they are at peace' (Wisdom 3.1-4); and this is the same *oppositio contrariorum* which she herself is using throughout this chapter, as she again joins together the two elements of compunction, sorrow and hatred for sin, and an increasing desire for God:

> ... evyr the more clerly that the soule seeyth the blyssefull chere by grace of lovyng, the mor it longyth to se it in fulhed, that is to sey in his owne lycknes ... for in þat precious syght ther may no woo abyde nor wele feyle (661.23).

She seems to be praying even as she writes; the sorrow which flows from the contemplation of her own sinfulness, as that which prevents her from seeing God's face, becomes the spiritual weeping which is the gift of tears:

> ... yett shuld we nevyr leue mornyng ne of gostely wepyng, þat is to sey of paynfull longyng, tyll whan we se verely the feyer blessedfull chere of oure maker (664.45).

And she refers again to Revelation XII, when she saw him in his glory, and was first taught that our soul will never be at peace or rest until it

---

[336] Ibid. 31.

comes into him who is the fulness of joy and true life (cf. 402.3 e.s.). So at last she feels that the question she posed in chapter 50 has been placed in its entire context and thoroughly elucidated, not only in the showings and all that she has been taught, but also through her continuing prayer of faith.

One task remains for her to perform. She must try in a practical way to set out more fully all that she has learned through her visions for the sake of those *þat for goddes loue hate synne and dyspose them to do goddes wylle* (667.15). In the short text at this point, she had first given a general description of wretchedness, observing that, if someone deliberately choose what is not good, he is loving sin — if, indeed, there be any such — and his pain is greater than all pains. She seems in fact to be addressing those who love God and hate sin, but yet sometimes fall into the sin they hate *by frelty or vnkynnynge* (272.52). In the long text she firmly abides by what God had shown her of sins in particular; *vnpacyens or slouth ... dispeyer or doughtfulle drede* (666.9) are both part of the frailty and ignorance referred to in the short text. As she had written in chapter 27, God had given her a general sight of sin, 'all that is not good' (cf. 405.15 e.s) She repeats this here in chapter 73, and adds: *but in specyall he shewde noone but theyse ij* (666.12) — that is, impatience and despair. Hence it is of these alone that she wishes to write. Impatience or 'grudging' is for her serious, because she sees it as a refusal to imitate Christ's own meekness and patience in his Passion, a rejection of his invitation, 'Come to me, all you who labour ...' (Matthew 11.28-29). The *doughtfulle drede* she makes oblique allusion to, in the Trinitarian context which she has pondered so long and so lovingly. 'Doubtful dread' is to refuse to share the life of the Trinity in faith, to refuse the Spirit who is the love of the Father for the Son, of the Son for the Father: *that he is alle loue and will do alle, there we fayle* (668.30; in the short text, this observation is not made to apply universally, but only to 'many men and women' — 274.19. Now her experience has shown her that she is one with all her brethren in their sin). 'Doubtful dread' is for her synonymous with the guilt she feels because

> we holde nott oure promise nor kepe oure clennes that oure lorde settyth vs in, but fall oftymes in to so moche wrechydnes that shame it is to say it (668.35).

Guilt for past sins and infidelities can often masquerade under the colour of humility, a fault to which religious are traditionally prone. There is only one true humility, and that is God's own, revealed in the incarnate Word, who comes to us out of love, to share with us his

Father's strength and his own wisdom:

> For loue makyth myght and wysdom fulle meke to vs; for ryght as by þe
> curtesy of god he forgetyth oure synne after the tyme that we repent vs, so
> wylle he that we forgett oure synne as agaynst oure vnskylfulle hevynesse
> and oure doughtfulle dredes (670.44).

So Julian offers us her own exegesis of Paul's *oppositiones* in I Corinthians
1.25: 'For the foolishness of God is wiser than men, and the weakness of
God is stronger than men'.

Chapter 74, which treats of love and fear, shows us two different
aspects of Julian's ability as theologian. First she deliberately uses
Scriptural and patristic allusions (cf. the annotations to pp. 671-672) to
draw the necessary distinctions between the schoolmen's *timor initialis,
timor serviliter servilis* and *timor filialis* or *castus*. But then, basing her contemplative thought on I John 4.18, and, perhaps, on Augustine's
exegesis (cf. 673.17 note), she uses all her rhetorical and lyrical skills to
describe how reverent dread can come to mean that experiential
knowledge of the triune God granted to his chosen as a foretaste of the
vision of the blessed, that special awareness of the fulfilment, now in
time, of the promise of divine indwelling: 'We shall come to him and
make our home with him' (John 14.21, 23). She is also, however,
describing the process of contemplative purification which demands a
progressive self-discernment. In the short text she had written in
general terms of the gift of discretion which enables us to unmask the
devil, when he disguises himself as an angel of light (cf. 277.26 e.s.).
Here in the long text she has recourse to the child-mother image, but
with all the weight of her teaching on God's motherhood to give it substance, as she appeals to God's everlasting goodness, and uses the Scriptural verb 'cleave' (675.38). It is Paul who sums up the whole tradition
of God's loving commerce with his people as he writes: Qui adhaeret
domino unus spiritus est (I Corinthians 6.17). And Julian's chapter ends
with a refutation, beautifully composed and expressed, of Peter
Abelard's condemned proposition, 'Quod etiam castus timor ex-
cludatur a futura vita':[337]

> For the kynde propyrte of drede whych we haue in this lyfe by the
> gracious werkyng of the holy gost, the same shall be in hevyn afore god,
> gentylle, curteyse, fulle swete; and thus we shalle in loue be homely and
> nere to god, and we in drede be gentylle and curtesse to god, and both in
> one manner, lyke evyn (676.43).

---

[337] Denzinger-Schönmetzer, 735.

Chapter 75 is perhaps Julian's most polished and precise theological reflection on the Trinitarian economy. It is based on Revelation IX, the intellectual vision which follows the locution *Arte thou well apayd that I sufferyd for thee?*, when she tells us that *my vnderstandyng was leftyd vppe in to hevyn* (382.2, 7 e.s.), and on Revelation XIII, the long text's development of the theme of Christ's 'ghostly thirst' (417.2 e.s.) This is monastic theology at its finest, and it has much in common with the principle which, Dumontier writes, 'furnishes the supreme explanation of the spirituality of St. Bernard, *Deus movet desiderans*'. 'The God who is desired and loved becomes a God of desire and love'.[338] Bernard uses the same Trinitarian and image-theology; and he too is writing of those who will be saved: 'Bernard affirms that the Father expects us and desires us ... there is the same desire in the Son, avid for us, rejoicing in us, eager for the day when he will enjoy the reward of his labours'.[339] This is precisely Julian's anagogy (cf. 679.11-680.15). Bernard adds: 'Expectat nos et spiritus sanctus: caritas et benignitas in qua praedestinati sumus ab aeterno; nec dubium quin praedestinationem suam velit impleri'.[340] This is in a sermon for Christmas Eve; and Julian, too, is recalling what she has been shown of the mother of the Christ-child in the time of his conception (483.5 e.s.), the quality of her reverent dread in a contemplation which anticipates the awesome joy of the Beatific Vision:

> it longyth to þe worthy maieste of god thus to be beholde of his creatures dredfully tremelyng and quakyng, for moch more of joy endlesly mer-veylyng of the greatnesse of god, þe maker, and of the lest parte of alle þat is made. For þe beholdyng of this makyth creature mervelous meke and mylde (681.31).

In chapter 76 Julian proceeds to argue that this reverent dread is the antithesis, the *oppositio* of sin. She recalls that God has shown her only those souls who dread him — our Lady and the procession of penitent-saints, those who truly have received the teaching of the Holy Spirit; for it is the Lord's promise that he will teach us all truth (John 16.13). Such souls hate sin more than any pain (the *ratio*), for they contemplate þe *kyndnesse of oure lorde Jhesu* (the *rationis confirmatio*). It is thus God's will that we pray to him for this teaching, in the consummate unitive prayer of petition for the Spirit of God (cf. Luke 11.13); and this is the *exornatio* of her argument (684.8-685.11).

---

[338] *Saint Bernard et la Bible,* 39.
[339] Ibid., 40.
[340] Ibid., 40 and note 4.

What follows, on how we are to behave when confronted with other men's sins (685.13 e.s.), seems to reflect Julian's experience as a spiritual director. Again, she constructs an *argumentatio perfectissima* (cf. 685.13 note). She implies in her *exornatio* that the counsellor is expected to share the fatherhood (and motherhood) of God. He must look upon *the feyerhede of god,* and behold his neighbour's sin

> with contrycion with him, with compassion on hym, and with holy desyer to god for hym (686.17).

These are the very gifts for which she had asked, before the revelations began, the three wounds of true contrition, kind compassion and earnest longing for God. Now she sees them as the components of reverent dread; and we see another measure of her spiritual stature. She knows how the graces she had asked for and had been given can be used, not merely for her own profit, but for the pastoral comforting and strengthening of other souls.

In the final section of this chapter, she rehearses how the contemplative penitent should exercise his faith, hope and charity when he is assailed by doubtful dread. Again, this is written in her capacity as a spiritual counsellor; she is speaking of and to

> þe creatures þat haue gevyn them selfe to serve oure lorde with inwarde beholdyng of his blessydfulle goodnesse (688.36).

At the end of chapter 76, Julian has insisted that doubtful dread is a diabolic temptation; and this leads her to reflect again on what she has seen of *the enmyte of the fende* (689.2) in chapter 77. As she writes of the devil's envy, she shares the cosmic view of the Book of Wisdom: the devil represents all wicked spirits and all wickedness, all that is corrupt in human nature. 'They did not know the secrets of God, nor did they hope for the wages of justice, nor did they esteem the honour of holy souls. For God created man incorruptible, and he made him to the image of his own likeness; but by the envy of the devil death came into the world' (Wisdom 2.22-24). Julian then proceeds to a contemplative review of the relationship of the Trinity, the *natura creatrix,* with fallen man (690.14-15). Just as in the previous chapter she imagined the tempter speaking (687.32 e.s.), so here she has the penitent resisting the temptation, not with the neurotic self-castigation which we find, for example, in the contemporary English version of the *Stimulus amoris,*[341] but with a gentle, peaceful contemplation in faith of Father, Son and Spirit:

[341] Kirchberger, *Goad,* 56-57.

> I knowe wele I haue deservyde payne; but oure lorde is almyghty, and may ponyssch me myghtly, and he is all wysdom, and can ponyssch me wysely, and he is alle goodnesse, and lovyth me tendyrly. And in this beholdyng it is spedfulle to vs to abyde (690.16; and cf. ibid. note).

Again she stresses that sorrow for sin, which is the beginning of reverent dread, is not only a compound of the gifts of the fear of the Lord and of hope, as the *Cloud*-author notes in his *Epistle of Prayer*,[342] but is based on the humility which she perceived so clearly in the soul of Mary at prayer. These are the virtues which constitute interior penance, the signs of the change of heart which will be the sinner's response to God's desire for him. Julian saw no other:

> For that pennance that man takyth vppon hym selfe, it was nott shewde me; that is to sey, it was not shewde me specyfyed. But this was shewde specially and hyghly and with fulle louely chere, that we shulde mekely and pacyently bere and suffer þat pennawnce þat god hym selfe gevyth vs, with mynde of hys blessyd passion (692.26).

Some commentators have seen, in Julian's statement, *This place is pryson, this lyfe is pennannce*(693.41),a veiled allusion to her state as an anchoress, especially as the sentiment closely resembles what the author of the *Ancrene Riwle* writes to his anchoresses. The present editors have offered arguments for another opinion.[343] In any case, Julian is here writing in the much wider context of the infinite depths of the Lord's compassion, as he turns his face to the world of men which is in process of being purified and enlightened by the Spirit, 'freed', as Paul writes, 'from the servitude of corruption to the freedom of the glory of God's sons' (Romans 8.21), the bliss of heaven. Julian reminds us here that the first revelations of Christ's sufferings made her 'choose him mightily for her heaven' (cf. 694.47 and note); and she has come to know by experience that though he is *souereyn homelyhed* (695.54), he is also mighty and dreadful, for all creation has its being in him.

*For vs behovyth verely to see þat of oure selfe we are ryght nought but synne and wrechydnesse* (698.18). As Julian continues, in these concluding chapters, to set down the practical spiritual counsel which is the authentic fruit of her intellectual visions of the Trinity and the incarnate Word, it has become her special concern to expose the heresy of Pelagianism and its watered-down version, semi-Pelagianism, which has always contaminated the atmosphere of consecrated life in the Church. The dif-

---

[342] Reynolds, xxxiii.
[343] 'Editing Julian of Norwich', 417-420.

ference between those who are *hyghest and nerest with god* and *the leste and the lowest of tho that shalle be savyd* (699.27), among whom she is happy to count herself in hope, is simply a matter of degree. All sinfulness is unlikeness to God; and in the clarity of contemplative vision, the distinctions of the moral theologians between sin and imperfection, between mortal and venial sin cease to have relevance. 'I am needy and poor' (Psalm 69.6). Julian echoes the Psalmist's sentiment, and applies it to all God's children, even those who appear to be specially favoured with contemplative graces:

> And herof was I lerned, though þat we be hyely lyftyd in to contemplacyon by the specialle gyfte of oure lorde, yett vs behovyth nedys therwith to haue knowyng and syght of oure synne and of oure febylnes; for without this knowyng we may not haue trew meknesse, and withoutyn this we may nott be safe (700.34).

Another such contemplative was St. Bernard, as he pondered, with Julian, the *oppositio contrariorum* he found within himself 'by the sweet gracious light of God himself':

> Through his good gift, then, I can sometimes think about my soul. And it seems to me that I find there two contraries. If I examine it truly, as it is in itself and with all that comes from itself, I can see nothing more than this. Is it necessary to make a catalogue of its miseries, except to say that it is weighed down with sins, shrouded in darkness ...?[344]

But for him, as for Julian, 'there is another opinion of us hidden in the heart of God':

> It is thus that you console, in your fatherly love, him whom you have brought to nothing by your truth, that he might grow to greatness in your heart who was so straitly confined in his own.[345]

Bernard is speaking of his God, who is the head of his body, the Church. Julian, too, who begins chapter 78 with yet another rendering of the Trinitarian formula, *ex Patre, per Filium, in Sancto Spiritu* (cf. 696.6-697.14 and note), knows that it is only of his gift that we see the whole truth of our need of him in our nothingness:

> Than are we moch bounde to god, that he wylle hym selfe for loue shewe it vs, in tyme of mercy and of grace (701.41).

'For whatever things were written were written for our teaching, that through patience and the comfort of the Scriptures we might have

---

[344] *In dedicatione ecclesiae V; Sermones,* ed. J. Leclercq and H. M. Rochais, 2 390.
[345] Ibid., 391.

hope' (Romans 15.4). As Julian in chapter 79 looks back over the long and complex revelation on the divine compassion (cf. 404.2 e.s.), she finds that it simply reinforces her knowledge of the sacred Scriptures, which she summarizes in one sentence which alludes to Paul:

> Alle this homely shewynge of oure curteyse lorde, it is a louely lesson and a swete gracious techyng of hym selfe, in comforthyng of oure soule (704.22).

She had at first agonized, when *he shewde me þat I shulde synne* (702.2), over the prospect of her personal infidelity, rather as did the apostles ('Is it I, Lord?') when the Lord said 'One of you is about to betray me' (Matthew 26.21). But now she has lived with and through her faithlessness, to find that God outreaches her with *the endleshed and the vnchanngeabylte of his loue, and also his grete goodnesse and his gracious inwardely kepyng* (703.16). This is a hope and a comfort which she shares with all God's people, his Church for which hope is the persevering response to his quality of mercy (cf. 702.5-703.8). To this hope belongs the patience which we need to have with ourselves in times of darkness, *whan we be fallen by freelte or blyndnes* (705.31); and Julian shows how patient endurance, commended and cultivated in the spirituality of the Old Testament as well as the New,[346] is related to the Lord's own patient longing for us, as was shown in the allegory of the lord and the servant. She had written that to her the servant's most astonishing pain *was that he leye aloone* (516.28). But even so she saw the lord *abydyng the servant whom he sent oute* (531.202), which she now knows to be the 'office and the working' here on earth (706.41) of the Spirit of both the Father and the Son.

In chapter 80, as she continues to instruct us on how God sees us and keeps us in our sinful human condition, Julian turns her attention to what she has learned about ministry, the ministry of Christ in his Church, that ministry which for us (and this applies with especial force to the contemplative) is primarily the worship of the Father by Christ in us, and their gaining for us, with the Spirit, our salvation. All the powers and gifts which we have received are designed to achieve this purpose, which is the reason for our existence; and they reflect the Trinitarian mystery:

> By thre thynges man stondyth in this lyfe, by whych iij god is wurschyppyd and we be sped, kepte and savyd (707.2).

---

[346] C. Spicq: 'Hupomone — Patientia'.

Through our higher powers of knowing and loving, through the teaching which Christ imparts in his word to the Church, through the sacramental presence of his Spirit, we are drawn into collaboration with God himself; 'we are God's fellow-workers' (I Corinthians 3.9). But, as always for Julian, it is God revealed in Christ who is the object of this contemplation, without which there is no ministry for his followers:

> Crist aloone dyd alle the grett werkes that longyth to oure saluation, and none but he; and ryghte so he aloone doth now in the last end, that is to sey he dwellyth here in vs, and rewlyth vs, and gemyth vs in this lyvyng, and brynggyth vs to his blesse (708.14),

where that ministry will have its fulfilment. It is a service as personal as the washing of the apostles' feet (John 13.4-8):

> so farforth that yf ther were none such soule in erth but one, he shulle be with that alle aloone, tylle he had brought it vppe to his blesse (709.19).

As Paul writes, in the same context of Christ's indwelling, 'he loved me and delivered himself for me' (Galatians 2.20).

> I beleue and vnderstonde the mynystracion of holy angelys, as clarkes telle, but it was not shewde me (710.22).

As the annotations to this passage indicate, Julian is showing a more than passing acquaintance with the body of Dionysian speculation which, by the mid-fourteenth century, was firmly entrenched in monastic theology. By far the most prolific commentator on the pseudo-Dionysian corpus, Thomas Gallus (or 'Vercellensis', as he came to be known to the later mediaeval exegetes), whose habit it was to gloss the Canticle of Canticles with the teaching of Denis's *Mystical Theology*, solved to his own satisfaction the problem to which Julian alludes when she writes:

> hym selfe is nerest and mekest, hyghest and lowest, and doyth all, and not onely alle that vs nedyth, but also he doyth alle that is wurschippefulle to oure joy in hevyn (710.23).

Christ is the one mediator, and with his Father and his Spirit 'cometh down to us to the lowest part of our need' (306.38). So Gallus writes of the hierarchies of the human mind (Julian's 'kindly reason') which Christ unifies and sanctifies, and thus he dispenses with any essential mediation through the angelic hierarchies.[347] If we had to classify the

---

[347] J. Walsh: 'Thomas Gallus et l'effort contemplatif', 20 e.s.

totality of Julian's teaching, we should have to speak of a 'mystique de la lumière' rather than 'de la ténèbre'. [348] However, we must at the same time observe the assurance with which Julian handles the key theological concept of *processus — reditus* (cf. e.g. 577.14 e.s.), which Aquinas made common currency in the thirteenth century, and her mastery of the influential Dionysian teaching in the *Divine Names* on the doctrine of appropriation (see notes to 722.2, 5, 723.8), though it must again be emphasized that she does not here reveal her sources, either directly or indirectly.

When she writes:

> there I sey he abydyth vs, monyng and mornyng, it menyth alle þe trew felyng þat we haue in oure selfe, in contricion and in compassion, and alle monyng and mornyng for we are nott onyd with oure lorde (710.26),

she is certainly treating of the mystery of Christ glorified and yet suffering with his members, as Paul encountered him on the Damascus road (Acts 9.5); and she has already expressed this with theological competence and precision in Revelation XIII:

> For as aneynst that Crist is oure hede, he is glorifyed and vnpassible; and as anenst his body, in whych alle his membris be knytt, he is nott ȝett fulle glorifyed ne all vnpassible (419.34).

Here, however, she is offering instruction for contemplative prayer, in which the soul must be prepared to move and to be moved from darkness into light, and to be exposed to the visitations of consolation and desolation, in which he is enabled to experience, in consciousness of his own sinfulness, that compassion for himself which is integral to the gift of loving sorrow, and is destined to become a sharing in the mystery of Christ's suffering compassion.

Julian concludes chapter 80 by recalling that the two particular sins which plague Christ's lovers, despair or doubtful dread, and all that is contained in the last capital sin, *accidie,* bruise the relationship between him and his Church, whether this concerns one soul or all souls. But she ends by stating firmly that on God's part, the covenant remains unshaken; he is everlastingly faithful:

> ... lastyngly he is with vs and tendyrly he excusyth vs, and evyr kepyth vs from blame in his syght (712.42).

And the compar, as is noted (712.38 note) emphasizes the Trinitarian nature of the presence. Now, in chapter 81, she reinforces this teaching

---

[348] J. Le Maître, J. Daniélou, R. Roques: 'Contemplation', DSp 2 1830-1911.

by cataloguing the various modes of this presence, with its transcendence as well as its immanence, as they were shown to her in the
revelations. It has also been noted how strong is the Johannine influence in this summary (cf. 713.2 note) and the emphasis which she
gives to the mode of presence which is his government and guidance of
man's spirit from within:

> He shewde hym dyuerse tymes reignyng, as it is a fore sayde, but pryn-
> cypally in mannes soule; he hath take there his restyng place and his wur-
> schypfulle cytte (714.9).

Yet it is not merely the vocabulary of mediaeval courtesy which Julian is
here employing. She is alluding to the Trinitarian glory which Irenaeus
long ago had called 'Man fully alive',[349] and of which Christ speaks at
the end of his high priestly prayer after the Eucharistic supper: '... that
they may see my glory which thou hast given me, because thou hast
loved me before the creation of the world... And I have made known
thy name to them and shall make it known, that the love with which
thou hast loved me may be in them, and I in them' (John 17.24, 26).
Rupert of Deutz had pointed out that the phrase 'the love with which
thou hast loved me' clearly referred, for the mediaeval exegete, to 'the
Holy Spirit, who is that love with which the Son loves the Father and
the Father the Son. Plainly and undoubtedly, the love of the Father and
the Son is the Holy Spirit, so that when Christ says "that the love with
which thou hast loved me may be in them, and I in them", it is as if he
were to say "that the Holy Spirit, the Paraclete, may come to them and
may teach them all truth, and when he shall have entered their hearts, I
too shall dwell there through faith and through that Spirit of love"'.[350]

Again, Julian's counsel is practical; the presence is dynamic, and
demands mutuality; and the right contemplative response to it is to
rejoice that the Spirit is at work in us in our penance:

> For he beholdyth vs so tendyrly that he seth alle oure lyvyng here to be
> penannce; for kynde longyng in vs to hym is a lastyng penannce in vs,
> whych penannce he werkyth in vs, and mercyfully he helpyth vs to bere it
> (715.17).

The process is that which Paul calls being 'transformed from glory into
glory, as by the Spirit of the Lord' (II Corinthians 3.18), *tylle what tyme
that we be fulfylled, whan we shulde haue hym to oure mede* (716.24).

---

[349] *Adversus haereses*, ed. Harvey, IV 7.
[350] *Commentariorum in Johannem* XX, ed. Haacke, 710.

The attitudes and dispositions which Julian expects from her readers, as they contemplate with her the indwelling as it has been revealed for them to her in the parable of the lord and the servant, is finely expressed here in one of the several forms of argumentation which she uses with increasing assurance to communicate our Lord's teaching in the showings. He had said to her, at the beginning of Revelation XIII,

> Synne is behouely, but alle shalle be wele, and alle shalle be wele, and alle maner of thynge shalle be wele (405.13).

Now she authoritatively refers this inevitability to the contemplative's passive purification, as she makes the Lord say:

> but for as moch as thou lyvyst nott with out synne, therfore thou arte hevy and sorowfulle, and if thou myghtest lyue without synne, thou woldest suffer for my loue alle the woo that myght come to the, and it is soyth. But be not to moch a grevyd with synne þat fallyth to þe agaynste thy wylle (717.4).

She is showing, too, the nature of the movement of this unitive prayer, how the purgative quality of this mourning for our sinfulness, when informed by the virtue of discretion, leads to illumination and then to union, and that these three stages of the interior life, though distinguishable, tend to fuse:

> He lovyth vs endlessly, and we synne customeably, and he shewyth it vs fulle myldely (718.11).

In reflecting that she was never shown anyone who *in erth ... is continually kepte fro fallyng* (720.27), she is opposing with her sound theology the Quietism which in her day was so rife (cf. 720.27 note). Pierre Adnès has recently written: 'Even with the saints, half-deliberated faults, spontaneous movements coming from instincts not yet sufficiently controlled, and various weaknesses often attest the persistence of an enfeebled will, the consequences of which have not yet been completely eliminated. This is why they never cease to fear, whilst still firmly hoping for their salvation'.[351]

This is exactly Julian's position:

> For in the beholdyng of god we falle nott, and in þe beholdyng of oure selfe we stonde nott (720.29).

She then constructs a series of oppositions, in order to illustrate how the progressive knowledge of the self in its sensuality, *the lower beholdyng*

---

[351] 'Impeccabilité', DSp 7 1620.

(721.36), which continues to find its prototype in Jesus's life in the flesh, is constantly purified and enlightened by what God shows us in contemplation of our life in him, which is *the hygher beholdyng* (721.35). Thus the process of unitive prayer is always constant, in that it moves from the tropological to the anagogical:

> But oure good lorde wylle evyr that we holde vs moch more in þe beholdyng of the hygher, and nought leue the knowyng of the lower in to the tyme that we be brought vppe aboue (721.38).

Julian had promised to write in these closing chapters of the long text as clearly and fully as she could of the most 'glorified' (cf. 402.3) of her visions. Now she finds herself able, in these last four chapters (83-86) to offer us a summary of the *thre propertees of god, in whych the strength and þe effecte of alle þe revelacion stondyth* (722.2). She writes too, by implication at least, of the spiritual senses with which she has been endowed in order to receive these showings. At the very beginning she had written of her desire for greater *mynde* and *felynge* for Christ's Passion (201.6, 9), and, contemplating the first revelations, she had come to realize that she was being enabled to respond to Paul's exhortation to all Christians:

> ... botte ylke saule aftere the sayinge of saynte Pawle schulde feele in hym þat in Criste Jhesu (234.25 and note).

Her *syght and ... feelyng* (723.11) were her continued response to the Trinitarian communication, the 'touching' of the intellectual visions which she had received. These 'touchings' she now calls *lyfe, loue and lyght* (722.5). They are the attributes appropriated to all the persons of the Trinity; she had regularly heard the preface of the Trinity sung in the Sunday Masses of ordinary time: 'et in personis proprietas, et in essentia unitas, et in maiestate adoretur aequalitas'. Her reason, the 'higher part' of her soul, *wolde be oonyd and clevyng to* these attributes *in oone goodnesse ... with alle þe myghtes* (723.8). For this 'higher part', which the author of the *Cloud*, using the Dionysian terminology which Bonaventure among others had adopted, called *þe souereyn poynte of þi spirit*,[352] is the apex both of the affections and of the intelligence, so that Julian

> behelde with reuerent drede, and hyghly mervelyng in the syght and in feelyng of the swete accorde that oure reson is in god, vnderstandyng that it is þe hyghest gyfte that we haue receyvyd, and it is growndyd in kynd (723.10).

[352] *Privy Counselling;* Hodgson, *Cloud,* 169.

Her definition here of faith, which she had previously described as the dynamic gift given by the Trinity as *natura creatrix* (cf. 578.20 e.s.) in virtue of the incarnate Word's taking of our sensuality, is one which spiritual theologians tend to describe as 'the spirit of faith': '... a living synthesis of light and of movement ... the impregnation of the human soul by faith in the soul's most spiritual faculties ... progress in the faith, in the sense that man is more completely submissive to God's invitations ... a perfecting of faith'.[353] Again, Julian's contemplation is strictly anagogical:

> And at þe end of woe, sodeynly oure eye shalle be opynyd, and in clernes of syght oure lyght shalle be fulle, whych lyght is god, oure maker, fadyr, and holy gost in Crist Jhesu oure savyour (724.21).

*Thys lyght is charite* (chapter 84, 726.2): that is, the luminous faith which is contemplative response and awareness is the virtue and gift of love. Julian's seeming lack of precision here might have been unacceptable to the dogmatic theologians of her own and later centuries, but it expresses the thought of the great Fathers, of the East as well as the West. So Gregory of Nazianzus writes: 'He who is loved will be loved. He who is loved is God's guest. And where God is, there, of necessity, is the light. And the first effect of the light is knowledge of the light. So love introduces knowledge'.[354] In the matter of the relationship between contemplation and charity, we expect Augustine and Gregory to be Julian's masters. 'The soul is close to God when it is pure; and as it remains united to love, so it is flooded by him somehow with an intelligible light, and, so illumined, it perceives, not with its bodily vision, but through him who is its principle, those reasons the sight of which make it most blessed'.[355] And it is Gregory's aphorism, 'Amor ipse notitia est',[356] which is the inspiration of all that William of St. Thierry taught on contemplative wisdom and charity; for example, in his *Speculum fidei*: 'There is an inward sense of the soul, for perceiving what is reasonable or divine or spiritual, which is the soul's understanding; for it is love which is a greater and more worthy sense, a purer understanding'.[357] Julian here, as she distinguishes between the light of contemplation *in via* and the vision of the blessed (cf. 726.4-5), emphasizes the contemplative effort; *it is such a lyghte in whych we may lyue*

---

[353] André de Bovis, 'Esprit de foi', DSp 5 611-612.
[354] *De virtute,* PG 37 731.
[355] Augustine, *Liber de diversis quaestionibus,* PL 40 31.
[356] Homily 27 *in Evangelia,* PL 76 1027.
[357] Ed. Déchanet, 154.

*medfully, with traveyle deseruyng þe wurschypfull thangke of god* (726.4), which ensures that God's desire for us will become a thanksgiving.

Chapter 85 seems to indicate that what Julian has written about God's properties and the relationship between faith and charity is itself the fruit of immediate contemplation on all the revelations, which are now through grace stored in her memory. Augustine, dealing with that contemplation towards which all understanding of Scripture moves, had written: Fidei fructus intellectus, ut perveniamus ad vitam aeternam, sed ille qui nobis modo evangelium dispensavit ... appareat.[358] This is, according to de Lubac, 'real' or practical anagogy; and he refers to Rupert of Deutz's prayer that we may be taken up to the heavenly Jerusalem, where the Word himself will be our light.[359] This is Julian's own sentiment:

> And therfore whan the dome is gevyn, and we be alle brought vppe aboue, than shalle we clerely see in god the prevytees whych now be hyd to vs (729.11).

And she concludes with the vision of Paradise reflected in the *Sanctus* of the Roman Mass (cf. 729.14 note), which itself might be called an anagogical gloss on Isaias's vision of the heavenly temple and of the Lord on his throne (Isaias 6.1-3).

Augustine Baker, to whom, along with his followers among the exiled English Benedictines we owe the preservation of Julian's long text, quotes the *Golden Epistle* of William of St. Thierry (in Baker's day still attributed to Bernard of Clairvaux) in praise of the contemplative life: Aliorum est deo servire; vestrum adhaerere. Aliorum est Deo credere, scire, amare, revereri; vestrum est sapere, intelligere, cognoscere, frui.[360] Julian, in her humble realization that she is still aspiring to that fullness of the life of prayer which must be *begonne by goddys gyfte and his grace* (chapter 86, 731.2) in this present moment, but which reaches out into God's eternal present, uses all William's verbs to describe it:

> For charyte, pray we alle to gedyr with goddes wurkyng, thankyng, trustyng, enjoyeng, for thus wylle oure good lord be prayde, by þe vnderstandyng þat I toke in alle his owne menyng (731.3).

It is only as we fulfil God's will in trusting him that he is the ground of the unitive prayer of petition — and here Julian is referring again to the

---

[358] *Enarrationes in Iohannem,* 22 2; cf. de Lubac, *Exégèse médiévale* 2 634.
[359] Ibid., 635 and note.
[360] *Holy Wisdom,* 15.

beginning of the great revelation on prayer (cf. 460.3-5) — that *he wylle geve vs grace to loue hym and cleve to hym* (732.9), and this whether we be *ex professo* contemplatives or not.

This lesson of love can be heard in its simplest form in the call to 'pray without ceasing'; and certainly all creatures, lettered or unlettered, are gifted by God for its performance, in one mode or another. But as this lesson was learned by Julian, it contains and demands far more, as the editors have sought to demonstrate in the annotations to her text. Jean Leclercq has written with great perception about the conflict that can arise, in monastic theology and living, between learning and the *beata conscientia,* the devotion to heavenly things, and how this conflict can be resolved. Readers of Julian's book must decide how closely Leclercq's description fits her:

> To combine a patiently acquired culture with a simplicity won through the power of fervent love, to keep simplicity of soul in the midst of the diverse attractions of the intellectual life and, in order to accomplish this, to place oneself and remain firmly on the plane of the conscience, to raise knowledge to its level and never let it fall below: this is what the cultivated monk succeeds in doing. He is a scholar, he is versed in letters, but he is not merely a man of science nor a man of letters nor an intellectual; he is a spiritual man. [361]

## 19 Conclusion

In this first critical presentation of the texts of the *Revelations,* the editors have attempted to show all the evidence which has persuaded them that those critics who have regarded Julian as a spiritual teacher of the first order have been right. Both versions demonstrate that she was a woman of deep learning, by no means outmatched by that, say, of the *Cloud* or of the *Scale*; and the sobriety of her piety and her intensely cultivated literary gifts saved her from the extravagances of the school of Richard Rolle. She was never, until the twentieth century, a popular author; and much of the admiration she has been paid in our own times has been evoked by qualities attributed to her which in truth were not hers. So far from being the simple, untutored devotee miraculously endowed by the Spirit, she had laboured long and hard to equip herself to speak to the Church with the Church's authentic voice. Some of her teachings as she enunciates them may at first startle; but no one of them in any way conflicts with her assurance that all which she

---

[361] *The Love of Learning,* 317.

was shown, and all that prayer had taught her of its meaning, is in total accord with every other truth which God has revealed to men. 'God our mother' is infinitely more than a whimsical and exotic devotion. Julian came to perceive it as she penetrated the mysteries of Trinity and of the incarnate Word; and she may have been helped to expound it by some of those who before her had been led along the same paths.

The internal evidence produced by objective study of the manuscripts shows that both texts are wholly free from invention or falsification. The essential difference between the short text (together with the other, as she first drafted it) and the long text (as it finally came to be written in the 'second edition') is that first she suppressed the sights and locutions which were then to her incomprehensible, but, in the end, she was made to see that this should not be, and was given the insights which enabled her to record the totality of her showings, and to demonstrate with a theologian's authority their authenticity.

Perhaps the most striking proof of that authenticity is that, although we know that for many years after her book was finished and published she was consulted as a spiritual director, we do not know that she ever wrote another word. The case of the writer who has scored one first great success and then finds, when he attempts to repeat it, that he can only repeat himself, because inspiration has run dry, is not peculiar to the literary world; some of the Church's most prolific teachers would enjoy greater reputations, had they remained content with their earlier works and thereafter kept silence. Julian, evidently, was indifferent to her fame. It is true that in the short text she shows apprehension of the hostility which her writings may arouse, but her fears are not for her own standing in men's eyes, but that what she knows to be divine truths be impugned as a silly woman's vapourings. Once she had revealed those truths as the Spirit had best helped her to do, that was, it seems, for her the end of the matter. The rest she left to God and his other servants.

How much is owed in this respect to Augustine Baker and his school has been shown. He had tried to teach his disciples to pray as Julian had prayed; and it was they who saw her greatness as a woman of prayer, and who venerated her as a saint. So doing, they rescued what might have disappeared altogether, and preserved in their copies the long text, with its unique record not only of what she was shown in May, 1373, but of the graces and the wisdom given to her in the twenty years which followed.

It has been remarked that it is probably well that we know virtually nothing of her external life. We may guess that she was careful to ensure that there remained no 'materials for her biography', just as in her book she asks us to forget that she wrote it and to remember that God inspired it. Any attempts whilst she was alive to pay her a saint's honours she would have found abhorrent — she knew too much about the 'discretion of spirits' — and evidently she was permitted to die and to rest in the obscurity she had sought.

The editors have considered themselves justified in presenting their own conjectures about matters which have importance for a proper evaluation of the *Revelations*, for they are convinced, and they hope that the evidence on which their convictions rest will convince others, that Julian was a great scholar. But about how she learned her Latin, with whom she studied Scripture and rhetoric, in which library she came upon William of St. Thierry, we can do no more than surmise. Nor would complete information tell us anything which we do not in effect already know. Whether it was Carrow or somewhere else which gave Julian her training is inessential. She had been schooled in 'the Abbey of the Holy Ghost'.

# A BOOK OF SHOWINGS

The short text
edited from
MS BM Additional 37790

7r   Here es a visio*n* schewed be the goodenes of god to a deuoute
woma*nn*, and hir name es Julyan, that is recluse atte Norwyche and ʒitt
ys o*nn* lyfe, anno do*m*ini mille*s*imo CCCC xiijº; in the whilke visyo*nn* er
fulle many comfortabylle wordes and gretly styrrande to alle thaye that
5   desires to be Crystes looverse.

I desyrede thre graces be the gyfte of god. The fyrst wa*s* to have
mynde of Cryste es passio*nn*. The seco*nn*nde was bodelye syeknes, and
the thryd was to haue of goddys gyfte thre wonndys. For the fyrste
come to my mynde with devoc*i*on; me thought I hadde grete felynge in
10   the passyo*nn* of Cryste, botte ʒitte I desyrede to haue mare be the grace
of god. Me thought I wolde haue bene that tyme with Mary Mawdeleyne and with othe*r*e that were Crystes loverse, that I myght have

---

1 *Here*: the scribe wrote 'ere', leaving blank a large space for a coloured initial. The
limner drew a 'T', below which a coloured 'H' has been added without cancellation of
the erroneous letter. Cf. Introduction, p. 1.

6 *I*: the limner's letter is 'S', with, in the rest of the space left by the scribe, a
coloured 'I', without cancellation of the 'S'.

---

3-4 *er fulle many comfortabylle wordes*: cf. II Corinthians 1.3-5: ... the Father of mercies
and God of all comfort, who comforts us in all our tribulations, that we also may be
able to comfort them who are in all distress ... for as the sufferings of Christ abound in
us, so also by Christ does our comfort abound.

6 *I desyrede thre graces ... as othere dyd that lovyd hym* (202.14): this corresponds with the
long text, 285.5-286.12.

*thre graces*: with Julian's account of her aspirations we may compare the *Fifteen Oes*, often in her day spuriously attributed to Bridget of Sweden, but anonymous and of the
mid-fourteenth century, as is suggested by many Latin manuscripts and by the English
version found in MS BM Royal 17.C.xvii. The first prayer, *O domine Jesu Christe, eterna
dulcedo te amantium* (Lorde Jh*e*su eu*er* lastyng swetnes of þam þ*at* þe luf) has: ... lorde I
be seke þe for þe mynd of this dyshese þ*at* þu sofurd be for þu was done on þe rode as
gyf me be for my dyyng v*err*ay contrycyon, clere schryfte and (f. 95ᶜ) worthy satys-
faccyon and all my syns full remyssyon. The earliest English verse translation of pseudo-
Bonaventure's *Meditationes de passione Christi* (see Introduction, p. 52) has: Behold þe
peines of þi sauiour / A*n*d crucifie þin herte wiþ gret dolour (MS Bodley 415, f. 83ᵈ).
This is the translator's addition; cf. Stallings, 111. Later, it says of Mary: Truli i*n* herte
she is crucified / Ful fein for sorowe she wlde ha died (ibid., f. 84ᵇ); cf. 202.23 note.

*to have mynde of Cryste es passionn*: cf. 285.5 and note.

10 *mare be the grace of god*: cf. 285.8 note.

11 *with Mary Mawdeleyne and with othere*: cf. John 19.25: Now there stood by the cross
of Jesus his mother, and his mother's sister, Mary of Cleophas, and Mary Magdalen ...

12 *that I myght have sene bodylye the passionn*: cf. Lamentations 1.12-18: O all you who
pass by the way, attend and see if there be any sorrow like my sorrow ... Hear, I pray
you, all you people, and see my sorrow; and also the opening of the English pseudo-
Bonaventure, *The Privity of the Passion*: Who so desyres to fynd comforthe and

sene bodylye the passionn of oure lorde that he sufferede for me, that I
myght have sufferede with hym as othere dyd that lovyd hym, not with-
15 standynge that I leevyd sadlye alle the peynes of Cryste as halye kyrke
schewys *and* techys, *and* also the payntyngys of crucyfexes that er made
be the grace of god aftere the techynge of haly kyrke to the lyknes of
Crystes passyonn, als farfurthe as man ys witte maye reche. Nouȝt withstondynge alle this trewe be leve I desyrede a bodylye syght, whare yn y
20 myght have more knawynge of bodelye paynes of oure lorde oure
savyoure, and of the compassyonn of oure ladye and of alle his trewe
loverse that were be levande his paynes that tyme and sythene;
for I wolde have beene one of thame and suffrede with thame. Othere

---

gostely gladnes in þe passione and in þe croysse of owre lorde Jhesu, hym nedis with a
besy thoghte for to duell in it and all oþer besynes forgette and sett at noghte; and
sothely I trowe fully þat who so wolde besy hyme with all his herte and all his mynde
and vmbethynke hym of this gloryus passione and all the circumstance thare off, it sulde
bryng hym and chaunge hyme in to a new state of lyfynge (Horstman, 1 198; Stallings,
95; Ragusa and Green, 317).

14 *not withstandynge*: cf. 285.11. The rest of this sentence is not in the long text. The
reason for its omission there may well be that the Lollard opinion that the use of art-
objects for devotional or meditative purposes is reprehensible, current when Julian first
wrote, had, twenty years later, been decisively rejected. Cf. J. Russell-Smith, 'Walter
Hilton and a Tract in Defence of the Veneration of Images'. Such an omission, had it
occurred in the short text, could have been caused through homoeotopy (*not withstandynge ... Nouȝt withstondynge*), but not in the long text, where the words do not occur.

16 *payntyngys of crucyfexes*: probably this is meant literally: 'pictures of the Crucifixion'
or 'painted crucifixes'; but see G. V. Smithers's learned article, 'Two Typological
Terms in the *Ancrene Riwle*', showing that there *peinture, peintunge* mean 'imitation in a
portrait', and that the author is reflecting ideas, possibly conveyed to him from Hugh of
St. Victor, as old as Plato on the 'idea or form' of an object, on the object itself and on
the object's imitation or representation. The *Riwle* and Julian make exactly the same
point: men's imaginings of heaven and hell (*Riwle*), an artist's representation of the
Crucifixion (Julian), are mere 'paintings', 'shadows' (*Riwle*), limited by human abilities
— *als farfurthe as man ys witte maye reche.*

19 *I desyrede a bodylye syght ... whene I were in threttye ȝeere eelde* (204.46): this corresponds with the long text, 286.12-288.39.

*whare yn y myght have more knawynge of bodelye paynes of oure lorde*: cf. Psalm 68.21: I
looked for one who would grieve together with me.

22 *be levande his paynes*: cf. 286.14: *lyuyng that tyme and saw his paynes*, clearly the
superior reading; but see 286.14 note.

23 *for I wolde have beene one of thame and suffrede with thame*: this 'Franciscan' aspiration,
characteristic of the religious enthusiasm of Julian's age, is often found in contemporary
literature. In the pseudo-Bonaventure *Meditationes de passione domini* we read:

syght of gode ne schewynge desyrede I never*e* none tylle atte the sawlle
25 wer*e* departyd frome the bodye, for I trayste sothfastlye that I schulde
be safe; and this was my menynge, for I wolde aftyr be cawse of that
schewynge have the more trewe mynde in the passio*nn* of Cryste. For the
seco*nn*de, come to my mynde with contricio*nn*, frelye with owtyn any
sekynge, a wylfulle desyre to hafe of goddys gyfte a bodelye syekenes,
30 and I wolde þ*at* this bodylye syekenes myght have beene so harde as to
97v    the dede, / so that I myght in the sekenes take alle my ryghtynges of
halye kyrke, wenande my selfe that I schulde dye, and that alle creatures
that sawe me myght wene the same, for I wolde hafe no comforth of no
fleschlye nothere erthelye lyfe. In this sekenes I desyrede to hafe alle
35 manere of paynes, bodelye *and* gastelye, that I schulde have ȝyf I
schulde dye, alle the dredes *and* te*m*pestes of feyndys, *and* alle maner*e* of

---

(Maria) cum filio pendebat in cruce, et pocius elegit mori cum ipso quam amplius vivere (Stallings, 113; Ragusa and Green, 335), which the English prose version modifies: For oure lady hange one þe rode with hire dere childe in soule... (Horstman, 1 206). In the versified English adaptation of pseudo-Bernard, *Liber de passione Christi*, Bernard is made to say to Mary: Allas, whine had þat bale be mine? / I wald haue standen whare þou stode (Horstman, 2 275). The Franciscan John Grimston (cf. 285.11 note) recorded an eight-line poem which contains: I wolde be clad in Cristis skyn, / Þat ran so longe on blode (C. Brown, XIV 88).

*Othere syght of gode ne schewynge desyrede I nevere none*: cf. 286.16. Julian does not need to say that in the event she was given much more than she had prayed for.

28 *with contricionn*: cf. 286.20. The long text, *for I would be purgied by the mercie of god* (131.10) makes plainer than this that such contrition was for her own past sins.

*frelye with owtyn any sekynge*: cf. 286.20. This notion was no product of her own fancy, but came by inspiration.

29 *of goddys gyfte a bodelye syekenes*: cf. the *Ancrene Riwle* on sickness as a divine gift (Day, 80-81). The author then links his readers' own sufferings with Christ's: Ouer alle oþere þouȝtes, in alle oure passions, þenkeþ euere inwardliche vppon godes pynen (Vernon MS, f. 380ᶜ; cf. Day 83). In this and subsequent quotations of the *Riwle* (as distinct from the *Wisse*), wherever possible the still unpublished version in Vernon has been quoted, with a reference to a published text, usually Mabel Day's, for those who may wish to read the quotation in its context. See Introduction, p. 77 n. 183.

31 *ryghtynges*: 'rites'. Cf. 287.23 note. NED does not record, or any verb 'to rite' from which a gerund could be made; but the parallel passage in the long text shows that even if this be Julian's (or a scribe's) nonce-word, it means 'rites, ceremonies'.

36 *alle the dredes and tempestes of feyndys*: cf. 287.27. Julian shared the belief common to her times that the departing soul is especially exposed to attack from the devil and his agents. Cf. Introduction. For this sense of 'tempest', cf. *A Book to a Mother*: for right as pilers beren vp an hous and maken hit strong to withstonde tempestes, so þese seuene vertues beren up mannes soule fro erþely loue and maken hire strong aȝen tempestes of þe seuene dedly synnes (McCarthy, 7). Its editor dates *A Book* c. 1380, before orthodox sympathizers with Wycliffe perceived that the Lollards were preaching heresy. If *A Book* came Julian's way, its anti-religious sentiments and its misogyny would be unlikely to commend it to her.

(oþere) paynes, safe of the owȝte passynge of the sawlle, for I hoped that
it myȝt be to me a spede whenn I schulde dye, for I desyrede sone to be
w*ith* my god.

40      This two desyres of the passyonn and of the seekenes I desyrede
thame with a condic*i*on, for me thought that it passede the comene
course of prayers; and therfore I sayde: Lorde, thowe woote whate I
wolde. Ȝyf it be thy wille that I have itt, grawnte itt me, and ȝyf it be
nouȝt thy wille, goode lorde, be nought dysplesede, for I wille nought
45 botte as thowe wille. This sekenes desyrede I yn my (ȝ)ought, þat y
myght have it whene I were in threttye ȝeere eelde. For the thirde, I
harde a man telle of halye kyrke of the storye of saynte Cecylle, in the

---

37 *oþere*: ms: þayre; cf. 287.28      *safe* interlineated with caret by the corrector     *hoped*: 'd' interlineated with caret by the corrector.
45 *ȝought*: ms: thought; cf. 288.39.
46 *in*: interl. by corrector.

---

37 *for I hoped that it myȝt be to me a spede*: by 'spede' Julian probably means that when
the actual day of her death came she would be strengthened by experience against
diabolical assaults; cf. 287.31 and note.
38 *for I desyrede sone to be with my god*: cf. 287.32, where the long text reads *to haue ben*.
But either text makes the same point: she is not asking for an early death, but that
when death comes she may go at once to God. Cf. Psalm 41.3: When shall I come and
appear before the face of God? This was recited in the rite for the blessing of the font
on Easter Eve; *Missale Romanum 1474*, 1 189.
42 *prayers*: cf. 288.36: *prayer*. That is probably the better reading; 'neither were ordinary petitions'.
*and therfore I sayde*: cf. 288.36 note.
43 *ȝyf it be thy wille that I have itt grawnte itt me / and ȝyf it be nouȝt thy wille goode lorde be
nought dysplesede / for I wille nought botte as thowe wille*: a *compar* with medial *repetitio* and
*conversio*.
43 *and ȝyf it be nouȝt thy wille*: cf. 288.37 note.
45 *yn my ȝought*: cf. 288.38, and 285.4 note. Though 'juventus', 'youth' could be used
then (as now) to indicate differing ages, it is more probable that Julian is looking back
to times when she had formed this desire to suffer when she was thirty years old, rather
than that she means 'When I was thirty years old I desired to have this sickness, whilst I
was still in my youth'.
46 *in threttye ȝeere eelde*: she probably specifies this to show that what she had prayed
for was answered in detail, and also to associate this event with the life of Christ.
Pseudo-Bonaventure had written: When he had spent twenty-nine years living in the
difficult and lonely manner that I have described, the Lord said to his mother: 'It is
time for me to go to glorify and manifest my Father ...' (Ragusa and Green, 102; cf.
Peltier 12 533).
46 *I harde a man telle of halye kyrke*: for this unique acknowledgement, reminiscent of
Margery Kempe, of a precise source of information, the long text substitutes *by the*

whilke schewynge I vndyrstode that sche hadde thre wonndys with a
swerde in the nekke, with the whilke sche pynede to the dede. By the
50  styrrynge of this I conseyvede a myghty desyre, prayande oure lorde god
that he wolde grawnte me thre wonndys in my lyfe tyme, that es to saye

---

*grace of god and teaching of holie church* (288.40), and then suppresses the allusion to St.
Cecilia's legend.

48 *sche hadde thre wonndys with a swerde in the nekke*: Julian's informant may have been
drawing on James of Voragine's *Legenda aurea*: Quam spiculator tribus ictibus in collo
percussit (ed. Lyons, 1493, f. ccix[d]). In *A Book to a Mother* (cf. 203.36 note) we have:
... so Katerine, Cecilie, Lucie and monye maidens more freel in kinde and lasse strong
in bodi schullen arise at þe dai of dome and condempne such bodiliche stronge men þat
dispisen chastite and Cristes techinge (McCarthy, 94).

50 *I conseyvede a myghty desyre ... with owtyn any meenn* (210.16): this corresponds with
the long text, 288.40-294.7.

51 *that he wolde grawnte me thre wonndys*: cf. the English *Stimulus amoris*: And ȝif þow be
þus turned in to hym thorouȝ helpe of grace, I may nouȝt trowe but þat þow shalt be
wounded with his woundes and ouer helte wyth peynes of his passioun (H. J. Kane, 15;
Kirchberger, 55). The notion of God 'wounding' the loving soul is a commonplace
among exegetes of Canticles 4.9, 5.7. Bernard of Clairvaux combines it ingeniously
with an allusion to Ezechiel 11.19, 36.26: ... movit et emollivit et vulneravit cor meum,
quoniam durum lapideumque erat et male sanum (Sermon 74.6, ed. Leclercq, Talbot
and Rochais, 2 243). But it is under the influence of early Franciscan spiritual writers,
and especially of pseudo-Bonaventure's *Meditationes*, that the idea grows that these
wounds will be St. Paul's 'stigmata' (cf. Galatians 6.17), that the soul can take active,
dolorous part in the Passion through meditation; and this account of Julian's early
aspirations without doubt shows such Franciscan influence. Cf. also Zacharias 13.6:
What are these wounds in the midst of thy hands? The notion of the 'three noughts'
may well have been suggested by a passage in the *Scale,* II chapter 21: ... meknes *and*
luf, þat is, I am noȝt, I haue noȝt, I coueite noȝt bot on (MS BM Harley 6579, f. 85[r]; Underhill, 305). This found its way into mediaeval English anthologies describing the contemplative life; see P. S. Jolliffe, 'Three Middle English Tracts ...' (In quoting the
heavily-edited fourteenth-century English version of the *Stimulus amoris, The Prickynge of
Love,* the editors regard its attribution to Walter Hilton as probable but not proven.
The many additions to and manipulations of the Latin text indicated by Clare Kirchberger in her edition are by someone deeply involved in spirituality, whose opinions,
so far as they can be determined by his treatment of another man's work, seem to coincide with what we find in the *Scale* and other treatises certainly written by Hilton. H. J.
Kane is less convinced. Rightly, he observes that of the three surviving manuscripts containing the attribution, two derive from a common source and so serve only as a single
witness, and that the third is an anthology of short extracts, a work of the type which
tended to encourage 'a tendency among medieval copyists to connect admirable
anonymous works with prestigious names' (xxxii). Having regard to Kane's other, less
forceful arguments against Hilton's authorship, the editors would add that Julian's
failure, if she knew the *Prickynge*, to name Hilton as the author is equally inconclusive.
The *Revelations* show her deep knowledge of several contemporary spiritual classics, but
no interest whatever in the names or personalities of their authors.)

the wonnd(e) of contricyoun, the wonnde of compassyoun *and* the wonnde of wylfulle langgynge to god. Ryght as I askede the othere two with a condyscion, so I askyd the thyrde with owtynn any condyscion. This two desyres before sayde passed fro my mynde, and the thyrde dwellyd contynuelye.

55

---

52 *wonnde*: ms: wonndys.     *and*: interl. by corrector with caret.
54 *so*: interl. by corrector with caret.

---

52 *the wonnde of contricyoun / the wonnde of compassyoun / and the wonnde of wylfulle langgynge to god*: a *compar* with *repetitio*.

54 *with owtynn any condyscion*: cf. 288.44, which adds that Julian asked for this *mightly*. The third petition, unlike the other two, she is certain is pleasing to God's will and thus needs no such condition.

56 *dwellyd contynuelye*: cf. 288.46 note.

Ande when I was thryttye wyntere alde and a halfe, god sente me a
bodelye syeknes in the whilke I laye thre dayes and thre nyghttes; and
on the ferthe nyght I toke alle my ryghttynges of haly kyrke, and wenyd
nought tylle haue lyffede tylle daye. And aftyr this y langourede furthe
5  two dayes *and* two nyghttes, *and* on the thyrde nyght I wenede ofte
tymes to hafe passede, and so wenyd thaye that we*re* abowte me. Botte
in this I was ryght sarye, *and* lothe thouȝt for to dye, botte for nothynge
98r  that was / in erthe that me lykede to lyeve fore, nor for nothynge that I
was aferde fore, for I tristyd in god. Botte it was fore I walde hafe
10  lyevede to have lovede god better and lange tyme, that (I) myght be the
grace of that lyevynge have the more knowynge and lovynge of god in
the blysse of hevene. For me thought alle the tyme that I hadd lyeve(d)
here so lytille and so schorte in the regarde of endeles blysse. I thouȝt

---

10 *I*: om. ms.
12 *hadd*: subst. corrector for 'wolde', exp.     *lyeved*: ms: lyeve.

---

2 *thre dayes and thre nyghttes*: cf. 289.3. Julian has the mediaeval fondness for triads;
but she may here wish to suggest analogy between her own experience, which at the
time she believed to be imminent death, and the 'triduum sacrum' between Christ's
death and the Resurrection. Ludolph of Saxony, whose *Vita Jesu Christi* was written
c. 1350 (and thereafter circulated throughout the West by the Carthusians) ends Book
II chapter li with a prayer which has: ... meque de hoc mundo transire non permittas
antequam per triduum poenitentiae ... peccata mea omnia deleas (Rigollot, 3 321).
  3 *ryghttynges*: cf. 289.4: *rightes*, and 203.31 note.
  6 *Botte in this I was ryght sarye ...*: on the rhetoric of this passage and the corresponding
figure in the long text, cf. 289.7 note.
  7 *for nothynge*: cf. 289.8: *for no payne.*
  *for nothynge that was in erthe that me lykede to lyeve for*: in *A Book to a Mother* (cf. 203.36
note) the disposition of Christ and of his persecutors are contrasted: Wronges hem
þouȝte þei schulde not suffre; what is more wrong þan to dampne an innocent as Crist
was? Bodili sorwes and peynes þei hateden; Crist was scourged ant turmented. Þei
dredden þe deþ; Crist wolde be slawe (McCarthy, 109-110).
  10 *lange*: cf. 290.10: *longer.*
  12 *that I hadd lyeved*: cf. 290.12; but the scribe's *that I wolde lyeve* is defensible: 'for all
the time that I should (ever) live'; cf. 208.22: *whilys my lyfe walde laste.* R. M. Wilson observes that *lyeve* could also be the substantive: 'all the time that I had life'.
  13 *so lityrlle and so schorte*: there may here be a reminiscence of Job 14.1 e.s. on the
brevity of human existence. Rolle opens his *Job*: Parce mihi domine, nihil enim sunt dies
mei. Exprimitur autem in his verbis humanae conditionis instabilitas, quae non habet in
hac miserabili valle manentem mansionem ... (H. E. Allen, *Rolle*, 143). The theme is
much elaborated in *The Bird with Four Feathers,* a rhymed 'tretys of *Parce michi domine*'
(Brown, XIV 208-215).

thus: Goode lorde, maye my lyevynge be no langere to thy worschippe?
15 And I was annswerde in my resone and be the felynges of my paynes
that I schulde dye; and I asentyd fully with alle the wille of mye herte to
be atte god ys wille.

Thus I endurede tille daye, and by than was my bodye dede fra the
myddys downwarde, as to my felynge. Than was I styrrede to be sette
20 vppe ryghttes, lenande with clothes to my heede, for to have the mare
fredome of my herte to be atte goddes wille, and thynkynge on hym
whilys my lyfe walde laste; and thay that were with me sente for the
personn, my curette, to be atte myne endynge. He come, and a childe
with hym, and brought a crosse; *and* be thanne I hadde sette myne
25 eyenn and myght nou3t speke. The persone sette the crosse before my
face, and sayde: Dow3tt*er*, I have brought the the ymage of thy
sauioure; loke there oponn *and* comforthe the þere with in reverence of
hym that dyede for the *and* me. Me thou3t þan that y was welle, for
myne eyenn ware sette vpwarde in to hevene, whethyr I trustede for to
30 come, botte nevere the lesse I assendyd to sette myne eyen in the face of
the crucyfixe 3if y myght, for to endure the langer in to the tyme of
mynn endyng, for me thought I my3t langyr endure to loke evyn forthe
than vppe ryght. Aftyr this my syght by ganne to fayle, and it was alle
dyrke abowte me in the chaumbyr, and myrke as it hadde bene nyght,
35 save in the ymage of the crosse ther*e* helde a commonn lyght, and I

15 *I (was)*: interl. by corrector with caret.
17 *be*: interl. by corrector with caret.

14 *maye my lyevynge be no langere to thy worschippe?* Julian may have had in mind Philippians 1.21-22: For to me to live is Christ, and to die is gain, and if to live in the flesh, this is to me the fruit of labour, and what I shall choose I know not. Ludolph of Saxony ends his *Vita*, I xlvii, with a prayer for freedom from sin and demonic temptation: ... meque ab eis liberatum usque in finem misericorditer custodi illaesum, ut ad tuam gloriam et proximorum utilitatem valeam verbis narrare ... (Rigollot, 2 21).
23 *my curette*: he is also called this in the long text, 290.20, but not, as here, *the persone*. The use of either term implies that he was a secular priest, unlike her other visitor later in the day whom she calls *a religiouse personn* (266.7; cf. 632.16). That the 'persone' is accompanied by a little boy as crossbearer (208.23), and that her mother (234.29) and others were at her bedside, suggests but not necessarily proves that at this time Julian was not living in enclosure as anchoress.
*and a childe with hym*: cf. 291.21, where this detail is omitted.
27 *in reverence of hym that dyede for the and me*: cf. 291.23, where these words are omitted.
31 *for to endure the langer in to the tyme of mynn endyng*: these words are not in the long text (cf. 291.26); and the similarity of the next clause suggests that they may be the result of dittography.
33 *was*: cf. 291.28 and note.

wyste nevere howe. Alle that was besyde the crosse was huglye to me,
as ȝyf it hadde bene mykylle occupyede with fendys.

Aftyr this the overe partye of my bodye beganne to dye, as to my
felynge. Myne handdys felle downe on aythere syde, and also for vn-
98v   powere my heede satylde downe / onn syde. The maste payne that I
41   felyd was schortnes of wynde and faylynge of lyfe. Than wende I
sothelye to hafe bene atte the poynte of dede. And in this sodeynlye alle
my payne was awaye fro me, and I was alle hole, and namely in the
overe partye of my bodye, as evere I was before or aftyr. I merveylede
45   of this channge, for me thought it was a pryue wyrkynge of god, *and*
nought of kynde; and ȝitte be the felynge of this ese I trystede nevere the
mare that I schulde lyeve, ne the felynge of this ese was ne fulle ese to
me, for me thouȝt I hadde leuere have bene delyverede of this worlde,
for my herte was wilfulle there to.

---

45 *pryue*: interl. corrector over 'journe', exp.

---

37 *as ȝyf it hadde bene mykylle occupyede with fendys*: this suggests mediaeval Crucifixion-
iconography. The Index of Christian Art writes: 'Often, in Italian and other representations, a devil or devils appear near the cross of the bad thief for the purpose of
removing his soul, while angels perform a similar function at the cross of the good
thief. In addition, mourning angels hover about the crucified Christ, and sometimes, as
in the Pisan fresco (Camposanto, 14th century), some of them almost surround the
devils'. Ludolph of Saxony, *Vita Jesu Christi* II lxiii 20, 'Diabolus supra crucem stetisse
fertur', writes of those exegetes who make the gigantic fish attacking Tobias a type of
the devil assailing the crucified Christ (Rigollot, 4 107).

39 *Myne handdys*: this graphic sentence is omitted in the long text; cf. 291.34.

45 *journe* (exp.): cf. 292.38. Perhaps A derives from a text with a reading < OE
dyrne, 'secret'.

48 *me thouȝt* ...: cf. 292.40, and Philippians 1.23: ... having a desire to be dissolved
and to be with Christ, a thing by far the better.

(iii)　　And sodeynlye co*mm*e vnto my mynde that I schulde desyre the
seconn*de* wonn*de* of our*e* lordes gyfte and of his grace, that he walde
fulfylle my bodye with mynde of felynge of his blessede passyo*nn* as I
hadde before prayede, for I wolde that his paynes ware my paynes, with

5　　compassyo*nn and* aftyrwarde langynge to god. Thus thou3t me that I
myght with his grace have his wonndys that y hadde before desyrede;
but in this I desyrede neu*er*e ne bodely syght ne no maner*e* schewynge of
god, botte co*m*passyo*nn* as me thought that a kynde sawlle myght have
with our*e* lorde Jh*es*u, that for love wolde be come man dedlye. With

10　　hym y desyrede to suffere, lyevande in dedlye bodye as god wolde gyffe
me grace. And in this sodaynlye I sawe the rede blode trekylle downe
fro vndyr the garlande, alle hate, freschlye, plentefully *and* lyvelye, ryght
as me thought that it was in that tyme that the garlonde of thornys was
thyrstede on his blessede heede. Ryght so, both god and man, the same

15　　sufferde for me. I conseyvede treulye *and* myghttyllye that itt was hym
selfe that schewyd it me with owtyn any mee*nn*; and than I sayde:

---

3 *mynde of felynge*: the long text's *mynd and feeling* (292.45) is probably superior.

8 *compassyonn as me thought*: cf. 293.49, and Ephesians 5.1-2: Be therefore followers of
Christ, as most dear children, and walk in love, as Christ also has loved us and has
delivered himself ...

9 *for love*: cf. 732.15-733.17 and note.

12 *garlande*: cf. 210.13, 294.5, 362.22. NED, s.v. Garland, *sb.*, 1 b, 'Christ's crown of
thorns', cites two examples, one from *Piers Plowman* B XVIII, and calls this usage 'obs.
rare'; but MED, gerlond 1(c), has five examples, not including this. Two others may be
added, Brown XIV 223, and Person, *Cambridge Middle English Lyrics,* 10. Mechtild of
Hackborn in her *Book of Special Grace,* I xxxiii, describes how in one vision Christ 'hadde
also in his hede a gerlande of dyuerse ande fulle fayre floures', which symbolized the
pains inflicted on his head; and in another vision, IV xxxiii, '... owre lorde apperede to
here ande helde in his blessede handdys a manere of a serkylle or a garlande of drye
tree', signifying man's heart, dried up in sin, which Christ will adorn with the roses of
grace (Halligan, 172, 540). There may be a satirical implication in this usage, contrasting Christ's wretchedness with worldlings' vanity. In one of its many reprehensions
of contemporary luxury, *A Book to a Mother* (cf. 203.36 note) has: Ne none nyce
dameselis wiþ garlondis of gold ne perlis ne filettis ne bonettis (McCarthy, 48-49). In the
Vulgate, 'corona' means both 'crown' and 'garland': illi quidem ut corruptibilem
coronam accipiant (I Corinthians 9.25). In a Marian lament, our Lady is made to say:
Hys chaplet ys thornys sore prykkyng (Wright: *Chester Plays,* 2 207).

16 *meenn*: 'intermediary'. Cf. NED Mean *n*² II-9ᵃ, where the first example is c. 1374
(Chaucer), the second, 9ᶜ, *Piers Plowman* A (i.e. c. 1370). MED mene, n. 3(a), 1389 *Guild
Return*: he þat is chose mene. Many other instances will be noted of Julian's very
modern and literary vocabulary.

*and than I sayde ... alle gostelye enmyes* (211.27): this corresponds with the long text,
296.16-297.27.

Benedicite domin*us*. This I sayde reu*e*rentlye in my menynge, with a
myghtty voyce, and fulle gretlye I was astonnyd for wonder*e and* mer-
veyle that y had that he wolde be so homblye with a synfulle creature
99r  lyevande in this wrecchyd flesch. / Thus I tokede it for that tyme that
21  oure lorde Jh*e*su of his curtayse love walde schewe me c*om*forthe before
the tyme of my te*m*ptacyo*n*n; for me thought it myght be welle that I
schulde be the suffyran*n*ce of god and with his kepynge be temptyd of
fendys or I dyede. With this syght of his blyssede passyo*n*n, with the
25  godhede that I saye in myn vndyrstandynge, I sawe that this was strengh
ynow3e to me, 3e, vnto alle creatures lyevande that schulde be saffe
agaynes alle the feendys of hell*e and* agaynes alle gostelye enmyes.

---

20 *flesch*: ms: fle- (which fills the line to its end) schly.

---

17 *Benedicite dominus*: cf. 296.16. For 'Benedicite' as a salutation or a blessing, cf. the
*Ancrene Riwle*: ... and goþ forþ mid godes dred to prest. Aller furst confiteor, and þer after Benedicite, þat he ou3te siggen (Vernon MS, f. 380ᶜ). For 'Benedicite' as a prayer
before eating, with the response 'Dominus', cf. J. Baudot, 'Bénédiction de la table ou
des aliments'. However, the 'Canticle of the Three Children' (Daniel 3.52 e.s.) was in
such frequent liturgical use, with its differing Latin beginnings, 'Benedicite omnia opera
domino', 'Benedicite dominum', 'Benedictus es domine' (cf. F. Cabrol, 'Benedicite et
Benedictus es Domine'), that it is hardly possible to decide what Julian actually said, and
whether it was in blessing, thanking or praising. It is however clear that this passage
provides no evidence for or against her being 'a woman that could no letter'.
   *This I sayde* ...: cf. 296.16 note.
  19 *homblye*: cf. 296.19: *homely*. Whether this is a spelling reflecting pronunciation
with 'momentary delabialisation', or a confusion of 'homely' with 'humbly', can only be
conjectured. R.M. Wilson suggests that *homblye* may represent the same ml > mbl
development as in NE 'bramble'; and this is supported by one spelling, 'homblynesse',
recorded by MED.
  23 *be the suffyrannce of god*: cf. 296.22. In the *Ancrene Riwle,* the 'fifth comfort against
temptation' is: þat he ne may no þing don vs bote be godes leue (Vernon MS, f. 382ᵈ; cf.
Day, 102). In MS Sidney Sussex 80, f. 101ᵛ, there is a prayer to the Virgin: O refugium
animarum, tibi supplico quatinus in tuo seruicio semper perseuerare valeam in
presenti, vt in exitu anime mee euadere possim terrorem maligni Sathane ...
  24 *With this syght* ...: this is a well-constructed *compar* which Julian has left unchanged
in the long text (296.23-297.27): *With this syght of his blyssede passyonn / with the godhede that
I saye in myn vndyrstandynge / I sawe that this was strengh ynow3e to me / 3e vnto alle creatures
lyevande that schulde be saffe / agaynes alle the feendys of helle / and agaynes alle gostelye enmyes.*
There is *repetitio (With ... with), conduplicatio (to me / 3e vnto alle),* and a second *repetitio
(agaynes ... agaynes).*
  25 *saye ... sawe*: 'saye' may mean 'I say' ( < OE secge) or 'I saw' ( < OE seah). Modern
English 'saw' is from the plural stem, OE sāwon. But the only other example in A, compared with 'sawe' (15×) is *I saye the bodylye syght* (217.2).
  *that this was strengh ynow3e to me*: cf. 296.24 note.

(iv)        And this same tyme that I sawe this bodyly syght, oure lorde schewyd
me a gastelye sight of his hamly lovynge. I sawe that he es to vs alle
thynge þat is goode and comfortabylle to oure helpe. He es oure
clethynge, for loove wappes vs and wyndes vs, halses vs and alle be
5      teches vs, hynges a boute vs for tendyr loove, that he maye nevere leve
vs. And so in this syght y sawe sothelye that he ys alle thynge that ys
goode, as to myne vndyrstandynge.
            And in this he schewyd me a lytille thynge, the qwantyte of a haselle
nutte, lyggande in the palme of my hande, *and* to my vndyrstandynge
10     that, it was as rownde as any balle. I lokede þer oponn and thought:
Whate maye this be? And I was annswerde gen*er*aly thus: It is alle that

---

2 *hamly*: scr.: Anly, which he has alt.
5 *vs (hynges)*: ms: vs vs.

---

1 *And this same tyme ... betwyxe my god and me* (213.21): this corresponds with the long
text (299.2-300.22).
    *this bodyly syght*: cf. 299.2: *this sight of the head bleidyng*, which is a reworking (by Julian
or another), probably to avoid any possible confusion with the preceding vision,
'ghostly in bodily lykenes' (297.29 and note) of Mary. In the contrast she makes here between the 'bodyly syght' and the 'gastelye sight of his hamly lovynge', Julian's per-
ceptions of the modes of the revelations is, like her language, careful and exact.
    3 *goode and comfortabylle*: that God is our comforter is found in the Old Testament as
well as the New: cf. e.g. Isaias 49.13, Zacharias 1.13, John 16.27, II Corinthians 1.3 e.s.
    *He es oure clethynge, for loove wappes vs*: cf. I John 4.8, 10: For God is love ... because he
has first loved us. Cf. 299.4, but the reading there, *He is oure clothing, that for loue*, seems
inferior, lacking the Johannine ring.
    5 *that he maye nevere leve vs*: Julian here seems to have in mind John 14.16-18: ... that
he may abide with you forever, the Spirit of truth ... because he shall abide with you
and shall be in you. I will not leave you orphans ...
    6 *he ys alle thynge that ys goode*: this may recall Christ's reply: Why do you ask me con-
cerning good? One is good, God (Matthew 19. 17).
    7 *as to myne vndyrstandynge*: that is, this is a 'gastelye sight'. Cf. 212.1 note.
    9 *lyggande in the palme of my hande*: cf. the Latin *Fifteen Oes*, (201.6 note): O Jhesu
mundi fabricator que*m* nulla diuisio uero intermino metitur, qui terram palmo con-
cludis ... (MS BM Royal 17 A xxvii, f. 91ᵛ); O Jhesu maker*e* of all*e* þe warlde whos
myght no thyng may mesur*e*, þat closes þe herth in þi hand ... (MS BM Royal 17 C xvii,
f. 95ᶜ).
    10 *it was as rownde as any balle*: cf. 299.10 note.
    *I lokede þer oponn and thought / Whate maye this be / And I was annswerde generaly thus / It
is alle that ys made*: a *compar* with *ratiocinatio*.
    11 *It is alle that ys made*: this and what follows is so close to the thought and language
of Wisdom 11.23-26 that it is hardly likely that this was not the source: For the whole
earth before thee is as the least grain of the balance, and as a drop of the morning dew
that falls down upon the earth. But thou hast mercy upon all, because thou canst do all
things, and overlookest the sins of men for the sake of repentance. For thou lovest all

ys made. I merveylede howe þat it myght laste, for me thought it myght falle sodaynlye to nought for litille. And I was annswerde in myne vndyrstandynge: It lastes and euer schalle, for god loves it; and so hath alle thynge the beynge thorowe the love of god.

15

In this lytille thynge I sawe thre partyes. The fyrste is that god made it, the seconnde ys that he loves it, the thyrde ys that god kepes it. Botte whate is that to me? Sothelye, the makere, the lovere, the kepere. For to I am substancyallye aned to hym, I may nevere have love, reste ne varray blysse; that is to saye that / I be so festenede to hym that thare be ryght nought that is made betwyxe my god *and* me. And wha schalle do this dede? Sothlye hym selfe be his mercye *and* his grace, for he has made me there to and blysfullye restoryd.

99v

21

In this god brought oure ladye to myne vndyrstandynge. I sawe hir gastelye in bodilye lyekenes, a sympille maydene *and* a meeke, 30nge of age, in the stature that scho was when scho conceyvede. Also god schewyd me in parte the wisdom *and* the trowthe of hir saule, whare yn I vndyrstode reuerente beholdynge, þat sche behelde hyre god, that ys

25

---

17 *(made) it*: interl. corrector w. caret.
28 *hyre*: ms: oure, exp., 'hyre' interl. corrector.

---

things that are, and hatest none of the things which thou hast made, for thou didst not appoint or make any thing hating it. And how could any thing endure if thou wouldst not, or be preserved if not called by thee?

16 *partyes*: cf. 300.17: *propreties*, and note. This A reading, though defensible, may be the result of a careless scribe's misinterpretation of 'p(ro)p(er)tyes'. Cf. 583.19: *I saw and vnderstode these thre propertes*. The *Cloud*-author writes, in *Privy Counselling*: ... whiche ben þe propirtees þat fallyn to þis perfeccion (Hodgson, *Cloud*, 153).

*The fyrste is that god made it / the seconnde ys that he loves it / the thyrde ys that god kepes it*: a *compar* with *complexio*.

17 *Botte whate is that to me?* Cf. 300.18 and note.

19 *love*: not in the long text. Cf. 300.20.

21 *And wha ... blysfullye restoryd*: not in the long text. Cf. 300.22.

24 *In this god brought ... the blyssede manhede of Criste* (214.36): this corresponds with the long text, 297.28-298.40. Cf. 297.28 note.

25 *gastelye in bodilye lyekenes*: cf. 297.29. As with the vision of Christ crowned with thorns, this is corporeal, but even whilst writing the short text, Julian knows that it is also 'gastelye', given not only for its own sake but to convey spiritual truths.

26 *in the stature that scho was when scho conceyvede*: in Julian's age it was generally received that this happened when Mary was a mere girl. Cf. MS Trinity College Dublin 423 (England, c. 1450), f. 105ᵛ: Sancta Maria fuit in etate quindecim annorum quando peperit Christum, postea mansit cum eo xxx annis in hoc seculo ... In the Christ Church, Dublin *Liber Niger* it is stated that she conceived at the age of twelve (E. Colledge: *The Latin Poems of Richard Ledrede*, 132 note).

28 *reuerente beholdynge*: in *Privy Counselling*, the *Cloud*-author writes: For þis same werk, 3if it be verrely conceyuid, is þat reuerent affeccion and þe frute departid fro þe tre þat

hir makere, mervelande with grete reuerence that he wolde be borne of
30  hir that was a sympille creature of his makynge. And this wysdome of
trowthe *and* knawande the gretnes of hir makere and the lytelle heede
of hir selfe that ys made, made hir for to saye mekely to the angelle
Gabrielle: Loo me here, goddys hande maydene. In this sight I sawe
sothfastlye that scho ys mare than alle þat god made benethe hir in wor-
35  thynes *and* in fulheede. For abovene hir ys nothynge that is made botte
the blyssede manhede of Criste. This lytille thynge that es made that es
benethe oure ladye saynt Marye — god schewyd it vnto me als litille as
it hadde beene a hasylle notte — me thought it myght hafe fallene for
litille.

---

30 *his makynge ... And this*: ms: his makynge. For this was hir mervelynge, that he that
was hir makere walde be borne of hir that was a sympille creature of his makynge. And
this ...

31 *and (knawande)*: interl. corrector w. caret.

32 *made hir for to*: scr.: made h (which reaches the ruled margin); the rest add.
corrector.

---

I speke of in þi lityl pistle of preier (Hodgson, *Cloud,* 154; and cf. *Deonise,* 56, where, in
the *Epistle of Prayer,* he quotes I Corinthians 6.17).

*beholdynge ... behelde*: the noun is complementary to *wisdom, trowthe,* and we must understand 'contemplation, contemplated'. Mary Baldwin ('Some Difficult Words in the
*Ancrene Riwle*'), demonstrates how often the *Riwle* uses 'bihalden' in this sense, and not
with any connotation of physical vision. One of her illustrations is: Þus lo þe articles ...
of oure bileaue onont godes monhead, hwa se inwardliche bihalt ham (Tolkien, 135).
Julian's vocabulary is a practical illustration of Richard of St. Victor's definition: Con-
templatio est libera mentis perspicacia in sapientiae spectacula ... (*Beniamin Major* 1 4,
PL 196 67).

29 *that he wolde be borne of hir that was a sympille creature of his makynge*: this is an 'oppositio contrariorum', of the Creator with the creature. So Richard Ledrede (ob. 1360)
in one of his Nativity poems had written: Fit magnus paruulus seruus et dominus /
Contentus continens breuis interminus / Antiquus nascitur distansque comminus / Ex-
celsus humilis et simplex geminus (ibid., 120 and notes). However, G. Rigg (*The Poems of
Walter of Wimborne,* 11-12) shows that Ledrede's asclepiadic verses are adaptations of
some of Wimborne's *Marie carmina.*

30 *his makynge ...*: the dittography which follows in the manuscript must derive from
an ancestor which had been collated with a long text copy, or vice versa. Cf. 297.34
and notes, Introduction, p. 19.

36 *This lytille thynge that es made that es benethe oure ladye*: cf. 300.23, where the
reference to Mary does not appear. In her reflection on the locution 'All shall be well'
(422.2), Julian speaks of *alle creaturys whych are beneth Crist* (424.25). Mary is also the
prototype of *mans soule ... a creature in god whych hath the same properties* (the divine attributes of truth and wisdom) *made* (484.13). It is doubtless this development in her
theology which leads her to remove the phrase in the long text as less than accurate.
See Introduction, IX 3.

40      In this blyssede revelacion god schewyd me thre noughtes of whilke
noušttes this is the fyrste that was schewyd me. Of this nedes ilke man
*and* woman to hafe knawynge that desyres to lyeve con*tem*platyfelye,
that hym lyke to noušt alle thynge that es made for to hafe the love of
god that es vn made. For this es the cause why thaye þat er occupyede
45   wylfullye in erthelye besynes *and* eue*r*mare sekes warldlye wele er
nought here of his in herte and in sawlle; for thaye love and seekes here
ryste in this thynge that is so lytille, where no reste ys yn, *and* knawes
noušt god that es alle myghtty, alle wyse and alle goode, for he is

_____

40 *In this blyssede revelacion* ...: this sentence is not in the long text; cf. 301.24. The
first 'nought' is this vision of all that is created (212.11); *fallen to nought* (300.23) is
probably a better reading than *fallen,* but in either text it is plain that it is creation *ex
nihilo* which Julian has in mind. The second 'nought' is probably sin (226.9), and the
third the impotent devil (227.31), whom Christ 'noughts', asking us to do the same
(228.40).

*noughtes*: 'nothings'. The numeral adjective shows that this is a plural noun, not the
adverbial genitive. The usage is rare but not without parallel. MED nought cites c.
1400 *Book of Vices and Virtues* 82.5: But wiþ-out witt and good auisement, þes þre þinges
beþ nouštes.

41 *Of this nedes ... to resayue gostlye reste* (216.53): this corresponds with the long text,
301.24-33.

42 *that desyres to lyeve contemplatyfelye*: cf. 301.24, where this clause is not found. This
could indicate that the ancestor of C, SS, P and W had been edited with secular as well
as religious readers in mind.

43 *that hym lyke to noušt*: 'that he find pleasure in despising', which shows that P's
*nought* (301.25) is infinitive, not adverb, as is also indicated by S1: *to nowtyn,* and S2: *to
noughten.*

*for to hafe the love*: cf. 301.25: *for to loue and haue,* which is probably superior. An ancestor of S1 evidently considered (though needlessly) that 'to love and have' was ob-
jectionable.

44 *thaye þat er occupyede ... wardlye wele*: not in the long text; cf. 301.26 and 215.42
note. The thought here on the rest which is to be found in God alone and not in worldly occupation is directly from Matthew 11.28-29: Come to me, all you that labour and
are burdened, and I will refresh you ... and you shall find rest for your souls. The
*Scale,* I chapter 3, has: Contemplatif lyfe ... longeš specialy to he*m* þe whilk forsaken for
þe loue of god all wordly ryches worschipes and outward bisynes and holly šyuen hem
bodie and soule ... to þe seruice of god by gostly occupacionn (MS Cambridge UL Add.
6686, p. 279; Underhill, 5).

45 *er nought here of his*: possibly corrupt. Probably 'be not all in ease' is superior (cf.
301.26), and *of his* should read 'at ease'. But Julian may be alluding to some such Scripture passage as: Has not God chosen the poor in this world ... heirs of the kingdom
which he has promised to those who love him? (James 2.5); and see also Galatians 3.29,
4.7, Romans 8.17, Titus 3.7. Cf. the *Treatise of Perfection*: And after as euery man sekys
and laborys to ouercomme hymselfe ... he felys hym inwardly towched, and swetly to
taste the frute of the sonne, thorowe the which taste the holy goste beres hym witnesse
to be eyre of god (Bazire and Colledge, *Chastising,* 254).

f. 100r  verraye reste. God wille be knawenn, *and* hym lykes þat / we reste vs in
50      hym; for alle that ar benethe hym suffyces nouȝt to vs. And this is the
        cause why that na saule ys restede to it be noghthed of alle that es
        made. Whenn he is noughthid for love, to hafe hym that is alle that is
        goode, than es he abylle to resayue gostlye reste.

---

49 *God wille be knawenn and hym lykes / þat we reste vs in hym for alle / that ar benethe hym suffyces nouȝt to vs*: a *compar* of three *cola*, with medial *repetitio* (*hym ... hym ... hym*). This echoes Augustine's 'Fecisti nos ad te ...' (*Confessions* I 1, probably one of the most frequently-quoted non-Scriptural sayings in the Christian world); and we may observe a very similar figure, a three-membered *compar* with *repetitio*, in Augustine's Latin: quia fecisti nos *ad te* / et inquietum est cor nostrum / donec requiescat *in te* (Knöll, 1).

51, 52 *noghthed, noughthid*: 'annihilated'. Cf. NED Nought, *v.*, where the first example is from the *Scale,* II 20, and MED, which adds 'nouȝtnyng (Parkminster: nowghtyng)' from the *Cloud* (Hodgson, 149). Though the examples from secular literature in NED, MED show that the term quickly gained currency in the sense of 'despise, dispraise', it would seem that it was first used, as here, by spiritual writers to render 'adnihilare'.

52 *that is goode*: not in the long text; cf. 301.32. This reading looks like some scribe-editor's superfluous addition; Julian is contrasting 'all that is made', which must be noughted if we are to have him 'who is all'.

(v)   And in that tyme that oure lorde schewyd this that I haue nowe
saydene in gastelye syght, I saye the bodylye syght lastande of the
plentyuouse bledynge of the hede, and als longe as y sawe that syght y
sayde oftynn tymes: Benedicite dominus. In this fyrste schewynge of
5   oure lorde I sawe sex thynges in myne vndyrstandynge. The furste is þe
takyns of his blysfulle passionn and the plentevous schedynge of his
precyous blode. The seconnde is the maydene, that sche ys his dere
worthy modere. The thyrde is the blysfulle godhede þat euer was *and* es
*and euer* schalle be alle myghty, alle wysdome *and* alle love. The ferthe
10   is alle thynge that he has made; it is mykille *and* fayre and large *and*
goode. Botte the cause why it schewed so lytille to my syght was for I
sawe itte in the presence of hym that es makere. For to a sawle that sees
the makere of alle thynge, alle that es made semy(s) fulle lytylle. The
fyfte es that he has made alle thynge that ys made for love, *and* thorowe
15   the same love it is kepydde, and euer schalle be with owtynn ende, as it

---

2 *in (gastelye)*: interl. corrector w. caret.        *saye*: not canc., but interl. corrector:
saw.
5 *þe*: interl. corrector w. caret.
11 *schewed*: add. marg. corrector w. caret.
13 *semys*: ms: semyd; cf. 318.12.

---

1 *And in that tyme ... of the hede* (217.3): this corresponds with the long text, 311.12-14.
2 *saydene*: 'said'. For the form, cf. NED, Say, *v*.¹, A.7., which quotes 1422, *Secreta
Secret.*: ... is largely Saydyn.
4 *In this ... or the same langer tyme* (218.22): this corresponds with the long text, 317.1-
319.21.
5 *sex thynges*: in neither text does the recapitulation which follows observe the
chronological order of the previous narrative. Julian seems to have regrouped the
revelations according to their modes: (1) 'bodily sights' — the 'tokens', the crown of
thorns and the bleeding; (2) 'ghostly in bodili likeness' — Mary; (3) 'ghostly sights' —
the Trinity, the 'homely loving', all creation in comparison with its creator, all created
for love, God is all that is good.
6 *the plentevous schedynge of his precyous blode*: this theme of the plenty of the blood shed
at the Passion occurs in the *Fifteen Oes* (cf. 201.6 note): O Jhesu verray *and* frutefull vine,
af mynd on þe ouerflowyng *and* þe plenteuus cheddyng of þine blode þat þou sched plen-
tewsly als grapes þat ere prast wen in þe crose þu trade þe prassure allone (cf. Isaias
63.3) and brog-/ht furth vntill vs water *and* blode ... (MS BM Royal 17 C xvii, f. 93ᶜ⁻ᵈ).
8 *þat euer was and es and euer schalle be / alle myghty alle wysdome and alle love*: *membrum*,
with *traductio* in the second *colon*.
11 *Botte the cause ...*: cf. 317.10 note.

is before sayde. The sexte es that god is alle thynge that ys goode, *and* the goodenes þat alle thynge has is he.

   And alle thynge oure lorde schewyd me in the fyrst syght, and gafe me space *and* tyme to behalde it. And the bodyly syght styntyd, *and* the
20 gastely syght dwellyd in myne vndyrstandynge, *and* I abade with reue*r*ente drede, ioyande in that I sawe *and* desyra*n*nde as y durste for to see mare, ʒif it ware his wille, or the same langer tyme.

---

17 *þat*: ms: of; 'þ*at*' interl. corrector.
18 *thynge (oure)*: interl. corrector: þis.

---

   16 *god is alle thynge that ys goode* ...: in general, Julian is here reflecting the common doctrine of the Western Church: God's goodness and his being are one and the same, and so it is with all that exists. 'Because God is good we exist, and in so far as we exist we are good'. This is the burden of chapter 4 of the *Divine Names* of pseudo-Denis. Cf. also *De Trinitate* VIII 3, Mountain and Glorie, 1 272: 'See good itself if you can; thus you will see God, not as a good distinct from another good, but as the good of every good'.

(vi)     Alle that I sawe of my selfe, I meene in the *pe*rsone of all*e* myne evy*n*n
cristene, for I am lernede in the gastelye schewynge of oure lorde that
he meenys so. And therfore I praye ʒowe alle for goddys sake, *and*
cownsayles ʒowe for ʒowre awne profyt, that ʒe leve the behaldynge of
ov    the wrechid wor(m)e, / synfulle creature, that it was schewyd vnto, *and*
6    that ʒe myghtlye, wyselye, lovandlye *and* mekelye be halde god, that of
his curtays love and of his endles goodnes walde schewe gene*r*alye this
visyo*n*n in comforthe of vs alle. *And* ʒe that hyerys and sees this visio*n*n
and this techynge that is of Jh*e*su Cryste to edificac*i*on of ʒoure saule, it
10   is goddys wille *and* my desyre that ʒe take it with als grete ioye and

---

1 *alle (myne)*: interl. corrector w. caret; marg.: all (in same hand as 'worme', 219.5;
cf. Introduction, p. 1).

5 *worme*: with 'wrechid' scribe filled last line, and added below 'worlde'. Cf. 211.20.
Contemp. hand (not the corrector's) add. marg.: worme.      *it*: add. corrector.

10 *desyre*: ms: desyrere.

---

1 *Alle that I sawe ... as he dyd to me* (220.11): this corresponds with the long text,
319.33-320.40.

*sawe*: cf. 319.33: *say*, and note. The conflict seems to have been caused by the different ME dialectal developments of OE seah, 'I saw', affected by sāwe, sāwon, 'thou
didst see, we saw'.

3 *And therfore I praye ʒowe alle ...*: what follows is very close to the *Chastising*, where
the author deals specifically with rapture and visions, and then continues: ... þenke þat
al þese ʒiftes whiche we receyue bien ʒoven to us not for oure meritis but for her grace
and for her profite ... and to þenke in oure owne synnes and vnworþinesse (Bazire and
Colledge, 184).

4 *cownsayles* (one of the many Northern dialect features of A): this use of the word
may indicate that Julian has no fears that she may be criticized for giving spiritual direction; by the time that she was ready to publish the short text, perhaps in the mid 1380s
(see Introduction), it may already have been known that she *was expert in swech thyngys
and good cownsel cowd ʒeuyn* (*Book of Margery Kempe*, 42).

5 *wrechid worme*: cf. 320.36: *wrech*. In the English *Stimulus amoris*, the translator interpolates the same words: A lorde hit is a gret mercy þat þou suffrest me a wrecchid
woorm for to walken vp on þe erþe (H. J. Kane, 157; Kirchberger, 170). In an English
prose commentary on the Benedictine Rule, where it cites Psalm 21.7, there is: And saie
als te prophete saide: Ego sum etc. Ic es wrmis and na man, and ut castyng o men. First
was ic hezed and siþin lazed þur scrifte and ouir cumin (Kock, 14; cf. Hanslik, 49).

6 *lovandlye*: not in the long text; cf. 320.37.

*be halde god*: see 320.37 note.

8 *And ʒe that hyerys ... of ʒoure saule*: not in the long text: cf. 320.39. Nor is, line 10,
*and my desyre*.

lykynge as Jhesu hadde schewyd it to ʒowe as he dyd to me. For the
schewynge I am not goode but ʒif y love god the better, and so may and
so schulde ylke man do that sees it and heres it with goode wille and
trewe menynge. And so ys my desyre that it schulde be to euery ilke
15  manne the same profytte that I desyrede to my selfe and þerto was
styrryd of god in the fyrste tyme when I sawe itte; for yt (ys) comonn
and generale as we ar alle ane, and I am sekere I sawe it for the profytte
of many oder. For sothly it was nought schewyd vnto me for that god
loves me bettere thane the leste sawlle that is in grace. For I am sekere
20  thare ys fulle many that nevere hadde schewynge ne syght botte of the
commonn techynge of haly kyrke that loves god better þan I. For ʒyf I
loke syngulerlye to my selfe I am ryght nought; botte in generalle I am
in anehede of charyte with alle myne evynn cristene. For in this
anehede of charyte standes the lyfe of alle mankynde that schalle be
25  safe. For god is alle that ys goode, and god has made alle that ys made,
and god loves alle that he has made, and ʒyf anye man or womann

---

16 *ys*: om. ms.
23 *cristene*: ms: cristende.

---

18 *for that*: 'because'; cf. 321.6: *that*. Either reading can be defended. The short text
makes Julian say that the revelations were not given to her because God loves her more
than any other soul in a state of grace, in P she says that the revelations did not show
her that God loves her more …; but note that C and S2 agree with A.

19 *For I am sekere* …: cf. the *Chastising*: Alle hooli men and wymmen, which I clepe
goddis chosen children, þouʒ þei wirche no myraclis, ne haue no spirit of profecie ne
reuelacions ne visions, ʒit her names bien writen in þe booke of lijf … (Bazire and
Colledge, 183-184). Ludolph of Saxony ends his *Vita*, II xli, with a prayer: Domine Jesu
Christe, mitis et humilis corde, funda cor meum in vera humilitate, et exclude a me om-
nem motum praesumptionis et superbiae, ut nunquam visiones desiderem aut
revelationes nec per aliquas tentationes seducar spirituales, quae me ducere quoquo-
modo possent in errores (Rigollot, 3 266).

23 *in anehede of charyte*: what follows is clearly inspired by Ephesians, chapter 4:
… supporting one another in charity … Cf. the *Cloud*: … þof al þei sie soche þinges wiþ
þeire bodely iʒen, it was schewyd bot in myracle and in certefiing of þing þat was
goostly … by miracle and in licnes for alle us þat ben abel to be sauid, þat ben onyd to
þe body of Criste goostly (Hodgson, 106-107).

25 *For god is alle that ys goode / and god has made alle that ys made / and god loves alle that
he has made*: a *compar* with initial *repetitio* (For god … and god … and god), medial *repetitio*
(alle … alle … alle) and *conversio* (ys goode … ys made … has made).

26 *and ʒyf anye … nouʒt in pees* (221.29): this passage, not reproduced in the long text,
is inspired by I John 3.14-17, 23-24: We know that we have passed from death to life,
because we love the brethren. He who does not love abides in death. Whoever hates
his brother is a murderer … How does the charity of God abide in him? … And this is
(God's) commandment, that we … love one another, as he has commanded us. And he
who keeps his commandments abides in him. Reflection may have suggested to Julian
that in this passage she had seemed to be reprehending her readers.

departe his love fra any of his evy*n* crysten, he loves ryght nought, for
he loves nou3t alle. And so that tyme he ys nou3t safe, for he es nou3t in
pees; and he that gen*e*raly looves his evy*n* crysty*n*n, he loves alle that
30  es. For in mankynde that schalle be saffe is co*m*prehende alle, that ys
alle that ys made and the makere of alle; for in manne ys god, *and* so in
man ys alle. And he þ*at* thus gen*e*ralye loves alle his evyn crystene, he
loves alle, and he that loves thus, he is safe. And thus wille I love, *and*
thus I love, and thus I am safe. For y mene in the perso*n*n of myne evyn
35  crystene, and the more I love of this lovynge whiles I am here, the mare
01r  I am lyke to the blysse that I / schalle have in hevene with owten ende,
that is god that of his endeles love wolde be come owre brothere *and*
suffer for vs. And I am sekere þ*at* he that behaldes it thus, he schalle be
trewly tau3t *and* myghttelye comforthtede, if hym nede co*m*forthe.

---

36 ms: that I (f. 101ʳ) that I.
39 *if*: by corrector over erasure.

---

29 *and he that generaly ... he loves alle* (221.33): this corresponds with the long text,
322.13-17.
30 *For in mankynde that schalle be saffe is comprehende alle / that ys alle that ys made and the
makere of alle / for in manne ys god and so in man ys alle*: a *compar* with *repetitio* and *conversio*.
*comprehende* ...: cf. *Privy Counselling*: He is þi being and in him þou arte þat at þou
arte ... and in þat he is one in alle and alle in him þat alle þinges han her beinges in him
and he is being of alle (Hodgson, *Cloud,* 136), and the *Cloud*: ... he is al comprehensible
at þe fulle, insomochel þat o louyng soule only in it self, by vertewe of loue, schuld comprehende in it hym þat is sufficient at þe fulle, and mochel more, wiþ oute comparison,
to fille alle þe soules and aungelles þat euer may be (ibid., 19).
32 *And he þat thus generalye loves* ...: this teaching on 'general love', not reproduced in
the long text, is very close to chapters 24 and 25 of the *Cloud* (Hodgson, 58-61). Note
especially: For alle men þink hym iliche sib unto him and no man fremmid (ibid., 59).
*And he þat thus generalye loves alle his evyn crystene / he loves alle and he that loves thus he is
safe*: a *compar* of two longer *cola*, with initial *repetitio* and medial: *And he ... loves ... loves ...
and he ... loves.*
33 *and he that loves thus ... and suffer for vs*: cf. 322.17. Julian is far from the only contemplative to have received assurances of her soul's salvation; but, again, she seems to
have judged this passage likely to arouse hostile response and therefore to have suppressed it. If taken out of its context and quoted without her qualification *For y mene in
the personn of myne evyn crystene,* it could have been misinterpreted.
35 *the mare I am lyke to the blysse that I schalle have in hevene*: cf. I Corinthians 13.10: But
when that which is perfect has come, that which is in part shall be done away.
37 *god that of his endeles love wolde be come owre brothere*: cf. Hebrews 2.17: It behoved
him in all things to be made like to his brethren ...
38 *And I am sekere ... nede comforthe*: this sentence corresponds with the long text,
322.17-19, though it has there been modified to *And I hope* ...
*he schalle be trewly tau3t*: cf. John 6.45: Every one who has heard of the Father and has
learned comes to me.

40 Botte god for bede that ʒe schulde saye or take it so that I am a techere,
for I meene nouʒt soo, no I mente nevere so; for I am a womann, leued,
febille *and* freyll*e*. Botte I wate wele, this that I saye, I hafe it of the
schewynge of hym tha(t) es sou*er*ayne techare. Botte sothelye charyte
styrres me to telle ʒowe it, for I wolde god ware knawenn, *and* mynn
45 evynn crystene spede, as I wolde be my selfe to the mare hatynge of
synne *and* lovynge of god. Botte for I am a womann, schulde I therfore
leve that I schulde nouʒt telle ʒowe the goodenes of god, syne that I
sawe in that same tyme that is his wille, that it be knawenn? And that
schalle ʒe welle see in the same matere that folowes aftyr, if itte be welle
50 and trewlye takynn. Thane schalle ʒe sone forgette me that am a wrecche, and dose so that I lette ʒowe nought, *and* behalde Jh*e*su that ys
techare of alle. I speke of thame that schalle be safe, for in this tyme

---

43 *that*: ms: thas.
49 *if*: interl. corrector w. caret.

---

40 *Botte god for bede* ...: from here to *techare of alle* (222.52) is not found in the long
text; cf. 322.19, 323.20. Again, this defence of herself, so like to Margery Kempe's, as a
woman who does not teach, may have been deleted as likely to antagonize male
readers; but, on the other hand, the notably more tranquil tone of the long text at this
point could suggest that in later years Julian had gained assurance. Plainly, Julian here
has in mind the prohibition in I Corinthians 14.34, as had the author of the *Riwle*: Sum
is so wel ileret oþer so wys iwordet þat heo ... bicomeþ mayster þat scholde beon ancre,
and lereþ hi*m* þat is icomen hire for to leren (Vernon MS, f. 374ᶜ; Day, 28).

41 *leued, febille and freylle*: this is no more than modest self-disparagement, and we are
not obliged to understand *leued* as meaning 'illiterate', any more than when Douglas
writes in his *Æneis* 'I say nocht this of Chaucer for offence / Bot till excuse my lawit in-
suffitience' (NED Lewd 2).

43 *of hym that es souerayne techare*: cf. Matthew 23.8: For one is your master.
*charyte styrres me*: cf. II Corinthians 5.14: For the charity of Christ presses us.

44 *I wolde god ware knawenn*: cf. Isaias 66.14: And the hand of the Lord shall be
known to his servants.
*and mynn evynn crystene spede*: cf. I Corinthians 12.7: ... the manifestation of the Spirit
is given ... for profit.

45 *hatynge of synne and lovynge of god*: cf. Psalm 96.10: You that love the Lord, hate
evil.

50 *Thane schalle ʒe sone forgette me that am a wrecche / and dose so that I lette ʒowe nought /
and behalde Jhesu that ys techare of alle*: a three-membered *compar* with *oppositio contrariorum*.

51 *dose*: this is the Northern plural imperative: 'and do this (forget me), so that I am
no hindrance to you'.
*behalde Jhesu that ys techare of alle*: cf. John 13. 13: You call me master and lord, and
you say well, for so I am; and Hebrews 12. 2: ... Jesus, the author and finisher of faith.

52 *I speke of thame ... haly kyrke techis* (223.54): this corresponds with the long text,
323. 20-23.

god schewyd me non othere; bot in alle thynge I lyeve as haly kyrke techis, for in alle thynge, this blyssede schewynge of oure lorde, I be 55 helde it as ane in god syght, and I vndyrstode neu*er* nathynge þer yn that stoneȝ me ne lettes me of the trewe techynge of halye kyrke.

(vii)     Alle this blyssede techynge of oure lorde god was schewyd to me in
thre partyes, that is be bodylye syght, and be worde formede in myne
vndyrstandynge, *and* be gastelye syght. Botte the gastelye syght I maye
nought ne can nought schewe it vnto ȝowe oponlye *and* als fullye as I
5   wolde; botte I truste in oure lorde god alle myghtty that he schalle of
his goodnes and for ȝoure love make ȝowe to take it mare gastelye and
mare swetly than I can or maye telle it ȝowe, and so motte it be, for we
are all*e* one in loove. And in alle this I was mekylle styrrede in charyte
to myne evy*n*n cristene, that thaye mygħt alle see and knawe þe same
f. 101v   that I sawe, for I walde that it ware comforthe to thame / alle as it es to
11   me; for this syght was schewyd in gen*e*ralle, *and* nathynge in specyalle.
Of alle that I sawe, this was the maste co*m*forthe to me, that oure lorde
es so hamlye *and* so curtayse, and this maste fillyd me with lykynge *and*
syekernes in saule. Than sayde I to the folke that were with me: Itt es to
15   daye domes daye with me. And this I sayde for I wenede to hafe dyed;
for that daye that man or womann dyes ys he demyd as he schall*e* be

---

6 *ȝowe*: ms: iȝowe.
12 *I*: interl. corrector w. caret.
13 *fillyd*: ms: fil-lyd; 'il' corrector over erasure.

---

1 *Alle this blyssede techynge ... maye telle it ȝowe* (224.7): this corresponds with the long text, 323.29-34.
7 *and so motte it be, for we are alle one in loove*: not in the long text; cf. 323.34.
8 *And in alle this ... nathynge in specyalle* (224.11): this corresponds with the long text, 319.21-25.
10 *for I walde that it ware comforthe to thame alle*: though Julian is very sure of her own place in contemplative life and its traditions, she is free of the guarded esotericism to be seen in some of even the most orthodox of her peers. For example, the *Cloud*-author writes that no-one must see his works except those who have forsaken the active life (Hodgson, 1-2).
11 *for this syght was schewyd in generalle / and nathynge in specyalle*: *oppositio contrariorum*.
12 *Of alle ... syekernes in saule*: this sentence corresponds with 313.31-34 in the long text.
14 *Than sayde I ... to hafe dyed* (225.20): this corresponds with 319.25-31 in the long text.
15 *domes daye with me*: the only example in NED of the meaning 'particular judgment' is 1579, Lyly: 'Dost thou not know that everyone's death day is his doomesday?' MED does not record the meaning. Hugh of St. Victor seems to have been the first theologian to distinguish clearly between the general and particular judgments, in *De sacramentis*, where he writes first 'de morientibus, seu de fine hominis', and then 'de fine saeculi'; but the terminology 'particular' and 'general' became current only with the scholastics. Cf. J. Rivière, 'Jugement'.

with owtynn eende. This I sayde for y walde thaye lovyd god mare *and*
sette the lesse pryse be the vanite of the worlde, for to make thame to
hafe mynde that this lyfe es schorte, as thaye myght se in ensampill*e* be
20  me; for in alle þis tyme I wenede to hafe dyed.

And aftyr this I sawe with bodely syght the face of the crucifixe that
hange before me, in whilke I behelde co*n*tynuely a party of his
passyo*n*n: despite, spittynge in sowlynge of his bodye *and* buffetynge in
his blysfulle face, *and* manye langoures and paynes, ma than I can telle,
25  and ofte chaungynge of coloure, and alle his blyssede face a tyme
closede in dry blode. This I sawe bodylye *and* hevelye *and* derkelye; and
I desyred mare bodelye lyght to hafe sene more clerelye. And I was
annswerde in my resone that ȝyf god walde schewe me mare he schulde,
botte me nedyd na lyght botte hym.

---

20 *þis*: 'is' interl. corrector.

---

17 *and sette the lesse pryse be the vanite of the worlde*: not in the long text; cf. 319.29.
21 *And aftyr this ... na lyght botte hym* (29): cf. 324.3-325.14.
23 *spittynge*: cf. 324.5 and note.
*sowlynge*: cf. 324.5 and note.
24 *langoures and paynes*: cf. 324.5: *languryng paynes*. Either reading is defensible. Cf.
Isaias 53.4: 'Surely he has borne our infirmities and carried our sorrows', which I Peter
2.24 relates to the Passion.
25 *ofte chaungynge of coloure*: cf. 233.2-8, 357.3-9, 11 and note. These descriptions
markedly resemble some lines from the 'imago pietatis' poem, *Brother, Abide*: 'My visage
changed to pale and blew as byse,/ My fleshe beganne to styff and waxid drye, / My
hart lokyd lyke a plommet of ise ...' (Brown, XV 174). Though the poet, like Julian,
may have known pseudo-Bonaventure (R. Woolf, *The English Religious Lyric,* 197 and
note 1), the *Meditations* are not here the source. Probably both writers are describing
contemporary art-objects, 'the payntyngys of crucyfexes that er made be the grace of
god' (202.16), such as the horrific illustrations from MS B.M. Add. 37049 reproduced
by R. Woolf; and Julian's intention plainly is to heighten the spiritual significance of the
contrast between this 'image of pite' and her visions of the risen and glorified Lord.
26 *dry blode*: pseudo-Bonaventure has a similar detail: 'his cloþes þat were drye and
bakene to his blessid body all abowte hyme in his blyssede blode' (Horstman 1 205;
Stallings, 111, Ragusa and Green, 333).
*hevelye*: cf. 325.11: swemly.
27 *I was annswerde in my resone*: here she seems to be trying to convey a reflective
process which is certainly, in her own consideration, assisted by grace, but which differs
greatly from the 'part' of the revelation which is 'by words formed in my understanding'. It also differs from where she says that there 'was brought to my mind
this word' (360.2), and 'I had a proffer in my reason' (370.6), both of which are also
'gracious' activities, but 'meditative' (discursive) rather than contemplative, acquired
rather than infused graces.
28 *ȝyf god walde schewe me mare he schulde / botte me nedyd na lyght botte hym*: a *compar.*
29 *me nedyd na lyght botte hym*: cf. 325.13 and note, and Psalm 22.1: 'The Lord rules
me, and I shall want nothing'.

(viii)     And aftyr this I sawe god in a poynte, that es in myne vndyrstandynge, by whilke syght I sawe that he es in alle thynge. I behelde
with vysemente, wittande and knawande in that syght that he dose alle
that es done. I merveylede in this syght with a softe drede, and thought:

5     Whate es synne? For I sawe trulye that god dothe alle thynge, be itt
nevere so litille, nor nathynge es done be happe ne be eventure, botte
the endeles forluke of the wysdome of god. Whare fore me behovede
nedes grawnte that alle thynge that es done es wele done, and I was
sekyr that god dose na synne. Þer fore it semed to me þat synne is nouȝt,

10     for in alle thys, synne was nouȝt schewyd me. And y walde no lengyr
mervelle of this, botte behalde oure lorde, whate he wolde schewe me.
*And* in anothyr tyme god schewyd me whate syne es, nakydlye be the
selfe, as y schalle telle aftyr warde.

---

9 *Þer fore ... thys, synne*: add., foot of page w. mark of om., corrector.
13 *warde*: ms: worde; 'a' interl. al. m.

---

1 *And aftyr this ... of the wysdome of god* (226.7): cf. 336.3-337.9.
*in a poynte*: 'in an instant'. Cf. NED Point *n¹* III 7, where the first example is 1382,
Wycliffe: 'At a poynt in a litil I forsoc þe' (Isaias 54.7: 'Ad punctum in modico dereliqui
te'). There is an earlier example in Rolle: and led þair dayes in lust and delyces, and in
a poynt þai fel intil hell (Margaret Amassian, ed.: *The Commandment*, where she observes
that Rolle is translating Job 21.13: And in a moment they go down to hell). He quotes
Job 20.5 in his *Exposicio* (cf. 263.1 note): In hiis quippe tormentis experimento
cognoscent quia *laus impiorum brevis est, et gaudium ypocrite ad instar puncti* (Murray, 19).
The *Speculum christiani*, which Holmstedt dated, on internal and manuscript evidence, as
of the second half of the fourteenth century, and which elsewhere quotes Rolle's *In-
cendium*, writes: thei ledde here dayes in lustes, lykynges and vanites, and thei descendyd
to helle in a poynte (204).
    5 *For I sawe trulye ...*: for this *ratiocinatio*, preserved in the long text, cf. 336.7 note.
    7 *forluke*: cf. MED for(e-lok, n. (2), '... divine prescience, divine providence', and
for(e-loken, v. The earliest example of the noun is 1357, the *Lay Folks' Catechism*. MED
calls the verb 'modelled on L provideo', and both entries indicate that the terms were
rare and generally confined to theological writings.
    *Whare fore me behovede nedes grawnte*: this is the logical concession of the proof, the an-
swer to the question in the *ratiocinatio*. For the legal term *concessio*, see *Ad Herennium*
I.xiv.24 (Marx-Trillitzsch, 20). Julian shows the same awareness of the philosophical
reasoning as she might have found in Chaucer's *Boethius*: Syn þat he ne may not done
yuel þat may done alle þinges ... deceiuest þou me, þat hast so wouen me wiþ þi
resouns (Morris, 105). Cf. 338.21 note.
    *Whare fore me behovede ... whate he wolde schewe me* (226.11): this corresponds with the
long text, 338.17-24.
    8 *alle thynge that es done es wele done*: cf. 338.18 note.
    9 *is nouȝt*: cf. 338.22: *is no dede*.
    12 *And in anothyr tyme ... as y schalle telle*: cf. 338.28-339.29.

And aftyr this I sawe be haldande the bodye plentevouslye bledande,
15  hate *and* freschlye and lyfelye, ryȝt as I sawe before in the heede. And
102r this was schewyd / me in the semes of scowrgynge, and this ranne so
plenteuouslye to my syght that me thought, ȝyf itt hadde bene so in
kynde, for þat tyme itt schulde hafe made the bedde alle on blode *and*
hafe passede o*n*n abowte.

20  God has made waterse plentuouse in erthe to oure servyce and to
owre bodylye eese, for tendyr love that he has to vs. Botte ȝit lykes hym
bettyr that we take fullye his blessede blode to wasche vs with of synne;
for thare ys no lykoure that es made that hym lykes so welle to gyffe vs.
For it is so plenteuouse and of oure kynde.

25  And aftyr this, or god schewyd me any wo(r)des, he suffyrde me to be
halde langere, and alle that I hadde seene, *and* alle that was there yn.
And than was with owty*n*n voyce *and* with owte openynge of lyppes formede in my sawlle this worde: Here *with* ys the feende ou*er* co*m*my*n*n.
This worde sayde oure lorde me(n)ande his passyo*n*n, as he schewyd me
30  before. In this oure lorde brought vnto my mynde *and* schewyd me a
perte of the fendys malyce, *and* fully his vnmyght, and for that he
schewyd me that the passyo*n*n of hym is ou*er*comynge of the fende. God

---

16 ms: schewyd (f. 102ʳ) schewyd.
25 *or*: ms: houre.    *wordes*: ms: wonndes; cf. 346.3.
29 *menande*: ms: mevande; cf. 346.8.

---

14 *And aftyr this ... the semes of scowrgynge*: cf. 342.3-4.
16 *semes*: cf. 342.3: *in semyng*, and note.
*and this ranne so plenteuouslye ... and of oure kynde* (227.24): cf. 342.9-343.18.
20 *God has made waterse*: see 343.13 note.
25 *And aftyr this ... lokene in goddys hande* (228.40): this corresponds with the long text, 346.3-347.18.
*or god schewyd me any wordes*: see 346.3 note.
26 *langere*: cf. 346.4: *a conveniable tyme*.
27 *with owtynn voyce ...*: see 346.6 note.
28 *Here with ys the feende ouer commynn*: the author of the *Ancrene Riwle* calls the Passion: herte scheld aȝeyn þe fent (he is alluding to Lamentations 3.65); and he continues: hef hit an heiȝ aboue*n* þin herte heued ... hold hit vp toȝeyn þe fend ... þe siȝt þer of one bringeþ hi*m* to fleon (Vernon MS, f. 385ᵈ; Day, 132).
29 *as he schewyd me before*: this is probably a general reference to the previous revelations of the suffering Christ, though it may allude to what she has just written, 227.21-22.
31 *the fendys malyce*: see 347.9 note.
*and fully his vnmyght*: see 347.9 note.
32 *the passyonn of hym ...*: see 347.10 note.

schewyd me that he hase nowe the same malyce that he had before the
incarnac*i*on, and als sare he traveyles, *and* als contynuelye he sees that
35 alle chosene saules eschapes hym worschipfullye. And that es alle his
sorowe; for alle that god suffers hym to do turnes vs to ioye *and* hym to
payne *and* to schame, and he has als mekylle sorowe when god gyffes
hym leve to wyrke as whe*n* he werkys nought. And that es for he maye
nevere do als ille as he wolde, for his myght es alle lokene in goddys
40 hande. Also I sawe oure lorde scorne his malyce and nought hym, and
he wille that we do the same. For this syght, I lugh3 myghttelye, and
that made tha*m*m to laugh3 that were abowte me; and thare laughynge
was lykynge to me. I thought y wolde myne evyn cristene hadde sene as
I sawe. Than schulde thaye alle hafe laughy*nn* with me. Botte I sawe
45 nou3t Cryste laugh3; neu*er* the lesse hym lykes that we laugh3 in com-
fortynge of vs, *and* er ioyande in god for the feende ys ou*er* comy*nn*.
*And* aftyr this I felle into a saddehe(d)e, *and* sayde: I see. I see thre
thynges: game, scorne and arneste. I see game, that the feende ys ou*er*-
f. 102v comenn, and I see scorne, / that god scornes hym and he schalle be
50 scornede, and I see arneste that he es ou*er*come*nn* be the passio*nn* of
oure lorde J*hesu* Cryste *and* be his dede, that was done ful erneste *and*
with sadde travayle.

---

36 *to (do)*: interl. corrector w. caret.     *vs*: corrector, over erasure.
47 *saddehede*: ms: sadde hete.     *I see (thre)*: interl. corrector w. caret.

---

35 *alle chosen saules*: cf. 347.13: *all sowles of saluacion*.
*And that es alle his sorowe*: St. Thomas taught that there is in the devil the sin of envy:
... est in angelo peccante malum invidiae secundum quod de bono hominis doluit
(*Summa theologiae* I.63.2 ad corpus).
40 *Also I sawe ... ys ouer comynn*: cf. 348.24-349.31.
44 *Botte I sawe nou3t Cryste laugh3*: Julian here is hinting at what in the long text she is
able to say with clarity (347.18): that there can be no 'laughing scorn' in God, even as
there can be no wrath; what she means when she there writes *I sawe hym scorne his malis*
(349.31) she explains as the quality of his unchanging *sothfastnesse*.
45 *neuer the lesse hym lykes that we laugh3*: in the long text this is changed to: *but wele I
wott that syght that he shewed me made me to laugh* (348.29-349.30).
47 *And aftyr this ... with saddle travayle*: cf. 349.36-350.41.
*saddehede*: cf. 349.36: *sadnes*; SS: *sadhede*. Plainly A's reading is a corruption of the
ancestor as represented by SS. NED, Sad, *adj*. and *adv*., II 10b, records 'sadde' (c. 1420),
'of a fire: violent'; but the A reading in its context is nonsensical. NED does not record
'Sadhead'.
48 *I see game that the feende ys ouercomenn / and I see scorne that god scornes hym and he
schalle be scornede / and I see arneste that he es ouercomenn be the passionn of oure lord Jhesu
Cryste*: a three-membered *compar* with *repetitio* (*I see ... I see ... I see ... ouercomenn ...
ouercomenn ... scorne ... scornes ... scornede*).

Aftyr this oure lorde sayde: I thanke the of thy servyce *and* of thy trauayle, *and* namly in þi ȝough.

---

53 *Aftyr this oure lorde ... in þi ȝough*: cf. 351.3-4 and note. Ludolph of Saxony ends his *Vita*, II xiv (in which he has commented on the parable of the workmen in the vineyard) with a prayer: Domine Jesu Christe, summe paterfamilias, tu me primo mane in vineam tuam conduxisti, dum me a juventute mea ad fidem et tuum servitium misericorditer vocasti (Rigollot, 3 98).

(ix)    God schewyd me thre degrees of blysse that ylke saule schalle hafe in
hevene that wilfullye hase servyd god in any degree heere in erthe. The
fyrste is the wyrschipfulle thankkynge of owre lorde god that he schall*e*
resayfe when he es delyu*e*rede fro payne. This thanke is so hy3e and so

5    wyrschipfulle that hym thynke it fylles hym, þow3 þare ware no mare
blys. For me thought that alle the payne *and* travayle that myght be suffyrde of alle lyffande men myght nought hafe deservede the thanke that
a man schalle hafe that wylfullye has servydde god. For the seconnde,
that alle the blyssede creatures þat er in hevene schalle see that wor-

10    schipfulle thankynge of oure lorde god. And he makys his servyce to
alle that er in heue*n*n knawe*n*n. And for the thyrde, that als new ande
als lykande as it es resayvede that tyme, ryght so schalle itt laste with
owte*n* ende, I sawe that goodelye and swetlye was this sayde *and*
schewyd to me, that þe age of eu*er*y ylk man schalle be knawen in

15    heue*n*n and rewardyd for his wilfulle seruyce and for his tyme, and
namely the age of thame þat wilfullye and frelye offers thare 3ought
vnto god es passande rewardede *and* wondyrlye thankkyd.

    And aftyr this oure lorde schewyd me a sou*e*rayne gastelye lykynge in
my sawlle. In this lykynge I was fulfillyd of eu*er*lastande sekernesse,
20    myghtlye festnede with owtyn any drede. This felynge was so gladde to
me and so goodly that I was in pee3, in ese and in ryste, so that þ*er*e was
nothynge in erthe that schulde hafe grevyd me.

    This lastyd botte a while, and I was turnede *and* lefte to my selfe in
hevynes and werynesse of my selfe and yrkesumnesse of my lyfe that vn-

---

7 *hafe (deseruede)*: add. marg. corrector.
14 *man*: interl. corrector w. caret.
21 *I was*: interl. corrector w. caret.

---

1 *God schewyd me ... or in heuenn knawenn* (230.11): cf. 352.13-23.
*thre degrees*: so the long text, 352.13. But 'degrees' is not here used in its commoner
sense of 'ascending scale', but to mean 'three separate categories'; and *in any degree* (line
2; cf. 352.14) means 'in any capacity'.
11 *And for the thyrde ... wondyrlye thankkyd* (230.17): this corresponds with the long text,
353.27-32.
17 *passande*: 'surpassingly'. Cf. NED Passingly, *adv.*, MED passaunt, adv. One of
MED's earliest examples is Rolle, *Form of Living*. Cf. MS Trinity College Dublin 70 (15th
century): Þese be þe ei3te tokenesse of mekenesse ... and for þis lownesse *and*
mekenesse he was passingli comendid of Crist.
18 *And aftyr this ... dryed to my sight* (233.10): cf. 354.3-357.11.
21 *goodly*: cf. 354.6: *goostely*. 'goodly' is the last word of the line, where the scribe
seems often prone to error: cf. 211.20, 219.5, 224.13, 230.7.

25  nethes I cowthe hafe pacyence to lyeve. Thare was none ese ne na comforthe to my felynge botte hope, faythe and charyte, and this y hadde in
trowthe botte fulle lytille in felynge. And an one aftyr god gafe me

103r  agayne the comforth and / the reste in saule, likynge and syekyrnesse so
blysfulle *and* so myghtty þat no drede, no sorowe, no payne bodylye no

30  gastelye that myght be sufferde schulde have dissesede me. And than
the payne schewyd agayne to my felynge, and than the ioye and the
lykynge, *and* than the tane *and* nowe the tothere, dyverse tymes, I suppose abowte twentye sythes. And in the tyme of ioye I myght hafe sayde
with Paule: Nathynge schalle departe me fro the charyte of Cryste; and

35  in payne y myght hafe sayde with saynte Petyr: Lorde, save me, I
perysche.

Þis visio*n*n was schewyd me to lere me atte my vndyrstandynge þat it
es nedefulle to ylke ma*n*n to feele on this wyse, sum tyme to be in comforthe *and* sum tyme to fayle *and* be lefte to hym selfe. God wille that

40  we knowe that he kepes vs eu*e*re lyke syekyr, in wele and in woo, *and* als
mykille loves vs in woo as in weele. *And* sum tyme for the profytte of his
saule a man es lefte to hymselfe; *and* to whethere synne es nought the
cause. For in this tyme I synnede nought wherefore I schulde be lefte to

---

31 *and the (lykynge)*: ms. and than the.

---

26 *botte hope, faythe and charyte*: again Julian adverts to I Corinthians 13.
*and this y hadde in trowthe botte fulle lytille in felynge*: 'I had faith in them, but I experienced little of them'.

33 *And in the tyme of ioye / I myght hafe sayde with Paule / Nathynge schalle departe me fro
the charyte of Cryste / and in payne / y myght hafe sayde with saynte Petyr / Lorde save me I
perysche*: a six-membered *compar* with *oppositio contrariorum*.

34 *Nathynge schalle departe me ...* : this is Julian's summary of Romans 8.35-39: Who
then shall separate us from the love of Christ? ... Neither life nor death ...

35 *Lorde, save me, I perysche*: again, this conflates Matthew 14. 30: Lord, save me, with
Matthew 8.25: Lord, save us, we perish.

40 *and als mykille loves us in woo as in weele*: not in the long text; cf. 355.24. But cf. the
apparatus to 354.1: S1: is of often tymes felyng of wele and wo. This shows that S1, or
an ancestor, had been collated with a copy of the short text.

42 *and to whethere synne es nought the cause*: this is modified in the long text: *all thogh hys
synne is nott evyr the cause* (355.25).
*to whethere*: this may mean 'in either case' or 'none the less'. NED does not notice under To or Whether; but in its discussion of 'whether'-forms, it cites OHG *diu hwiduru,
tho-hwidaro*, and cross-refers to Though-whether, 'Notwithstanding'. But the antecedent
of *whethere* is probably 'consolation and dereliction', *in woo as in weele*, and 'in either
case' is more suited to Julian's logical and categorizing temper.

my selfe, ne also I deseruede nouȝt to hafe this blysfulle felynge; botte
45  frelye god gyffeȝ wele when hym lykes, and suffers (vs) in wa sum tyme,
and bothe es of love. For it is godys wille that we halde vs in comforthe
with alle oure myght, for blys es lastande with owtynn ende, and paynn
es passande *and* schalle be brought to nought. There fore it es nought
goddys wille that we folowe the felynges of payne in sorowynge and in
50  mournynge for thaim, botte sodaynlye passe ou*er and* halde vs in endelesse lykynge, that es god alle myghtty our*e* lover*e and* kepar*e*.

---

45 *us*: om. ms.
50 *thaim*: 'im' by corrector over erasure.

---

45 *suffers vs*: cf. 356.290: *sufferyth vs*.
46 *of love*: cf. 356.29: *one loue*.
48 *There fore it es nought goddys wille* ...: cf. *Bonum est*: ... he is neuer angri ne wroþ, ne
stured þoru frouwardnes of wil aȝeynes god ne mon; and also for he feleþ no desyr in
him self vnneþes to eny þing þat is, but holdeþ him payed with al as hit is, ful louynd-
liche vnbidynge þe wil of vr lord, lest crauynde of god in special and most hauynde of
him in general, þat bereþ his bodilych lyf as a cros on his bak, miȝtiliche with paceince,
euer redi for to dyen whon his tyme comeþ, þat haþ lost sauour of þis world and liueþ
in continuel longyng to heuenlich blis (Wallner, 59-60).
51 *alle myghtty oure lovere and kepare*: not in the long text; cf. 356.35.

(x)     Aftyr this Cryste schewyd me a partye of his passyone nere his dyinge.
I sawe that swete faace as yt ware drye and bludyelesse with pale
dyinge, sithenn mare dede, pale, langourrande, and than turnede more
dede to the blewe, *and* sithene mare blewe, as the flesche turnede mare
5  deepe dede. For alle the paynes that Cryste sufferde in his bodye
schewyd to me in the blyssede faace als farfurthe as I sawe it, and
namelye in the lyppes. Thare I sawe this foure colourse, thay that I
sawe be forehand, freschlye *and* ruddy, lyflye *and* lykande to my syght.
*3v  This / was a hevy channge to see, this deepe dyinge, and also the nese
10  c(lu)nge and dryed to my sight. This lange pynynge semede to me as he
hadde bene a seuenn nyght dede, alle waye sufferannde payne, *and* me
thought the dryinge of Crystes flesche was the maste payne of his
passionn and the laste. And in this dryhede was brouȝt to my mynde
this worde that Cryste sayde: I thryste. For I sawe in Criste a doubill*e*
15  thyrste, ane bodylye, ane othere gastelye. This worde was schewyd to
me for the bodylye thirste, and for the gastelye thyrste was schewyd to
me als I schalle saye eftyr warde; and I vndyrstode of bodelye thyrste

---

3 *dede*: second 'de' corrector over erasure.

8 *ruddy*: 'dy' corrector over erasure.

10 *clunge*: ms: channgede.

15 *schewyd to me*: 'schewyd' last word of line (cf. 230.21 note); 'to' add. marg., not by usual corrector.

---

2 *bludyelesse*: not recorded in NED, and this is the only example in MED. It is probably a scribe's error for 'bludlesse'. Cf. 357.4: *blodeles*, with which C, SS agree.

10 *clunge*: A's *channgede* is certainly erroneous, as are P's *cloeggeran* and C's *cloggering*. The only sense given is by S1's *clonge*, S2's *clange* (357.10 app.), 'shrivelled'. Cf. NED Cling *v.* 12, and 364.43, 46 note. Cf. also 359.28: *clongyn*.

*This lange pynynge ... sufferannde payne*: cf. 358.24-359.26.

11 *and me thought ... and weyght of the bodye* (234.21); cf. 359.29-360.9.

13 *And in this dryhede ... maye nouȝt be tolde* (234.25): this corresponds with the long text, 364.46-49.

*dryhede*: cf. NED Dryhede: a. 1300, *E. E. Psalter* 66.6: Whilk þat tornes þe se / In mikel drihed for to be (Qui convertit mare in aridam).

14 *I thryste*: John 19.28. The English verse *Meditationes de passione Christi* has: A a how strong was þan his pine / Thogh hit be expowned *in* a sermoun / That he þristede soules saluacioun / ȝit truli þe manhede þristede on rode / For he was ful drie for faute of blode (MS Bodley 415, f. 84^d). Cf. Stallings, 115, and see also 153, where she adduces Bonaventure's *Vitis mystica*, stressing the greater importance of Christ's 'ghostly thirst'; but for pseudo-Bonaventure, as for Julian, the thirst is 'double'.

17 *als I schalle saye eftyr warde*: cf. 249.13 e.s.

that the bodye hadde of faylynge of moystere, for the blessede flesche *and* banes ware lefte allane with owtynn blode *and* moystere. The
20    blyssyd bodye dryede alle ane lange tyme, with wryngynge of the nayles and paysynge of the hede and weyght of the bodye, with blawynge of wynde fra withoutynn that dryed mare and pyned hym with calde, mare thann mynn herte can thynke, *and* alle othere paynes. Swilke paynes I sawe that alle es to litelle þat y can telle or saye, for itt maye nouȝt be
25    tolde, botte ylke saule aftere the sayinge of saynte Pawle schulde feele in hym þat in Criste Jhesu. This schewynge of Criste paynes fillyd me fulle of paynes, for I wate weele he suffrede nouȝt botte aneȝ, botte as he walde schewe yt me and fylle me with mynde as I hadde desyrede before. My modere that stode emangys othere and behelde me lyftyd
30    vppe hir hande before m(y) face to lokke mynn eyenn, for sche wenyd I had bene dede or els I hadde dyede; and this encresyd mekille my sorowe, for nouȝt withstandynge alle my paynes, I wolde nouȝt hafe beenn lettyd for loove that I hadde in hym. And to whethere, in alle this tyme of Crystes presence, I felyd no payne, botte for Cristes paynes; þan
35    thouȝt me I knewe ful lytylle whate payne it was that I askyd, for me

---

21 *hede*: 'ede' by corrector over erasure.
30 *my*: ms: me.
35 *ful lytylle*: ms: fully tylle.

---

18 *faylynge of moystere*: cf. the *Fifteen Oes* (201.6 note): ... þu was hungen on heght and þi tendyre flesche wanysched, þe moyster of þi bowels dryed *and* þe marrowe of þi bones oute dwyned (MS BM Royal 17 C xvii, f. 96ᵈ).

   21 *and paysynge of the hede*: not in the long text; cf. 360.9.

   *with blawynge of wynde ... maye noȝt be tolde*: cf. 364.46-49. The English verse *Meditationes de passione Christi* has: On a cold morning at prime of daie / The prestes *and* princes gunne hem araie (MS Bodley 415, f. 83ᵃ). The Latin reads: Mane autem tempestive ... (Stallings, 105). Julian's account combines both traditions.

   25 *botte ylke saule ... Criste Jhesu*: not in the long text; cf. 364.49-50.

   *saynte Pawle*: Philippians 2.5: For let this mind be in you which was also in Christ Jesus (Hoc enim sentite in vobis quod et in Christo Jesu). Julian's syntax exactly reproduces that of the Vulgate. She is probably thinking of the connexion she so often makes between 'mind' and 'feeling'. Cf. I Corinthians 2.16: We have the mind of Christ (Habemus sensum Christi).

   26 *This schewynge ... desyrede before*: cf. 364.50-52.

   29 *My modere ... And to whethere*: not in the long text; cf. 364.52.

   30 *for sche wenyd ...*: 'for she thought that I was already dead, or else had just died'. It is noteworthy that this is the only allusion in the revelations to any relative.

   33 *And to whethere*: cf. 231.41: 'and with regard to either'. Julian is suffering 'in Christ Jesus', as St. Paul enjoins (cf. 234.25 and note). The cause of her suffering is neither her own sickness nor the sorrow she feels when she can no longer see Christ, but only the pains of his Passion.

   *in alle this tyme ... to hafe dyede bodylye* (235.42): cf. 364.52-365.63.

thought that my paynes passede any bodylye dede. I thouȝt: Es any payne in helle lyke this payne? And I was annswerde in my reso*n*ne that dyspayre ys mare, for that es gastelye payne. Bot bodilye payne es nane mare than this; howe myght my payne be more than to see hym that es
04r alle my lyfe, alle my blys *and* alle mye / ioye suffyr? H(ere) felyd I sothfastlye that y lovede Criste so mekille aboue*n* my selfe that me thought it hadde beene a grete eese to me to hafe dyede bodylye.

Here yn I sawe in partye the co*m*passyo*n*n of oure ladye saynte Marye; for Criste *and* scho ware so anede in loove that þe gretnesse of hir loove was the cause of the mykille hede of hir payne. For so mykille as scho lovyd hym mare than alle other*e*, her payne passed alle othere. And so alle his disciples *and* alle his trewe lovers suffyrde paynes mare than thare awne bodelye dying. For I am sekyr be my*n*n awne felynge that the leste of thame luffed hym mare than thaye dyd tha*m*m selfe. Here I sawe a grete anynge be twyx Criste and vs; for when he was in payne we ware in payne, and alle creatures that myght suffyr payne soffyrde w*ith* hym. And thaye that knewe hym nouȝt, this was thare payne,

---

39 *payne be more*: 'payne' is the last word of the line (cf. 230.21 note); 'be more' add. marg. corrector.

40 *suffyr? Here:* ms: suffyrde hir.

49 *hym*: interl. corrector w. caret.

50 *a*: interl. corrector w. caret.

---

36 *Es any payne in helle lyke this payne?* This seems to be a blend of Lamentations 1.12: Attend and see if there be any sorrow like to my sorrow, and Psalm 17.6: The sorrows of hell encompassed me. In the *Chauncoun de noustre dame,* Mary says to Christ on the Cross: Bot hit be þe pine of helle, / Of more pine ne wot I non (C. Brown, XIII 88).

37 *that dyspayre ys mare, for that es gastelye payne*: cf. 365.58: *Helle is a nother peyne, for ther is dyspyer.*

38 *Bot bodilye payne ... my ioye suffyr?* (235.40). This corresponds, but with considerable differences, with 365.58-61. Here she is distinguishing between the pain of loss and the pain of sense, whereas in the long text she seems to realize that a further distinction is necessary: there are pains which lead to salvation.

39 *hym that es alle my lyfe, alle my blys and alle mye ioye*: *conversio.*

40 *suffyr? Here*: cf. 365.61.

43 *Here yn I sawe ... the mykille hede of hir payne*: cf. 366.2-4.

45 *For so mykille ... alle othere*: not in the long text; cf. 366.4.

46 *And so alle his disciples ... thaye dyd thamm selfe*: cf. 366.10-367.12.

50 *Here I sawe ... soffyrde with hym*: cf. 367.14-16.

52 *And thaye that knewe hym nouȝt, this was thare payne*: this has been transferred to 367.23.

that alle creatures, sonne *and* the mone, with drewe thare seruyce, and
so ware thaye alle lefte in sorowe for the tyme. And thus thaye that
55  lovyd hym sufferde payne for luffe, *and* thay that luffyd hym nought
sufferde payne for faylynge of comforthe of all*e* creatures.

In this tyme I walde hafe lokyd besyde the crosse, botte I durste
nouȝt, for I wyste wele whilys I lukyd vppo*n*n the crosse I was sekyr
and safe. Therfore I walde nought assente to putte my sawle in per*i*lle,
60  for besyde the crosse was na syekernesse, botte vglynesse of feendes.

Than hadde I a pr*o*fyr in my resone, as ȝyf it hadde beene frendlye.
I(t) sayde to me: Luke vppe to heve*n*n to his fadere. Than sawe I wele
with the faythe that y felyd that thare ware nathynge be twyx the crosse
*and* heue*n*n that myght hafe desesyd me, and othere me behovyd loke
65  vppe or els annswere. I answerde *and* sayde: Naye, I may nought, for
thowe erte myne heuen. This I sayde for I walde nouȝt; for I hadde
levyr hafe bene in that payne to domysdaye than hafe comme*n*n to
hevene othere wyse than be hym. For I wyste wele he that bought me so
sare schulde vnbynde me when he walde.

---

56 *of alle*: corrector over erasure.
60 *syekernesse*: 'r' interl. corrector w. caret.
62 *It*: ms: I.

---

53 *sonne and the mone … of alle creatures*: this corresponds, but with many differences,
with 367.17-24.

57 *In this tyme … and in wa* (237.6): cf. 370.2-371.20.

60 *besyde the crosse was na syekernesse*: this is a commonplace in liturgical hymnology for
Passiontide and feasts of the Holy Cross; it is also summed up in the adaptation of
Galatians 6.14 (But God forbid that I should glory, save in the cross of our Lord Jesus
Christ …) for the introit for Maundy Thursday and Holy Cross feasts: Nos autem
gloriari oportet in cruce domini nostri Jesu Christi, in quo est salus, vita et resurrectio
nostra, per quem salvati et liberati sumus.

*vglynesse of feendes*: cf. 209.37: *mykylle occupyede with fendys*, and note.

65 *for thowe erte myne heuen*: the antecedent of 'thowe' appears to be Christ and his
Cross, just as for Paul (I Corinthians 1.23) 'Crux Christi' and 'Jesus crucifixus' are
synonymous.

69 *schulde vnbynde me*: Julian here seems to have in mind the cure, in Luke chapter 13,
of the woman who 'was bowed together, nor could she look up at all. When Jesus saw
her, he called her to him, and said to her: Woman, you are delivered from your in-
firmity'. This was a Sabbath healing, and Jesus replied to his critics: … ought not this
daughter of Abraham, whom Satan has bound, see, these eighteen years, be loosed
from this bond on the Sabbath day? It is, however, the Lord himself who has bound
Julian, in response to her request for sickness.

(xi)      Thus chese I Jhesu for my heuenn, whamm I saw onlye in payne at

04v      that tyme. Me lykede non othere hevene / than Jhesu, whilke schalle be
         my blysse when I am thare; and this has eure beene a comforthe to me,
         that I chesyd Jhesu to my hevene in alle tyme of passyonn and of

5        sorowe. And that has beene a lernynge to me that I schulde euermare
         do so, and chese anly hym to my heuen in wele and in wa. And thus
         sawe I my lorde Jhesu langoure lange tyme, for the anynge of the
         godhede, for love gafe strenght to the manhede to suffyr mare than alle
         men myght. I mene nought anly mare payne anly than alle men myght

10       suffyr, bot a(lso) that he suffyrde mare payne than alle men that euer
         was fra the fyrste begynnynge to the laste daye. No tonge maye telle ne
         herte fully thynke the paynes that oure savyoure sufferde for vs, haf-
         fande rewarde to the worthynes of the hyest worschipfulle kynge and to
         the schamefulle dyspyttous and paynefulle dede. For he that was hieste

---

1 *saw*: by corrector over longer erasure.
10 *bot also*: ms: bot (last word of line; cf. 230.21 note) anly.

---

1 *chese*: cf. 371.15: *was I lernyd to chese*.

*whamm I saw onlye in payne*: she is grateful that she made the choice before she saw
Christ glorified (cf. Revelation XII, 402.2 es.s). But in the long text she is careful to add
that the choice was only *by his grace* (371.18).

6 *And thus sawe I ... and witterlyest dyspyside*: cf. 374.2-375.9.

10 *bot also*: cf. 374.5.

11 *No tonge maye telle ne herte fully thynke*: this seems to be a clear reminiscence of the
*Jubilus*: Nil canitur suauius, / Auditur nil iocundius, / Nil cogitatur dulcius / Quam
Iesus dei filius (Wilmart, 'Le "Jubilus" sur le nom de Jésus', 146-147). Of the many
English versions current in Julian's time, the closest is that in the Vernon MS: Jhesu, no
song mai be swettore / Ne þouȝt in herte blisfollere / Nouȝt may be feeled lihtsomere /
Þen þou, so swete a louyere (f. 298ᶜ; Horstman 2 12). An Anglo-French version reads:
Ren nest chanté tant bonement / Ne oï tant ioïusement / Ne pur pensé plus dulcement
/ Que le fiz deu omnipotent (Wilmart, 252). There is a similar reminiscence in Prologue
I of Mechtild of Hackborn's *Book of Special Grace*: ... howe many gyftes he hath putte in
a mannes sawle whiche loues hym trewlye no tonge maye telle (Halligan, 66). The
*Speculum christiani* writes: ... the wondyrful blis of the hye kyngedome of heuen and ...
the dredful and horrible payne of the depe pitte of helle, the which be more than tonge
may telle or eyre may here or ee may see or hert may thynke (Holmstedt, 114-116), and
*The Charter of the Abbey of the Holy Ghost* concludes: ... more ioye and blisse þan eiȝe may
see or tonge telle or hert thenke (MS Stonyhurst XXIII, f. 60ᵇ; Horstman 1 362). Both
*Speculum* and *Charter* are alluding also to I Corinthians 2.9: But as it is written: 'That eye
has not seen nor ear heard ...', which is quoting Isaias 64.4: They have not heard ...
the eye has not seen ... what things thou hast prepared for them.

15  *and* worthyest was fullyest noghthede *and* witt*er*lyest dyspyside. Botte
the loue that made hym to suffere alle this, it passes als fare alle his
payns as heue*n* es abouen*n* erthe. For the paynes was a dede done in a
tyme be the wyrkynge of love, botte luffe was w*i*thowtyn*n* begynnynge
*and* es and evere schalle be with owtyn*n* any ende.

---------------

15 *was fullyest noghthede and witterlyest dyspyside*: 'was most completely brought low,
most utterly despised'; cf. 375.9: *was foulest condempnyd and vtterly dyspysed*, where the SS
variants to 'foulest', 'condempnyd' and 'vtterly', agreeing with A, suggest that they and
the short text share the better readings.

*Botte the loue ... with owtynn any ende*: cf. 386.46-387.49.

*Botte the loue that made hym to suffere alle this / it passes als fare alle his payns as heuen es
abouenn erthe / For the paynes was a dede done in a tyme be the wyrkynge of love / botte luffe was
withowtynn begynnynge / and es and evere schalle be with owtynn any ende*: a *compar* of five
*cola*. In the first two we have *oppositio*: *loue / suffere ... heuen / erthe*, to treat of the
Hypostatic Union. Then the next three express the Trinitarian *operatio ad extra*. In
*loue ... love* there is *gradatio*, and, in *paynes done in a tyme ... loue / luffe ... withowtyn begynnynge*, a form of *chiasmus*.

xii)   And sodaynlye, me behaldande in the same crosse, he chan*n*chede in
to blysfulle chere. The chawngynge of his chere chan*n*gyd my*n*ne, and I
was alle gladde *and* mery as yt was possybill*e*. Than brought oure lorde
merelye to my mynde: Whate es any poynte of thy payne or of þy grefe?
5   And I was fulle merye.

Than sayde oure lorde, askande: Arte thou wele payde that I suffyrde
for the? Ʒa, goode lorde, quod I; gramercy, goode lorde, blissyd mut
thowe be. Ʒyf thowe be payede, quod oure lorde, I am payede. It is a
ioye and a blysse and ane endlesse lykynge to me that eu*er* y suffyrde
10   passyo*n*n for the, for Ʒyf I myght suffyr mare, I walde suffyr. In this
felynge myne vndyrstandynge was lyftyd vppe in to heue*n*n, and thare I
sawe thre hevens; of the whilke syght I was gretlye merveylede, and /
5r   thought: I sawe thre heve*n*ns, and alle of the blessyd manhede of
Cryste. And nane is mare, nane is lesse, nane is hiare, nane is lawere,
15   botte evene like in blysse.

For the fyrste heue*n*n schewed Criste me his fadere, bot in na bodelye
lyknesse, botte in his p*ro*pe*r*te and in his lykynge. The wyrkynge of the
fadere it is this: that he gyffes mede tille his so*n*ne Jhe*s*u Criste. This
gyfte and this mede is so blysfulle to Jhe*s*u that (his) fadere myght haffe
20   gyffene na mede that myght hafe likede hym bette*r*e. For the firste
heue*n*n, that is blissynge of the fadere, schewed to me as a heue*n*n, and

19 *his*: om. ms.

1 *And sodaynlye ... was fulle merye*: cf. 379.7-11.

2 *The chawngynge of his chere channgyd mynne*: cf. Ecclesiastes 8.1: The wisdom of a
man shines in his countenance, and the most might will change his face.

6 *Than sayde oure lorde ... we er his crowne* (240.25): cf. 382.2-384.22.

10 *for Ʒyf I myght suffyr mare, I walde suffyr*: Sr. Mary Arthur Knowlton comments (122)
on the similarity of this to Christ's reproach in C. Brown's *Woefully Arrayed*: What myght
I suffer more / þen I haue sufferde, man, for þe? (XV 157); and she suggests a common
source in the Good Friday *Improperia*: Quid ultra debui facere tibi et non feci? (*Missale
Romanum 1474*, 1 171); the allusion is to Isaias 5.4: What is there that I ought to do
more to my vineyard that I have not done? Cf. William Herebert's translation: What
more shulde ich hauen ydon / þat þou ne hauest nouth underuon? (C. Brown, XIV,
18).

13 *sawe*: cf. 383.9: *see*; but S2 reads: *saw*.

14 *And nane is mare / nane is lesse / nane is hiare / nane is lawere*: a four-membered *compar* with *repetitio* and *oppositio contrariorum*.

17 *lykynge*: cf. 383.13: *wurkyng*, and note.

*The wyrkynge ... I walde suffyr mare* (240.28): this corresponds with the long text, 383.14-
385.26.

19 *his fadere*: cf. 383.16.

21 *blissynge*: cf. 384.18: *plesyng*.

itt was fulle blysfulle. For he is fulle blyssede with alle the dedes that he
has done abow3te oure saluaci*o*n, wherefore we ere nought anely his
thurgh byingge botte also be the curtayse gyfte of his fadere. We er his
25  blysse, we er his mede, we er his wyrschippe, we er his crowne.

This that I saye is soo grete blysse to J*hesu* that he settys atte nought
his travayle and his harde passio*nn* and cruell*e* and schamefulle dede.
And in this wordes: 3yf I myght suffyr mare, I walde suffyr mare, I sawe
sothly that 3if he myght dye als ofte als fore eu*er* ilke man anes that
30  schalle be safe, as he dyd anes for alle, love schulde neu*er* late hym hafe
reste to he hadde done it. And whe*nn* he hadde done it, he walde sette
it atte nought for luff, for alle thyn(k)e hym botte litylle in regarde of
his love. And that schewed he me wele, sobarly sayande this worde:
3yffe I myght suffere mare. He sayde nought: 3if it ware nedfull*e* to suf-
35  fyr mare, botte: 3if I myght suffyr mare; for thow3 it be nought
nedefulle, and he myght suffyr mare, mare he walde. This dede and this
werke abowte our*e* saluaci*o*n was als wele as he myght ordayne it. It
was done als wyrschipfullye as Cryste myght do it; and in this I sawe a
fulle blysse in Cryste, botte this blysse schulde nought hafe bene done
40  fulle 3yf it myght any bettere hafe bene done þa*nn* it was done. And in
this thre wordes: It is a ioye, a blysse and ane endeles likynge to me,
ware schewed to me thr*e* hevens, as thus. For the ioye I vndyrstode the
plesannce of the fadere, for the blysse the wirschippe of the so*nn*e, and
for the endeles lykynge the haly gaste. The fadere is plesed, the so*nn*e ys

---

30 *dyd*: alt. al. m. (not corrector's) w. caret and interl.: *dyed*.
32 *thynke*: ms: thynge.

---

22 *blyssede*: cf. 384.19: *plesyde*.
*that he has done*: cf. 384.19: *that Jhesu hath done*.
24 *We er his blysse / we er his mede / we er his wyrschippe / we er his crowne*: a *compar* with *repetitio*.
26 *This that I saye ... he hadde done it*: cf. 384.24-385.28.
28 *And in this wordes*: cf. 239.10.
*3yf I myght ... the haly gaste lykes* (241.45): this corresponds with the long text, 387.49-389.6.
31 *And whenn he hadde done ... of his love*: cf. 385.32-33.
32 *thynke*: cf. 230.5.
33 *And that schewed he ... haly gaste lykes* (241.45): cf. 387.49-389.6.
*wele, sobarly*: cf. 387.50: *fulle swetely*, and 269.25 and note.
40 *And in this thre wordes*: the 'thre wordes' evidently are *It is a ioye, (It is) a blysse*, and *(It is) ane endeles likynge to me*. Julian often uses 'word' to mean 'saying'; cf. 242.18, 249.12 and note, 250.29.
42 *For the ioye I vndyrstode ...*: for this figure, perfectly preserved in the long text, cf. 389.3 note.
44 *The fadere is plesed ...*: for this figure in the long text, cf. 389.5 note.

45 worschippyd, the haly gaste lykes. Jhesu wille that we take heede to this
blysse that is in the blyssedfulle trinite of oure saluacionn, and that we
05v lyke als mekylle / with his grace whyles we er here. And this was
schewyd me in þis worde: Erte þow wele payed? Be the tothere worde
that Cryste sayde: ȝyf þou be payed, I am payd, he schewed me the vn-
50 dyrstandynge, as ȝyf he had sayde: It is ioye and lykynge enough to me,
and I aske nought els for my travayle botte that I myght paye the. Plentyuoslye and fully was this schewyd to me.

Thynke also wyselye of the gretnesse of this worde: That euer I suf-
fred passionn for the; for in that worde was a hye knawynge of luffe
55 and of lykynge that he hadde in oure saluacion.

_45 Jhesu wille ... with his grace_: cf. 391.25-27, inc.: _A, Jhesu, wylle we ..._
_47 whyles we er here_: not in the long text; cf. 391.27.
_And this was shewyd ... that I myght paye the_: cf. 392.32-36.
_48 in þis worde_: cf. 239.6.
_the tothere worde_: cf. 239.8.
_51 Plentyuoslye and fully ... in oure saluacion_: cf. 393.43-46.
_53 of this worde: That euer_: cf. 393.45: _of thys worde, evyr_. The reference to the short text
is to 239.9.

(xiii)      Fulle merelye and gladlye oure lorde lokyd in to his syde and behelde
and sayde this worde: Loo how I lovyd the, as ȝyf he hadde sayde: My
childe, ȝif thow kan nought loke in my godhede, see heere how I lette
opyn my syde and my herte be clovene in twa and lette oute blude and
5    watere, alle þat was thare yn; and this lykes me and so wille I that it do
the.

        This schewed oure lorde me, to make vs gladde and mery. And with
the same chere and myrthe he loked downe on the ryght syde and
brought to my mynde whare oure ladye stode in the tyme of his
10   passionn, and sayde: Wille thowe see hir? And I annswerde and sayde:
Ȝa, goode lorde, gramercy, gyf it be thy wille. Ofte tymes I prayed it,
and wened to haffe sene here in bodely lykenes; botte I sawe her nought
soo. And Jhesu in þat worde schewed me a gastelye syght of hire. Ryght
as I hadde before sene hire litille and sympille, ryght so he schewed here
15   than, hye and nobille and gloriouse and plesannte to hym abouen alle
creatures. And so he wille that it be knawynn that alle tha that lykes in
hym schulde lyke in hire, and in the lykynge that he hase in hire and scho
in hym. And in that worde that Jhesu sayde: Wille þu see hire? me
thought I hadde the maste lykynge that he myght hafe gyffenn me with
20   the gastelye schewynge that he gafe me of hire. For oure lorde schewed
me nothynge in specyalle botte oure lady saynte Marye, and here he
schewyd me in thre tymes. The fyrste was as sche consayved, the

---

2 *he*: ms: he (end of line; cf. 230.21 note) he hadde.

---

1 *Fulle merelye and gladlye ... and behelde*: cf. 394.3.
*oure lorde lokyd in to his syde*: this is one of many indications (cf. 394.3 note) that Julian
has in mind the iconography of the Sacred Heart, as she makes plain when she continues: *see heere how I lette opyn my syde and my herte be clovene in twa*. The wound in the
side reveals the pierced heart. So in one stanza of the *Song of Love-Longing*, copied,
c. 1400, into MS BM Add. 37787, we read: Jhesu of loue I se toknyng: / Þyn armus
sprad to loue clippyng, / Þyn hed bowet to swete kussyng, / Þi side al open to loue
schewyng (Nita S. Baugh: *A Worcestershire Miscellany*, 134).
2 *and sayde this worde ... My childe*: cf. 395.15.
4 *be clovene in twa*: cf. 395.10.
7 *This schewed oure lorde ... Wille thowe see hir?*: cf. 397.30-398.5.
10 *And I annswerde ... scho in hym* (242.18): cf. 400.24-31.
13 *Ryght as I hadde before sene hire litille and sympille*: cf. 213.24 e.s., 213.26 note.
18 *And in that worde ... was I lerede*: cf. 400.35-402.4.
19 *the maste lykynge*: cf. 401.36: *the most lykyn worde*.
22 *The fyrste was as sche consayved / the seconnde ... / and the thryd ...*: the enumeration of
the three *cola* produces an effect of *similiter cadens*.

seconnde was as scho were in hire sorowes vndere the crosse, and the
thryd as scho is nowe in lykynge, wirschippe / and ioye.

And eftyr this oure lorde schewyd hym to me mare gloryfyed as to my
syght than I sawe hym before, and in this was I lerede that ilke saule
contemplatyfe to whilke es gyffenn to luke and seke god schalle se hire
and passe vnto god by contemplacionn. And eftyr this techynge,
hamelye, curtayse and blysfulle, and verray lyfe, ofte tymes oure lorde
Jhesu sayde to me: I it am that is hiaste. I it am that þou luffes. I it am
that thowe lykes. I it am that þowe serves. I it am þat þou langes. I it am
that þowe desyres. I it am that thowe menes. I it am þat is alle. I it am
that haly kyrke preches the and teches the. I it am that schewed me are
to the. Thies wordes I declare nought botte for ilke man, eftyr the grace
that god gyffes hym in vndyrstandynge and lovynge, resayfe tham in
oure lordes menynge.

And eftyr oure lorde brought vnto my mynde the langynge that I
hadde to hym before; and I sawe that nathynge letted me bot synn, and
so I be helde generallye in vs alle, and me thought ȝyf synn hadde

23 *vndere the crosse*: the Vulgate's preposition is 'juxta' (John 19.25); but an English poem in a fourteenth-century manuscript has this rubric: Crisostomus et ymaginatur de planctu virginis quod beata virgo stat sub cruce dicens filio suo sic: O fili, agnosce matrem *et cetera* (Brown, XIV 228, 285). Julian may have known the *Chauncoun de noustre dame*, Stond wel, moder, ounder rode, / Bihold þi child wiþ glade mode (C. Brown, XIII 87).

26 *that ilke saule contemplatyfe*: cf. 402.4: *that oure soule*: and cf. 215.42 note.

27 *schalle se hire and passe vnto god by contemplacionn*: the 'learning' in the long text is quite different; cf. 402.4-5. But we find the same notion that one's last days may be graced by a vision of Mary in a prayer, *Obsecro te domina Maria*, common in French books of hours and doubtless also known in England: ... et in nouissimis diebus ostende michi faciem tuam et denuncia michi diem et horam obitus mei ... et uitam eternam michi tribuas ... (MS Trinity College Dublin 102, f. 28). In MS 51 of the Fitzwilliam Museum, Cambridge, a book of hours which James dated 1440-1450, in the 'Oratio ... de septem verbis Christi in cruce pendentis', here, as commonly — but spuriously — attributed to Bede, there is a rubric stating that 'if it be said every day, the devotee "per triginta dies ante obitum suum uidebit gloriosam uirginem Mariam in auxilium sibi preparatam"' (James, *Fitzwilliam* 128).

29 *hamelye, curtayse ... are to the*: cf. 402.6-403.11.

*ofte tymes ... are to the* (243.34): this corresponds with the long text, 402.6-403.11.

30 *I it am*: cf. 402.7, where the long text repeats twice. Here the *repetitio* is ten-fold.

34 *Thies wordes ... resone and dyscrecionn* (244.45): this corresponds with the long text, 403.16-405.11.

*Thies wordes I declare nought botte for ilke man*: she is reporting these locutions, not because she considers them any mark of special favour to her, but as they are applicable and acceptable to every loving soul, a qualification she is several times careful to make. Cf. 220.18 and note, 321.2 and note.

37 *And eftyr ... that me neded* (244.47): cf. 404.3-405.12.

40  nought bene, we schulde alle hafe bene clene and lyke to oure lorde as
he made vs. And thus in my folye before this tyme ofte I wondrede why,
be the grete forseande wysdome of god, syn was not lettede; for than
thought me that alle schulde hafe bene wele.

45  This styrrynge was mekylle to forsayke; and mournynge and sorowe I
made therfore with outyn resone and dyscrecionn of fulle grete pryde.
Neuer the lesse Jhesu in this visionn enfourmede me of alle that me
neded. I saye nought that me nedes na mare techynge, for oure lorde
with the schewynge of this hase lefte me to haly kyrke, and I am
hungery and thyrstye and nedy and synfulle and freele, *and* wilfully sub-
50  myttes me to the techynge of haly kyrke with alle myne euencrystenn in
to the ende of my lyfe.

He annswerde be this worde and sayde: Synne is behouelye. In this
worde: Synne, oure lorde brought to my mynde generallye alle that is
nought goode: the schamefulle dyspyte and the vtter noghtynge that he
55  bare for vs in this lyfe and in his dyinge, and alle the paynes and
passyons of alle his creatures, gastelye and bodelye. For we are alle in
party noghted, and we schulde be noghted, folowande oure maister

---

45 *of fulle grete pryde*: not in the long text; cf. 405.11.

46 *Neuer the lesse Jhesu ... that me neded* (244.47): this corresponds with the long text,
405.11-12.

47 *I saye nought ... ende of my lyfe*: not in the long text; cf. 405.12.

48 *... hase lefte me to haly kyrke ... the techynge of haly kyrke*: cf. the *Ancrene Riwle*: ȝe schul
bi leeue habben þat al þat holy chirche deeþ, redeþ oþer syngeþ *and* alle hire sacremens
strengþeþ ou gostliche (Vernon MS, f. 384ᶜ; Day, 120). Julian may have in mind John
14.18: I will not leave you orphans.

*I am hungery and thyrstye and nedy and synfulle and freele*: this is *continuatio*. Cf. Psalm
69.6: I am needy and poor; O God, help me.

52 *He annswerde ... not me for synne* (246.77): cf. 405.12-407.38.

*Synne is behouelye*: 'sin is necessary'. Cf. 405.13, *behouely* C( =U), *behoveful*, S1 ( =S2),
*behovabil*, and MED *bihoveli*, adj. (c.). As when she goes on, *than euer was the synne of
Adam harmfulle* (247.13), Julian seems to be alluding to the 'necessarium Ade peccatum'
of the *Praeconium paschale*; cf. 412.12 note. Piers Plowman B.V. quotes from the
*Praeconium* and draws the same optimistic conclusion as Julian: 'Now god' quod he, 'that
of thi goodnesse . gonne the worlde make, / And of nauȝte madest auȝte . and man
moste liche to thi selue, / And sithen suffredest for to synne . a sikernesse to vs alle, /
And al for the best, I bileue . what euere the boke telleth, / *O felix culpa! o necessarium
peccatum Ade!* (Skeat, 1 176).

*In this worde ... his blyssyd wille* (245.71): this corresponds with the long text, 405.14-
407.33.

54 *vtter noghtynge*: cf. 405.16: *vttermost trybulation*: but SS agree with A.

56 *For we are alle in party noghted / and we schulde be noghted / folowande oure maister Jhesu
to we be fulle purgede / that is to say to we be fully noghted / of oure awne dedely flesche / and of
alle oure inwarde affeccionns whilke ere nought goode*: a *compar* of six *cola*, two short followed
by a longer, repeated, with *conversio* (*noghted ... noghted ... noghted*) and *traductio* (*nought*).

57 *noghted*: cf. 406.19: *trobelyd*: again, SS agree with A.

₆v Jhesu to we be fulle purgede, that is to say to we be fully / noghted of
oure awne dedely flesche, and of alle oure inwarde affeccionn(s) whilke
60 ere nought goode.

And the behaldynge of this with alle the paynes that euer ware or euer
schalle be, (and with alle thys I vnderstode the passion of Criste for the
most payne and ovyr passyng,) and this was schewed me in a toch, and
redely passed ouere into comforth. For oure goode lorde god walde
65 noght that the saule ware afferdede of this vglye syght. Botte I sawe
noght synne, fore I lefe it has na manere of substannce, na partye of
beynge, na it myght nought be knawenn bot be the paynes that it is
cause of. And this payne, it is sumthynge, as to my syght, for a tyme, for
it purges vs and makes vs to knawe oureselfe and aske mercye; for the
70 passionn of oure lorde is comforth to vs agaynes alle this, and so is his
blyssyd wille to alle that schalle be saffe. He comfortes redely and
swetlye be his wordes, and says: Botte alle schalle be wele, and alle
maner of thynge schalle be wele.

---

59 *affeccionns*: ms: affeccio*nn*.
62 *and with alle ... passyng*: om. ms; cf. 406.23.

---

58 *that is to say to we be fully noghted*: not in P, but preserved (or supplied) in SS; cf.
406.20.

*noghted of oure awne dedely flesche*: cf. the *Scale*, II chapter 24: þis noȝt I mene þus, þat a
soule may ... not be drifen ageyn þe wille ne drawen downe bi maistrie for to þinken or
liken or louen with clefyng of affeccioun to ony synne or veynly ony erþly þinge (MS BM
Harley 6579, f. 91ʳ; Underhill, 323).

63 *in a toch*: cf. 406.24. The sense here seems to be 'brief mention, hint'. MED
suggests that this is also the meaning in Gawain 1301: Bi sum towch of summe tryfle at
sum talez ende; and in Capgrave's *Chronicle*: that whanne I loke upon hem and have a
schort touch of the writing; and observes that this sense of the verb first appears in the
late fourteenth century: 1387 *Trevisa*: as it is itouched in þe bygynninge of þe firste in þe
þridde prefas.

71 *He comfortes redely ... and says*: this corresponds with the long text, 407.32-33.

72 *Botte alle ... not me for synne* (246.77): this corresponds with the long text, 407.33-38.

*Botte alle schalle be wele, and alle maner of thynge schalle be wele*: this is probably the most
famous of all Julian's locutions, owing its celebrity in modern times partly to T. S.
Eliot's use of it in 'Little Gidding' (*Four Quartets*). In the long text, it becomes one of the
*Leitmotive*; cf. 405.13, 417.4, 422.2, 618.46, and its final resolution: *And then shalle none of
vs be steryd to sey in ony thyng: Lorde, yf it had ben thus, it had ben wele. But we shalle alle sey
with one voyce: Lorde, blessyd mott thou be, for it is thus, it is wele* (729.13). There is remarkable similarity to certain manuscripts of the *Scale*, I chapter 33: with mekenes of hert
treistand also sykerly in þe mercie of oure lord þat he schal make it gode, more þen þou
knoweȝ or feleȝ; and if þou do þus, all schal be wel ... bot þoȝ þou fall an oþere tyme in
þe same, ȝee an hunderth tymes, a thousand tymes, ȝit do as I haue seid,

Thyes wordes ware schewed wele tenderlye, schewande na ma(ne)re
75 of blame to me na to nane that schalle be safe. Than were it a grete
vnkyndenesse of me to blame or wondyr of god for my synnes, synn he
blames not me for synne. Thus I sawe howe Cryste has compassyonn of
vs for the cause of synne; and ryght as I was be fore with the passyonn
of Cryste fulfilled with payne and compassion, lyke in þis I was in party
80 fyllyd *with* compassionn of alle mynn euenncristene; and than sawe I
that ylke kynde compassyonne that man hase of his evencristene *with*
charyte, þat it is Criste in hym.

---

74 *manere*: ms: mare.
79 *lyke in þis ... compassionn (of)*: added at foot of page with marks of correction,
corrector.

---

and all schal be wel (MS Cambridge UL Add. 6686, p. 304). Evelyn Underhill, who did
not use Add. 6686, reports, 75 note 2, that Harley 2387 and Lambeth 472 also 'insert'
the first 'all schal be wel'; but we must await a critical edition of *Scale* I to know
whether this is a matter of interpolation or omission. If indeed some scribe-editor did
interpolate the first occurrence of the phrase, it can only have been to make the passage
resemble Julian even more. Michael Sargent points out to the editors that the locution
seems also to be the inspiration for the burden of a fifteenth-century carol (punning on
the name 'Noel'): Now is well and all is well, / And right well, so have I bliss; / And
sithen all things are so well, / I rede we do no more amiss (Rickert, 173).
74 *manere*: cf. 407.35.
77 *Thus I sawe ... alle mynn euenncristene*: cf. 408.2-5.
79 *lyke in þis ... compassion*: cf. 408.4.
80 *and than sawe I ... Criste in hym*: cf. 410.21-22.

xiv)    Bot in this (I) schalle studye, behaldande generallye, drerelye *and*
mournande, sayande thus to oure lorde in my menynge with fulle grete
drede: A, goode lorde, howe myght alle be wele for the grete harme
that is comonn by synne to thy creatures? And I desired as I durste to
5    hafe sum mare open declarynge whare *with* I myght be hesyd in this.
And to this oure blyssede lorde annswerde fulle mekelye and with fulle
lovelye chere, and schewed me that Adammes synne was the maste
harme that euer was done or ever schalle to the warldes ende. And also
he schewed me that this is opynnly knawyn, in alle haly kyrke in erthe.
10    Forthermare he lered me that I schulde be halde the gloriouse asethe,
for this aseth makynge is mare plesande to the blissede godhede and
mare wyrschipfulle to mannes saluacionn with owtene comparysonn
107r    than euer was the synne of Adam harmfulle. Þanne / menes oure
blyssede lorde thus in this techynge, that we schulde take hede to this:
15    For senn I hafe made wele the maste harme, it is my wille that þowe
knawe þerby that I schalle make wele alle that is the lesse.
He gaffe me vndyrstandynge of twa partyes. The ta party is oure
savioure and oure saluacionn. This blyssed party is opynn and clere and
fayre and lyght and plentiouse, for alle mankynde that is of goode wille
20    or þat schalle be es comprehendyd in this partye. Here to ere we
byddynn of god and drawenn and consayled and lered inwardlye be the
haly gaste *and* outwarde by haly kyrke by the same grace. In this wille

---

1 *I*: ms: ӡe.
9 *knawyn*: ms: knawynge.
14 *blyssede lorde*: ms: lorde blyssede.

---

1 *Bot in this ... as he schalle thanne haffe* (250.18): cf. 412.2-418.20.
*I schalle studye*: cf. 412.2: *I stode.* That the short text employs the future tense and the
long text the past seems to indicate that the fifteen years' meditation which Julian
records separate the two texts.

3 *A, goode lorde ...*: cf. 412.3, where in the long text Julian has retained the *exclamatio*,
used to introduce a *ratiocinatio*.

7 *Adammes synne was the maste harme that euer was done*: cf. Romans 5.12: As by one
man sin entered into this world, and by sin death ...

18 *This blyssed party is opynn and clere and fayre and lyght and plentiouse*: this is *continuatio*.
Julian is thinking of the initial revelation of the Nativity: An angel of the Lord stood by
them, and the brightness of God shone round about them ... (Luke 2.9), and the gloss
on this in Hebrews 1.1-3: God ... in these days has spoken by his Son, who is the
brightness of his glory and the full expression of his being.

oure lorde that we be occupyed, enioyande in hym, for he enioyes in vs.
And þe mare plentyouslye that we take of this with reuerence and
25  mekenesse, the mare we deserve thanke of hym, and the mare spede to
oure selfe, and thus maye we saye, enioyande: Oure parte is oure lorde.

The tother parte is spared fra vs and hidde, that is to saye alle that is
besyde oure saluacionn. For this is oure lordys prive consayles, and it
langes to þe ryalle lordeschyp of god for to haue his prive consayles in
30  pees, and it langes to his seruanntys for obedyence and reuerence nought
to wille witte his councelle.

Oure lorde has pite and compassyonn of vs for that sum creatures
makes thamm so besy þer yn; and I am sekyr ȝyf we wyste howe mekille
we schulde plese hym and ese oure selfe for to lefe it, we walde. The
35  sayntes in heuenn wille nathynge witte bot that oure lorde wille schewe
thame, and also there charyte and þer desyre is rewlyd eftyr the wille of
oure lorde; and þus awe we to wille to be lyke to hym. And than schalle
we nathynge wille ne desyre botte the wille of oure lorde, as he does,
for we er alle ane in goddys menynge.
40  And here was I lered that we schalle anely enioye in oure blessid
sauioure Jhesu and trist in hym for alle thynge.

---

28 *and it langes ... consayles (in)*: added at foot of page with marks of correction, corrector.

37 *to wille to be*: ms: to wille ne to be.

---

26 *Oure parte is oure lorde*: cf. Psalms 15.5: The Lord is the portion of my inheritance and my cup, 118.57, 141.6 and *Piers Plowman* C VI 61 (Skeat, 1 120), where the context suggests that the poet, quoting *Dominus pars hereditatis mee*, is alluding to his own reception of minor orders.

28 *For this is oure lordys prive consayles / and it langes to þe ryalle lordeschyp of god / for to haue his prive consayles in pees / and it langes to his seruanntys for obedyence and reuerence / nought to wille witte his councelle*: a *compar* of three shorter *cola* enclosing two longer, with *conversio* (*consayles ... consayles ... councelle*) and *repetitio* (*and it langes ... and it langes*).

37 *wille ne ... hym* (ms): this seems to suggest an infinitive 'wilne' < OE wilnian and a non-Northern dative pronoun 'hem' in an ancestor.

38 *as he does*: cf. 416.23: *lyke as they do*. This reading in the short text is supported by several places in Scripture: John 8.29: I do always the things that please him; John 4.34: My meat is to do the will of him who sent me; Matthew 6.9: Thus therefore shall you pray ... Thy will be done; Matthew 26.39: Not as I will but as thou wilt.

xv)      And thus oure goode lorde answerde to alle the questyons and doutes
that I myght make, sayande fulle comfortabelye on this wyse: I wille
make alle thynge wele, I schalle make alle thynge wele, I maye make alle
thynge wele and I can make alle thynge wele; and þowe schalle se þat
5    thy selfe, that alle thynge schalle be wele. There he says he maye, I vndyrstande for the fadere; and þere he says he can, I vndyrstande for the
07v   sonne; and þer he says: / I wille, I vnderstande for the hali gaste; and
þere he says: I schalle, I vndirstande for the vnyte of the blyssede trinyte,
thre persones in a trewthe; and there he says: Thowe schalle se thy selfe,
10   I vndyrstande the anynge of alle mankynde that schalle be sayfe in to
the blysfulle trinyte.

         And in this fyve wordes god wille be closed in ryste and in pees. And
thus has the gastely thyrst of Cryste ane ende. For this is the gastely

---

4 þat: interl. w. caret, corrector.

---

2 *I wille make alle thynge wele, I schalle make alle thynge wele, I maye make alle thynge wele
and I can make alle thynge wele*: cf. Introduction, VIII; this is a subtle example of *complexio*, which Sr. Frances Nims defines as 'repetition of both initial and final words in
successive clauses'. In pointing out Julian's employment of such rhetorical devices (cf.
e.g. the notes to 260.29, 263.17, 269.37, 271.26) the editors have been much helped by
Sr. Frances's valuable information.
4 *and þowe schalle se þat thy selfe / that alle thynge schalle be wele*: a two-membered *compar*,
the second echoing the *complexio* of the preceding figure.
5 *There he says he maye / I vndyrstande for the fadere / and þere he says he can / I vndyrstande for the sonne / and þer he says I wille / I vnderstande for the hali gaste / and þere he
says I schalle / I vndirstande for the vnyte of the blyssede trinyte / thre persones in a trewthe / and
there he says Thowe schalle se thy selfe / I vndyrstande the anynge of alle mankynde that schalle be
sayfe / in to the blysfulle trinyte*: a twelve-membered *compar*, combining, reworking and
augmenting the two previous figures, with a new *repetitio* (*There he says ..., I vndyrstande ...*).
12 *fyve wordes*: 'I wille', 'I schalle', 'I maye', 'I can', 'þowe schalle se'. Cf. 240.40 note.
*wille be closed*: cf. 418.13: *wyll that we be enclosyd*; but SS agree with the short text.
Julian was too good a theologian to suppose that the divine rest and peace can in any
way be disturbed; what she means is that God wishes to be surrounded by the rest and
peace of his earthly creatures, who should cease to torment themselves, as, she tells us,
the notion of sin had tormented her until now.
13 *For this is the gastely thyrste*: this is the explanation she promised when she quoted
John 19.28 and wrote: *For I sawe in Criste a doubille thyrste, ane bodylye, ane othere gastelye ...*
(233.14). We find the same exegesis in the English *Fifteen Oes* (cf. 212.9 note): *O Jhesu þe
welle of vnwastand pyte, þat of inwarde affeccyon of luf sayd in þe cros: I thyrst, þat (is)
to say þe hele of mankynde...* (MS BM Royal 17 C xvii, f. 96ª).

thyrste, the luff langynge, and that lastes and euer schalle to wee see that
15  syght atte domesdaye; for we that schalle be safe, and schalle be Crystes
ioye and his blysse, ere ʒit here, and schalle be vnto the daye. Therefore
this is the thyrste, the falynge of his blysse, þat he has vs nought in hym
als haelye as he schalle thanne haffe.

Alle this was schewed me in the schewynge of compassionn, for þat
20  schalle sese atte domesdaye. Thus he hath rewthe and compassionn of
vs, and he has langynge to hafe vs, botte his wysdome and his love suffers nought the ende to comme to the beste tymm. And in thies same
fyve wordes before sayde: I make alle thynge wele, I vndyrstande a
myghtty comforthe of alle the werkys of oure lorde that ere for to
25  comme; for ryght as the blissyd trinyte made alle thynge of nought,
ryght soo the same blyssed trinyte schalle make wele alle that es nought
wele. It is goddys wille that we hafe grete rewarde to alle the dedys that
he has done, for he wille that we knawe there by alle that he schalle do;
and þat schewyd he me in this worde that he sayde: And þou schalle see
30  thy selfe that alle manere of thynge schalle be wele. This I vndyrstande

---

14 *the luff langynge*: this cliché for 'the pangs of (unrequited) love' must have been
known to every amateur of secular poetry and song in the fourteenth century. Cf.
*Alysoun*: 'Ich libbe in loue longinge / For semlokest of alle þynge' (G. L. Brook: *The
Harley Lyrics*, 33), and *Now Springs the Spray*: 'Þe clot him clingge! Wai es him i louue
longinge / Sal libben ai!' (K. Sisam: *Fourteenth Century Verse and Prose*, 163). It is found in
a spiritual context in 'Swete Jhesu now wol I synge / To þe a song of loue longinge'
(Vernon MS, f. 298ᵇ; Horstman, 2 9).

15 *atte domesdaye*: cf. 418.16, and 224.15 note.

16 *and schalle be vnto the daye*: cf. 418.17: *and some be to come, and so shalle some be in to
that day*; that gives notably better sense, and we may suppose that the text here has suffered through homoeotopy. But this may be a reminiscence of Canticles 2.17 and II
Peter 1.19: ... until the day dawn and the day star arise in your hearts.

17 *the falynge of his blysse*: cf. 418.19-20, which seems inferior, and may represent the
editing of someone who could not understand 'falynge': 'this is Christ's thirst and the
incompleteness of his joy, that he does not now possess us in himself as wholly as he
then will'.

19 *Alle this was schewed ... to the beste tymm* (250.22): this corresponds with the long text,
421.50-53.

22 *And in thies same fyve wordes ... for to comme* (250.25): this corresponds with the long
text, 423.20-22.

*thies same fyve wordes ... I may make alle thynge wele*: cf. 240.40 note. Here Julian seems
to be using 'word' in its primary sense; and evidently she calls these 'five words'
because she regards *alle thynge* as a single compound noun, a view commonly reflected
in mediaeval scribal practice.

25 *for ryght ... nought wele* (250.27): this corresponds with the long text, 424.35-37.

27 *It is goddys wille ... he schalle do* (250.28): this corresponds with the long text, 429.28-
30.

29 *in this worde*: cf. 249.4.

in twa manerse: ane, I am wele payed that I wate it noght, anothere, I
am gladde and mery for I schalle witte itt. It is goddys wille that we
witte that alle schalle be wele in generalle, botte it is nought goddys
wille that we schulde witte it nowe botte as it langes to vs for the tyme,
35   *and þat* is the techynge of haly kyrke.

---

31 *ane I am wele payed that I wate it noght / anothere I am gladde and mery for I schalle witte*
*itt*: Julian expounds the *twa manerse* in a two-membered *compar*, with *traductio* (*wate ...*
*witte*).

33 *botte it is nought goddys wille that we schulde witte it nowe*: cf. Matthew 24.36: But of
that day and hour no one knows, no, not the angels of heaven, but the Father alone.

(xvi)     God schewyd me fulle grete plesannce that he has in alle men and
womenn that myghttelye and mekelye and wyrschipfullye takes the
prechynge and the techynge of haly kyrke, for he is haly kyrke. For he is
f. 108r   the grownde, he is the substannce, / he is the techynge, he is the
5    techare, he is the ende, he is the myddes wharefore ilke trewe sawlle
trauaylles; and he is knawenn and schalle be knawenn to ylke saule to
whame the haly gaste declares it. And I am sekyr that alle tho that sekes
thus schalle spede, for thay seke god.

     Alle this that I hafe nowe sayde, and mare that I schalle saye eftyr, es
10   comforthynge agayne synne; for fyrst when I sawe þat god does alle that
es done, I sawe nought synne, and than sawe I that alle is wele. But
when god schewyd me synne, than sayde he: Alle schalle be wele.

     And when god alle myghttye hadde schewed me plentyuouslye *and*
fully of his goodnesse, I desyred of a certayne *personn* that I lovyd howe
15   it schulde be with hir*e*; and in þis desyre I lettyd my selfe, for I was
noght taught in this tyme. And than was I answerde in my reson*n*, als it
ware be a frendfull*e* man: Take it gen*er*ally, and be halde the curtayssy
of thy lorde god as he schewes it to the, for it is mare worschippe to god
to be halde hym in alle than in any specyalle thynge. I assentyd, and þer
20   with I lered that it is mare wyrschippe to god to knawe alle thynge in

---

1 *God schewyd me ... Alle schalle be wele*: cf. 431.15-433.13.

2 *and mekelye and wyrschipfullye*: cf. 431.16: *and wysely*.

3 *he is the grownde / he is the substannce / he is the techynge / he is the techare / he is the ende
/ he is the myddes / wharefore ilke trewe sawlle trauaylles*: a *membrum* of seven *cola* with
*repetitio*.

5 *myddes*: cf. 431.18: *mede*.

12 *Alle schalle be wele*: cf. 245.73

14 *personn*: cf. 432.3: *creature*.

15 *I lettyd my selfe*: she sees her anxiety for the soul she loved as a disabling imperfection. Ludolph of Saxony ends his *Vita*, I liv, with a prayer which asks: Da michi
affectionem carnalis propinquitatis et amorem corporalis delectationis omnino relin-
quere, teque super omnia diligere ..., where 'carnalis propinquitas' means 'close ties of
blood'. In chapter liv, commenting on Matthew 10 and Luke 12 and 14, Ludolph,
dealing with 'He who loves father or mother more than me is not worthy of me', writes
of 'inordinatus propinquorum amor' as the 'primum impedimentum perfectionis et
sequelae Christi' (Rigollot, 2 62).

16 *als it ware be a frendfulle man*: cf. 432.7: *mene*. Either reading is defensible, that of P
the more probable. This is an entirely different 'mode', in which it is not God himself
who speaks. The locution comes as it were from a well-disposed intermediary (or
'human being').

20 *lered*: cf. 432.10: *lernyd*. NED Lere *v*. 3 and 4 shows that the sense 'learn' is well
established in Middle and early New English.

generalle than to lyke in any thynge in specialle. And ȝyf I schulde do wysely eftyr this techynge I schulde nought be glad for nathynge in specyalle, na desesed for na manere of thynge, for alle schalle be wele.

God brought to my mynde that I schulde synne; and for lykynge that
25  I hadde in behaldynge of hym, I entendid nought redely to that schewynge. And oure lorde fulle curtayslye abayde to I walde entende, and than oure lorde brought to mynde with my synnes the synne of alle myne even cristen, alle in generalle and nathynge in specialle.

----

24 *God brought ... wirschippe to mann* (255.17): cf. 442.2-445.3.

26 *fulle curtayslye*: cf. 442.4: *fulle marcifully*, and note to 442.3.

*abayde*: NED, Abide, *v.*, quotes 1375, Barbour *Bruce*: abaid.

*to I walde*: cf. 442.4: *and gaue me grace for*.

27 *and than oure lorde ... in specialle*: this has been reworked in the long text: cf. 442.4-7.

*with my synnes the synne of alle myne even cristen*: cf. 442.6 and note.

(xvii)    Iff alle oure lorde schewyd me that I schulde synne, be me allay*nn* I
vnderstode alle. In this I consayved a softe drede; and to this oure lorde
answerde me thus: I kepe the full*e* sekerly. This worde was sayde to me
with mare love *and* sekernes of gastely kepynge than I ca*nn* or maye

f. 108v    telle. For as it was be / fore schewed to me that I schulde synne, ryght

6    so was the comforth schewed to me: sekernesse of kepynge for alle
myne evencrist*en*. What may make me mar*e* to luff myne evenc*r*isten
than to see in god that he loues alle that schalle be safe, as it ware alle a
saulle? And in ilke saule that schalle be sayfe is a goodely wille that

10    neu*er* assentyd to synne, na neu*er* schalle. For as þ*er* is a bestely wille in
the nether*e* p*ar*ty that maye wille na goode, so is thare a goodely wille in

---

7 *What may ... evencristen (than)*: add. head of page w. marks of omission, corrector.

---

1 *Iff alle*: cf. 442.8: *Though*, and NED, If, *conj.*, 8 a, 'All if, if all'.
*I (vnderstode)*: cf. 442.8: *is*.
2 *a softe drede*: Julian can so qualify 'dread' because presently she will distinguish between fear which is good and that which is not. In chapter xx she writes that the soul
should *luff and lyke hymm* (God) *and nought drede bot hymm* (265.45), and in chapter xxv
she categorizes *foure maner of dredes*, of which the best is *reuerente drede ... of luffe* (276.1-
17; cf. 442.9, 630.25, 671.2-673.19).
3 *I kepe the fulle sekerly*: cf. 443.13: *suernesse of kepyng*, and note.
9 *in ilke saule that schalle be sayfe is a goodely wille ...*: cf. 443.16, and Introduction, 117-
118. William of St. Thierry's Latin is: Magna enim voluntas ad deum amor est; dilectio,
adhaesio sive conjunctio; charitas, fruitio. Unitas vero spiritus cum deo homini sursum
cor habenti, proficientis in deum voluntatis est perfectio, cum jam non solummodo vult
quod deus vult, sed sic est non tantum affectus sed in affectu perfectus ut non possit
velle nisi quod deus vult. Velle autem quod deus vult, hoc est jam similem deo esse;
non posse velle nisi quod deus vult, hoc est jam esse quod deus est, cui velle et esse id
ipsum est. Unde bene dicitur quod tunc plene videbimus eum sicuti est, cum similes ei
erimus (I John 3.2); hoc est, erimus quod ipse est (PL 184 348).
10 *For as þer is a bestely wille*: cf. MED's quotation, s.v. best(e)li, adj., of a Lollard version of I Corinthians 15.44: If there is a beestly body, there is and a spiritual body ...,
and the *Scale*, II chapter 13: þe sensualite ... comon*n* to man *and* to best ... þe whilk
sensualite, whan it is vnskilfully *and* vnordinatly rewled, is made þe (f. 75ᵛ) ymage of syn
(MS BM Harley 6579; Underhill, 272).
*For as þer is a bestely wille / in the nethere party / that maye wille na goode / so is thare a
goodely wille / in the ouer partye / that maye wille nane euille*: a six-membered *compar* with *oppositio contrariorum* (a bestely wille / a goodely wille, the nethere party / the ouer partye, na goode /
nane euille) and *traductio* (a ... wille / maye wille).
11 *so is there a goodely wille*: cf. the *Scale*, II chapter 35: God wirkiþ in vs al boþe goode
wil *and* goode werk as seynt Poul seiþ: ... it is god þat wirkiþ in vs good wille *and*
fulfillyng of gode wil (MS BM Harley 6579, f. 114ᵛ; Underhill, 390). Cf. Philippians
2.13.

the ouer partye that maye wille nane eville, botte euer goode, na mare
than the persones of þe blissed trinyte. And this schewyd oure lorde me
in the holehed of luffe, that we stande in his sight, ȝa, that he luffeȝ vs
15   nowe als wele whiles we ere here as he schalle do when we ere thare
before his blissed face.

Also god schewed me that syn is na schame, bot wirschippe to mann,
for in this sight mynn vnderstandynge was lyfted vp in to hevenn; and
thann comm verrayly to my mynde David, Peter and Paule, Thomas of
20   Inde and the Maudelaynn, howe thaye er knawenn in the kyrke of erth
with thare synnes to thayre wirschippe. And it is to thamm no schame
that thay hafe synned — na mare it is in the blysse of heven — for thare
the takenynge of synne is tourned into wirschippe. Right so oure lorde
god schewed me thamm in ensampille of alle othere that schalle cum

---

12 *that maye wille nane eville, botte euer goode*: cf. *Contemplations of the Love and Dread of God*: ... mannes wyll is ordeyned fyrst and dysposed with the grace of god that he shall wyll good (Horstman, 2 92).

*na mare than the persones of þe blissed trinyte*: cf. 443.20: *And therfore we be that he lovyth, and endlesly we do that he lykyth.*

17 *is*: cf. 445.2: *shalle be.*

18 *for in this sight ... lorde god schewed*: cf. 446.12-447.18.

19 *comm verrayly*: cf. 446.13: *god brought merely.* Either reading can be defended. Julian is convinced of her visions' objective reality; and the 'great penitents' can be the cause of joy for other sinners, also seeking God's forgiveness.

*David, Peter and Paule ...*: cf. 446.15 e.s., where the long text adds St. John of Beverley. The support of an argument with *exempla* from classical literature was a rhetorical device well known to spiritual and secular authors. *The Chastising of God's Children*, on the efficacy of self-distrust, has: We han ensamplis herof in the olde lawe, how Dauid þat was so hooli fel, hou Salamon þat was so wijs fel ... (Bazire and Colledge, 212). In *Sir Gawain and the Green Knight*, the discomfited hero consoles himself with the thought that greater men than he had been tricked by women: For so watz Adam in erde with one bygyled, / And Salamon with fele sere, and Samson eftsonez — / Dalyda dalt hym hys wyrde — and Dauyth þerafter / Watz blended with Barsabe ... (Tolkien and Gordon, 66; for further literature, cf. Burrow, *A Reading of 'Sir Gawain'*, 146-149 and notes). Margery Kempe makes the same point as Julian: Haue mend ... what Mary Mawdelyn was, Mary Eypcyan, Seynt Powyl, and many oþer seyntys þat arn now in hevyn, for of vnworthy I make worthy and of synful I make rytful (Meech and Allen, 49).

20 *the kyrke of erth*: cf. 446.11: *holy church in erth*, 446.17: *the chyrch on erth*. For such terms to convey the notion of the 'ecclesia militans', MED quotes Wycliffe: al holi chirche in erþe, and Trevisa: Holy chirche here in erþe.

22 *for thare ... into wirschippe*: cf. 447.21. Julian has already observed that sin can be known only by the pain which it causes (245.67-68), and that she *sawe a grete anynge be twyx Criste and vs; for when he was in payne we ware in payne, and alle creatures that myght suffyr payne soffyrde with hym* (235.50). Here she develops her thought further, by using the word *takenynge*, and concludes by calling sins *wonndes* (256.38), which *er sene before god nowht as wonndes bot as wyrschippes*, honourable scars which are the stigmata of every penitent sinner who enjoys the beatific vision.

25 thedyr. Synn is the scharpyste scourge that any chosenn saule maye be
bette with, whilke scourge it alle for bettes mann *and* womann, and alle
for brekes thamm, *and* noghteʒ hym selfe in thare awne syght sa fare
forth that hym thynke that he is noght worthy bot as it ware to synke in
to helle; botte when contricionn takes hym be the towchynge of the haly
30 gaste, than turnes he bitternesse into hope of goddys mercye. And than
begynnes his wonndys to hile and the sawlle to qwykkynn, turnyd in to
the lyfe of haly kyrke. The haly gaste leddes hymm to confessyonn,
wilfully to schewe his synnes nakedly *and* trewly with grete sorowe and
grete schame that he hase swa defowled the fayre ymage of god. Than
35 he takes pennannce for ylke a synne eniewnyd be his domesmann that is
growndyd in haly kyrke be the techynge of the haly gaste. Be this
medycynn behoues euer ilke synfulle sawlle be heled, *and* namlye of syn-
f. 109r nes that ere dedely in the selfe. / Thouʒ he be heled, his wonndes er
sene before god nowht as wonndes bot as wyrschippes. And so onn
40 contrarye wyse, as it es punysched here with sorowe and with penannce,
it schalle be rewarded in heuen be the curtayse loue of oure lorde god
alle myghttye, that wille that nane that commes thare lese his travayle.
      That mede that we salle resayfe thare salle nought be litelle, bot it
schalle be hy, gloriouse and wirschipfulle. And so schalle alle schame
45 turne in to wyrschyppe *and* in to mare ioye. And I am sekere be mynn
awne felynge, the mare that ilke kynde saule sees þis in the kynde *and*
curtayse love of god, the lathere es hym for to synne.

---

25 *Synn is the scharpyste ... and alle for brekes thamm*: cf. 449.2-4.
27 *and noghteʒ hym selfe in thare awne syght*: cf. 449.4: *and purgyth hym in hys owne syght*;
the SS readings evidently derive from 'noghteʒ'.
*hym selfe in thare awne syght*: the numbers of the pronouns are confused. If the ar-
chetype were composed in the East Midland dialect, it probably had 'hemselfe' and
'here'; cf. E. Colledge and C. Smetana: 'Capgrave's *Life of St. Norbert*', 428-429. As do
many other defects of this text, this seems to result from bungled translation into
Northern dialect.
*sa fare forth ... of the haly gaste* (256.36): cf. 449.4-450.13.
29 *botte*: cf. 449.6: *tylle*.
30 *he*: cf. 449.7: *the*. In the long text we must understand *turnes* as intransitive,
whereas here it is transitive, and the antecedent of *he* is *the haly gaste*.
35 *eniewnyd*: MED, enjoinen, -ien, v., records forms 'eniunʒe', 'iniunyd'.
36 *Be this medycynn ... lese his travayle*: cf. 452.30-35.
37 *and namlye of synnes that ere dedely in the selfe*: not in the long text; cf. 452.31.
40 *it es*: cf. 452.32: *we be*.
43 *That mede ... and in to mare ioye* (256.45): this corresponds with the long text,
452.38-453.40.
*That mede that we salle resayfe thare salle nought be litelle / bot it schalle be hy gloriouse and
wirschipfulle*: a *compar* with *oppositio contrariorum*.
45 *mare*: not in the long text; cf. 453.40.
*And I am sekere ... to synne* (256.47): this corresponds with the long text, 457.33-35.

(xviii)    Bot ȝyf thowe be styrred to saye or to thynke: Senn this is sothe, þan
ware it goode for to synne for to hafe the mare mede, be ware of this
styrrynge and dispice it, for it is of the enmy. For whate saule that
wilfully takys this styrrynge, he may neuer be safe to he be amendyd as
5    of dedely synne. For ȝyf it ware layde before me, alle the payne that is
in helle and in purgatorye and in erth, dede and othere and synne, I had
leuer chese alle that payne than synne. For synne is so vyle and so
mykille for to hate that it maye be likened to na payne whilke payne es
nought synn. For alle thynge is goode botte synne, and nathynge is
10    wikkyd botte synne. Synne es nowthere deed no lykynge, botte when a
saule cheses wilfully synne, that is payne, as fore his god, atte the ende
he hase ryght nought. That payne thynke me the herdeste helle, for he
has nought his god. In alle paynes a saule may hafe god botte in synne.
   And als myghtty and als witty as god is for to safe mann, als willy he
15    is. For Criste hym selfe is grownde of alle the lawe of crysten menn, and
he has tawht vs to do goode agaynes eville. Here may we see that he es
hym selfe this charite, and does to vs as he teches vs to do; for he wille
that we be lyke to hym in anehede of endeles luffe to oure selfe and to
oure  even cristenn. Na mare than his love es broken to vs for oure
20    synne, na mare wille he that oure love be brokenn to oure selfe ne to
oure even cristenn; botte nakedlye hate synne and endelesslye love the
saule as god loves it. For this worde that god sayde es ane endelesse
comforth, that kepes vs fulle sekerlye.

---

1 þan: add. marg. corrector.

---

1 *Senn this is sothe ... of the enmy* (257.3): this corresponds with the long text, 456.27-30.
5 *For ȝyf it ware layde ... es nought synn* (257.9): this corresponds with the long text,
457.35-458.39.
6 *and synne*: cf. 458.37: *than synne (we)*. The reading here, which avoids the repetition
of 'than synne', is superior.
9 *For alle thynge ... botte synne* (257.10): this corresponds with the long text, 458.40-41.
10 *Synne es nowthere deed no lykynge, botte when a saule cheses wilfully synne, that is payne, as
fore his god, atte the ende he hase ryght nought*: this passage is not in the long text (cf. 458.41
e.s.), where Julian appears to have omitted it as a reflection of her own, not founded
on the showings; for when she tells us that she desired some sight of hell or purgatory
'for learning', she adds: *I ne culde se of thys ryght nouȝt* (427.8).
14 *And als myghtty ... as god loves it* (257.22): this corresponds with the long text,
458.44-459.53.
*And als myghtty and als witty / as god is for to safe mann / als willy he is*: a *compar* with
*repetitio* (als ... als ... als) and *similiter cadens*: (witty ... willy).
22 *For this worde ... sekerlye* (257.23): this corresponds with the long text, 459.53-54.
*For this worde*: cf. 254.3.
23 *that kepes*: the reading is defensible, but cf. 459.54: *I kepe the fulle truly*, which
suggests a possible emendation: that he kepes. Cf. 254.3-5.
*that kepes vs fulle sekerlye*: cf. 443.13: *suernesse of kepyng*, and note.

(**xix**)      Aftyr this oure lorde schewed me for prayers. I sawe ij condicions in
f. 109v    thamm that prayes, aftyr that I hafe felyd in my selfe. Ane / es thaye
wille nought praye for nathynge that may be botte that thynge that es
goddes wille and his wirschippe; anothere is that thay sette thamm
5      myghttelye *and* contynuely to be seke that thynge that es his wille and
his wirschippe. And þat es as I hafe vndyrstandide be the techynge of
haly kyrke; for in this oure lorde lered me the same, to hafe of goddes
gyfte faith, hope and charyte, and kepe vs there in to oure lyves ende.
And in this we say Pater noster, Aue and Crede with devocionn as god
10     wille gyffe it. And thus we praye fore alle oure evenn cristenn, and for
alle manere of menn that god es wille es, for we walde that alle maner

---

1 *for*: ms: foure.

---

1 *Aftyr this oure lorde* ...: from here to ... *is þe saule aned to god* (262.78) corresponds
with the long-text version of the fourteenth revelation (460-474); the many differences
between them are one of the most striking examples of Julian's growth as a spiritual
theologian and as a contemplative. Cf. Introduction, p. 113 e.s.
   *foure* (ms): the context does not support this, and cf. 460.3: *for prayer*, 'about prayer'.
   2 *aftyr that I hafe felyd in my selfe*: in the long text she substitutes *in our lordes menyng*
(460.4), not simply, it would seem, to draw attention away from herself, but because
she now knows that she must first reflect on what she saw and heard, before she turns
to her own experience.
   *thaye wille nought praye for nathynge that may be botte that thynge that es goddes wille*: cf.
Romans 12.2: ... that you may prove what is the good and the acceptable and the perfect will of God. Julian here seems to be referring all prayer to the first three petitions
of the Pater Noster (Matthew 6.9-10).
   4 *anothere is that they sette thamm myghttelye and contynuely to be seke that thynge that es his
wille and his wirschippe*: cf. 332.68: *And this vision was a lernyng to my vnderstandyng that
the contynually sekyng of the soule plesyth god moch*.
   5 *to be seke that thynge that es his wille and his wirschippe*: cf. Ecclesiasticus 2.19: They that
fear the Lord will seek after the things that are well pleasing to him.
   9 *And in this we say Pater noster, Aue and Crede*: Julian is probably alluding to the
people's devotions during Mass. In *The Lay Folks' Mass Book* they are directed to recite
the Our Father, Hail Mary and Creed at the beginning of Mass (Simmons, 10), during
the offertory (24), at the elevation (26) and at the end of Mass (58).
   10 *And thus we praye fore alle oure evenn cristenn, and for alle manere of menn that god es
wille es*: this is the tenor of the silent petitions to be said during the canon of the Mass:
Oure sib men and oure wele willandes, / Oure frendes, tenandes and seruandes /
... Riche men and pore, grete and smalle, / I pray þe, lord, for hom alle (Simmons, 34).
In the *Mirror of St. Edmund* we read: ... we suld gedyre all men with vs in oure prayers,
for all ere oure brethire, crystende and vncristende (Horstman 1, 231).
   11 *that god es wille es*: sc. 'for whom salvation is God's will', a frequent qualification of
Julian's; cf. e.g. 222.51, 240.29.

of menn and womenn ware in the same vertu and grace that we awe to desyre to oure selfe. Botte ȝitt in alle this oft tymes oure triste is nowht fulle, for we ere nouȝt sekare that god almyghtty hyeres vs, as vs thynke for oure vnworthynesse and fore we fele ryght nought; fore we ere als barayne and als drye oftymes eftyr oure prayers as we ware before. And thus in oure felynge oure foly es cause of oure waykenesse, for thus hafe I felede in my selfe. And alle this brought oure lorde sodaynlye to my mynde, and myghttely and lyfely *and* comfortande me agaynes this maner of waykenesse in prayers, and sayde: I am grownde of thy besekynge. First it is my wille that þou hafe it, *and* syne I make the to will it, *and* syne I make the to be seke it. *And* ȝif þou beseke, howe schulde it than be that þou schulde nought hafe thy besekynge? And thus in the fyrste resonn with the thre that folowe eftere, oure lorde schewed a myghty comfort.

And the fyrst þare he says : And þowe beseke, thare he schewes fulle grete plesannce and endelesse mede that he wille gyffe vs for oure besekynge. And in the fourte resonn thare he sais : Howe schulde it

---

21 *syne (I make the to will)*: 'y' by corrector over one erased letter.
28 *fourte*: 'fort' and 'u' interl. w. caret, by corrector, over 'sext', erased.

---

13 *Botte ȝitt in alle this oft tymes ... to my mynde* (259.19): this corresponds with the long text, 460.5-461.10.

*oure triste is nowht fulle*: the *Mirror of St. Edmund* has: Certayne trayst es contende in þis worde *noster*, for if he be ours, þan may we sekerly trayst in hym þat he es haldene till vs (Horstman 1, 233).

17 *And thus in oure felynge / oure foly es cause / of oure waykenesse / for thus hafe I felede / in my selfe*: a *compar* of five *cola*, with *traductio (felynge ... felede)* and *adnominatio (felynge ... foly)*. The long text preserves the figure intact: 460.8.

20 *and sayde: I am grownde ... thy besekynge* (260.29): this corresponds with the long text, 461.10-14.

*and sayde*: the long text has: *and shewed theyse wordes and seyde* (461.10). Cf. 258.1 note.

21 *First it is my wille that þou hafe it / and syne I make the to will it / and syne I make the to be seke it*: a *compar* with initial *repetitio (and syne ...)*, medial *repetitio (I make the ...)*, and *traductio (my wille / to will)*.

22 *And ȝif þou beseke*: this is repeated exactly, 259.26: *And the fyrst þare he says: And þowe beseke*; but cf. 461.13 and 17, where SS have *besekyst ... besekyst*, but P and C have *sekyst ... beseke*. There can be little doubt of the short text's superiority, or that Julian means 'Provided that you beseech' (subjunctive), not 'and you do beseech' (indicative).

25 *a myghty comfort*: the long text adds: *as it may be sene in the same wordes* (461.15).

28 *fourte*: this has been allowed to stand; but for reasons why Julian probably wrote 'second' (or 'other'), see 461.14, 19 and notes.

than be þat þou schulde noght hafe thy besekynge? þare he schewes a
30  sobere vndertakynge, for we tryste nou3t als myghtelye als we schulde
do. Thus wille oure lorde that we bath praye *and* triste, for the cause of
the resones befor sayde is to make vs myghty agaynes waiknesse in oure
prayers. For it is goddis wille that we pray, and þer to he styrres vs in
thies wordes befor sayde, for he wille þat we sekere to hafe oure
35  prayere, for prayer pleses god. Prayer pleses mann with hym selfe, and
f. 110r  makes hym sobure *and* meke that before hand / was in strife *and*
travayle. Praiere anes the saule to god, for þow3 the saule be euer lyke
god in kynde and in substannce, it is oft vnlike in condicionn thurgh
synn of mannes party. Than makes prayer þe saule like vnto god, when
40  the sawlle wille as god wille, and than es it lyke to god in condicion as it
es in kynde. And thus he teches vs to pray and myghttely tryste that we
schalle hafe that we praye fore, for alle thynge that es done schulde be
done þow3 we neuer prayed it. Botte the luff of god es so mykille that he

---

29 *þare he schewes ... we schulde do*: not in the long text. This again she omits as a reflection of her own, and not what she saw. Cf. 511.9: *nor I se nott the shewyng to vs no manner
of blame*.

*a sobere vndertakynge*: 'a serious rebuke'. Cf. NED Undertaking, *vbl. sb.* † 2, b, the first
example c. 1430; the second, c. 1440, glossed 'deprehencio', from the King's Lynn
*Promptorium Parvulorum*. This is the figure known as *interrogatio* (erotema).

31 *Thus wille oure lorde ... strife and travayle* (260.37): There is correspondence between
this passage and the long text, 469.15-18. There is, however, no equivalent for the short
text's observation: *Prayer pleses mann with hym selfe*.

34 *he wille þat we be sekere to hafe oure prayere*: cf. Matthew 21.22: And whatever things
you shall ask in prayer, believing, you shall receive.

35 *for prayer pleses god*: cf. I Timothy 2.1-3: ... supplications, prayers, intercessions
and thanksgivings ... for this is good and acceptable in the sight of God our saviour.

37 *Praiere anes the saule ... betwix god and mannes saule* (261.54): this corresponds with
the long text, 475.2-476.17.

39 *Than makes prayer þe saule like vnto god*: cf. 475.4: *Than is prayer a wytnesse*, and 475.3
note.

40 *and than es it lyke to god in condicion as it es in kynde*: cf. 475.5: *and comfortyth the conscience and ablyth man to grace*.

42 *for alle thynge*: 'even though something'. Cf. NED All, *a.*, *sb.*, and *adv.* 9.c, For,
*prep.* and *conj.* 23.

*alle thynge that es done schulde be done þow3 we neuer prayed it*: not in the long text (476.7),
where it would have been otiose, in the light of her reflection on what God showed —
that it is pleasing to him for us ask him what he wishes to do for us.

43 *the luff of god es so mykille*: this observation is Julian's constant and persistent inspiration. In the long text she replaces it with *he beholdyth vs in loue*, seemingly because,
for her, God's beholding us signifies his great and active love. Cf. Genesis 1.31: And
God saw all the things that he had made, and they were very good.

haldes vs p*arcyn*ers of his goode deede; and þ*er*fore he styrres vs to praye
45   that hy*m* lykes to do, for whate prayer*e* or goode will*e* that we hafe of
his gyfte, he wille rewarde vs *and* gife vs endelese mede. And this was
schewed me in this worde: And þou beseke it.

In this worde god schewed me so grete plesannce *and* so grete
lykynge, as ȝif he ware mekill*e* behaldene to vs for ilke goode dede that
50   we do, all*e* ȝif it es he that does it. And for that we beseke besily to do
that thynge that hym lykes, as ȝif he sayde: Whate myght þowe plese me
mare than to bisike bisily, wisely *and* wilfullye to do that thynge that I
wille do? And thus makes prayer*e* accorde betwix god *and* mannes
saule, for whate tyme that mannes saule es hamelye with god, hym
55   nedes nought to praye, botte be halde reu*er*entlye whate he s(ee)s. For
in alle this tyme that this was schewed me, I was noght stirred to praye,
botte to hafe alle waye this welle in my mynde for comforth, that when
we see god we hafe that we desyre, *and* than nedes vs nought to praye.
Botte when we se nought god, than nedes vs to pray for faylynge *and* for

---

55 *sees*: ms: says.

---

44 *he styrres vs to praye that hym lykes to do*: cf. 476.8, and John 16.26-27: ... You shall
ask in my name, and I do not say to you that I will ask the Father for you. For the
Father himself loves you ...

46 *he wille rewarde vs and gife vs endelese mede*: cf. 476.10, and Matthew 19.27-29:
... What therefore shall we have? Everyone who has left house or brothers or sisters or
father or mother or wife or children or lands for my sake shall receive a hundredfold
and shall possess everlasting life.

47 *in this worde: And* ...: cf. 259.22.

50 *alle ȝif it es*: cf. 476.13: *and yet it is.*
*besily*: cf. 476.14: *myghtly*; and so 261.52, 476.16.

52 *I wille do?* Cf. 476.16: *I wyll haue doen?*

53 *And thus makes prayere accorde betwix god and mannes saule, for whate tyme that mannes
saule es hamelye with god* ...: cf. what is called in MS BN Fonds anglais 41 (the hand of
which is probably ante 1400), as in other manuscripts: ... þese eiȝte chapitris necessarie
for men *and* wo*m*men þ*at* ȝeuen he*m* to p*er*feccioun, which was fou*n*den in maistir
Lowys de Fontib*us* book, and maistir Watir Hiltonn, chanou*n* of Thurkartonn, trans-
latide it in to english tu*n*ge for þe comown profyȝt (f. 155ʳ) ... Ther is þre mane*r* trans-
foormynge of þe soule ... (f. 152ʳ) ... Anoþir is forto be *transfoormyd with* god, *and* þ*at*
is wha*n*ne his soule is oonyd wiþ Crist, *and* riȝt hoomly w*ith* him. Cf. Jones, 103.

54 *for whate tyme ... nought to praye*: not in the long text; cf. 476.17 e.s., where Julian
develops the same thought at greater length.

55 *sees*: the manuscript reading is plainly corrupt, and must be emended, either to
*saye*, 'he saw' (cf. 217.2 and note), or, more probably, *sees*. Julian is writing of that
moment of infused contemplative prayer when the soul rests in the beholding of him
for sight of whom the unitive prayer of petition is made; cf. 477.18-479.36.

57 *welle*: probably not adverb but noun, 'this good'. Cf. 263.5.

59 *Botte when we se ... euer ylyke in love*: cf. 478.28-479.33.

60    habelynge of oure selfe to Jhesu. For whenn a saule es tempted, trubled
      *and* lefte to it selfe be vnreste, than es it tyme to pray and to make hym
      selfe symple and boxsomm to god. Bot he be boxomm, na maner of
      prayer makes god souple to hym, for he is euer ylyke in love. Botte in
      the tyme that man is in synne he is so vnmyghttye, so vnwyse *and* so
65    vnluffande that he can nought love god ne hym selfe.

      The maste myschefe that he hase es blyndnesse, for he sees nought
      alle this. Than the hale luffe of god alle myghty that euer is ane gyffes

f. 110v    hym sight / to hym selfe; and thann wenes he that god ware wrathe with
      hym for his synne. And than is he stirred to contricionn, and be con-
70    fessyonn and othere goode dedys to slake the wrathe of god, vnto the
      tyme he fynde a reste in saule *and* softnesse in conscience; and than hym
      thynke þat god hase for gyffynn his synnes, and it es soth. And than is
      god in þe sight of ⟨the⟩ saule turnede in to the behaldynge of the saule,
      as ʒif it had bene in payne or in presonn, sayande thus: I am gladde that
75    þou erte commen to reste, for I hafe euer loved the *and* nowe loves the,
      and þou me. And thus with prayers, as I hafe before sayde, *and* with
      othere goode werkys þat ere custummab⟨ylle⟩ be the techynge of haly
      kyrke, is þe saule aned to god.

---

73  *the*: om. ms.
77  *custummabylle*: ms: custummabelye.

---

60 *habelynge*: cf. 478.29: *vnablynes*. Either reading can be defended, and this can
mean: 'We need to pray, because we are deficient, and for strengthening of ourselves'.
But it cannot mean, as MED suggests, citing this passage, 'making oneself fit or worthy';
Julian was no semi-Pelagian. SS, we should observe, agree with A.

*For whenn a saule es tempted* ...: see the *Scale*, I chapter 89: Crie to hym by grete desires
and sihʒynges þat he wil helpe þe bere þis heuy birþen of þis ymage ... It may so be þat
þou schalt fele peyn and soroe ... for þou schalt vnderstond þat þere may no soule lyue
withouten grete peyn, bot if he haue rest and delite ... in his creatour (MS Cambridge
UL Add. 6686, p. 358; Underhill, 213-214).

62 *symple*: cf. 478.31 note. The reading here is defensible and has been retained; but
'supple and buxom' is more suggestive. NED, Supple, *a*.4, 'Yielding readily to per-
suasion or influence; compliant', has as its first example: c. 1340 Hampole *Prose Treat.*
... Forto breke downe the vnbuxomnes of the body ... that itt myght be souple and
redy, and not moch contrarious to the spirite in gostely wyrkynge.

*Bot he be boxomm*: not in the long text; cf. 479.32.
64 *he is so vnmyghttye ... es blyndnesse*: cf. 496.17-19.
68 *and thann wenes he ... and it es soth*: cf. 454.5-10.
69 *and be confessyonn and othere goode dedys*: not in the long text; cf. 454.7.
71 *hym thynke*: cf. 454.9: *hope we*.
72 *And than is god ... and þou me*: cf. 454.10-455.15.
75 *to reste*: cf. 455.13 and note.
*for I hafe ... and þou me*: cf. 455.14 and note.
76 *And thus with prayers ... aned to god*: not in the long text; cf. 455.15.

(xx)     Before this tyme I hadde ofte grete langynge *and* desyred of goddys
gyfte to be delyue*r*ed of this warlde and of this lyfe, for I schulde be
with my god in blysse whare I hope sikerlye thurgh his me*r*cye to be
with owte*n*n ende. For ofte tymes I behelde the waa that is here and the
5    weele *and* the blyssede beynge thare; *and* ჳyf thare hadde bene na pay*n*n
in erthe bot the absence of oure lorde god, me thouჳt sum tyme it ware
mare than I myght bere. And this made me to mourne *and* beselye
lange.
     Than god sayde to me, for pacience *and* for suffera*n*nce, thus:
10   Sudanly thowe schalle be takene fra alle thy payne, fra alle thy dissese
*and* fra alle thy waa. *And* þow schalle comme*n*n vp aboue*n*n, and thowe
schalle hafe me to thy mede, and þowe schalle be fulfyllede of ioye and
blysse, *and* þowe schalle neu*er* hafe na man*er* of payne, na man*er* of
sekenes, na man*er* of myslykynge, na wantynge of wille, botte eu*er* ioye
15   *and* blysse with oute*n*n ende. Whate schulde it than greve the to suffyr a
while, se*n*n it is my wille and my wirschippe?
     Also in this reso*n*n: Sudanly þou schalle be take*n*n, I sawe how god
rewardys ma*n*n of the pacience that he has in abydynge of goddes wille
in his tyme, and þ*at* ma*n*n lengthes his pacyence owe*r*e the tyme of his
20   lyffynge for vnknawynge of his tyme of passynge. This is a grete pr*o*fytte,

1 *Before this tyme ... it schalle be nouჳt*: cf. 619.5-620.11.

*ofte*: not in the long text; cf. 619.5.

*and desyred of goddys gyfte to be delyuered of this warlde*: Rolle, in his *Exposicio super secundum versiculum Cantici Canticorum* (Hope Allen called this work *Comment on the Canticles*,
Rolle, 63 et passim, Sr. Elizabeth Murray entitles her edition *Richard Rolle's Comment on
the Canticles*, but they should have avoided this misnomer and have followed this
colophon from the Dublin manuscript) writes: ... quia tunc cum gaudio morimur
quando delicias eterni amoris canentes solam in deo delectacionem contemplamur
(Murray, 4).

2 *for I schulde be ... with owtenn ende*: not in the long text; cf. 619.6.

11 *And þow schalle commenn vp abouenn / and thowe schalle hafe me to thy mede*: a compar
with *repetitio* (*And þowe ...*).

12 *and þowe schalle be fulfyllede of ioye and blysse / and þowe schalle neuer hafe na maner of
payne*: a *compar* with *repetitio* and *oppositio contrariorum*.

13 *na maner of sekenes / na maner of myslykynge / na wantynge of wille*: a *compar* with
*repetitio*.

17 *resonn*: cf. 621.22: *worde*, and note. Julian probably here has in mind the
rhetoricians' *ratiocinatio*, 'reasoning by question and answer'. *Whate schulde it than greve
the ...? ...Sudanly þou schalle be taken* ... NED, Reason, *sb.*[1], MED, resoun, do not record
this specific use; the nearest is NED's 19, 'the act of reasoning or argumentation'. The
probability is that, as with *contraryte* (cf. 372.24 note) and *profyr* (370.6 note), Julian was
obliged to invent her own rhetorical terminology. See Introduction, 48-49.

for ȝif a mann knewe his tyme, he schulde noght hafe pacience owere
þat tyme. Also god wille that whiles the saule es in the bodye, that it
seme to it selfe that it es euer atte the poynte to be takenn. For alle þis /
f. 111r  lyfe (and) this langoure that we hafe here is bot a poynte, and whenn we
25  ere takene sodaynly oute of payne in to blysse, it schalle be nouȝt.
    And þerfore sayde oure lorde: Whate schulde it than greve the to suf-
fere a while, senn it is my wille *and* my wyrschippe? It is goddys wille
that we take his behestys and his confortynges als largelye and as
myghtelye as we maye take thame; and also he wille þat we take oure
30  abydynge and oure desese als lyghtelye as we maye take thamm, and
sette thamm atte nought. For the lyghtlyere we take thamm, the lesse
price we sette be thamm for luff, the lesse payne salle we hafe in the
felynge of tham, and the mare thanke we schalle hafe for thamm.
    In this blyssed revelacionn I was trewly taught that whate mann or
35  wommann wilfully cheses god in his lyfe, he may be sekere that he is
chosene. Kepe this treulye, for sothly it is god ys wille that we be als
sekere in tryste of the blys in heuenn whiles we ere here as we schulde
be in sekernesse whenn we ere thare.
    And euer the mare likynge and the ioye that we take in this sekernesse
40  with reuerence and mekenes, the bettere likes hym. For I am sekyr, ȝif

---

23 *seme*: ms: semenn.
24 *and*: ms: in.

---

23 *seme*: cf. 622.27.
*For alle þis lyfe and this langoure that we hafe here is bot a poynte*: of the many places in
Scripture dealing with the brevity of human existence, Julian most probably has in
mind here I Peter 1.5-6: ... the last time, in which you will greatly rejoice, if now for a
little time you must be made sorrowfull (... *modicum nunc si oportet contristari* ...)
For *poynte*, 'instant', cf. 226.1 note.
24 *and (this)*: cf. 622.28.
25 *it schalle be nouȝt*: the antecedent of *it* appears to be *blysse*; but cf. 622.30: *than payn
shall be nought*.
26 *And þerfore sayde oure lorde*: not in the long text; cf. 625.59.
27 *It is goddys wille ... the bettere likes hym* (264.40): cf. 626.61-628.8.
29 *þat we take oure abydynge* ... : the *Ancrene Riwle* offers similar advice: ... eueneþ al
ȝor wo, seeknesse and oþer what, wrong of word and of werk and al þat mon may
þolen, to þat þat he þolede, and ȝe schul lihtlice iseon how luytel hit recheþ (Vernon MS,
f. 380ᶜ; Day, 83).
35 *his*: cf. 627.3: *this*.
*that he is chosene*: cf. 627.3: *þat he is louyd without end, with endlesse loue that werkyth in him
þat grace*. Cf. 221.33 note. It will be observed that S1's introductory paragraph (627.1
app.) says the same as the short text: *is sekir to be savid*.
37 *schulde*: probably error for 'schulle'; cf. 627.6: *shalle*.
40 *For I am sekyr ... bodelye seknes* (266.1): not in the long text; cf. 628.8.

thare hadde nane ben bot I that schulde be safe, god wolde hafe done
alle that he hase done for me. And so schulde ilke saule thynke in
knawynge of his lovere, forgettande ʒif he myght alle creatures, *and*
thynkkande that god hase done for hym alle that he hase done. And
45  thys thynke me schulde styrre a saule for to luff *and* lyke hymm, *and*
nought drede bot hymm; for it is his wille that we witte that alle the
myght of oure enmye is loken in oure frendes hande. And þerfore a
saule that wate sekerlye this schalle nought drede botte hym that he
loves, and alle other dredes sette thamm emange passyons and bodelye
50  sekenesse *and* ymagynacions.

And þerfore ʒif a mann be in so mekylle payne, in so mekylle waa *and*
in so mekylle deseses that hym thynke that he can thynke ryght nought
bot that þat he is in or that he feles, als sone as he maye, passe lyghtlye
ower and sette it atte nouʒt. And why? For god wille be knawen; for
11v  ʒyff we knewe hym *and* luffed hym we schulde hafe / pacience and be in
56  grete reste, *and* it schulde be lykynge to vs, alle that he does. And this
schewed oure lorde me in thies wordes þat he sayde: Whate schulde it
than greve the to suffyr a while, senn it is my wille and my wirschippe?
And here was ane ende of alle þat oure lorde schewed me that daye.

---

51 *in so mekylle payne / in so mekylle waa / and in so mekylle deseses*: a *compar* with *repetitio*.
57 *in thies wordes*: cf. 263.15.

(xxi) And efter this sone I felle to my selfe *and* to my bodelye seknes, vnderstandande that I schulde life, *and* as a wrech heuyed and mo*ur*ned for
the bodely paynes that I feled, and thou3t grete irksumnes that I schulde
langer*e* lyffe. And I was als barane and drye as 3if I hadde neu*er* had
5 comforth before bot litill*e*, for fallynge to my paynes *and* faylynge of
gastelye felynge.

Than*n* co*m*m a religiouse p*er*son*n* to me and asked me howe I farde,
and I sayde that I ha(dd)e raued þat daye. And he lugh lowde *and*
ent*er*lye. And I sayde: The crosse that stode atte my bedde feete, it bled
10 faste; and with this worde the p*er*son*n* that I spake to wex alle sadde *and*
m*er*uelande. And on*n* ane I was sare aschamed for my reklessenes, *and* I
thou3t thus: this man takys it sadlye, the leste worde that I myght saye,
that says na mare þ*er*to. And when I sawe that he toke it so sadely *and*
*with* so grete reu*er*ence, I wex ryght gretly aschamed, and walde haffe
15 bene schryfen*n*. Bot I couth tell*e* it na preste, for I thoght, howe schulde
a p*re*ste leue me? I leued nought oure lorde god. This I leued sothfastlye for the tyme that I sawe hym, and so was than my wille *and* my
menynge eu*er* for to do with owten*n* ende. Bot as a fule I lette it passe
fro my mynde.

---

2 *heuyed*: ms: that heuyed.
8 *hadde*: ms: hafe.

---

1 *vnderstandande that I schulde life*: cf. 632.10: *soone I feelt that I should life longer.*
2 *and as a wrech ... the bodely paynes* (266.3): this corresponds with the long text,
632.13-14.
*heuyed and mourned*: cf. 632.14: mornyd hevyly; but SS agree with A.
4 *And I was als barane ... bot litille*: cf. 632.12-13.
7 *Thann comm a religiouse personn...in my throte* (267-27): this corresponds with the long
text, 632.16-635.3.
8 *hadde*: cf. 632.16-633.17: *and I seyde I had ravyd today* (though this has its own mixture of direct and oblique speech).
9 *enterlye*: plainly superior to P: *inwardly* (633.17). Cf. MED enterli adv. 1: c. 1440
*PLAlex*: Þay saw Alexander wepe so enterely, and the incipit of a prayer in MS Glasgow
Hunterian V. 6. 22, f. ii^r: Lord Jhesu Crist, I thanke þe enterely þat þou for me beganne
to suffre ... For precisely the same force of the adjective, cf. a Marian complaint: Y
wylle love yowrys with hert entere (Wright: *Chester Plays*, 2 209). The SS 'inderly'
readings derive from some manuscript agreeing with A.
*The crosse that stode atte my bedde feete*: this may be identical with *the crucifixe that hange
before me* (225.21, and cf. 324.3), of the face of which Julian says that she had 'bodely
syght'; but the suspended crucifix may be part of her imaginative vision, a 'bodily
lykenes' as was that of Mary; cf. 297.29.
13 *says*: probably superior to 633.22: *sawe.*

20　Loo I, wrich! This was a grete synne *and* a grete vnkyndnes, that I for
folye of felynge of a litill*e* bodely payne so vnwyselye lefte for the tyme
the comforth of alle this blissede schewynge of oure lorde god. Here
maye ʒe see whate I am of my selfe; b*o*tte here in walde nought oure
curtayse lorde leue me. And I laye stille till*e* nyght, t*r*istande in his m*er*-
25　cye, and than I beganne to slepe.

And in my slepe atte the begynnynge me thought the fende sette hym
in my throte and walde hafe st*r*angelede mé, b*o*tte he myght nought.
Than I woke oute of my slepe, *and* vnnethes hadde I my lyfe. The p*er*-
sones that ware with me behelde me and wette my temples, and my
30　herte bega*n*n to comforth. And o*n*n ane a lytell*e* smoke come in atte the
112r　dore with a grete hete / and a fowle stynke. I sayde: Benedicite
d*o*min*us*! Is alle o*n*n fyre that is her*e?* And I wened it hadde bene a
bodely fyre that schulde hafe brenned vs to dede. I asked tha*m*m that
ware with me ʒyf thaye felyd any stynke. Thay sayde naye, thay felyd
35　nane. I sayde: Blissede be god! for than wiste I wele it was the fende
was co*m*me*n*n to tempest me. And onane I tuke þa that oure lorde
hadde schewed me on the same daye with alle the fayth of hali kyrke,
for I holde it as bathe ane, *and* fled þe*r*to as to my comforth. And alsone
alle vanysched awaye, *and* I was brought to gret reste and pees, w*i*th
40　outene seknes of bodye or drede of conscyence.

---

26 *And in my slepe*: cf. 635.2 and note.
27 *and walde ... myght nought*: cf. 636.10-11.
28 *Than I woke*: cf. 636.13-637.14: *And oure curtesse lorde gaue me grace to wake.*
*and vnnethes ... haymelyeste hame* (268.14): cf. 637.14-641.16.
31 *a fowle stynke*: cf. 637.17.
36 *to tempest*: 'assail'. Cf. NED Tempest, *v.*, MED tempest; their earliest example is c.
1374 Chaucer *Boethius* II iv 38. Cf. 637.21: *tempte*; but SS agree with A.
*þa*: 'those things', to which *for I holde it as bathe ane* seems to refer; but cf. 638.22: *I
toke me to that.*
38 *and fled þerto as to my comfort*: Julian may have had in mind some such Scriptural
passage as Psalm 54.8-9: Lo, I have gone far off, fleeing away, and I abode in the
wilderness. I waited for him who has saved me ...
*alsone*: 'at once'. 'From phrase al sone; partly confused with a(l)s sone, esp. as conj.;
mostly Northern' (MED, where all examples are of the fifteenth century).

(xxii)     Bot than lefte I stylle wakande, and than owre lorde openedde my
gastely eyenn *and* schewyd me my saule in myddys of my herte. I sawe
my saule swa large as it ware a kyngdome; and be the condicions that I
sawe þerin me thought it was a wirschipfulle cite. In myddys of this cite
5    sittes oure lorde Jhesu, verraye god *and* verray mann, a fayre personn
and of large stature, wyrschipfulle, hiest lorde. And I sawe hym cledde
solemplye in wyrschippes. He sittes in the saule euenn ryght in pees *and*
reste, and he rewles *and* ȝemes heuenn *and* erth and alle that is. The
manhede w*ith* the godhede sittis in reste, and the godhede rewles *and*
10   ȝemes w*ith* owtynn any instrumente or besynes. And my saule (is)
blisfullye occupyed with the godhede, that is sufferaynn myght, sufferayne wisdomme, sufferayne goodnesse.
     The place that Jhesu takes in oure saule he schalle neu*er* remove it
with owtynn ende, for in vs is his haymelyeste hame, *and* maste lykynge
15   to hym to dwelle in. This was a delectabille syght *and* a restefulle, for it
is so in trowth with owtenn ende; and the behaldynge of this whiles we
er*e* here es fulle plesannde to god and fulle grete spede to vs. And the
saule that thus behaldys, it makys it lyke to hym that is behaldene, and
anes in reste *and* in pees. And this was a singuler*e* ioye *and* a blis to me
20   that I sawe hym sitte, for the behaldynge of this sittynge schewed to me
sikernes of his endelesse dwellynge; and I knewe sothfastly that it was he
f. 112v   that schewed me / alle before. And whenn I hadde behaldenn this with

---

10 *is* om. ms.

---

1 *Bot than lefte I stylle wakande*: not in the long text; cf. 639.2.
*lefte*: for this intransitive use, 'to remain', cf. NED Leave *v.* 1, +III 12.
4 *In myddys of this cite / sittes oure lorde Jhesu / verraye god and verray mann / a fayre personn and of large stature / wyrschipfulle hiest lorde*: a five-membered *compar* giving *membrum*
with *oppositio contrariorum* in the middle *colon*.
6 *cledde solemplye in wyrschippes*: this seems to echo Psalm 92.1: The Lord has reigned,
he is clothed with beauty.
10 *is blisfullye*: cf. 640.12: *þe soule is*. An alternative emendation would be 'was'.
14 *for in vs is his haymelyeste hame*: *tautologia*, 'a repetition of the same statement' (NED).
*maste lykynge to hym to dwelle in*: not in the long text; cf. 641.17. Cf. Proverbs 8.31: My
delights were to be with the children of men.
15 *This was a delectabille syght ... dispayre, as me thouȝt* (270.8): cf. 644.46-648.8.
16 *so in trowth*: not in the long text; cf. 644.46.
20 *for the behaldynge*: cf. 645.51 and note.
21 *I knewe sothfastly*: cf. 645.52 and note.

fulle avisement, thann schewed oure lorde me wordys fulle mekely, with
owtynn voyce *and* with owtenn openynge of lyppes, as he hadde done
25 before, and sayde fulle soberlye: Witte it welle, it was na rauynge that
thowe sawe to day, botte take it and leue it and kepe þe ther to, and þou
schalle nought be ouercomenn.

This laste wordes ware sayde to me for lernynge of fulle trewe sikernes that it is our lorde Jhesu that schewed me alle; for ryght as in the
30 fyrste worde that oure lorde schewed me, menande his blissyd passionn:
Here with is the fende ouercomenn, ryght so he sayde in the laste worde
with fulle trewe sikernesse: Thow schalle nought be ouercommen. And
this lernynge and this trewe comforthe, it es generalle to alle myne euen-
cristenn, as I haffe before sayde, *and* so is goddys wille.
35 And this worde: Thowe schalle nought be ouercommenn, was sayde
fulle scharpely and fulle myghtely, for sekernes and comforth agayne
alle tribulacions that maye comm. He sayde nought: Þou salle not be
tempestyd, thowe schalle not be trauayled, þou schalle not be desesed;
bot he sayde: Þou schalle nouȝt be ouercommen. God wille that we take
40 hede of his worde, and that we be euer myghtty in sekernesse, in wele
and in waa, for he luffes vs and likes vs, and so wille he that we luff hym
and lyke hym and myghtely triste in hym, and alle schalle be wele.
And sone eftyr alle was close, *and* I sawe na mare.

---

26 *þe*: interl. corrector w. caret.
37 *Þou salle not (be tempestyd)*: add. marg. corrector w. caret.

---

23 *oure lorde me wordys*: cf. 645.53-54: *oure good lorde wordes*; there has evidently been
some corruption, but where and of what nature is hard to say.
25 *soberlye*: cf. 646.55: *swetely*. Cf. also 240.33, 387.50 and notes.
29 *that it is*: cf. 646.59: *þat is*, evidently the inferior reading.
*the fyrste worde*: cf. 227.28.
37 *He sayde nought / Þou salle not be tempestyd / thowe schalle not be trauayled / þou schalle
not be desesed / bot he sayde / Þou schalle nouȝt be ouercommen*: a six-membered *compar* with
*repetitio* (þou salle not ...).
38 *tempestyd*: cf. 647.68: *trobelyd*.
39 *Þou schalle nouȝt be ouercommen*: cf. the *Chastising*: whanne he seiþ þat ȝe entre nat
into temptacion, ȝe schal vndirstonde þat ȝe be nat ouercomen wiþ temptacion (Bazire
and Colledge, 96, and notes, 259, for analogues from Tertullian onwards).
40 *his*: cf. 647.70: *this*.
*sekernesse*: cf. 647.71: *feytfull trust*; SS: *sekir*.
42 *myghtely triste in hym*: cf. 649.11.

(xxiii)      After this the fende comm agayne with his heete and with his stynke,
           *and* made me fulle besye. The stynke was so vile and so paynfull*e*, and
           the bodely heete also dredfulle *and* trauaylous; *and* also I harde a bodely
           iangelynge *and* a speche, as it hadde bene of two bodyes, and bathe to
      5    my thynkynge iangled at anes, as ȝif thay had haldene a *p*arliamente
           with grete besynes, and alle was softe mutterynge. And I vnderstode
           nouȝt whate thay sayde, botte alle this was to stirre me to dispayre, as
           me thouȝt; and I triste besely in god *and* comforthede my sawlle with
           bodely speche, as I schulde hafe done to another*e* person*n* tha*n*n my
      10   selfe that hadde so bene travaylede. Me thought this besynes myght
   f. 113r  nought be / lykned to na bodely besenes. My bodely eyȝen*n* I sette on
           the same crosse that I hadde sene comforth in before that tyme, my
           tu*n*ge I occupyed with speche of Cristes passion*n* *and* rehersynge of the
           faith of hali kyrke, and my herte I festende on god with alle the triste
      15   and alle the myght that was in me. And I thouȝt to my selfe, menande:
           thowe hase nowe grete besynes; walde þou nowe fra this tyme eu*er* mar*e*
           be so besy to kepe the fro synne, this ware a soferayne *and* a goode oc-
           cupacion*n*. For I trowe sothlye, ware I saffe fra synne I ware fulle saife
           fra alle the fendes of helle *and* enmyse of my saule.

      20        And thus thay occupied me alle the nyght and on*n* the morn*n* tille it
           was aboute pryme dayes; and tha*n*n on*n* ane thay ware alle gane and
           passed, and þ*er*e lefte nathynge bot stynke; and that lasted stille a while.
           And I scorned thame, and thus was I delyu*er*ed of tha*m*m be the v*er*tu of
           Cristes passion*n*. For tharewith is the fende ou*er*commen*n*, as Criste
      25   sayde before to me.

---

        4 *iangelynge and a speche*: cf. 648.4: *talkyng*. SS agree with *iangelynge*.
        5 *iangled*: cf. 648.5: *talkyd*. Again, SS agree with A. In a satiric macaronic poem, *On
        Chattering in Church*, the poet says to the women so reprehended: For his loue þat ȝou
        der boȝth, / Hold ȝou stil and iangel noȝth, / Sed prece deponentes (C. Brown, XV
        277).
        6 *mutterynge*: cf. 648.7: *whystryn*; SS: *muttering*.
        8 *and I triste ... sayde before to me* (270.25): cf. 649.11-651.16.
        11 *My bodely eyȝenn ... before to me* (270.25): this corresponds with the long text, 650.2-
        651.16.
        14 *I festende*: cf. 650.4: *to fasten*, which seems inferior.
        18 *I trowe sothlye*: cf. 651.9: *I thought faythfully*.
        20 *thay*: cf. 651.11: *he*.
        21 *aboute pryme dayes*: 'soon after sunrise'. Cf. NED Prime *n.*[1] IV 11; but this is not
        the sense of the only instance there. Yet cf. MED prime, n.: c. 1450 *Mirour Saluacioun*: In
        the houre of pryme dayes thyne hoege luf shewed thow me.
        23 *thame ... thamm*: cf. 651.14: *hym* (bis).

A wriched synne, whate ert þou? Thowe er nought. For I sawe that
god is alle thynge; I sawe nought the. And when I sawe that god hase
made alle thynge, I sawe the nought. And when I sawe that god is in
alle thynge, I sawe the nought. And whenn I sawe that god does alle
30  thynge þat is done, lesse and mare, I sawe the nought. And when I sawe
oure lorde Jhesu sitt in oure saule so wyrschipfully, and luff and lyke
and rewle and ʒeme alle that he has made, I sawe nouʒt the. And thus I
am sekyr þat þou erte nouʒt, and alle þa that luffeʒ the and lykes the and
folowes the and wilfully endes in the, I am sekyr thay schalle be brought
35  to nought with the and endleslye confownded. God schelde vs alle fra
the. Amen pour charyte.

And whate wrecchednesse is I wille saye, as I am lernede be the
schewynge of god. Wrecchydnesse es alle thynge that is nought goode,
þe gastelye blyndehede that we falle in to in the fyrste synne, and alle
40  that folowes of that wrecchydnesse, passions and paynes gastelye or
bodely, and alle that es in erth or in othere place whilke es nouʒt goode.

---

26 *A wriched synne ... wee er in pees* (272.56): not in the long text; cf. 651.16, and Introduction, p. 51-52. In the long text Julian writes: *I culde haue no pacience for grett feer
and perplexite* (511.22), and this magnificent apostrophe to sin ably expresses the fear
and perplexity she then felt. Reflection, however, leads her to conclude that the
problem is humble and common (cf. 512.29-31), so that even before she announces the
solution in the parable of the lord and the servant, the apostrophe no longer expresses
her illumined thought and feelings, and in the interests of truth she suppresses what is,
stylistically, one of her finest passages, with its adroit combination of *conversio*, ('Thowe
er *nought*', 'I sawe *nought* the', 'I sawe the *nought*' ...), with *exclamatio* ('A wriched
synne ...') and *repetitio* ('And when I sawe ...', 'And whenn I sawe ...').

37 *And whate wrecchednesse is ... wee er in pees* (272.56): this passage appears to have
been replaced in the long text by the disquisition on the contraries, 659.2-665.58. As
this stands, it is a philosophical and theological reflection of quality, reasoned and written with care and skill. But again, as with the apostrophe to sin (cf. 271.26 note), Julian
has not hesitated to sacrifice it, in the light of what she has learned through the
parable.

39 *þe gastelye blyndehede*: cf. 662.35.
*blyndehede*: NED quotes Rolle's Psalter, 96.2: for thaire blynhede he semys myrk.
*in the fyrste synne*: Julian's description of the miseries of sin has much in common with
what Hilton writes at the beginning of the *Scale*, Book II: þat is, oure lord god schope
man in soule to his owne ymage and liknes. Þis is þe ymage þat I haue spokyn of. Þis
ymage made to þe image of god in þe first schapynge was wnderly faire and briʒt, ful of
brennande loue and gostly lyʒt, bot þorw synne (f. 63ᵛ) of þe first man Adam it was dif-
figured and forschapyn in to a noþer liknes, as I haue before said, for it fel fro þat
goostly liʒt and þat heuenly fode in to pynful mirknes and lust of þis wrecchid liif, exiled
and flemed oute fro þe heritage of heuen þat it schuld haue had if it had stonden stille,
in to þe wrecchednesse of þis erþe and afterward in to þe prisoun of helle, þer to haue
ben wiþ outen ende, fro þe whilk prisoun to þat heuenly heritage it miʒt neuer haue
come agayn, bot if it had ben reformed to þe first schap and þe first liknes (MS BM
Harley 6579; Underhill, 226).

f. 113v   And than may be asked of this: whate er we? / And I answere to this:
ȝif alle ware departed fra vs that is nouȝt goode, we schulde be goode.
Whenn wrechidnesse is departed fra vs, god and the saule is alle ane,

45   and god and man alle ane. Whate is alle in erthe that twynnes vs? I answere and saye, in þat that it serues vs it is goode, and in that that it
schalle perisch it (is) wricchednes, and in that that a mann settys his
herte þer oponn othere wyse than thus, it is synne. And for þat tyme that
mann or womann loves synne, ȝif any be swilke, he is in payne that

50   passes alle paynes; and whenn he loves nouȝt synne, botte hates it and
luffeȝ god, alle is wele. And he that trewlye doeȝ thus, þowȝ he synn
sum tyme by frelty or vnkunnynge in his wille, he falles nought, for he
wille myghtely ryse agayne and behalde god, whamm he loves in alle his
wille. God has made thamm to be loved of hym or hire that has bene a

55   synnere, bot euer he loves and euer he langes to hafe oure luffe; and
when we myghttely and wisely luffe Jhesu, wee er in pees.

Alle the blissede techynge of oure lorde god was schewed to me be
thre partyes, as I hafe sayde before, that es to saye be the bodely sight,
and be worde formed in mynn vndyrstandynge, and by gastelye syght.

60   For the bodely sight, I haffe sayde as I sawe, als trewlye as I cann. And
for the wordes fourmed, I hafe sayde thamm ryght as oure lorde

---

47 *is (wricchednes)*: om. ms.

---

42 *And than may be asked of this whate er we? / And I answere to this ȝif alle ware departed
fra vs / that is nouȝt goode we schulde be goode*: a *compar* with *ratiocinatio* and *conversio* (*goode ...
goode*).

45 *Whate is alle in erthe that twynnes vs? / I answere and saye / in þat that it serues vs it is
goode / and in that that it schalle perisch it is wricchednes / and in that that a mann settys his herte
þer oponn / othere wyse than thus it is synne*: again, a *compar* with *ratiocinatio* and *oppositio contrariorum*.

*twynnes*: 'separates'. NED's first example of the verb is from the Titus MS of the *Ancrene Riwle*, a synonym of Nero's 'to dealed', and it is noteworthy how many early examples in NED, MED are from spiritual writings. Cf. MED, ab 1440, Thornton MS: *and
suffire me neuer mare to twyne fra the* (which translates a petition of the *Anima Christi*).

51 *And he that trewlye doeȝ thus / þowȝ he synn sum tyme by frelty / or vnkunnynge in his wille
/ he falles nought for he wille myghtely ryse agayne / and behalde god whamm he loves in alle his
wille*: a *compar*, with *oppositio*, *traductio* and *inclusio*.

*And he that trewlye doeȝ thus*: the *Cloud*-author teaches much the same, in different
terms, when he writes that the sudden thought of anything bodily or worldly — as opposed to anything good, pure and spiritual — will hinder those 'þat han in a trewe wile
forsaken þe woreld' unless it is immediately suppressed (Hodgson, 35-36).

57 *Alle the blissede techynge ... be alle evenn* (274.17): cf. 666.2-668.26.

schewed me thame. And for the gastely sight, I hafe sayde som dele, bot I maye neu*er* fully tell*e* it; and þ*er*fore of this gastely sight I am stirred to say more, as god will*e* gyfe me grace.

---

62 *schewed*: so the long text, 666.6. NED, Show, 23., quotes *The Mirror of Our Lady*: And my mouthe shall shew thy praysynge (et os meum annuntiabit laudem tuam); but it is more probable that Julian means, as usually, 'revealed'. The words were *formed in mynn vnderstandyng* (cf. 666.3-4). She has already used this formula: 224.2-3, 323.30; and she has also employed the verb: *or god schewyd me any wordes* (227.25; cf. 346.3). There she carefully specifies: *with owtynn voyce and with owte openynge of lyppes* (227.27; cf. 346.6). We may properly call these 'locutions', because that is the form which the revelations suggested to Julian's reason and in which she reports them; but she nowhere claims that they in any way resembled, for example, Joan of Arc's 'voices', and had she been asked, as Joan was to be, in what language she had been 'spoken' to, she could have shown the futility of the question.

(xxiv)    God schewed me twa maners of sekenes that we hafe, of whilke he
wille that we be amended. The tone es inpacyence, for we bere our
trauaylle and oure payne heuely. The tothere is dispayre of doutefulle
drede, as I schalle saye efterwarde. And thiese twa er it that moste

5  travayles vs and tempestes vs, as by that oure lorde schewed me, and

f. 114r  maste lefe to hym that thiese be amendede. I speke of swylke / menn
and womenn that for goddes love hates synne and dysposes thamm to
do goddes wille. Thann ere thiese twa priue synnes and maste besye
aboute vs. Therefore it is goddys wille that thay be knawenn, and thann

10  schalle we refuse thamm as we do othere synnes.

And thus fulle mekelye oure lorde schewed me the pacience that he
hadde in his harde passyonn, and also the ioye and the lykynge that he
hafes of that passionn for love. And this he schewed me in ensampille
that we schulde gladlye and esely bere oure paynes, for that es grete

15  plesynge to hym and endelesse profitte to vs. And cause why we ere
travayled with thamm is for vnknawenge of luffe. Þowȝ the persones in
the blissede trinyte be alle evenn in properte, luffe was moste schewed to
me, that it is moste nere to vs alle. And of this knawynge er we moste
blynde, for many menn and womenn leues that god is alle myghty and

---

13 *this*: 'i' corrector, over one erased letter.
16 *vnknawenge*: 'g' corrector, over one erased letter.
18 *of*: interl. corrector w. caret.

---

1 *God schewed me ... as I schalle saye afterwarde* (l. 4): this corresponds with the long text, 666.9-11.
*of whilke he wille that we be amended*: not in the long text; cf. 666.9.
3 *of*: cf. 666.11: *or*. Either reading is defensible.
5 *and maste lefe to hym*: cf. 667.14-15: *of whych he wylle*.
8 *Thann ere thiese twa priue synnes and maste besye aboute vs*: cf. 667.16: *Than by oure gostly blyndhed and bodely hevynesse we are most enclynyng to theyse*.
16 *vnknawenge*: this compound, to acquire celebrity through its use in the title of the *Cloud*, is first recorded by NED and MED in *The Prick of Conscience* and Rolle's *Psalter*.
17 *in properte*: cf. 668.26: *in the selfe*.
*luffe was moste schewed to me*: cf. 668.26: *the soule toke most vnderstandyng in loue*.
18 *that it is moste nere ... synnes before done* (275.25): not in the long text; cf. 668.27.
19 *many menn and womenn ...*: cf. 668.29: *some of vs*. In the long text, characteristically, Julian includes herself; and so throughout the revised text on 'doubtfull dread'.
*that god is alle myghty and may do alle / and that he is alle wisdome and can do alle / botte that he is alle love and wille do alle*: a three-membered *compar* with *repetitio* (*that ... and that ... botte that*) and *conversio* (*may do alle ... can do alle ... wille do alle*).

20 may do alle, and that he is alle wisdome and can do alle, botte that he is
alle love *and* wille do alle, þar thay stynte. And this vnknawynge it is
that most lettis goddes luffers, for whenn thay be gynn to hate synne
and to amende thamm by the ordynannce of holye kyrke, ȝit þere dwelles
a drede that styrres thamm to behaldynge of thamm selfe and of þer syn-
25 nes before done. And this drede þay take for a mekenesse, bot this is a
fowlle blyndehede and a waykenesse; and we cann it nouȝt dispyse, for
ȝif we knewe it, we schulde sodaynly dispice it as we do ane othere
synne þat we knawe, for it commes of the enmy, *and* it is agayne the
trewthe. For alle the propertees of the blissed trinite, it is goddes
30 wille that we hafe moste sekernesse in lykynge and luffe.

For luffe makes myght *and* wisdome fulle meke to vs; for ryght as be
the curtasye of god he for gettys oure synne for tyme we repente vs,
right so wille he that we fore gette oure synne and alle oure hevynesse
and alle oure dowtefulle dredes. /

---

27 *it, we*: ms: it (þat — exp.) we.

---

25 *And this drede ... mekillehede of luffe* (276.17); cf. 669.39-673.19.
þay: cf. 669.39: *we*.
26 *waykenesse*: cf. 669.40 and note.
28 *of the enmy*: cf. 669.41: *thorugh lack of true jugment*; and cf. the SS readings.
30 *sekernesse in lykynge and luffe*: cf. 669.43: *feythfulnes and lykyng in loue*. SS support 'sekernesse'; but P's 'and lykyng in' seems superior to A.
32 *for tyme*: cf. 670.45: *after the tyme*. This seems the better reading; but cf. 272.48: *And for þat tyme ...*

(**xxv**)

f. 114v    Fore I saw foure man*er* of dredes. One is drede of a fray, that co*m*mes
to a ma*n*n sodanly be frelty. This drede is good, for it helpes to purge a
ma*n*n, as does bodely seknes or swylke oder*e* payne that is nought
synne; for alle swylke paynes helpes ma*n*n ʒif thay be paciently take*n*n.

5    The secunde is drede of payne, whar by a ma*n*n is styrred *and* wakned
fro slepe of sy*n*n; for man þ*at* is harde in slepe of sy*n*n, he is nouʒt able
for þe tyme to resayfe the soft comforth of the hali gaste, to he hafe
gety*n*n this drede of payne *and* of the fyre of purgatory. And this drede
styrres hy*m*m to seke comforth and m*er*cy of god; and thus this drede

10    helpys hym as ane a*n*ntre, and ables hym to hafe cont*ri*cio*n*n be the
blysfulle techynge of the hali gaste. The thyrde is a doutfull*e* drede; for
þowʒ it be litill*e* in the selfe, *and* it ware knawe*n*n, it is a spice of
dispayre. For I am sekyr that alle doutefulle dredes god hates, and he
wille þat we hafe tha*m*m dep*ar*ted with trewe knawynge of lyfe. The

15    fourthe is reu*er*ente drede, for þare is na drede that pleses hy*m*m in vs
bot reu*er*ente drede, and that is fulle swete and softe for mekill*e*hede of
luffe. And ʒit is this reu*er*ente drede and luffe nought bathe ane, bot
thay er twa in p*ro*p*er*te and in wyrkynge, *and* nowther*e* of tha*m*m may be
hadde with owty*n*n othere.

20    Therfore I am sekyr*e*, he þat luffeʒ, he dredes, þowʒ he fele bot litill*e*.
Alle dredes other*e* tha*n*n reu*er*ente dredes that er p*ro*ferde to vs, þowʒ
thay co*m*m vnder*e* the coloure of halynes, thay er*e* not so trewe; and

---

1 *saw*: cf. 671.2: *vnderstonde.*

8 *the fyre of purgatory*: cf. 672.9-10: *gostly enemys.*

10 *anntre*: cf. 672.11: *entre.*

11 *techyng*: cf. 672.12: *touchyng.*

*for þowʒ it be ... knawynge of lyfe*: cf. 673.13-17, which differs considerably.

13 *alle doutefulle dredes god hates*: Julian has many Gospel texts to support her asser-
tion; for example, Peter's fear and doubt at Christ's prophecy of his passion receives the
response: Get behind me, Satan; you are a scandal to me (Matthew 16.21-23).

14 *lyfe*: cf. 673.15: *loue.*

16 *fulle swete and*: not in the long text; cf. 673.19.

*mekillehede*: cf. 673.19: *swetnesse.*

17 *And ʒit is this ... may thaye be knawenn* (277.22): cf. 674.27-675.33.

20 *Therfore I am sekyre / he þat luffeʒ / he dredes / þowʒ he fele bot litille*: a *compar* with
*chiasmus.*

21 *þowʒ thay comm vndere the coloure of halynes*: evidently Julian, of whom Margery
Kempe was to say that she was a skilled spiritual counsellor, was acquainted already
with the problems of scrupulosity.

hereby may thaye be knawe*n*n and discerned, whilke is whilke. For this
reue*r*ente drede, the mar*e* it is hadde, the mar*e* it softes and comfortes
25  *and* pleses and restes; and the false drede, it travayles and tempestes *and*
truble*s*. Than is this the remedye, to knawe tha*m*m bath *and* refuse (th)e
fals, righte as we walde do a wikkyd spiritte that schewed hym in likne*s*
of a goode angell*e*. For ryght as ane ille spyrit, þow3 he co*m*m vnder*e*
the coloure and the liknes of a goode angell*e* his daliannce *and* his
30  wirkynge, þow3 he schewe neue*r* so fayre, fyrst he travayles *and* tempes
*and* trubles the pe*r*so*n*n that he spekes with, and lettes hym and lefe3 /
115r  hym alle in vnreste; and the mar*e* that he co*m*mone3 with hym, the mar*e*

---

26  *the (fals)*: ms: 3e.

---

23  *and discerned, whilke is whilke*: cf. 675.33: *on sonder*.

*discerned*: cf. III Kings 3.9 (Solomon's prayer for wisdom): Give therefore to thy servant an understanding heart, to judge thy people and discern between evil and good.
MED's earliest example of this precise sense is c. 1450 (1410), Walton, *Boethius*.

*For this reue*r*ente drede* ...: the rest of the short text is not found in the long.

*For this reue*r*ente drede* ...: the language here is similar to that of the *Cloud*: ... lerne
þee to loue listely wiþ a softe and a demure contenaunce, as wel in body as in soule, and
abide curesly and meekly þe wil of oure lorde (Hodgson, 87).

26  *refuse the fals ... in liknes of a goode angelle*: cf. II Corinthians 11.13-14: For such false
apostles are deceitful workmen, transforming themselves into the apostles of Christ;
and no wonder, for Satan himself transforms himself into an angel of light. Cf. *A
Treatise of Discretion of Spirits*: ... it is ful needful and speedful to knowe his queintyse and
not for to vnknowe his doelful deseites. For somtyme he wol, þat wickid cursid wi3t,
chaunge his licnes into an aungel of li3t, þat he may vnder colour of vertewe do more
dere (Hodgson, *Deonise*, 85).

*3e* (ms): though '3' is occasionally found as a 'th'-symbol, it does not appear to be this
scribe's practice.

28  *For ryght as ane ille spyrit* ...: Julian offers the same advice as the author of the *Ancrene Riwle*, but without his embellishments. Cf. the *Scale*, I, chapter 10: For as a gode
aungel come3 with ly3t, so can þe deuel ... Whose hade feled boþe, he schuld kun tell
whilk were gode *and* whilk were yuell, bot he þat neuer feled neiþir, or elles bot þat
one, may ly3tly be deceyued (MS Cambridge UL Add. 6686, p. 284; Underhill, 20).

30  *tempes*: there seems no need to emend to either 'temptes' or 'tempestes'. MED
quotes the Göttingen *Cursor Mundi*, l. 170: 'temped' (past participle).

32  *the mare he travayles hym* ...: cf. the *Scale*, II chapter 27: þi mirknes of *t*raueilend
desire *and* þi blynde trust in god ... schal tu*r*ne in to clere knowynge *and* in to sikirnes
of luf. And þi lord god schal gife rest to þe (Isaias 57.11) ... þi pyneful dredis *and*
doutes *and* wicked spirites ... alle þese schal weiken *and* lesen mikel of her my3t, for þu
schalt be hid in rest fro hem (MS BM Harley 6579, f. 78*r*; Underhill, 344-345).

he travayles hym and the farther*e* is he fra pees. Þer*f*ore it is goddes
will*e* and oure spede that we knawe tha*m*m thus ysundur*e*; for god will*e*
35　eu*er* that we be seker*e* in luffe, *and* peessabill*e* *and* ristefull*e* as he is to vs,
and ryght so of the same condicio*n*n as he is to vs, so will*e* he that we be
to our*e* selfe and to our*e* even christe*n*n. Amen.

Explicit Juliane de Norwych